Celebrate Today!

JOHN KREMER

More Than

4,000

Holidays,

Celebrations,

Origins, and Anniversaries

PRIMA PUBLISHING

PRIMA PUBLISHING and colophon are trademarks of Prima Communications, Inc.

Library of Congress Cataloging-in-Publication Data

Kremer, John
    Celebrate today! : more than 4,000 holidays, celebrations, origins, and anniversaries / by John Kremer.
        p.   cm.

    ISBN 0-7615-0330-7
    1. Holidays.   2. Special days.   3. Anniversaries.   I. Title.
GT3930.K74 1995
394.2—dc20   95-40486
                                                        CIP

96 97 98 99 00 AA 10 9 8 7 6 5 4 3 2 1
Printed in the United States of America

How to Order:
Single copies may be ordered from Prima Publishing, P.O. Box 1260BK, Rocklin, CA 95677; telephone (916) 632-4400. Quantity discounts are also available. On your letterhead, include information concerning the intended use of the books and the number of books you wish to purchase.

Contents

Introduction

Welcome to *Celebrate Today!*, the book that presents over 4,000 holidays, celebrations, origins, anniversaries, and other special events.

I've always tried to follow the old maxim that "Today is the first day of the rest of your life!" To me, that means that every day is special, and therefore I should make the best use of it that I can. The best use anyone can make of a day is to enjoy it—and then spread that joy to others.

In reading this book, you should be able to find at least one reason for celebrating each day. On most days, I offer you ten or more reasons, one of which will surely appeal to you. Use that reason to bolster you throughout the day—even if you don't get to take the day off.

HOW TO USE THIS BOOK

Some of the events listed here are serious, some are funny, some are neutral. Take what you like, and use it to make each day special. Here are just a few of the ways different people might use this book to make their days special:

Teachers Use these special events and days to create attractive bulletin boards, to make reading assignments or other classroom activities more interesting, or to use as a springboard for discussing current events and issues.

Students Use a special day or anniversary as the theme for show-and-tell presentations. Or use this book to find out what makes your birthday so special.

Recreation leaders Find a whole year's worth of reasons to get out and play! And inspire others to do the same.

Sales managers Use these daily reminders to inspire your sales force or to lighten up a long meeting.

Meeting planners and groups Create themes that will pull people into your meetings and have them coming back for more.

Speakers Start your speeches by loosening up the crowd with a short tidbit on one or more of the special celebrations happening today. Or use one of the quirkier days to add humor or a light aside to your talk.

Authors Find article ideas, creative inspiration, query-letter punchlines, or promotional tie-ins.

Librarians Create interesting displays or bulletin boards based on interesting events of the day. Suggest discussion themes for your reading groups.

Media representatives Use *Celebrate Today!* for lifestyle bits, historical event listings, daily calendar items, and theme sections. Morning drive-time hosts can give their listeners reasons to take the day off.

Publicists Tie in your news releases to these special days and events, thus making any story more timely and intriguing. Or lighten up your cover letters with little tidbits from this book. Or, better yet, sponsor your own special day, week, or month to bring more attention to your product, service, or cause.

Retailers Create window displays, aisle talkers, in-store promotions, unusual ads, sales promotions, or publicity tie-ins.

Everybody else Use the daily bits of information in this book to find a good excuse to take the day off or, at the very least, to throw a great party!

HOW TO SPONSOR YOUR OWN SPECIAL DAY

If you'd like to sponsor a special day or celebration that will be featured in future editions of this book, send the following information to John Kremer at Open Horizons, P.O. Box 205, Fairfield, IA 52556-0205 (e-mail: JohnKremer@bookmarket.com):

- the name of your special event
- a detailed description of the event
- the sponsor's name
- your address and phone number
- your fax number and/or e-mail address
- the date(s) of your event (if the date changes from year to year, how do you determine the change?)

What more can you do? Do what others do. If you want your special day or event to be recognized, publicize it. Also, get other people to endorse it. Hire a celebrity spokesperson. Or encourage a mayor, governor, or the president to sign an official proclamation recognizing your event. It's done all the time. You can do it, too!

SPECIAL EVENTS DATA FILES

All of the daily details in this book are available in an even larger computer data file—more than 5,675 events and counting! If you'd like the most up-to-date listing, all sortable by subject interest, order the Special Events Data File for only $32.50 postpaid. Order from Open Horizons, P.O. Box 205, Fairfield,

National Volunteer Blood Donor Month

Recognizes those who donate blood on a regular basis. *Sponsor:* American Association of Blood Banks, 8101 Glenbrook Road, Bethesda, MD 20814; 301-907-6977; Fax: 301-907-6895.

National Yours, Mine, and Ours Month

Promotes blending families and creating positive step-family relationships. *Sponsor:* Parenting without Pressure. ✉

Prevention of Cruelty to Your Money Month

Also known as Second Hand But Simply Grand, promotes the use of second hand clothing in establishing your personal style. (Note that the sponsor will be moving in May of 1996). *Sponsor:* Now Is Your Time, Patricia Reynolds, Director, 340 N Dearborn #223, Kankakee, IL 60901; 815-933-6109.

Thyroid Awareness Month

Promotes awareness of thyroid diseases, which affect 7 million Americans. *Sponsor:* American Association of Clinical Endocrinologists, Interscience Communications, Radio City Station, P.O. Box 1512, New York, NY 10101-1512; 212-468-3612; Fax: 212-468-3620.

January 1

Braille Literacy Week

For a free Braille Alphabet Card, send a postcard to the address below. Always celebrated the week of Louis Braille's birthday (January 4, 1809). *Sponsor:* American Foundation for the Blind, 15 West 16th Street, New York, NY 10011; 212-620-2000; Fax: 212-727-7418.

Diet Resolution Week

During the first 7 days of the year, start watching your weight by eating unprocessed, high-complex carbohydrate foods. What counts is the type, not the amount, of food you consume. Slim down with whole grains, legumes, fresh fruit, and vegetables. *Sponsor:* Vegetarian Awareness Network, P.O.

Box 321, Knoxville, TN 37901; 800-872-8343.

Ellis Island opened (1892)

Over 20,000,000 immigrants were processed at Ellis Island for entrance into the U.S.; it is now a museum. *Contact:* Statue of Liberty, Ellis Island Foundation, 52 Vanderbilt Avenue, New York, NY 10017-3898; 212-883-1986; Fax: 212-883-1069. Ellis Island information: 212-363-3200.

Emancipation Proclamation issued (1863)

President Lincoln issued the proclamation that freed the slaves in the northern states.

European Economic Community started operation (1958)

First scheduled airline service began in 1914

The world's first scheduled airline service began between Tampa and Saint Petersburg, Florida.

Imani—Faith Day

The seventh day of Kwanzaa; the day for you to renew your faith in what you believe.

International Carnivorous Plant Society founded (1990)

National Environmental Policy Act (1970)

This made it government policy to protect the environment. *Contact:* Council on Environmental Quality,

722 Jackson Place NW, Washington, DC 20503-0001; 202-395-5750; Fax: 202-456-6546.

New Year's Day

Start the year off right, resolve to make this the best year of your life. The world's most widely celebrated holiday, New Year's was set on January 1 by Julius Caesar because that was the date the Roman consuls took over their duties.

North American Free Trade Agreement (NAFTA)

Took effect in 1994; created the world's largest free-trade zone by eliminating trade barriers between the U.S., Canada, and Mexico.

Party Party Day

An excuse to have a party once a month. *Sponsor:* Bonza Bottler Day. ✉

Postum Cereal's Birthday

C. W. Post created the first batch of Postum cereal in Battle Creek, Michigan, in 1895. *Contact:* General Foods, 250 North Street, White Plains, NY 10625; 914-335-2500; Fax: 914-335-3511.

Solemnity of Mary, Mother of God

The Roman Catholic Church holy day that replaced the Circumcision of Christ feast.

Universal Letter-Writing Week

Get to know people around the world by writing letters to them. Celebrated the first 7 days in January. *Sponsor:* International Society of Friendship and Good Will. ✉

Z Day

Honors those who end up last when placed in alphabetical order. *Sponsor:* Tom Zager, P.O. Box 875, Sterling Heights, MI 48310; 313-268-2856.

January 2

First black president of a white university (1970)

Clifton R. Wharton, Jr., became president of Michigan State. *Contact:* Michigan State University, John A. Hanna Building, East Lansing, MI 48824; 517-355-1855; Fax: 517-336-2069.

First commemorative stamps issued in U.S. (1893)

Commemorated Columbus's voyage. *Contact:* U.S. Postal Service. ✉

First no-fault divorce law passed (1971)

First religious services broadcast (1921)

Contact: KDKA Radio, 1 Gateway Center, Pittsburgh, PA 15222; 412-392-2200; Fax: 412-392-3207.

First spacecraft to orbit the sun (1959)

The Russian satellite *Luna I* was launched; it overshot the moon and became the first spacecraft to orbit the sun. *Contact:* NASA. ✉

Georgia Ratification Day

Georgia became the fourth state to ratify the U.S. Constitution in 1788. *Contact:* Georgia Tourist Division, 285 Peachtree Center Avenue, P.O. Box 1776, Atlanta, GA 30301; 404-656-3590; 800-847-4842; Fax: 404-651-9063.

National Science Fiction Day

On the birthday of Isaac Asimov, celebrate the one form of fiction that he helped to create—science fiction. Asimov was born in 1920, near Smolensk, Russia. *Sponsor:* The Life of the Party. ✉

National Woman's Party formed (1913)

This party was founded to take direct action in getting women the right to vote. *Contact:* National Woman's Party, 144 Constitution Avenue NE, Washington, DC 20002; 202-546-1210.

Saint Adelard Feast Day
Saint Adelard, exiled because of his advice, took up gardening. He is considered a patron saint of gardening.

January 3

Alaska Admission Day
Alaska became the 49th state in 1959. *Contact:* Alaska Division of Tourism, P.O. Box 110801, Juneau, AK 99811-0801; 907-465-2010; 800-200-1160; Fax: 907-465-2287.

Apple Computer incorporated (1977)
Contact: Apple Computer, One Infinite Loop, Cupertino, CA 95014; 408-996-1010; 800-776-2333; Fax: 408-974-6412.

Congress assembles
The 20th Amendment mandates that Congress assemble on this day.

Dragnet premiered (1952)
This realistic cop drama first appeared on NBC-TV. It premiered as a radio show on KFI radio (June 3, 1949) and was carried by NBC radio starting on July 7, 1949. *Contact:* NBC-TV. ✉

Drinking straw patented (1888)
Patented by Marvin Stone of Washington, D.C.

March of Dimes campaign organized (1938)
Raises funds to fight polio. *Contact:* March of Dimes Foundation, 1275 Mamaroneck Avenue, White Plains, NY 10605; 914-428-7100; Fax: 914-997-4662.

Oleomargarine patented (1871)

San Francisco Name Day
The small town of Yerba Buena became the city of San Francisco in 1847. *Contact:* San Francisco Visitors Bureau, Holiday Plaza, First Floor, 900 Market Street, San Francisco, CA 94103; 415-974-6900.

Super Soakers Birthday
These popular water guns first went on sale in 1991.

Tom Sawyer's Cat's Birthday
This day campaigns against those who do things the hard way, especially bureaucrats. *Sponsor:* Puns Corp. ✉

January 4

Appendectomy Day
In 1885, Dr. William Grant of Davenport, Iowa, performed the first appendectomy.

Birthday of the Blender (1910)

Braille Day
On the birthday of Louis Braille (1809), we honor the blind. Louis Braille invented the raised alphabet for the blind. He was born in Coupvray, France.

Elizabeth Ann Seton Feast Day
Founder of the American Sisters of Charity, she died in 1821; was the first American-born saint (canonized on September 14, 1975). She was born in New York City.

Get Out Your Boxer Shorts Day
On the birthday of Floyd Patterson, celebrate the world of boxing. Patterson, one of the great heavyweight champions, was born in 1935, at Waco, North Carolina. *Sponsor:* The Life of the Party. ✉

Short People Day
On the birthday of General Tom Thumb (1838), we celebrate all short people.

Trivia Day
Celebrates those who have filled their heads with useless facts. *Sponsor:* Puns Corp. ✉

Utah Admission Day (1896)
Utah became the 45th state. *Contact:* Utah Travel Council, Council

Hall, Capital Mall, Salt Lake City, UT 84114; 801-538-1030; Fax: 801-538-1399; 800-200-1160.

January 5

First woman governor inaugurated (1925)
Nellie Ross of Wyoming was inaugurated as the first female governor in the U.S.

$5 per day minimum wage anniversary (1914)
Henry Ford announced that he would pay workers $5.00 per day.

George Washington Carver Day
Born into slavery just before the end of the Civil War, he died in 1943. An agricultural scientist, inventor, and teacher, he developed new uses for peanuts, potatoes, and wood.

Twelfth Night
The evening before Epiphany marks the end of the 12 days of Christmas. This day is also known as 12th Day Eve.

Wolf Moon
The full moon of January is the wolf moon, symbolic of strength, confidence, and protection.

January 6

Dorm room refrigerator invented (1956)

Epiphany (the 12th day of Christmas)
Celebrates the visit of the Magi to baby Jesus. This day is also known as Three Kings Day or the Feast of the Magi.

First round-the-world commercial air flight
Pan Am Pacific Clipper started out on its around-the-world flight on December 2, 1941, and arrived back in New York City on January 6, 1942.

Leisure Suit Saturday
The last National Leisure Suit Convention will be held at the Val Air Ballroom near Des Moines, Iowa in 1996. *Sponsor:* Van and Bonnie in the Morning, Van Harden, Producer, WHO-AM Radio, 1801 Grand Avenue, Des Moines, IA 50309-3362; 515-242-3500; Fax: 515-242-3798.

New Mexico Admission Day
New Mexico became the 47th state in 1912. *Contact:* New Mexico Tourism Division, 491 Old Santa Fe Trail, Santa Fe, NM 87501; 505-827-7400; 800-545-2040; Fax: 505-827-0396.

Sherlock Holmes's Birthday (1854)
The world's first consulting detective, Holmes is the most famous fictional character in history.

Take a Poet to Lunch Day
On the birthday of Carl Sandburg (1878), take a starving poet to lunch. An American poet and biographer of Lincoln, he was born in Galesburg, Illinois. *Sponsor:* The Life of the Party. ✉

January 7

Egyptian New Year's Day (Sekhmet)

First ant farm sold in America (1958)

First balloon flight across the English Channel (1785)
John Jeffries, a Boston doctor, and Jean-Pierre Blanchard, a Frenchman, made this flight, crossing from Dover, England, to Calais, France.

First commercial bank opened in the U.S. (1782)
Philadelphia's Bank of North America was the first commercial bank in the U.S.

First passage through the Panama Canal (1914)

First U.S. presidential election (1789)
Americans voted for president for the first time.

Millard Fillmore's Birthday (1800)
The 13th President of the U.S. was born in Summerhill, New York.

National Law Enforcement Training Week
Always the first full week in January.

National Pass Gas Day
Celebrates the birthday of the founder in a very explosive way. Come on baby, light my fire! *Sponsor:* Camp Chaos, ABC Radio Z Rock, Chaz Fernandez, 13725 Montfort Drive, Dallas, TX 75240; 214-991-9200.

National Word Processing Transcriptionist Week
Recognizes the contribution of word processing personnel in all areas of business and health care. *Sponsor:* Norfolk Regional Center, Norma Rohlff, Word Processing, P.O. Box 1209, Norfolk, NE 68701-1209; 402-370-3203.

Saint Aldric Feast Day
Saint Aldric (aka Saint Elric) is a patron saint of those suffering from asthma.

Someday We'll Laugh about This Week
Ninety percent of all New Year's resolutions are violated within a week. Why not laugh about it now? For an information packet on the positive power of humor, send SASE and $1.01 to The Humor Project. *Sponsor:* The Humor Pro-ject, Joel Goodman, 110 Spring Street #D, Saratoga Springs, NY 12866; 518-587-8770; Fax: 518-587-8771; e-mail: DRJ3@aol.com.

Tarzan comic strip first appeared (1929)

Transatlantic telephone service began (1927)

Service was inaugurated between London and New York.

January 8

AT&T Divesture Anniversary (1982)
To settle an antitrust suit, AT&T agreed to divest itself of its local telephone companies, the Baby Bells. *Contact:* American Telephone & Telegraph, 32 Sixth Avenue, New York, NY 10013; 212-387-5400; Fax: 212-226-4935.

Battle of New Orleans (1815)
American forces defeated a British attack on New Orleans 2 weeks after the War of 1812 had ended. *Contact:* New Orleans Tourist Commission, 1520 Sugar Bowl Drive, New Orleans, LA 70112; 504-566-5011; 800-345-1187; Fax: 504-566-5046.

First all-woman state supreme court (1925)

Hold onto Your Head Day
Mary, Queen of Scots, was executed on this day. *Sponsor:* The Life of the Party. ✉

National Clean Off Your Desk Day
On the second Monday in January, everyone should be able to see the top of their desk. *Sponsor:* National Association of Professional Organizers, 1033 La Posada Drive #220, Austin, TX 78752-3880; 512-206-0151.

National Joygerm Day
Find every moaner and groaner and turn them around with a smile, a hug, or a grin. For a whee-they're-free! membership card, send an SASE to Joygerms Unlimited. *Sponsor:* Joygerms Unlimited, Joan White, Director, P.O. Box 219, Eastwood Station, Syracuse, NY 13206; 315-472-2779.

Rock 'n' Roll Day
On the birthday of Elvis Presley (1935), the King of Rock 'n' Roll, we honor rock'n' roll music and musicians. Elvis was born in Tupelo, Mississippi. Also known as Blue Suede Shoes Day. *Sponsor:* Open Horizons. ✉

Show and Tell Day at Work
On the second Monday in January, take your nifty new gifts to work so you can share your good fortune

with the gang at the office. *Sponsor:* Wellness Permission League. ✉

War on Poverty declared (1964)
In his State of the Union address, President Johnson declared war on poverty.

January 9

Aviation in America Day
The first balloon flight in the U.S. was made by Jean Pierre Blanchard in 1793.

Choreographers Day
George Balanchine, one of the world's greatest choreographers, was born in 1904 in Saint Petersburg, Russia; we recognize and honor all choreographers.

Connecticut Ratification Day
One of the original 13 states, Connecticut became the fifth state to ratify the U.S. Constitution in 1788. *Contact:* Connecticut Department of Tourism, 865 Brook Street, Rocky Hill, CT 06067; 203-258-4290; 800-282-6863.

First income tax imposed (1799 in England)

First women's golf tournament (1811)
Organized in Scotland. *Contact:* Ladies Professional Golf Association, 2570 Volusia Avenue, Daytona Beach, FL 32114; 904-254-8800.

Richard Milhous Nixon's Birthday (1913)
The 37th President of the U.S., was born in Yorba Linda, California. In 1974, he became the first President to resign.

What You Don't Know Day
On the second Tuesday of every month, go to the library and research things you don't know anything about. Keep learning. Note that the sponsor suggests you do this at least once a month on the second Tuesday. *Sponsor:* All My Events. ✉

January 10

Black Scientist Day
On the birthday of George Washington Carver, we honor all black scientists. Carver, born in 1864 in Diamond Grove, Missouri, was famous for producing synthetic products from peanuts, potatoes, and wood.

First subway passenger train opened (1863)
London's Metropolitan railway opened as the first underground subway.

League of Nations created (1920)
Fifty nations (but not the U.S.) signed a covenant to avoid war. This agreement created the League of Nations, the forerunner of the United Nations.

Make Your Dreams Come True Day
Celebrated on the second Wednesday in January.

Standard Oil incorporated (1870)
John D. Rockefeller incorporated Standard Oil. Standard was the first major oil company. The Standard Oil company was broken into smaller companies when, on May 15, 1911, the Supreme Court ruled it was in violation of the Sherman Anti-Trust Act.

United Nations General Assembly first meeting
Met for the first time in 1946, in London, England. *Contact:* United Nations. ✉

"Where's the Beef?" Day
In a 1984 television commercial, Clara Peller, Wendy's spokesperson, first uttered those immortal words, "Where's the beef?" *Contact:* Wendy's International, 4288 W Dublin-Granville Road, Dublin, OH 43017; 614-764-3100; Fax: 614-764-3459.

✉ Addresses for frequently cited organizations are gathered on pages vii–viii.

Women's Suffrage Amendment introduced (1878)

An amendment to the U.S. Constitution was introduced into the Senate. The amendment was finally passed in 1910.

World's first great oil gusher (1901)

The world's first oil boom town, Beaumont, Texas, grew as a result of the first great oil gusher, Spindletop. Anthony F. Lewis drilled the well. *Contact:* Beaumont Visitors Bureau, 801 Main Street #100, P.O. Box 3827, Beaumont, TX 77704; 409-880-3749; 800-392-4401; Fax: 409-880-3750.

January 11

Family Communications Day

On the second Thursday in January, turn off the TV, stay home, and have fun as a family. Talk. Reconnect. *Sponsor:* Texas PTA, Deborah Glover, 408 West 11th, Austin, TX 78701; 512-476-6769; Fax: 512-476-8152.

First real American discotheque opened (1963)

The Whiskey-A-Go-Go opened on Sunset Boulevard in Los Angeles, California.

International Thank You Day

Thank someone today who has done you a favor in the past. Call, write, fax, or e-mail to say thanks! *Sponsor:* All My Events. ✉

Pharmacists Day

Take time to thank your local druggist on the second Thursday in January. *Sponsor:* Mary Mashall Manor, Connie Heidebrecht, Activity Director, 810 North 18th Street, Marysville, KS 66508.

Send a Dollar to the Treasury Day

On the birthday of Alexander Hamilton, America's first treasurer, send an extra dollar to the U.S. Treasury. It needs all it can get. Hamilton was born in 1755, in the British West Indies. *Sponsor:* The Life of the Party. ✉

Smoking May Be Hazardous to Your Health Day (1964)

U.S. Surgeon General Luther Terry issued the first government report saying that smoking may be hazardous to your health. *Contact:* U.S.

Surgeon General, Humphrey Building, 200 Independence Avenue, Washington, DC 20201; 202-690-6467.

Use More of Your Mind Day

This is the birthday of William James (1842) who said that "we only use 10% of our minds..." *Sponsor:* Open Horizons. ✉

January 12

All in the Family premiered (1971)

This comedy premiered on CBS-TV. *Contact:* CBS-TV. ✉

First public museum in America (1773)

Opened in Charleston, South Carolina.

First woman elected to the U.S. Senate (1932)

Hattie Caraway was the first woman to be elected to the U.S. Senate.

Gals Night Out

The second Friday night of every month is reserved for women to have a special night out together. Note: This monthly event will be listed only once in this book. *Sponsor:* All My Events. ✉

Lift Every Voice and Sing Day

Written by James Weldon Johnson with music by Rosamond Johnson, this Negro national anthem was first performed by 500 school children in 1900.

Work Harder Day
This is Rush Limbaugh's birthday, and in 1993 he declared that on this day everybody should work harder! *Contact:* Rush Limbaugh Show, The EIB Network, 2 Penn Plaza, 17th Floor, New York, NY 10021; 212-613-3800.

January 13

Accordion patented (1854)
Anthony Foss patented the accordion.

Bald Eagle Appreciation Days
These days, held on a mid-January weekend, honor and celebrate the American bald eagle. *Sponsor:* Keokuk Tourism Bureau, 401 Main, Keokuk, IA 52632; 800-383-1219.

Door-to-Door Salespeople Day
On the birthday of Alfred Fuller (1885) of Fuller Brush fame, we honor all door-to-door salespeople. Alfred Fuller was born in Kings County, Nova Scotia.

First ad for a radio (1906)
Scientific American carried the first advertisement for a radio, a $7.50 Telimco. *Contact: Scientific American,* Ad Department, 415 Madison Avenue, New York, NY 10017-1179; 212-754-0550; Fax: 212-355-6245.

First black to play in an NBA all-star game (1953)
Don Barksdale became the first black to play in an NBA all-star game. *Contact:* National Basketball Association, 645 Fifth Avenue, 15th Floor, New York, NY 10022; 212-826-7000; Fax: 212-826-0579.

First radio broadcast (1910)
Lee Deforest arranged the first public radio broadcast in New York City. The broadcast featured Enrico Caruso and other singers from the Metropolitan Opera.

First woman to conduct the Metropolitan Opera (1976)
Sarah Caldwell conducted *La Travista. Contact:* Metropolitan Opera Association, Lincoln Center, New York, NY 10023; 212-799-3100; Fax: 212-870-7416.

Stephen Foster Memorial Day
This is the anniversary of the death of Stephen Foster in 1864; he was the first popular songwriter in the U.S. Among other songs, he wrote "Oh! Susanna" and "Camptown Races."

Strive and Succeed Day
Strive and succeed on the birthday of Horatio Alger (1834), author of many inspiring novels for young boys. *Sponsor:* Open Horizons. ✉

January 14

Cuckoo Dancing Week
The week of the 18th celebrates the movies of Laurel and Hardy (Oliver Hardy was born in 1892). "The Dancing Cuckoos" was their theme song. This week was originally sponsored by William Rabe.

First constitution in America (1639)
The Fundamental Orders, adopted by representatives of several counties in Connecticut, became the first constitution adopted in America.

First moving assembly line (1913)
Henry Ford introduced the moving assembly line for automobiles. *Contact:* Ford Motor Company, American Road, Dearborn, MI 48121-0000; 313-332-3000; Fax: 313-845-8981.

Healthy Weight Week
During the third week of January, work toward achieving a healthy weight by eating better and exercising. For a free report on *A New Look at the Problems of Weight Loss,* write to *Healthy Weight Journal. Sponsor: Healthy Weight Journal,* Frances Berg, Editor, 402 South 14th Street, Hettinger, ND 58639; 701-567-2646.

International Printing Week
During the week of the 17th, Benjamin Franklin's birthday, celebrate the printing trade. *Sponsor:* International Association of Printing House Craftsmen, 7042 Brooklyn Boulevard, Minneapolis, MN 55429-1370; 612-560-1620.

National Book Week

The third full week in January promotes the reading of books. *Sponsor:* National Book Foundation, 260 Fifth Avenue #904, New York, NY 10001; 212-685-0261; Fax: 212-213-6570.

National Pizza Week

Formerly sponsored by Pizza Hut on the third week in January, this week celebrates America's favorite party food.

Printers Ink Week

Held the week of Benjamin Franklin's birthday, celebrates printing, especially colorful printing. *Sponsor:* National Association of Printing Ink Manufacturers, Heights Plaza, 777 Terrace Avenue, Hasbrouck Height, NJ 07604; 201-288-9454.

Ratification Day (1874)

The U.S. ratified the Treaty of Paris, thereby officially ending the Revolutionary War.

Roman New Year

The Roman Era year of 2749 begins in 1996.

The Simpsons cartoon TV show premiered (1990)

Contact: Fox Broadcasting, 10201 W Pico Boulevard, Los Angeles, CA 90035; 310-277-2211.

Take a Missionary to Lunch Day

On the birthday of Albert Schweitzer, take a missionary to lunch. Schweitzer won the 1952 Nobel Peace Prize for his missionary work in Africa, he was born on this day in 1875 at Kayserberg, Upper Alsace. *Sponsor:* The Life of the Party. ✉

Today Show premiered (1952)

The *Today Show* was the longest-lasting of the morning TV news shows. *Contact:* NBC-TV. ✉

Traitor's Day (1741)

Celebrated on the birthday of America's greatest traitor, Benedict Arnold.

January 15

Basketball's Official Birthday (1892)

The rules of basketball were first published in Springfield, Massachusetts. *Contact:* Basketball Hall of Fame, 1150 W Columbus Avenue, P.O. Box 179, Springfield, MA 01101; 413-781-6500.

Elementary School Teacher Day

Celebrate your children's teachers on the third Monday in January. *Sponsor:* Dawn T. Brue, 2006 NW 55th Avenue #H5, Gainesville, FL 32653.

First dental gold inlay (1907)

First Superbowl game (1967)

The Green Bay Packers defeated the Kansas City Chiefs 35-10. *Contact:* National Football League. ✉

Human Relations Day

Celebrated the same day as Martin Luther King's birthday holiday. *Sponsor:* Flint Community Schools, Staff Development Office, 923 E Kearsley Street, Flint, MI 48502; 810-760-1122.

Humanitarian Day

On Dr. Martin Luther King's birthday (1929), we wear white to honor all humanitarians. *Sponsor:* Global Committee Commemorating, Kingdom Respect Days, P.O. Box 21050, Chicago, IL 60621; 312-737-7328.

Junk Food News Alert Day

On the third Monday in January, the top 10 junk food news stories of the past year are announced. *Sponsor:* Project Censored, Carl Jensen, Director, Sonoma State University, Rohnert Park, CA 94928; 707-664-2500; Fax: 707-664-2505.

Man Watchers' Appreciation Week

Turn the tables on men, and take a look. Celebrated the second full week in January (starting with a Monday), when the 10 most watchable men are named. *Sponsor:* Man Watchers International, Suzy Mallery, President, 12021 Wilshire Boulevard #371, Los Angeles, CA 90025; 310-826-9101; e-mail: smallery@aol.com.

Martin Luther King Jr.'s Birthday (celebrated)

Federal holiday honoring the black civil rights leader, who was born in 1929 in Atlanta, Georgia.

Pentagon completed (1948)

The world's largest office building was completed.

Procrastinator's New Year

If you are a procrastinator, you should be getting around to celebrating the new year. Do it today. Or tomorrow. No hurry. *Sponsor:* The Life of the Party. ✉

Steam elevator patented (1861)

Elisha Otis patented the steam elevator.

January 16

Book Publishers Day

On the birthday of John Kremer (1949), author of *1001 Ways to Mar-*ket Your Books and *Book Marketing Made Easier*, all book publishers are honored. *Sponsor:* Book Marketing Update. ✉

First non-stop, around-the-world flight (1957)

First photofinish camera installed at a racetrack (1936)

Installed at the Hialeah Race Course in Florida.

Gulf War began (1991)

The beginning of Desert Storm operation's flights over Iraq.

"Love a Mystery" radio show premiered (1939)

One of the longest-running mystery radio shows. *Contact:* NBC-TV. ✉

National Good Teen Day

Founded by an Ohio school teacher, this day has been approved by Congress.

National Nothing Day

Harold Pullman Coffin, a journalist, created this day in 1973. This is a day to sit without celebrating, observing, or honoring anything.

Prohibition began (1920)

The 18th amendment prohibited the selling of alcoholic beverages. Prohibition was ratified in 1919 and took effect one year later.

Religious Freedom Day

In 1786, Virginia adopted a law guaranteeing religious freedom. Virginia's law became the model for the first amendment of the Constitution of the U.S.

Rid the World of Fad Diets and Gimmicks Day

On the Tuesday of Healthy Weight Week, the Slim Chance Awards are given out to the worst weight loss promotions of the past year. *Sponsor:* Healthy Weight Journal, Frances Berg, Editor, 402 South 14th Street, Hettinger, ND 58639; 701-567-2646.

There's No Business Like Show Business Day

On the birthday of Ethel Merman, celebrate the world of show business. Merman was born in 1909, in Queens, New York. *Sponsor:* The Life of the Party. ✉

U.S. Civil Service Commission established (1883)

January 17

Benjamin Franklin's Birthday (1706)

Born in Boston, Massachusetts, Benjamin Franklin was the author of *Poor Richard's Almanac*, signer of both the Declaration of Independence and the U.S. Constitution, scientist, inventor, diplomat, publisher, and philosopher.

Fire from the Sky Day

This day commemorates the 1966 Palomares hydrogen bomb incident, where 4 hydrogen bombs fell from an American B-52 bomber during a refueling accident over the skies of Spain. Two of the bombs spilled radioactive plutonium over the Palomares area.

First meeting of the UN Security Council (1948)
Contact: United Nations. ✉

Good Luck Day
Honors Felicitas, the Roman goddess of good luck.

Maintenance Day
On the third Wednesday in January, honor all janitors and building maintenance workers. *Sponsor:* Blue Valley Nursing Home, Jim Heidebrecht, Maintenance Superintendent, Blue Rapids, KS 66411; 913-363-7777.

Not the Big One Yet Day (1994)
Southern California experienced a major earthquake that destroyed many of its freeways. But, and here's the good part, it wasn't the big one—where California is predicted to slide into the ocean.

Professional Boxers Day
On the birthday of Muhammad Ali, 3-time winner of the heavyweight title, we honor all professional boxers. Ali was born as Cassius Clay in 1942, in Louisville, Kentucky.

Saint Anthony Feast Day
Saint Anthony, patriarch of all monks, is also patron of domestic animals and grave diggers.

World Championship Snow Sculpting Contest
Held on the third weekend in January, determines the international champion. *Sponsor:* Breckenridge Resort Chamber, John Hendryson, P.O. Box 1909, Breckenridge, CO 80424; 303-453-2913; 800-221-1091; Fax: 303-453-7238.

January 18

First aircraft landing on a ship (1911)
Eugene Ely landed his airplane on the deck of the *USS Pennsylvania.*

First black cabinet member (1966)
Robert Weaver, Secretary of Housing and Urban Development, became the first black cabinet member in U.S. history. *Contact:* Department of Housing and Urban Development, 451 Seventh Street SW, Washington, DC 20410-0001; 202-708-1112; Fax: 202-708-0299.

Guys Night Out
The third Thursday night of every month is reserved for men to have a night out doing guy things. Note: This monthly event will be listed only once in this book. *Sponsor:* All My Events. ✉

Healthy Weight, Healthy Look Day
Thursday of Health Weight Week is a day to honor women of all sizes and more important, a day to promote a more realistic look for all women. *Sponsor:* Healthy Weight Journal, Frances Berg, Editor, 402 South 14th Street, Hettinger, ND 58639; 701-567-2646.

Pooh Day
Honors the birthday of Alan Alexander Milne, author of the *Winnie the Pooh* stories. Milne was born in 1882 in London, England.

Pulsars first identified (1969)
First identified by University of Arizona astronomers. *Contact:* University of Arizona, Tucson, AZ 85721; 602-621-2211; Fax: 602-621-9098.

Sundance Film Festival
Held in Park City, Utah, from Thursday through Sunday of the last week and a half of January. It is the most important and largest festival featuring the work of independent filmmakers in America. *Sponsor:* Sundance Institute, P.O. Box 16450, Salt Lake City, UT 84116; 801-328-3456.

Thesaurus Day
On the birthday (1779) of Peter Roget, author of the major thesaurus, we celebrate all the-

sauruses. *Sponsor:* Book Marketing Update. ✉

Vacuum tube developed (1903)

This development allowed for more effective transmission of radio signals, including the message President Theodore Roosevelt sent to King Edward VII on this date.

January 19

Black Publishers Day

On the birthday of John H. Johnson, editor and publisher of *Ebony* and *Jet* magazines, we honor all black publishers. Johnson was born in 1918.

Confederate Heroes Day

On the birthday of General Robert E. Lee (1807), Confederate heroes are honored. This public holiday is observed by some states on the third Monday in January. Also known as Robert E. Lee's Birthday or Lee-Jackson-King Day.

Horror Novels Are Horrendous Day

On the birthday (1809) of Edgar Allan Poe, author of many horror tales, we honor all horror novelists who scare the dickens out of us. *Sponsor:* Book Marketing Update. ✉

Tin Can Day

The tin canning process was patented on this day in 1825.

January 20

First traffic rules published (1900)

Writing in a small horse magazine, *Rider & Driver*, William Phelps Eno introduced the first rules for facilitating the flow of traffic. Among the rules: drivers must stay to the right, signal for turns, be licensed, and follow a speed limit.

Hot and Spicy Food International Day

The third Saturday in January celebrates hot and spicy foods from around the world. *Sponsor:* Thai Network, Prasong Nurack, 215 E Walnut Street, Des Moines, IA 50309; 515-282-0044.

National Learn to Ski Day

Learn how to sky on the third Saturday in January.

Reindeer Day

Saint Sebastian Feast Day

Martyred by being shot full of arrows; Saint Sebastian is the patron saint of archers, athletes, and soldiers. He is also patron saint of Rio de Janeiro, Brazil.

Sign of Aquarius

The astrological sign of Aquarius, the water carrier, runs from January 20th to February 19th. Aquarians are unselfish, generous, and idealistic.

Stay Young Forever Day

Celebrate older people on the birthday of comedian George Burns. He was born Nathan Birnbaum in 1896 in New York City. *Sponsor:* The Life of the Party. ✉

World's largest limited-class speed sled-dog derby

Weather permitting, this derby is held the third weekend in January. Contact these men for more information and possible change of dates due to weather: Val Lougheed 705-286-1119 or Jack Brezina 705-286-1288. *Sponsor:* Minden Sled Dog Derby, P.O. Box 97, Minden, Ontario, K0M 2K0 Canada; 705-286-1760; 800-461-7677.

January 21

Amateur Athletic Union founded (1888)

Contact: Amateur Athletic Union, 3400 West 86th Street, Indianapolis, IN 46268; 317-872-2900; Fax: 317-875-0548.

Birthday of the American Novel

The first novel published in America, *The Power of Sympathy, or the Triumph of Nature*, was published in 1789. *Contact:* Book Marketing Update. ✉

Birthday of the Atomic Submarine (1954)

The *USS Nautilus*, the first atomic submarine, was launched in Groton, Connecticut.

Celebrity Read a Book Week

During the last full week of January. *Sponsor:* Choo Choo Child Care Center, Anne L. Haas, 16107 Elliott Pkwy, P.O. Box 250, Williamsport, MD 21795; 301-582-4894; Fax: 301-582-4896.

Celtic New Year

Today is the first day of Luis (Rowan), the first month in the Celtic Tree Calendar.

First wide body jet put into service (1970)

Pan Am flew the first commercial flight of the Boeing 747.

Health Awareness Week

Always celebrated during the week with the fourth Wednesday in January.

Kiwanis International founded (1915)

The first Kiwanis Club was formed in Detroit, Michigan. *Contact:* Kiwanis International. ✉

Microwave oven invented (1967)

National Activity Professionals Week

The week of the fourth Friday in January honors activity directors at nursing homes, senior citizens centers, etc. *Sponsor:* National Association of Activity Professionals, 1225 Eye Street NW #300, Washington, DC 20005; 202-289-0722; Fax: 202-842-0621.

National Glaucoma Awareness Week

Especially during the last full week in January, make sure you get an eye exam. Note that African-Americans are 15 times more likely than the general population to go blind from glaucoma. *Sponsor:* Prevent Blindness America. ✉

National Handwriting Analysis Week

Your handwriting is a written expression of your personality at a given moment. A professional analyst knows for sure. This week is always celebrated the week of the 23rd, John Hancock's birthday. *Sponsor:* American Handwriting Analysis Foundation, P.O. Box 6201, San Jose, CA 95150; 408-377-6775; Fax: 408-377-3739.

National Hugging Day

Share hugs with anyone willing to accept them. The most Famous Huggers of the Year are also announced on this date. *Sponsor:* Kevin Zaborney, 1418 22nd Street, Port Huron, MI 48060; 810-982-8436.

National Meat Week

During the last week of January, encourage the consumption of beef and pork.

National Sanctity of Human Life Day

Always celebrated on the third Sunday in January.

Ramadhan, Muslim month of fasting, begins

During this month of purification, the ninth month of the Islamic calendar, Muslims don't eat or drink during daylight hours; they also abstain from smoking, gambling, and sex. The Koran was first revealed to Muhammad during this month. 1997: January 10. 1998: December 31.

Saint Agnes Feast Day

Saint Agnes is the patron saint of girls, virgins, girl scouts, betrothed couples, and bodily purity. If girls fast for 24 hours and then eat an egg with salt on the eve of her feast day, they will dream of their future husbands.

World Championship Snowmobile Derby

Held the third weekend in January, these races determine the world champion of snowmobile racing. *Sponsor:* Eagle River Derby Races, P.O. Box 1447, Eagle River, WI 54521; 715-479-4424; Fax: 715-479-9711.

World Religion Day

First established in 1950, the third Sunday in January is dedicated to working toward a unified world through religion. This day proclaims the oneness of all religions. *Sponsor:* Baha'i National Center. ✉

Worldwide Kiwanis Week

The week of January 21 promotes lasting relationships among the world's Kiwanis clubs. *Sponsor:* Kiwanis International. ✉

January 22

Ampere Day

Andre Ampere, founder of the science of electrodynamics, was born in 1775, in Lyons, France. The ampere, the unit of electrical current, was named for him.

Answer Your Cat's Question Day

Think about what your cat's question is and then answer it. *Sponsor:* Wellness Permission League. ✉

First nude beach opened in the U.S. (1952)

Roe vs Wade Anniversary (1972)

This Supreme Court decision legalized women's right to abortions. *Contact:* U.S. Supreme Court. ✉

Rowan & Martin's Laugh-In premiered (1968)

Dick Martin and Dan Rowan starred in this wacky show. *Contact:* NBC-TV. ✉

Saint Vincent Feast Day

Saint Vincent is the patron saint of wine growers. If the sun is seen on this day, good wine crops will grow during the coming season.

January 23

20th Amendment to the Constitution ratified (1933)

Set the inauguration date as January 20th and fixed the succession of president-elects. This amendment was formally adopted on February 6, 1933.

24th Amendment to the Constitution ratified (1964)

Eliminated poll taxes and other prerequisites of voting in U.S. elections.

Barney Miller premiered (1975)

This honest comedy about police life aired on ABC. *Contact:* ABC-TV. ✉

Barney's Birthday

Barney, the purple dinosaur, is over 2,000,000 years old, and no one is sure when he was born. His birthday is celebrated on the 23rd of every month. Note: This monthly event will be listed only once in this book. *Sponsor:* The Lyons Group, P.O. Box 9000, Allen, TX 75002; 800-791-8093.

First woman to receive a medical degree in America (1849)

Elizabeth Blackwell graduated from the Medical Institution of Geneva, New York.

National Handwriting Day

On the birthday of John Hancock (1737), the first signer of the Declaration of Independence, celebrate good handwriting. This day encourages people to write neatly so others can easily read it. Also known as Practice Your Penmanship Day.

✉ Addresses for frequently cited organizations are gathered on pages vii–viii.

JANUARY   15

National Pie Day

Celebrate the joys of baking and eating pies. The best way to round out a square meal is with a triangle of pie. *Sponsor:* Charlie Papazian, P.O. Box 1825, Boulder, CO 80306-1825; 303-665-6489.

Roots miniseries premiered (1977)

The miniseries, which traced a black family from Africa to modern-day America, began the first day of a record-setting run. At the time, it was the most-watched television miniseries in history. *Contact:* ABC-TV. ✉

Tupperware invented

The original party plan food saver. Earl Tupper bought his first manufacturing plant in 1942, and Tupperware was introduced to the public in 1945. *Contact:* Tupperware U.S., P.O. Box 2353, Orlando, FL 32802-2353; 407-826-4568; Fax: 407-826-4459; 800-858-7221.

January 24

Boy Scout's Birthday

The first troop was organized by Robert Baden-Powell in England in 1908. *Contact:* Boy Scouts of America. ✉

California Gold Discovery Day

In 1848, gold was discovered at Sutter's Mill near Coloma, Califor-nia. Also known as Go for the Gold Day. *Contact:* California Division of Tourism, P.O. Box 1499, Sacramento, CA 95812-1499; 916-322-3402; 800-462-2543.

First beer in cans sold (1935)

First heart transplant operation (1964)

This operation was unsuccessful; it was performed at the University Hospital in Jackson, Mississippi. *Contact:* University of Mississippi, School of Medicine, 2500 N State Street, Jackson, MS 39216; 601-984-1010; Fax: 601-984-1013.

First ice cream bar patented (1922)

Christian Nelson of Onawa, Iowa, patented the Eskimo Pie.

National School Nurse Day

Since 1977, the fourth Wednesday of January has provided recognition to school nurses. *Sponsor:* National Association of School Nurses,

P.O. Box 1300, Scarborough, ME 04070-1300; 207-883-2117.

Saint Francis de Sales Feast Day

Patron saint of journalists, authors, the deaf, and the Catholic press.

TV Game Show Day

On the birthday of Mark Goodson (1915), we celebrate all television game shows. He created such shows as *The Price Is Right, What's My Line, Family Feud, I've Got a Secret*, and *Password*.

World's deadliest earthquake (1556)

An earthquake in the Shensi Province of China killed 830,000 people.

January 25

A Room of One's Own Day

Find a private place to enjoy silence and aloneness. *Sponsor:* Wellness Permission League. ✉

Conversion of Saint Paul

This feast day celebrates the conversion of Saint Paul from persecutor of Christians to one of the founders of the Christian faith as we know it.

Elvis Presley's first #1 hit released (1956)

"Heartbreak Hotel" was released by RCA. It became a number one hit on May 3, 1956.

Emmy Awards Birthday

The first Emmys were given out in 1949. *"Pantomine Quiz Time"* on KTLA won for the best show; Shirley Dinsdale and her puppet Judy Splinters won for best personality. *Contact:* Academy of TV Arts & Sciences, 522 Lankershim Boulevard, Burbank, CA 91601; 818-754-2800; Fax: 818-761-2827.

First Black Women's Rights Convention (1851)

This convention was held in Akron, Ohio.

First televised presidential news conference (1961)

President Kennedy held the first live TV news conference.

First transcontinental commercial jet flight (1959)

American Airlines flew a Boeing 707 on this flight. *Contact:* American Airlines, P.O. Box 619616, Dallas, TX 75261; 817-963-1234.

First transcontinental phone call (1915)

This call was placed between New York and San Francisco. Alexander Graham Bell inaugurated the service.

Fluoride Day

In 1945, Grand Rapids, Michigan, was the first city to add fluoride to the city's drinking water. *Contact:* Grand Rapids Visitors Bureau, 140 Monroe Center NW #300, Grand Rapids, MI 49503-2246; 616-459-8287; 800-678-9859; Fax: 616-459-7291.

National Clashing Clothes Day

On the fourth Thursday in January, beat the mid-winter doldrums by wearing clashing clothes to work. Formerly sponsored by the Shane Hill Nursing Home.

United Mine Workers of America founded (1890)

On this date in 1946, the United Mine Workers joined the American Federation of Labor. *Contact:* United Mine Workers of America, 900 15th Street NW, Washington, DC 20005; 202-842-7200; Fax: 202-842-7342.

January 26

All You Can Eat Day

Every month, on the 26th, take a homeless person out to lunch. Let them eat all they can eat. Note: This monthly event will be listed only once in this book. *Sponsor:* All My Events. ✉

Backwards Day

On the last Friday in January, look back on your accomplishments. Eat backwards, dress backwards. *Sponsor:* Unity Lutheran School, Pamela Wolfe, 5401 S. Calhoun, Fort Wayne, IN 46807; 219-747-2958.

Black Woman Aviator Day

We honor all black women who fly. Bessie Coleman was the first; she was born on this day in 1892.

Electric dental drill patented (1875)

George Green of Kalamazoo, Michigan, patented the electric dental drill.

First prohibition law passed in the U.S. (1838)

Tennessee passed the first prohibition law.

Michigan Admission Day

In 1837, Michigan became the 26th state of the U.S. *Contact:* Michigan Travel Bureau, 300 S. Capitol Avenue #F, Lansing, MI 48909; 517-373-0670; 800-543-2937; Fax: 517-373-0059.

National Activity Professionals Day

The fourth Friday in January honors activity directors at nursing homes, senior citizens centers, etc. *Sponsor:* National Association of Activity Professionals, 1225 Eye Street NW #300, Washington, DC 20005; 202-289-0722; Fax: 202-842-0621.

Saint Paula Feast Day

Because she achieved so much after the death of her husband, she is considered the patron saint of widows.

Spouse's Day

On the fourth Friday in January, spouses should share jobs and responsibilities in order to show their appreciation for each other. Formerly sponsored by WCUZ Radio, Grand Rapids, Michigan.

January 27

Electric light patented (1880)

Thomas A. Edison received a patent for the electric incandescent light.

First state university founded (1785)

The University of Georgia was the first state university. *Contact*: University of Georgia, 114 Academic Building, Athens, GA 30602; 706-542-2112; Fax: 706-542-6578.

First tape recorders sold (1948)

Jewish Music Season

Formerly sponsored by the Jewish Music Council, these days celebrate Jewish music. The season is held from the Saturday before the full moon in January to the eve of Israel's Independence Day (April 23).

Mad Tea Party Day

On the birthday of Lewis Carroll, author of *Alice's Adventures in Wonderland*, we celebrate life with a mad tea party. Carroll, whose real name was Charles Lutwidge Dodgson, was born in 1832, in Cheshire, England.

Mozart's Birthday

Wolfgang Amadeus Mozart, one of the world's greatest composers, was born in Salzburg, Austria, in 1756; celebrate by playing the piano.

Thomas Crapper Day

Honors the anniversary of the death of Thomas Crapper in 1910. He was the primary inventor of the modern flush toilet (February 3, 1837).

Vietnam War ended (1973)

A cease-fire agreement was signed by the U.S., North and South Vietnam, and the Viet Cong to end the war in Vietnam. This agreement ended the longest foreign war in U.S. history.

January 28

Challenger Space Shuttle Explosion (1986)

The space shuttle *Challenger* exploded within seconds after its launch; 7 people were killed. *Contact*: NASA. ✉

First commercial radio station to air a CD (1983)

WDHA of Dover, New Jersey, was the first.

First commercial telephone switchboard (1878)

First daily college newspaper (1878)

The oldest college daily was *The Yale News*. *Contact*: Yale University, The Yale News, Yale Station, P.O. Box 209007, New Haven, CT 06520-9007; 203-432-2424; Fax: 203-432-7425.

First Jewish Supreme Court judge (1916)

Louis Brandeis was appointed as the first Jewish judge of the U.S. Supreme Court. *Contact*: U.S. Supreme Court. ✉

First ski tow started running in Vermont (1938)

Free African Society founded (1787)

Worked to outlaw slavery; organized by Absalom Jones and Richard Allen in Philadelphia, Pennsylvania.

National Kazoo Day

To promote the use of kazoos with music-loving stroke patients. *Sponsor*: Leader Nursing and Rehab Center, 1070 Stouffer Avenue, Chambersburg, PA 17201; 717-263-0436.

National Popcorn Day

Eat a big bowl of popcorn as you watch the Superbowl. *Sponsor*: KMJC Radio, Polly Peterson, 100 E Kimberly, Davenport, IA 52806.

National Spieling Day

Celebrate America's national past-time—blathering. *Sponsor:* Donahue Brothers Productions, Bill Donahue, 7626 SE Alder, Portland, OR 97215; 503-254-5315; e-mail: wfd13@aol.com.

Saint Thomas Aquinas Feast Day

Patron saint of students, academics, Roman Catholic schools, colleges, universities, booksellers, philosophers, theologians, and pencil makers.

Superbowl Sunday

Sponsor: National Football League.
✉

U.S. Coast Guard established by Congress (1915)

Contact: U.S. Coast Guard, 2100 Second Street SW, Washington, DC 20593; 202-267-2229.

"We Are the World" was recorded (1985)

30 music superstars gathered together to record "We Are the World" to raise funds for starving Africans.

January 29

American League organized (1900)

Organized in Philadelphia, Pennsylvania. *Contact:* American League, 350 Park Avenue, 18th Floor, New York, NY 10022; 212-339-7600; Fax: 212-935-5069.

American Music Awards Ceremony

The winners of these awards covering all categories are selected by consumers. Dick Clark Productions also produces the Golden Globe and American Country Music Awards ceremonies. *Sponsor:* Dick Clark Productions, 3003 W Olive Avenue, Burbank, CA 91505; 818-841-3003.

Baseball Hall of Fame established (1936)

Established in 1936, it was dedicated in 1939. *Contact:* National Baseball Hall of Fame, Main Street, P.O. Box 590, Cooperstown, NY 13326; 607-547-9988.

First country to curb use of aerosol cans (1978)

Sweden was the first country to curb the use of aerosol cans to help preserve the ozone layer.

First Librarian of Congress appointed (1802)

President Thomas Jefferson appointed John Beckley as the first Librarian of Congress. *Contact:* Library of Congress, 101 Independence Avenue SE, Washington, DC 20540-0001; 202-707-5000; Fax: 202-707-5844.

First members of Baseball and Football Halls of Fame

Members of the Baseball Hall of Fame were first named in 1936 (Ty Cobb and Babe Ruth were among the first honorees). Members of the Football Hall of Fame were first named in 1963.

Kansas Admission Day (1861)

Kansas became the 34th state. *Contact:* Kansas Travel & Tourism Division, Kansas Department of Commerce, 700 SW Harrison #1300, Topeka, KS 66603; 913-296-2009; 800-252-6727; Fax: 913-296-6988.

National Puzzle Day

Honors creators of puzzles and games. *Sponsor:* Jodi Jill Features, Carol Handz, 1705 14th Street #321, Boulder, CO 80302; 303-441-7877; 303-575-1319.

Think Hawaii Day

On the birthday of Tom Selleck, star of *Magnum, P.I.,* celebrate the island state of Hawaii. Selleck was born in 1945, in Detroit, Michigan. *Sponsor:* The Life of the Party. ✉

William McKinley's Birthday
The 25th President of the U.S. was born in 1843, in Niles, Ohio.

January 30

Festival of Peace
Honors Pax, the Roman goddess of peace.

First jazz record cut in U.S. (1917)

Franklin Delano Roosevelt's Birthday
The 32nd President of the U.S was born near Hyde Park, New York, in 1882.

Let It Be Day
In 1969, the Beatles gave their last public performance on their rooftop in London, England. The concert was cut short by police responding to complaints from neighbors. ✉

The Lone Ranger first aired (1933)
The first episode was broadcast on WXYZ Radio in Detroit, Michigan. Contact: WXYZ Radio, 20777 West Ten-Mile Road, Southfield, MI 48037; 810-827-7777; Fax: 810-827-4454.

Mahatma Gandhi assassinated (1948)
Mahatma Gandhi was assassinated in New Delhi, India. Gandhi, one of this century's greatest political leaders, espoused a nonviolent means of effecting political change.

Tet Offensive Anniversary
In 1968 the Viet Cong violated their own cease-fire agreement during the Tet holidays to attack major cities and other sites all over South Vietnam. While the Viet Cong lost 40,000 soldiers, this offensive was credited with turning American public opinion.

World's largest maritime disaster (1945)
When a Soviet submarine torpedoed the German passenger ship *Wilhelm Gustoff*, 7,700 people drowned in the Baltic Sea.

January 31

Animal in Space Day
In 1961, the U.S. recovered the first large animal it launched into space. Ham, a chimpanzee, returned to Earth after successfully transmitting signals from outer space. *Contact:* NASA. ✉

First daytime soap opera on TV (1949)
These Are My Children was the first daytime soap opera broadcast on TV. It was broadcast from the NBC station in Chicago, Illinois. *Contact:* NBC-TV. ✉

First McDonald's in the Soviet Union (1990)
McDonald's opened its first fast-food restaurant on Pushkin Square in Moscow. *Contact:* McDonald's Corporation, 1 McDonald's Plaza, Oak Brook, IL 60521; 708-575-3000; Fax: 708-575-5700.

First successful U.S. satellite launch (1958)
The Explorer I was the first successful satellite launched by the U.S. During this trip, it discovered the Van Allen Belt. *Contact:* NASA. ✉

Jackie Robinson's Birthday
The first African-American to play major league baseball. He broke a color barrier that has enabled thousands of blacks to play professional sports. Robinson was born in 1919, in Cairo, Georgia.

Saint John Bosco Feast Day
Patron saint of editors, publishers, and apprentices.

Twist-off bottle cap invented (1956)

Westerns Are Wonderful Day
On the birthday (1875) of Zane Grey, we celebrate western novels and stories of the Old West. *Sponsor:* Book Marketing Update. ✉

FEBRUARY

AMD Awareness Month
Age-related macular degeneration is the #1 cause of blindness among older Americans. More than 13 million Americans over the age of 40 show signs of this disorder. *Sponsor:* Prevent Blindness America. ✉

America Loves Its Kids Month

American Heart Month
Volunteers educate people door-to-door on the importance of taking care of our circulatory systems. *Sponsor:* American Heart Association, 7272 Greenville Avenue, Dallas, TX 75231-4596; 214-373-6300; 800-242-8721; Fax: 214-706-1341.

American History Month
First proclaimed in 1956, promotes the study of American history. *Sponsor:* Daughters of American Revolution, 1776 D Street NW, Washington, DC 20006-5392; 202-628-1776; Fax: 202-879-3261.

An Affair to Remember
Keep the romance sizzling, have an affair with your spouse this month. *Sponsor:* Monogamous Male Association, Rose Smith, P.O. Box 81064, Albuquerque, NM 87198-1064; 505-899-3121; Fax: 505-899-3120.

Black History Month (1926)
Celebrates achievements of black Americans. Also known as Afro-American History Month. February includes the birthdays of Abraham Lincoln and Frederick Douglas. *Sponsor:* Association for the Study of Afro-American Life and History, 1407 14th Street NW, Washington, DC 20005; 202-265-1441.

Canned Food Month
Promotes the convenience and nutrition of canned food. *Sponsor:* Canned Food Information Council, 500 N Michigan Avenue #200, Chicago, IL 60611; 312-836-7279; Fax: 312-836-6060.

Celebration of Chocolate
Celebrate hot chocolate, boxed chocolates, fudge, chips, and cookies. *Sponsor:* Pinehill Bed & Breakfast, Sharon Burdick, Innkeeper, 400 Mix Street, Oregon, IL 61061; 815-732-2061.

Creative Romance Month
To encourage couples to feed the flames of romance. *Sponsor:* Celebrate Romance, Eileen Buchheim, 5199 E Pacific Coast Hwy #303A, Long Beach, CA 90804-3398; 714-459-7620; 800-368-7978.

Great American Pies Month
Promotes America's favorite dessert. *Sponsor:* Borden Inc., Product Publicity (Eagle Brand), 180 E Broad Street, Columbus, OH 43215-3367; 614-225-4037; Fax: 614-225-7680.

Human Relations Month
Promotes better understanding among different peoples and races. *Sponsor:* New Hanover Human Relations Commission, 320 Chestnut Street #409, Wilmington, NC 28401; 910-341-7171; Fax: 910-341-4040.

Humpback Whale Awareness Month
Distribution of information on the humpback whale. *Sponsor:* Sea Life Park—Hawaii, 41-202 Kalanianaole Highway #7, Waimanalo, HI 96795-1897; 808-259-7933; Fax: 808-259-7373.

International Boost Your Self-Esteem Month

Build self-esteem; make your dream a reality. *Sponsor:* Valla Dana Fotiades, P.O. Box 812, West Side Station, Worcester, MA 01602-0812; 508-799-9860.

International Embroidery Month

In appreciation of embroidery and monogramming. *Sponsor:* Stitches Magazine, 5660 Greenwood Plaza Blvd #350, Englewood, CO 80111; 303-793-0448; Fax: 303-793-0454.

Life Rhythms and Health Month

Encourages awareness of the importance of body rhythms. *Sponsor:* International Health Association for Practical Application of Biological Rhythms, Thomas Reynolds, Director, 1537A Fourth Street #183, San Rafael, CA 94901.

Marfan Syndrome Awareness Month

40,000 people in the U. S. have Marfan syndrome, a genetic disorder of the connective tissue. *Sponsor:* National Marfan Foundation, 382 Main Street, Port Washington, NY 11050; 516-883-8712; 800-862-7326; Fax: 516-883-8712.

Month of Love and Romance

Celebrate love and romance for the entire month of Valentine's. *Sponsor:* Delacorte Books, Bantam Double-day Dell, 1540 Broadway, New York, NY 10103; 212-354-6500; 800-223-6834; Fax: 212-782-9700.

National Blah Buster Month

Think Spring! Celebrate that winter's almost over. *Sponsor:* Blahco Creative Group, James Kells Ward, 3796 E Velocipede Pike, Liberty, IN 47353.

National Cat Health Month

Sponsor: American Veterinary Medical Association, Edelman Public Relations, 300 E Randolph Drive, 63rd Floor, Chicago, IL 60601; 312-240-3000; Fax: 312-240-2900.

National Cherry Month

It's George Washington's birthday month; use canned, frozen, or dried tart cherries in your favorite pie, crisp, cobbler, bread, or other recipe. For a free 36-page recipe book, write to the Cherry Marketing Institute. *Sponsor:* Cherry Marketing Institute, Jane Baker, Domestic Marketing, 2220 University Park Drive #200, Okemos, MI 48864; 517-347-0100; Fax: 517-347-0605.

National Children's Dental Health Month

Designed to educate children about proper eating and brushing habits. For a copy of *Casper's Dental Health Activity Book,* send 35¢ to the Health Education Department at the following address. *Sponsor:* American Dental Association, 211 E Chicago Avenue #2038, Chicago, IL 60611-2678; 312-440-7649; 800-621-8099.

National Community College Month

National Condom Month

Sponsor: Pharmacists Planning Service. ✉

National Cruise Vacation Month

Sponsor: Cruise Lines International, Diana M. Orban Associates, 60 East 42nd Street, New York, NY 10165; 212-557-8448.

National Fiber Focus Month

Eat more fiber for better health. *Sponsor:* General Mills, Fiber One Cereal Department, P.O. Box 1113, Minneapolis, MN 55440; 612-540-4520.

National Grapefruit Month

Sponsored by the Florida Department of Citrus.

✉ Addresses for frequently cited organizations are gathered on pages vii–viii.

National Macadamia Nut Month

Celebrates the discovery of macadamia nuts in Australia in 1850.

National Snack Food Month

Enjoy America's salty, crunchy, munchy snacks. *Sponsor:* Snack Food Association, 1711 King Street #1, Alexandria, VA 22314; 703-836-4500; Fax: 703-836-8262.

National Weddings Month

The month of romance; most engagements take place between Christmas and Valentine's Day. Also the time when most brides start planning for summer weddings. *Sponsor:* Association of Bridal Consultants, 200 Chestnutland Road, New Milford, CT 06776-2521; 203-355-0464; Fax: 203-354-1404.

National Wild Bird Feeding Month

Help birds make it through the winter, put out extra bread crumbs or seeds for them to eat. *Sponsor:* National Bird-Feeding Society, Sue Wells, 2218 Crabtree Lane, Northbrook, IL 60062-3520; 708-272-0135.

Potato Lovers Month

For free potato information and the most current educational materials for teachers, send a request (with your grade level) to the National Potato Board. *Sponsor:* National Potato Board, 1385 S Colorado Boulevard #512, Denver, CO 80222; 303-369-7783.

Responsible Pet Owner Month

Take care of your pets. *Sponsor:* American Society for the Prevention of Cruelty to Animals, 424 East 92nd Street, New York, NY 10128; 212-876-7700.

Return Shopping Carts to the Supermarket Month

An amnesty month to allow people to return milk crates, bread trays, and shopping carts. *Sponsor:* Illinois Food Retailers Association, Anthony Dinolfo, Director, 8148 S Homan Avenue, Chicago, IL 60652; 312-737-6540.

Self-Help and Advice Books Month

Celebrates books and writers on psychology, relationships, family, aging, sex, parenting, education, recovery, etc. *Sponsor:* Book Marketing Update. ✉

Sleep Safety Month

Improve safety in the bedroom, especially for children. *Sponsor:* Sleep Products Safety Council, 333 Commerce Street, Alexandria, VA 22314; 703-683-8371; Fax: 703-683-4503.

World Understanding Month

During the month of Valentine's Day, Brotherhood/Sisterhood Week, and International Friendship Week, we work toward greater understanding among all people.

World Wide Innovation Month

Celebrate creativity and innovation during this month. *Sponsor:* The Innovative Thinking Network, Joyce Wycoff, 101 E. Victoria #33, Santa Barbara, CA 93101; 805-963-9151; Fax: 805-963-8220; e-mail: staff@thinksmart.com.

February 1

Auto Insurance Day

Travelers Insurance issued the first auto insurance policy in Buffalo, New York, in 1898. *Contact:* Travelers Insurance Company, 1 Tower Square, Hartford, CT 06183-0001; 203-277-0111; 800-243-0191; Fax: 203-277-7979.

Be an Encourager Day

Send a note, make someone's favorite food, offer a smile or hug, give a small gift that says "thanks for being here." *Sponsor:* Liz Curtis Higgs, P.O. Box 43577, Louisville, KY 40253-0577; 502-254-5454; Fax: 502-254-5455.

First armored car introduced (1920)

First children's music book (1831)

First federal penitentiary completed (1906)

First modern automobile patent (1898)

First motion picture censorship board appointed (1914)

First motion picture studio (1893)
The Black Maria studio was created by Thomas Edison in West Orange, New Jersey.

First single record released (1949)

First steamboat patent (1788)

First U.S. dental college (1840)

Frankly, I Don't Give a Damn Day
Clark Gable, who uttered those immortal words in Gone with the Wind, was born in 1901, in Cadiz, Ohio. Do whatever you like today.

Inspire Your Employees to Excellence Day
Celebrated on the first weekday in February. Encourage your employees to do their best; make your organization so attractive to them that they'll never want to leave. Sponsor: CBT Recruitment & Retention, Carolyn B. Thompson, 221 Vermont Road, Frankfort, IL 60423; 815-469-1162; Fax: 815-469-0886.

National Freedom Day
Abraham Lincoln approved the 13th Amendment in 1865, abolishing slavery.

National Women and Girls in Sports Day
Celebrated on the first Thursday in February.

No Talk Day
Celebrated on the first Thursday in February, recognizes the importance of written communications. Sponsor: Garner Elementary School, Marilyn Bachelor, Teacher, 3116 Wilman Drive, Clio, MI 48420.

Robinson Crusoe Day
In 1709, Alexander Selkirk was rescued; his adventures formed the basis for Daniel Defoe's novel, Robinson Crusoe.

Saint Brigid Feast Day
The patron saint of cows, the dairy, and milk. A house decorated with Saint Brigid's cross is said to be protected from harm; also patron saint of Ireland, New Zealand, fugitives, newborns, nuns, and poultry raisers.

Sit-In Against Discrimination Day
In 1960, 4 black college students sat down at a Woolworth's lunch counter and ordered coffee. They were refused service, so they sat there as a form of nonviolent protest. Their example inspired sit-ins all over the South.

Supreme Court convened for the first time (1790)
Convened at the Royal Exchange Building on Broad Street in New York City. Contact: U.S. Supreme Court. ✉

Women's Heart Health Day
At the beginning of American Heart Month, remember that heart disease is the number one killer of women. Sponsor: Charlotte Libov, 71 Judson Lane, Bethlehem, CT 06751; 203-266-5904; e-mail: 75260.2606@compuserve.com.

February 2

Candlemas Day
Celebrates both the presentation of Jesus in the temple 40 days after his birth; and the purification of Mary, his mother. Also known as the Purification of Mary; old English name is Wives' Feast Day.

Crown bottle cap patented (1892)

Export-Import Bank established (1934)
Established by President Franklin Delano Roosevelt to encourage trade. *Contact:* Export-Import Bank of the U.S., 811 Vermont Avenue NW, Washington, DC 20571; 202-566-8990; 800-424-5201; Fax: 202-566-7524.

First close-up in movie history (1893)
The close-up was of a man sneezing. It appeared in the movie *The Record of a Sneeze*, which was made at Thomas Edison's Black Maria studio. It is also the first movie to be copyrighted.

First lie detector test (1935)

First person to pole vault over 16 feet (1962)
John Uelses performed this vault at Madison Square Garden in New York City.

Groundhog Day
If the groundhog sees its shadow on this day (that is, if the sun shines today), winter will continue for another 6 weeks.

Longest work stoppage in sports history ended
On April 2, 1995, after 234 days and no World Series, Major League baseball players and owners agreed to end the longest baseball strike in history. *Contact:* Major League Baseball. ✉

National League formed (1876)
This was the first professional baseball league. *Contact:* National League, 350 Park Avenue, 18th Floor, New York, NY 10022; 212-339-7700; Fax: 212-935-5069.

Party Party Day
An excuse to have a party once a month (when the day equals the month). *Sponsor:* Bonza Bottler Day. ✉

Treaty of Guadalupe Hidalgo (1948)
The U.S.-Mexico war ended with the signing of this treaty. Mexico ceded California, Nevada, Utah, Arizona, parts of Colorado, New Mexico, and Wyoming to the U.S.

U.S. Army Dental Corps established by Congress (1901)
Contact: Department of the Army, Pentagon SAPA-CR, Room 3E718, Washington, DC 20310; 703-695-0363; Fax: 703-693-5737.

World Shovel Race Championships
Spectators can join in on these world championships. Of course, they have little chance of winning against the pros who use modified snow shovels. Always held on the first weekend in February. *Sponsor:* Angel Fire Resort, P.O. Box B, Angel Fire, NM 87710; 800-633-7463.

February 3

15th Amendment to the Constitution ratified (1870)
Granted all citizens the right to vote, regardless of race or color; took effect on March 30, 1870.

16th Amendment to the Constitution ratified (1913)
Granted Congress the power to levy taxes on income.

American Painters Day
On the birthday of American illustrator Norman Rockwell (born 1894 in New York City), we honor all American painters. Go to your favorite museum and enjoy the great art that is freely available to you. *Sponsor:* Open Horizons. ✉

The Day That Music Died

In 1959, Buddy Holly, Richie Valens, and the Big Bopper died in an airplane crash outside Clear Lake, Iowa. According to Don McLean's song, "American Pie," this is the day that music died.

First paper money issued in America (1690)

Massachusetts issued the first paper money in America. *Contact:* Massachusetts Tourism Office, 100 Cambridge Street, 13th Floor, Boston, MA 02202; 617-727-3201; 800-447-6277; Fax: 617-727-6525.

Flush Toilet Birthday (1837)

Thomas Crapper was the primary inventor of the modern flush toilet.

Income Tax Birthday

The 16th Amendment was ratified in 1913, and granted Congress the power to tax income. Okay, maybe you don't want to celebrate today. *Contact:* Internal Revenue Service. ✉

Saint Blaise Feast Day

Patron saint of throats and throat ailments. On this feast day, Catholics have their throats blessed.

Saranac Lake Winter Carnival

From the first Saturday in February to the following Sunday, America's oldest winter festival features an ice palace, lots of games and activities, and a carnival ball. *Sponsor:* Chamber of Commerce, 30 Main Street, Saranac Lake, NY 12983; 518-891-1990; 800-347-1992.

Speed Weeks

From the first Saturday in February until 2 weeks later, the Daytona International Speedway hosts IMSA Grand Prix of Endurance Race. *Sponsor:* Daytona International Speedway, P.O. Box 2801, Daytona Beach, FL 32120-2801; 904-254-6782.

Trade relations with Vietnam reopened (1993)

Contact: Socialist Republic of Vietnam, Mission to the United Nations, 20 Waterside Plaza, New York, NY 10010; 212-679-3779; Fax: 212-686-8534.

World Championship Hoop Dance Contest

Since 1990, Native American hoop dancers compete for the world championship on the first weekend in February. *Sponsor:* Heard Museum, 22 E Monte Vista Road, Phoenix, AZ 85004; 602-252-8840.

February 4

Apache Wars begin (1861)

Apache chief Cochise was arrested for rading a ranch. After escaping, he declared war on the U.S.; it lasted for 25 years.

Boy Scouts of America Anniversary Week

Chartered by Congress in 1910. Boy Scouts Week is held during the week of the 8th. *Sponsor:* Boy Scouts of America. ✉

Chaste Moon

The full moon of February is the chaste moon, symbolic of strength and fertility; also known as the Snow Moon in the American backwoods tradition.

Circle K International Week

First full week in February honors college students who volunteer their help. *Sponsor:* Circle K International, Kiwanis International. ✉

Confederate States of America founded (1861)

Founded in Montgomery, Alabama.

Festival of King Frost

Designed to fight the boredom of winter with a celebration asking for a quick arrival of spring.

First Winter Olympics (1932)

The first Winter Olympics were held in Lake Placid, New York.

Contact: U.S. Olympic Committee. ✉

**Interstate Commerce
Act enacted (1887)**
The Interstate Commerce Commission was the first federal regulatory commission in the U.S. *Contact:* Interstate Commerce Commission, 12th St. & Constitution Avenue NW, Washington, DC 20423-0001; 202-927-7119; Fax: 202-927-5984.

**Liberia founded as home
for freed slaves (1822)**
The American Colonization Society founded the African state of Liberia as a home for freed U.S. slaves. *Contact:* Republic of Liberia Embassy, 5201 16th Street NW, Washington, DC 20011; 202-723-0437.

Muffin Mania Week
Always celebrated the first full week in February.

**National Burn
Awareness Week**
During the first week in February, make sure your family is safe by burn-proofing your home. Look for danger spots, exposed heaters, etc.

**National Crime
Prevention Week**
The first full week in February is designed to stimulate year-around crime prevention activities. *Sponsor:*

The National Exchange Clubs, C Neal Davis, 3050 Central Avenue, Toledo, OH 43606-1700; 419-535-3232; Fax: 419-535-1989.

**National Homemade
Soup Day**
Sponsor: The Life of the Party. ✉

NFL Pro Bowl
The Sunday after the Superbowl, the best players of the National Football League come together to play the all-star game of football. *Contact:* National Football League. ✉

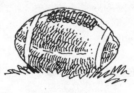

**Our Town opened on
Broadway (1938)**
Thornton Wilder's play about small town life.

Torture Abolition Day
In 1985, 20 countries (not the U.S.) signed a United Nations charter against torture. *Sponsor:* United Nations. ✉

USO Birthday
Since 1941, the USO has been entertaining armed services personnel away from home.

February 5

**American Statistical Society
incorporated (1841)**
Contact: American Statistical Association, 1429 Duke Street, Alexandria, VA 22314-3402; 703-684-1221; Fax: 703-684-2037.

**Dietary Managers' Pride in
Food Service Week**
The first week in February (Monday to Friday) honors dietary managers and others working in institutional food service. *Sponsor:* Dietary Managers Association, One Pierce Place #1220, Itasca, IL 60143-1277; 708-775-9200; Fax: 708-775-9250.

**Eating Disorders
Awareness Week**
During the first full week in February, starting with Monday, take time to become more aware of eating disorders. *Sponsor:* Eating Disorders Awareness and Prevention Association, Anita Sinicrope; 412-922-5922.

**First educational television
station (1932)**
W2XAB in New York City was the first.

**First gas company
incorporated (1817)**

Home Run Hitters Days
On the birthdays of Hank Aaron and Babe Ruth, we honor all home run hitters. Henry Aaron was born

on February 5, 1934, in Mobile, Alabama; George Herman Ruth was born on February 6, 1895, in Baltimore, Maryland.

Longest War in History ended (1985)
The Third Punic War began in 149 B.C. and ended in 1985 (2131 years later). The war ended when the mayors of Rome and Carthage finally signed a treaty in 1985.

Mandatory screening of airline passengers (1972)
Airline passengers and luggage screening was required by the federal government to cut down on hijacking.

National School Counseling Week
Celebrated the first full week of February; promotes school counseling programs and services. *Sponsor*: American School Counselors Association, 5999 Stevenson Avenue, Alexandria, VA 22304; 703-823-9800; Fax: 703-461-3569.

National Wildlife Federation founded (1936)
Contact: National Wildlife Federation, 1400 16th Street NW, Washington, DC 20036-2217; 202-797-6800; 800-432-6564; Fax: 202-797-6646.

No Memo! Day
On the first Monday of every month, don't write any memos! *Sponsor*: All My Events. ✉

Saint Agatha Feast Day
Patron saint of foundry workers, jewelers, nurses, miners, and Alpine guides. She's also patron saint of Malta, and helps those with breast diseases.

Tu B'Shevat
Jewish Arbor Day, or New Year of the Trees, to show respect to trees and other plants. Celebrated the 15th day of Shevat in the Hebrew calendar. 1997: January 23; 1998: February 11.

Weatherman's Day
On the birthday of early American weatherman, John Jeffries (1744), we celebrate and honor all meteorologists.

February 6

First railroad charter in the U.S. (1815)
Received by John Stevens.

Massachusetts Ratification Day
One of the original 13 states, in 1788 Massachusetts was the 6th state to ratify the Constitution. *Contact*: Massachusetts Tourism Office, 100 Cambridge Street, 13th Floor, Boston, MA 02202; 617-727-3201; 800-447-6277; Fax: 617-727-6525.

Mid-Winter's Day Celebration
This day is approximately halfway between the winter solstice and the vernal equinox. *Sponsor*: The Fifth Wheel Tavern, Richard Ankli, 639 Fifth Street, Ann Arbor, MI 48103; e-mail: rankli@umich.edu.

Ronald Wilson Reagan's Birthday
The 40th President of the U.S. was born in Tampico, Illinois, in 1911. At 73, he was the oldest person ever elected President.

Saint Amand of Maastricht Feast Day
Patron saint of bartenders and innkeepers (hotel workers).

February 7

11th Amendment to the Constitution ratified (1795)
Affirmed the power of the states by prohibiting suits against them.

Ballet debuts in the U.S. (1827)
Ballet was introduced at the Bowery Theater in New York City. The first ballet performed was *The Deserter*.

Beatles began first U.S. tour (1964)

The first tour began in New York City when the Beatles landed at Kennedy Airport. On February 9, they made their first appearance on *The Ed Sullivan Show*.

First astronauts to fly freely in space (1984)

Two American astronauts from the space shuttle *Challenger* were the first humans to fly freely in space. *Contact:* NASA. ✉

Great American Pizza Bake

During the 7 days before Valentine's Day, pizza parlors and other restaurants create healthy pizza recipes to help people control their cholesterol. *Sponsor:* Cholesterol Council of America, Frederick S. Mayer, President, PPSI, P.O. Box 1336, Sausalito, CA 94966; 800-523-2222; Fax: 415-332-1832

Largest Snowfall Anniversary (1916)

78 inches of snow fell on Alaska.

Little House Day

On the birthday of Laura Ingalls Wilder (1867), we celebrate home and family life. Wilder's Little House books for children featured stories about the life of the Ingalls family.

Main Street USA Day

On the birthday of Sinclair Lewis (1885), celebrate small towns everywhere! Sinclair Lewis was born at Sauk Center, Minnesota.

Monopoly game mass marketed (1935)

Invented on March 7, 1933. *Contact:* Parker Brothers, 50 Dunham Road, Beverly, MA 01915; 508-927-7600; Fax: 508-921-3066.

National Hangover Awareness Day

Celebrated the day after Babe Ruth's birthday (1895); he was known for his hangovers. *Sponsor:* WRNX/WTTT, Brian McCullough, P.O. Box 67, Amherst, MA 01004; 413-256-6794; Fax: 413-256-3171.

Put Your Gun Away Day

On this day, Los Angeles banned the sale of semi-automatic weapons. *Sponsor:* The Life of the Party. ✉

February 8

The Birth of a Nation (1914)

D. W. Griffin's classic movie premiered in Los Angeles.

Boy Scout Day

Boy Scouts of America was chartered by Congress in 1910. *Sponsor:* Boy Scouts of America. ✉

First execution by gas (1924)

For killing his wife, Gee Jon was the first. Took place at the Nevada State Prison.

Fountain pen invented (1883)

Louis Waterman invented the fountain pen.

Opera debuts in the U.S. (1735)

The Hob in the Well was performed at the Courtroom in Charleston, South Carolina.

Rebel Without a Cause Day

On actor James Dean's birthday, of *Rebel Without a Cause* fame, we celebrate young rebels who burn out so young. Dean was born in 1931, in Fairmont, Indiana.

Saint Jerome Emiliani Feast Day

Patron saint of orphans and abandoned children.

Science Fiction Is So Fantastic Day

On the birthday of Jules Verne (1828), the father of science fiction, we honor all science fiction authors and celebrate science fiction and fantasy books, magazines, and movies. *Sponsor:* Book Marketing Update. ✉

Stars & Stripes first published (1918)

This was the first newspaper published by the U.S. Army; it was discontinued after World War I. In 1942, the European edition resurfaced; in 1945, a Pacific edition was published. *Contact:* Stars & Stripes, Washington News Bureau, Chuck

Vinch, P.O. Box 46095, Washington, DC 20050; 703-697-6695.

Sweater Day
On Lana Turner's birthday, wear a special sweater! Turner, the "Sweater Girl," was born Julia Jean Mildred Frances in 1920, in Wallace, Idaho. *Sponsor:* The Life of the Party. ✉

War Is Hell Day
William Tecumseh Sherman was the Union general who declared that "war is hell." Today, on his birthday, we are reminded of the horrors of war. Sherman was born in 1820, in Lancaster, Ohio.

February 9

Federal Narcotics Prohibitions Act passed (1909)
Contact: Drug Enforcement Agency, 700 Army Navy Drive, Arlington, VA 22202-0000; 202-307-1000; Fax: 202-307-8320.

First Negro League player elected to Hall of Fame
Leroy "Satchel" Paige became the first baseball player from the Negro Leagues to be elected to the Baseball Hall of Fame. *Contact:* Baseball Hall of Fame, Main Street, P.O. Box 590, Cooperstown, NY 13326; 607-547-9988.

Fish Protection Office established (1880)
Contact: Fish & Wildlife Service, 1849 C Street NW, Room 3240, Washington, DC 20240-0001; 202-208-4131.

National Kraut and Frankfurter Week
Celebrate this great food combination during the 10-day period that begins the 2nd Friday in February, and ends the following Sunday. *Sponsor:* Pickle Packers International, DHM Group, Department K, P.O. Box 767, Holmdel, NJ 07733; 908-975-9675; Fax: 908-946-3343.

Saint Apollonia Feast Day
Legend has it that before being martyred, all her teeth were knocked out. For this reason she is patron of dentists. She is also looked to for relief from toothaches.

Turn Off Your TV Day
On the second Friday in February, protest the violence, sex, and vulgarity of network and cable TV by turning off your set. *Sponsor:* Morality in Media, Robert Peters, 475 Riverside Drive, New York, NY 10115; 212-870-3222; Fax: 212-870-2765.

U.S. Weather Bureau began operations (1870)
For a free pamphlet, *What's the Weather,* send an SASE to Air France Distribution Center, 2039 Ninth Avenue, Ronkonkoma, NY 11779. *Contact:* National Weather Service, 1325 East-West Highway, Silver Spring, MD 20910-0000; 301-427-7689; Fax: 301-427-2610.

William Henry Harrison's Birthday
The 9th President of the U.S. was born in 1773, in Charles County, Virginia.

February 10

25th Amendment to the Constitution ratified (1967)
Provides for presidential succession and disability.

All the News That's Fit to Print Anniversary (1897)
The *New York Times'* slogan first appeared. *Contact:* New York Times, 229 West 43rd Street, New York, NY 10036; 212-556-1234; Fax: 212-556-7126.

The Death of a Salesman opened on Broadway (1949)

Fire extinguisher patented (1863)

First American to run a mile under 4 minutes (1962)
In Los Angeles, California, Jim Beatty became the first American to accomplish this.

First electric arc light used (1879)
First used in a California theater.

First gold record (1942)
Glen Miller's "Chattanooga Choo-Choo" was the first song to reach a million dollars in sales and earn a gold record.

First singing telegram (1933)
Produced by Postal Telegram Company of New York City. Also see July 28.

Spanish-American War ended (1899)
President McKinley signed the Treaty of Paris, ending the Spanish-American War.

Styrofoam cooler invented (1957)

Tinhorn Politician Day
American journalist and editor William Allen White coined the term, "tinhorn politician." He was born on this day in 1868, in Emporia, Kansas.

February 11

Beatles record their first album (1963)

Celebration of Love Week
Love makes the world a better place; always celebrated the week of Valentine's Day. *Sponsor:* International Society of Friendship and Good Will. ✉

Child Car Safety Week
Take time during the second full week in February to make sure your children are secure in their child safety seats before you start your car. Be sure their safety seats are in good condition.

First bicycle club (1878)

First female jockey to ride against males in U.S. (1969)
Diana Crump was the first.

First hospital in the U.S. (1751)

First Soviet commercial satellite mission (1990)
In 1990, a Soyuz TM-9 was launched from the Baikonur launching site with the intention of manufacturing industrial crystals in the weightlessness of space. It was the first for-profit venture of the Soviet space program. *Contact:* Russian Federation Embassy, 1125 16th Street NW, Washington, DC 20036; 202-628-7551.

First state to abolish slavery (1777)
Vermont was the first.

Japan launches its first spacecraft (1970)
The launching of Osumi made Japan the 4th country to send a satellite into space. *Contact:* Japanese Embassy, 2520 Massachusetts Avenue NW, Washington, DC 20008; 202-939-6700.

La-Z-Boy chair invented (1948)
Sit back and relax today. *Contact:* La-Z-Boy Chair Company, 1284 N Telegraph Road, Monroe, MI 48161; 313-242-1444; Fax: 313-241-4422.

Love and Laughter Keeps Us from Getting Dizzy Week
During this week of Valentines, remember Victor Borge's assertion that laughter is the shortest distance between 2 people. For a free live-love-laugh info packet, send a $1.01 SASE to The Humor Project. *Sponsor:* The Humor Project, Joel Goodman, 110 Spring Street #D, Saratoga Springs, NY 12866; 518-587-8770; Fax: 518-587-8771; e-mail: DRJ3@aol.com.

Male Centerfold Day
On Burt Reynolds's birthday, celebrate male centerfolds everywhere. Born in 1936 in Waycross, Georgia, he was one of the first *Playgirl* centerfolds. *Sponsor:* The Life of the Party. ✉

National Future Homemakers of America Hero Week
The week of Valentine's Day spotlights home economics education. *Sponsor:* Future Homemakers of America, 1910 Association Drive,

Reston, VA 22091; 703-476-4900; Fax: 703-860-2713.

National Inventors Day
We honor all inventors on the birthday of Thomas Alva Edison (1847), America's greatest inventor.

National New Idea Week
The week of Thomas Alva Edison's birthday encourages people to think more creatively and to develop new ideas.

Political Prisoners Release Day
In 1990, Nelson Mandela was released from a South African prison after 27 years. Now he's the leader of his country. On this day, we work to get all political prisoners released so they can live their full potential.

Vocational/Technical Education Week
Celebrated the second full week in February.

Week of Kindness
People are working toward a congressional resolution supporting this week (held the week of the 14th). *Sponsor:* The Crusaders TV Show, Bonnie View Productions.

White Shirt Day
The United Auto Workers and General Motors settled a major strike in 1937. Blue collar workers wear white shirts on this day to celebrate their victory. *Contact:* United Auto Workers, 8000 East Jefferson, Detroit, MI 48214; 313-926-5000.

World Marriage Day
On the second Sunday in February, celebrate married people everywhere. The sponsor changes every year. *Sponsor:* World Marriage Day, Bill and Cathy Thurnau, 1594 Woodmills Drive E, Cordova, TN 38018; 901-759-2294.

February 12

Abraham Lincoln's Birthday
One of America's greatest presidents was born in 1809.

Clean Out Your Computer Day
On the second Monday in February, take time to organize your computer files and delete those not needed. *Sponsor:* Institute for Business Technology, Ira Chaleff, 513 Capitol Court NE, Washington, DC 20002; 202-544-0097.

Export-Import Bank incorporated (1934)
Contact: Export-Import Bank of the U.S., 811 Vermont Avenue NW, Washington, DC 20571; 202-566-8990; 800-424-5201; Fax: 202-566-7524.

First automobile race around the world began
In New York City in 1908.

First puppet show in the U.S. (1738)

NAACP founded (1909)
The National Association for the Advancement of Colored People was founded by 60 people in 1909. *Contact:* NAACP, 4805 Mount Hope Drive, Baltimore, MD 21215; 410-358-8900; Fax: 410-358-2332.

National Bird Dog Field Trials
February 12 through 23. These field trials help select the national champion bird dog. *Sponsor:* National Field Trial Championship Association, P.O. Box 389, Grand Junction, TN 38039; 901-878-1067; Fax: 901-878-1068.

National Croquet League established (1880)
First national croquet association; has been superceded by the U.S. Croquet Association, which was founded in 1976. *Contact:* U.S. Croquet Association, 500 Avenue of the Champions, Palm Beach Gard,

✉ Addresses for frequently cited organizations are gathered on pages vii–viii.

FL 33418; 407-627-3999; Fax: 407-624-3128.

Safetypup's Birthday
Safetypup promotes child safety. *Sponsor:* National Child Safety Council, 4065 Page Avenue, P.O. Box 1368, Jackson, MI 49204-1368; 517-764-6070.

Saint Julian the Hospitaller Feast Day
A fictitious saint, he is patron saint of boatmen, travelers, and inn-keepers.

February 13

ASCAP founded (1914)
The American Society of Composers, Authors, and Publishers was founded in New York City. *Contact:* ASCAP, 1 Lincoln Plaza, New York, NY 10023-7142; 212-621-6000; Fax: 212-724-9064.

First black professional basketball team organized
In 1923, "The Rennaissance" was organized.

First magazine published in America (1741)
Andrew Bradford published *The American Magazine.*

First public school in America opened (1635)
The Boston Latin School was the first.

Get a Different Name Day
If you dislike your name, you may use a different name today. *Sponsor:* Wellness Permission League. ✉

Saint Agabus Feast Day
A Jewish convert to Christianity, Saint Agabus foretold many events. He is considered a patron saint of fortune-tellers.

Women's Marine Corps created (1943)
Contact: U.S. Marine Corps Headquarters, Washington DC 20380-0001; 202-443-2258; Fax: 202-695-7366.

February 14

Apple parer patented (1803)
Invented by Moses Coats.

Arizona Admission Day
Arizona became the 48th state of the U.S. in 1912. *Contact:* Arizona Office of Tourism, 1100 W Washington Street, Phoenix, AZ 85007; 602-542-8687; Fax: 602-542-4068.

Ferris Wheel Day
The birthday of George Washington Ferris (1859), inventor of the Ferris Wheel.

First porpoise born in captivity (1940)

First President to be photographed (1849)
James Polk was the 1st president to be photographed while in office.

First Tarzan movie released (1918)

First Vietnam P.O.W.s return to the U.S. (1973)
American P.O.W.s held by North Vietnam arrived at Travis Air Force Base in the U.S.

Great Emancipator Day
Frederick Douglas was born in 1817, in Tuckahoe, Maryland; he was an outstanding orator, journalist, and anti-slavery leader.

Hug-In
On the closest weekday to February 14th, hug people. *Sponsor:* University of South Carolina, Anthony Rice, 200 Miller Road, Sumter, SC 29150; 803-775-6341; Fax: 803-775-2180.

Lawrencium produced (1961)
This is element 103 on the Periodic Chart of Elements.

League of Women Voters founded (1920)
Founded in Chicago, Illinois, at the convention of the National American Women's Suffrage Association. *Contact:* League of Women Voters, 1730 M Street NW, 11th Floor, Washington, DC 20036-4587; 202-429-1965; Fax: 202-429-0854.

National Condom Week
The week of the 14th to the 21st promotes the use of condoms, the best way to prevent pregnancy and

sexually transmitted diseases. *Sponsor:* Pharmacists Planning Service. ✉

National Have a Heart Day

To celebrate life and create a new consumer consciousness concerning the consequences of our cuisine choices for the environment, world hunger, animal welfare, and human health. A vegetarian diet can prevent and even reverse heart disease. *Sponsor:* Vegetarian Awareness Network, P.O. Box 321, Knoxville, TN 37901; 800-872-8343.

National Salute to Hospitalized Veterans Day

Oregon Admission Day

Oregon was the 33rd state of the U.S. *Contact:* Oregon Tourism Division, 775 Summer Street NE, Salem, OR 97310; 503-986-0000; 800-547-7842; Fax: 503-986-0001.

Race Relations Day

Some churches celebrate Valentine's Day to emphasize the importance of harmonious race relations.

Read to Your Child Day

Motto: Show your kids you love them: Read to them! For a free packet of materials about reading aloud, send a self-addressed, business-size envelope to Dee Anderson, Children's Librarian, 1023 25th Street #1, Moline, IL 61265; 309-755-9614.

Skeezix Wallet's Birthday

The first comic strip character to grow and age, was found on the doorstep of Walt and Phyllis Wallet in 1921. This *Gasoline Alley* character went through childhood, high school, marriage, military service, and parenthood.

Telephone patent applied for (1876)

Alexander Graham Bell and Elisha Gray both applied for patents today (Bell a few hours before Gray). The U.S. Supreme Court eventually ruled that Bell had invented the telephone. *Contact:* U.S. Supreme Court. ✉

U.S. Department of Commerce and Labor formed (1903)

Contacts: Department of Commerce, 14th Street and Constitution Avenue, Washington, DC 20230; 202-482-2000; Fax: 202-482-3772. Department of Labor, 200 Constitution Avenue NW, Washington, DC 20210; 202-219-7316; 202-219-7312.

Valentine's Day

Feast day of Saint Valentine, patron saint of lovers and romance. The first valentine card was probably sent by the Duke of Orleans while he was imprisoned in the Tower of London in 1415.

February 15

Erector Set Day

On the birthday of Alfred C. Gilbert (1884), inventor of the Erector Set, build new creations with your Erector Set. He was born in Salem, Oregon. Salem's celebration is held on the Saturday nearest President's Day. *Contact:* Gilbert House Children's Museum, 116 Marion Street NE, Salem, OR 97301; 503-371-3631.

First adhesive postage stamps in the U.S. (1842)

A private mail service issued the first adhesive postage stamps. The U.S. Post Office issued its first stamps on July 1, 1847. *Contact:* U.S. Postal Service. ✉

First black to direct a major orchestra (1968)

Henry Lewis was director of the New Jersey Symphony. *Contact:* New Jersey Symphony Orchestra, 50 Park Place, 11th Floor, Newark, NJ 07102; 201-624-3713; Fax: 201-624-2115.

Galileo's Birthday

Galileo was born in 1564; he devised the first astronomical telescope in 1609.

Jewelry Day

On the birthday of Charles Tiffany, the famous American jeweler, bedeck yourself! Tiffany was born in

1812, at Killingly, Connecticut. *Sponsor:* The Life of the Party.

Lupercalia
An ancient Roman fertility rite that might have established some Valentine's Day traditions; also a day when animals help humans.

Maple Leaf Flag Day
In 1965, Canada inaugurated its Maple Leaf flag. The design was actually approved on December 15, 1964. *Contact:* Canadian Embassy, 501 Pennsylvania Avenue NW, Washington, DC 20001; 202-682-1740.

Nirvana Day
Celebrates the death of Buddha, who according to Buddhist belief, was the first person to reach a state of nirvana (a state of enlightenment where one is free from the cycle of birth and death). *Contact:* Buddhist Churches of America, 1710 Octavia Street, San Francisco, CA 94109-4341; 415-776-5600.

Remember the Maine Day (1898)
The battleship *Maine* was blown up in the harbor of Havana, Cuba. This incident precipitated the Spanish-American war.

Susan B. Anthony Day
On the birthday of Susan B. Anthony (1820), work for women's issues and recognize women's rights.

Susan B. Anthony was the first U.S. woman to have her likeness on a coin. This day is a holiday in Florida and Minnesota.

Synthetic diamonds created (1955)

Women allowed to argue cases before Supreme Court (1879)
Congress passed a law giving women attorneys the right to argue cases before the U.S. Supreme Court. *Contact:* U.S. Supreme Court.

February 16

911 Birthday
The first 911 emergency phone system in the U.S. was established in Haleyville, Alabama.

Cultural Diversity Day
A day to raise younger people's awareness of the value of cultural

diversity. *Sponsor:* Westboro Youth & Family Services, Explorer Post 24, 34 W Main Street, Westboro, MA 01581; 508-366-3090; Fax: 508-366-3099.

Documentary Film Day
Robert J. Flaherty is called the father of the documentary film. His films inlcude *Nanook of the North* and *Moana.* Flaherty was born on this day in 1884, in Iron Mountain, Michigan.

Federal Crop Insurance Corporation created (1938)
To protect farmers from poor crop production due to bad weather, Congress created this corporation. *Contact:* Federal Crop Insurance Corp., 2101 L Street NW #500, Washington, DC 20037; 202-254-4581; Fax: 202-254-8356.

Fidel Castro became premier of Cuba (1959)

First fruit tree patent issued (1932)

God Bless You Day
In 600, Pope Gregory the Great issued a papal decree declaring that "God bless you!" is the proper response to a sneeze.

I Got You Babe Day
Spend a little extra time with your someone special to celebrate the birthday of singer and politician

 Addresses for frequently cited organizations are gathered on pages vii–viii.

Sonny Bono; he was born in 1935, in Detroit, Michigan. *Sponsor:* The Life of the Party. ✉

Koran Day
The Koran was first revealed to the Prophet Muhammad on the 27th night of the month of Ramadan. Muslims commemorate this event by reading the Koran during the last ten days of Ramadan.

Ladies Home Journal first published (1883)
Contact: Ladies Home Journal, 100 Park Avenue, New York, NY 10017-5599; 212-953-7070; Fax: 212-351-3650.

National Slap a Cop Day
On the birthday of Zsa Zsa Gabor, who was prosecuted for slapping a traffic cop, give your favorite police officer a pat on the back, in support of your local police.

Nylon fiber patented (1937)
Invented by Wallace H. Carothers, nylon was the first human-made fiber. Nylon was first commercially produced in a DuPont plant in Arlington, New Jersey, on February 24, 1938. *Contact:* E. I. duPont de Nemours & Company, 1007 Market Street, Wilmington, DE 19898; 302-774-1000.

What's My Line premiered on CBS-TV (1950)
John Daly hosted this quiz show. *Contact:* CBS-TV. ✉

February 17

First gas lit street (1817)

First successful submarine attack (1864)
The Confederate submarine *Hunley* sank the *U.S. Housatonic* during the Civil War.

First woman judge in the U.S. (1870)
Esther Morris of South Pass, Wyoming, was appointed the first woman judge.

I've Got a Rash I Can't Explain Day
If your boss won't let you take the day off, just tell him that you have a rash you can't explain *and* it's contagious; then offer to shake his or her hand. That should get you the day off. *Sponsor:* KCAQ-FM, The Woody Show, Jewel Langway, Producer, 1701 Pacific Avenue #270, Oxnard, CA 93033; 805-483-1000; Fax: 805-483-6555.

Marian Anderson's Birthday
The first African-American singer to appear with the Metropolitan Opera, was born in 1902 in Philadelphia, Pennsylvania. She was hired by the Metropolitan Opera on October 7, 1954.

National Congress of Mothers founded (1897)
The forerunner of the PTA was founded in Washington, DC. *Con-tact:* National PTA, 330 N. Wabash Avenue #2100, Chicago, IL 60611-3690; 312-670-6782; Fax: 312-670-6783.

National FFA Organization Awareness Week
During the week of Washington's birthday, from Saturday to Saturday, the Future Farmers of America celebrate their organization. If Washington's birthday falls on a Saturday, the week starts the previous Saturday. *Sponsor:* Future Farmers of America, 5632 Mt. Vernon Memorial Highway, P.O. Box 15160, Alexandria, VA 22309-0160; 703-360-3600.

National PTA Founder's Day
The Parent/Teachers Association was founded in 1897 by Phoebe Apperson Hearst and Alice McLellan Birney. *Sponsor:* National PTA (see previous address).

Newsweek first published (1933)
Contact: Newsweek Magazine, 444 Madison Avenue, New York, NY

10022-6999; 212-350-4000; 800-631-1040; Fax: 212-421-4993.

Sardines first canned (1876)
Sardines were first canned in Eastport, Maine.

Vacuum Your Cat Day
Sponsor: The Life of the Party. ✉

Voice of America first broadcasted to the Soviet Union (1947)
Contact: Voice of America, 330 Independence Avenue SW, Washington, DC 20547-0001; 202-619-3117.

World Championship Crab Races
Always held on the weekend of President's Day. *Sponsor:* Crescent City, Chamber of Commerce, 1001 Front Street, Crescent City, CA 95531; 707-464-3174; 800-343-8300; Fax: 707-464-9676.

February 18

Adventures of Huckleberry Finn published (1885)

American Wine Appreciation Week
Always the last full week in February.

Brotherhood/Sisterhood Week
The National Conference, founded in 1927, fights bias, bigotry, and racism; promotes understanding and respect among all races, religions, and cultures through advocacy, education, and conflict resolution. Always the week of the third Monday in February. *Sponsor:* National Conference of Christians & Jews, 71 Fifth Avenue, New York, NY 10003; 212-206-0006.

First 3-D movie released (1953)
The first feature-length 3-D movie was *Bwana Devil*. People had to wear special glasses to see the effects.

First cow to fly (1930)
Elm Farm Ollie took a flight over the city of Saint Louis, Missouri.

First tintype camera patented (1856)

Health Education Week
The third full week in February promotes healthy lifestyle choices. *Sponsor:* New York State Health Department, Corning Tower Building #1084, Albany, NY 12237; 518-474-5370.

Homes for Birds Week
Take time during the third full week in February to build, clean out, or fix up your bird houses and other homes for wild birds. For a free booklet, *Homes for Birds*, write to the Consumer Information Center, Pueblo, CO 81009. Ask for booklet 582Z. *Sponsor:* Wild Bird Marketplace, 710 W Main Street, P.O. Box 1184, New Holland, PA 17557; 717-354-2841; Fax: 717-355-0425.

International Friendship Week
The last full week in February promotes international friendship through use of the international language, Esperanto. First celebrated in 1969, this week was created by Erik Carlen of Sweden. *Sponsor:* International Society of Friendship and Good Will. ✉

Longest walk anniversary (1978)
Native Americans began walking across the U.S. to highlight their plight.

Lunar New Year
Celebrated at sunset on the day of the new moon in the sign of Aquarius.

National Engineers Week
George Washington was a military engineer and land surveyor; we honor professional engineers during the week of his birthday. *Sponsor:* Society of Professional Engineers, 1420 King Street, Alexandria, VA 22314-2715; 703-684-2800.

National Pancake Week
Celebrates Pancake Tuesday and promotes the history of pancakes. *Sponsor:* Bisquick Baking Mix, General Mills, 1 General Mills Blvd.,

Minneapolis, MN 55426; 612-540-2470; 800-328-6787.

National Visiting Nurse Association Week
Celebrated the third full week in February.

Oldest existing yacht club in U.S. formed (1839)
The Detroit Boat Club was formed in Detroit, Michigan.

Pay Your Bills Week
During the third full week in February, educational programs are given to teach consumers the value of a good credit rating and the importance of paying bills on time. *Sponsor:* American Collectors Association, P.O. Box 39106, Minneapolis, MN 55439-0106; 612-926-6547; Fax: 612-926-1624.

Pluto discovered (1930)
Discovered by Clyde Tombaugh at the Lowell Observatory in Flagstaff, Arizona. *Contact:* Lowell Observatory, 1400 W Mars Hill Road, Flagstaff, AZ 86001; 602-774-3358.

Vacuum cleaner, improved version, patented (1901)
H. Cecil Booth patented a dust removing suction cleaner in 1901.

Vietnamese New Year (Tet)
On the day of the lunar new year, Vietnamese people celebrate the most important holiday of their year. *Contact:* Socialist Republic of Vietnam, Mission to the United Nations, 20 Waterside Plaza, New York, NY 10010; 212-679-3779; Fax: 212-686-8534.

Wheel of Fortune Day
Celebrate *Wheel of Fortune* on the birthday of Vanna White, classic letter turner. White was born in 1957, in North Myrtle Beach, South Carolina. *Sponsor:* The Life of the Party. ✉

February 19

Chinese New Year (Sun Nin)
Celebrated at sunset on the day of the new moon in the sign of Aquarius. 1996: the year of the rat; 1997: ox; 1998: tiger; 1999: rabbit; 2000: dragon; 2001: snake; 2002: horse; 2003: sheep; 2004: monkey; 2005: rooster; 2006: dog; 2007: pig.

Eid al-Fitr
On the 1st day of the 10th month of the Islamic lunar calendar, Muslims celebrate the end of Ramadan, the month of fasting. One of two holidays celebrated throughout the Islamic world. Also known as Idu'l Fitar.

First Pan African Congress held (1919)
Held in Paris, France.

First prize inserted into a Cracker Jack box (1913)

First state to ban alcoholic beverages (1881)
Kansas was the first state to ban the sale of all alcoholic beverages.

First statewide teachers strike in the U.S. (1968)
Florida's teachers went out on strike.

Iwo Jima Landing Anniversary
In 1945, U.S. troops landed on Iwo Jima. The taking of the island was one of the hardest fought battles of the Pacific phase of World War II.

Japanese Internment Anniversary
In 1942, President Roosevelt signed an executive order placing 110,000 Japanese Americans into concentration camps. People feared that those interred would aid the Japanese during World War II.

Knights of Pythias founded (1864)
The social fraternity was founded in Washington, D.C. *Contact:* Knights of Pythias, 2785 E Desert Inn Road #150, Las Vegas, NV

89121; 702-735-3302; Fax: 702-735-3302; 800-655-6599.

Phonograph patented (1878)
Thomas Edison patented the phonograph in 1878.

Presidents' Day
The third Monday honors all American presidents, especially the two greatest, George Washington and Abraham Lincoln.

Solar System Day
This day honors the birthday of Nicolaus Copernicus, who discovered that the Earth revolves around sun. This Polish astronomer is sometimes known as the father of modern astronomy. Copernicus was born on February 19, 1473, at Torun, Poland.

Temporary Insanity Day
In 1859, Dan Sickles was acquitted of murdering his wife's lover on grounds of temporary insanity. His case was the first time this defense was used successfully in the U.S.

February 20

A Holiday of Firsts
On the day that John Glenn became the first American to orbit the Earth (1962), create your own first!

Do something today that you've always wanted to do. *Sponsor:* A Pilgrim's Almanac. ✉

Airship patented (1900)
In 1900, J. F. Pickering, a black inventor, received a patent for his airship invention.

First American to orbit Earth (1962)
John Glenn, Jr., aboard Friendship 7, was the first American to orbit the Earth. *Contact:* NASA. ✉

First federal post office established (1792)
Contact: U.S. Postal Service. ✉

First square-bottom paper bag machine (1872)

Hydraulic elevator patented (1872)

International Pancake Day
A pancake race is held between the women of Liberal, Kansas, and those of Olney, England. On Shrove Tuesday (also, Pancake Tuesday), the day before Lent, people have celebrated by eating lots of food in preparation for the fasting of Lent. *Sponsor:* International Pancake Race, Rosalee Phillips, Secretary, P.O. Box 665, Liberal, KS 67905-0665; 316-624-6427.

Mardi Gras (Shrove Tuesday)
The day before Ash Wednesday is a time of feasting and celebration. Have a party! Also known as Carnival (in Brazil), Fastnacht (in Switzerland), or Fat Tuesday.

Pizzaaahlympics
February 20 to 23. During Pizza Expo, world championship contests are held for making the largest, fastest, and highest pizzas. Also sponsored by *Pizza Today* magazine. *Sponsor:* Pizza Expo, National Association of Pizza Operators, P.O. Box 1347, New Albany IN 47151; 812-949-0909.

Sign of Pisces
The astrological sign of Pisces, the fish, runs from February 20 to March 20. Pisces people are sympathetic, sensitive, and timid.

Student Volunteer Day
Today we thank students for giving their time to improve their communities. 1996 is the 10th anniversary of this day. *Sponsor:* Susquehanna

University, Student Life Office, Center for Volunteer Programs, Selinsgrove, PA 17870; 717-372-4139; Fax: 717-372-2745.

Toothpick manufacturing machine patented (1872)
Silas Noble and James Cooley invented the toothpick manufacturing equipment.

February 21

Alka Seltzer introduced (1931)
Oh, what a relief it is! *Contact:* Bristol-Meyers Squibb, 345 Park Avenue, New York, NY 10154; 212-546-4000; Fax: 212-546-4020.

Ash Wednesday
Marks the beginning of Lent, a period of abstinence from rich foods and luxury.

First American president to visit China (1972)
President Nixon visited Beijing, becoming the 1st American president to visit the Republic of China; also the first visit by an American president to a country not officially recognized by the U.S.

First burglar alarm installed in the U.S. (1838)
E. T. Holmes installed the first burglar alarm in Boston, Massachusetts.

First female telegrapher (1846)
Sarah Bagley of Lowell, Massachusetts, was the first female telegrapher.

First self-propelled locomotive (1804)
The first self-propelled locomotive on rails was demonstrated in Wales.

First woman to graduate from dental school (1866)
Lucy Hobbs graduated from dental school in Cincinnati, Ohio.

I've Got Your Number Day
The first telephone book was published in 1878 in New Haven, Connecticut. *Sponsor:* The Life of the Party. ✉

Last green and yellow Carolina parakeet died (1918)

Malcolm X assassinated (1965)
Black activist Malcolm X renounced the Black Muslims; he was shot by 3 Black Muslims in 1965. Malcolm X formed the Organization for Afro-American Unity.

The New Yorker Magazine's Birthday
The first issue of *The New Yorker* was published in 1925. *Contact:* The New Yorker magazine, Inc., 20 West 43rd Street, New York, NY 10036; 212-840-3800; Fax: 212-536-5735.

Polaroid Land camera first demonstrated (1947)
Edwin Land first demonstrated his new camera; it could produce a black and white photograph in 60 seconds. *Contact:* Polaroid Corporation, 549 Technology Square, Cambridge, MA 02139; 617-577-2000; Fax: 617-577-3624.

Washington Monument dedicated (1885)

February 22

Boy Scouts Founder's Day
Robert Baden-Powell, founder of the Boy Scouts, was born in 1857, in London, England. *Sponsor:* Boy Scouts of America. ✉

First chinchilla farm established (1923)
Established in Los Angeles, California.

First five & dime opened (1879)
F. W. Woolworth opened the first five and dime in Utica, New York. *Contact:* F. W. Woolworth, 233 Broadway, New York, NY 10279; 212-553-2000; Fax: 212-553-2042.

First joint stock company in America (1875)
The American Manufactory of Woolens, Linens, and Cottons became the first joint stock company formed in America.

First Presidential radio broadcast from the White House (1924)

Calvin Coolidge made the first broadcast.

First Thanksgiving Day

The first public observance of Thanksgiving took place in 1631 in the Massachusetts Bay Colony.

French Fry Friday

Formerly sponsored by Lamb-Weston, this day celebrates french fries, one of America's favorite foods. Eat some today! Always celebrated on the 4th Friday of February.

George Washington's Birthday

The father of our country was born in 1732 in Westmoreland County, Virginia. For a free *George Washington Biography Booklet*, send $1.00 for shipping to Mount Vernon Ladies Association, Education Department, Mount Vernon, VA 22121.

Invite an Atheist to Lunch Day

On the birthday of Arthur Schopenhauer (1788), famous philosopher and atheist, invite an atheist to lunch. Schopenhauer was born in Danzig, Germany. *Sponsor:* The Life of the Party. ✉

National Ski Association founded (1904)

Now known as the U.S. Skiing Association; founded in Ishpeming, Michigan. *Contact:* U.S. Skiing Association, P.O. Box 100, Park City, UT 84060; 801-649-9090; Fax: 801-649-3613.

Popcorn introduced to colonists (1630)

Quadequina brought popcorn to the first Thanksgiving celebration in the Massachusetts Bay Colony.

Saint Margaret of Cortona Feast Day

A prostitute turned penitent, Saint Margaret is patron saint of prostitutes who despair of making a change.

February 23

Aluminum manufacturing process developed (1886)

America's largest pub dart tournament

The 24th annual open dart tournament will be held from February 23 to 25, 1996. *Sponsor:* Blueberry Hill Dart Tournament, Joe Edwards, Blueberry Hill, 6504 Delmar, Saint Louis, MO 63130; 314-727-0880; Fax: 314-727-1288.

Federal Radio Commission created (1927)

President Coolidge signed a bill creating the Federal Radio Commission, which later became the Federal Communications Commission. *Contact:* Federal Communications Commission, 1919 M Street NW, Washington, DC 20554; 202-632-7000; Fax: 202-653-5402.

First easy divorce law in the U.S. (1915)

Nevada passed a law that made divorce possible after only 6 months of residency.

First shelling of the U.S. mainland during WW II (1942)

A Japanese submarine shelled an oil refinery near Ellwood, California.

Rotary Club founded (1905)

Paul Harris and 3 friends founded the first Rotary Club in Chicago, Illinois. *Contact:* Rotary Clubs International, 1560 Sherman Avenue, Evanston, IL 60201; 708-866-3000; Fax: 708-328-8554.

Salk vaccine first used (1954)

The polio vaccine was first used to inoculate school children in Pittsburgh, Pennsylvania.

Tennis Day

Walter Wingfield of Pimlico, England patented lawn tennis in 1874.

For a free booklet, *Introduction to the Rules of Tennis*, send an SASE to U.S. Tennis Association, Publications Department, 70 W. Red Oak Lane, White Plains, NY 10604-3602.

Tootsie Roll introduced (1896)
Leo Hirschfield brought the recipe for Tootsie Rolls from his native Austria. He made the candy bits in his kitchen behind his candy store, where he sold the Rolls for a penny each. *Contact:* Tootsie Roll Industries, 7401 S. Cicero Avenue, Chicago, IL 60629; 312-838-3400; Fax: 312-838-3534.

February 24

First perforated postage stamp (1857)
Contact: U.S. Postal Service. ✉

First record album to go platinum (1976)
The Eagles Greatest Hits became the first U.S. album to sell 2,000,000 copies.

First rocket launched into space (1949)
A 2-stage rocket was launched from the White Sands proving grounds in New Mexico. It reached an altitude of 25 miles. *Contact:* NASA. ✉

First U.S. Court of Claims created (1855)
Contact: U.S. Claims Court, 717 Madison Place NW, Washington, DC 20005; 202-219-9697.

First Voice of America broadcast (1942)
Contact: Voice of America, 330 Independence Avenue SW, Washington, DC 20547-0001; 202-619-3117.

Gregorian Calendar Day
Pope Gregory XIII issued a papal bull in 1582 adopting a new calendar. It is the most widely used calendar in the world, and was adopted by the U.S. in 1752.

Hadassah founded (1912)
Hadassah, founded by Henrietta Szold and the Daughters of Zion Study Group in 1912, is the world's largest Zionist women's organization in the world. It promotes better education, health care improvement, vocational training, and other social issues. *Contact:* Hadassah, 50 West 58th Street, New York, NY 10019; 212-303-8153.

National Obnoxious Day
You can be as obnoxious as you want on this day. *Sponsor:* The Life of the Party. ✉

Null and Void Day
The U.S. Supreme Court ruled in 1803 that an act of Congress was null and void because it conflicted with the U.S. Constitution. This was the most important ruling upholding the supremacy of the Constitution. *Contact:* U.S. Supreme Court. ✉

Steam shovel patented (1839)

World Championship Hog Calling Contest
Held on the last Saturday in February. Contest office: Weatherford Daily News, P.O. Box 191, Weatherford, OK 73096; 405-772-3301.

World Championship Snowmobile Drag Races
Held on the fourth Saturday in February, on Lake Minocqua. The world champion snowmobile drag racer is determined. *Sponsor:* Minocqua Cup, Arbor-Vitae/Woodruff Chamber, P.O. Box 226, Woodruff, WI 54568; 715-356-6266; 800-876-8818.

World's Greatest Clam Chowder Cookoff
On the last Saturday in February, over 80 teams compete for the title of world's greatest clam chowder cook. There are separate catagories for restaurants and individuals; Boston and Manhattan style. *Sponsor:* Santa Cruz Beach Boardwalk, 400 Beach Street, Santa Cruz, CA 95060-5491; 408-423-5590; Fax: 408-423-5875.

February 25

Colt revolver patented (1836)
Samuel Colt patented his 6-shooter revolver.

Don't Fence Me in Day
Congress passed a law prohibiting the fencing of public lands in 1885.

First black to serve in the U.S. Senate (1870)

Hiram Revels, a Republican from Mississippi, became the first black to serve in the U.S. Senate.

First Pan American Games began (1951)

The first Pan American Games began in Buenos Aires, Argentina.

First power-driven vacuum cleaner (1902)

Hubert Booth of London, England, built the first powered vacuum cleaner.

First practical electrical motor patented (1837)

Thomas Davenport of Rutland, Vermont, patented the first practical electric motor.

First state to tax gasoline (1919)

Oregon was the first state to tax gasoline (one cent per gallon).

First Timberland Protection Act passed (1879)

Congress passed the first Timberland Protection Act in 1879.

First U.S. aircraft carrier (1933)

The first U.S. aircraft carrier was the *USS Ranger.*

First U.S. Cabinet meeting held (1793)

The first Cabinet meeting was held in President Washington's home.

Go to the Opera Day

On the birthday of Enrico Caruso, the great operatic tenor, go to the opera and enjoy some good music. Caruso was born on February 25, 1873, at Naples, Italy. *Sponsor:* The Life of the Party. ✉

I Am the Greatest Day

In 1964, Muhammed Ali won the world heavyweight boxing championship by knocking out Sonny Liston in the 7th round. Ali is the only boxer to win the heavyweight title three times.

U.S. Steel incorporated (1901)

The first billion-dollar corporation was incorporated by J. P. Morgan in 1901. *Contact:* U.S. Steel, 600 Grant Street, Pittsburgh, PA 15219; 412-433-1121; Fax: 412-433-5733.

February 26

Blue Jeans Monday

Levi Strauss, creator of the world's first blue jeans, was born in 1829, in Bavaria. The name of this day changes with the day of the week on which this date falls. *Contact:* Levi Strauss & Company, 1155 Battery Street, San Francisco, CA 94111-1264; 415-544-6000; 800-USA-LEVI; Fax: 415-544-3939.

First black middleweight boxing champion (1926)

Theodore "Georgia Deacon" Flowers was the first black middleweight boxing champion.

First cartoon shown in a movie theater (1909)

Glass-blowing machine patented in U.S. (1895)

Grand Canyon National Park established (1919)

Contact: Grand Canyon National Park, P.O. Box 129, Grand Canyon, AZ 86023; 602-638-7888.

February 27

22nd Amendment to the Constitution ratified (1950)

Limits U.S. presidents to 2 terms in office.

First black church in U.S. established (1794)

First black to win a medal at Winter Olympics

Debi Thomas, by winning a silver medal at the 1988 Winter Olympics, became the first black to win a medal at any winter olympics. *Contact:* U.S. Olympic Committee. ✉

First practical cigar-rolling machine (1883)
The cigar-rolling machine was patented by Oscar Hammerstein.

Gulf War ended (1991)
With the liberation of Kuwait City, the war ended about 40 days after it began. It would have resulted in a complete defeat of Iraq if the U.S. had continued to press its advantage.

National Read Your Warranty Day
On the birthday of consumer advocate Ralph Nader, take your car in for a check-up. Make sure your car is safe. Nader was born in 1934, in Winsted, Connecticut. *Sponsor:* The Life of the Party. ✉

February 28

Final episode of M*A*S*H (1983)
The final episode was the most watched series TV show ever. *Contact:* CBS-TV. ✉

First chartered passenger railroad in U.S. (1827)
B&O Railroad was the first railroad in the U.S. chartered to carry passengers. *Contact:* B&O Railroad Museum, 901 W Pratt Street, Baltimore, MD 21223; 410-752-2490; Fax: 410-752-2499.

First killer whale born in captivity (1977)
The whale did not survive.

Republican Party began (1854)
Fifty people in Ripon, Wisconsin, called for the forming of a new party. *Contact:* Republican National Committee, 310 First Street SE, Washington, DC 20003; 202-863-8500; Fax: 202-863-8820.

February 29

Bachelors Day
An old Scottish and Irish tradition says that women may propose marriage on this date.

First black actress to win an Oscar (1940)
Hattie McDaniel won an Oscar for her work in *Gone with the Wind*.

Leap Year Day
According to legend, any enterprise begun on February 29th is sure of success.

National Rift in the Time Continuum Day
On this day, you don't have to be on time for work. Indeed, you can take the entire day off, especially if today is your birthday. *Sponsor:* WBVP-AM, The Dimitri Show, Loretta Hardt and Dimitri, 1316 7th Avenue, Beaver Falls, PA 15010; 412-846-4100; Fax: 412-843-7771.

Save the Rhino Day
On February 29th when available; otherwise, May 1st. Rhinos are nearly extinct! Work with your local zoo to find out what you can do to help save these incredible creatures. *Sponsor:* Really, Rhinos!, Judyth Lessee, Founder, P.O. Box 40503, Tucson, AZ 85717-0503; 520-318-2954; Fax: 520-795-6177; e-mail: rinophyl@rtd.com.

MARCH

American Red Cross Month
Have a heart, and give blood. A Presidential Proclamation was issued in 1943. *Sponsor:* American Red Cross Headquarters, 8111 Gatehouse Road, Falls Church, VA 22042; 703-206-6000; Fax: 703-206-7507.

Cataract Awareness Month
This month increases awareness of cataracts, including how to prevent them and how to treat them. *Sponsor:* Prevent Blindness America. ✉

Gardening, Nature, and Ecology Books Month
Read a book about gardening, nature, ecology, botany, agriculture, or biology. *Sponsor:* Book Marketing Update. ✉

✉ Addresses for frequently cited organizations are gathered on pages vii–viii.

Herb Month in Missouri
Sponsor: Ozark Regional Herb Growers, Ozark Exotica, Route 3, Box 3500, Theodosia, MO 65761; 417-273-4949.

Humorists Are Artists Month
Recognizes the contributions of humorists. *Sponsor:* Lone Star Publications of Humor, Lauren Barnett, P.O. Box 29000, San Antonio, TX 78229.

Irish-American Heritage Month
The month of Saint Patrick's Day.

Mental Retardation Awareness Month
Promotes the needs and abilities of America's citizens with mental retardation. *Sponsor:* The Arc National Headquarters, 500 E. Border Street #300, Arlington, TX 76010; 817-261-6003; Fax: 817-277-3491.

Music in Our Schools Month
Music has been a part of public school curriculums since 1838; it is an important aspect of a balanced education. *Sponsor:* Music Educators National Conference, 1806 Robert Fulton Drive, Reston, VA 22091; 703-860-4000; 800-336-3768; Fax: 703-860-1531.

National Chronic Fatigue Syndrome Awareness Month
Promote awareness of CFS and related diseases. *Sponsor:* National Chronic Fatigue Syndrome Association, 3521 Broadway #222, Kansas City, MO 64111; 816-931-4777.

National Craft Month
Enjoy some crafts this month. *Sponsor:* Hobby Industry Association, 319 E. 54th Street, Elmwood Park, NJ 07407; 201-794-1133; Fax: 201-797-0657.

National Feminine Empowerment Month
Promotes the empowerment of the feminine principle, spirituality, mental health, physical health, and Jungian psychology. *Sponsor:* Jean Benedict Raffa, 17 S. Osceola Avenue, Orlando, FL 32801; 407-426-7077; Fax: 407-649-8601.

National Frozen Food Month
To spotlight the benefits of frozen foods. *Sponsor:* National Frozen Food Association, 4755 Linglestown Road #300, Harrisburg, PA 17112; 717-657-8601; Fax: 717-657-9862.

National Hemophilia Month

National Middle School Month
This month celebrates the students and teachers of middle schools.

National Noodle Month
By law, a noodle must contain egg to be called a noodle. Noodles are low fat, low calorie, low sodium, but rich in vitamins. *Sponsor:* National Pasta Association, 2101 Wilson Boulevard #920, Arlington, VA 22201; 703-841-0818; Fax: 703-528-6507.

National Nutrition Month
Promotes educating people about the importace of healthy eating. *Sponsor:* The American Dietetic Association, National Center for Nutrition, 216 W. Jackson Boulevard #800, Chicago, IL 60606-6995; 312-899-0040; Fax: 312-899-1739.

National Peanut Month
Spotlights America's favorite nut. *Sponsor:* Peanut Advisory Board, 1950 N. Park Place #525, Atlanta, GA 30309; 404-933-0357; Fax: 404-933-0796.

National Pothole Month
Do your best to avoid this month's deepest holes.

National Professional Social Work Month
Honors all social workers for their contributions to society. *Sponsor:* National Association of Social Workers, 750 First Street NE, Washington, DC 20002; 202-408-8600; Fax: 202-336-8310.

National Sauce Month
Celebrate the sauces that are used in cooking. *Sponsor:* The Alden Group, 52 Vanderbilt Avenue, New York, NY 10017 (also sponsored by

Martini and Rossi Vermouth); 212-867-6400; Fax: 212-986-5988.

National Talk with Your Teen about Sex Month

Promotes frank and open talk between parents and teens about sex. *Sponsor:* Parenting without Pressure. ⊠

National Women's History Month

Honors all women in history, including those who have made significant public contributions as well as those whose impact was felt exclusively by their families. Send for their *Women's History Catalog.* *Sponsor:* National Women's History Project, 7738 Bell Road, Windsor, CA 95492; 707-838-6000; Fax: 707-838-0478.

Poison Prevention Awareness Month

To spread the word about how poisonings can be prevented. *Sponsor:* Poison Prevention Week Council, P.O. Box 1543, Washington, DC 20013; 301-504-0580.

Rosacea Awareness Month

Promotes awareness of the common skin disease, Rosacea. *Sponsor:* National Rosacea Society, Sam Huff, 220 S. Cook Street #201, Barrington, IL 60010; 708-382-8971; Fax: 708-382-5567.

Youth Art Month

Promotes the importance of art in education. Send for a booklet of ideas. *Sponsor:* Council for Art Education, 100 Boylston Street #1050, Boston, MA 02116; 617-426-6400; Fax: 617-426-6639.

March 1

Art Week

The first week in March focuses attention on how artists make the world a better place. Formerly sponsored by Richard Falk, who died in 1994.

Civil Rights Act of 1875 Anniversary

First black woman to receive a medical degree (1864)

Rebecca Lee received her medical degree from the New England Female Medical College in Boston, Massachusetts.

First human-made object on another planet (1966)

Venera 3, a USSR satellite, crashed into Venus. *Contact:* NASA. ⊠

First parachute jump from an airplane (1912)

Albert Berry made this jump at Jefferson Barracks, Missouri.

International Monetary Fund began operation (1947)

Contact: International Monetary Fund, 700 19th Street NW, Washington, DC 20431; 202-623-7000; Fax: 202-623-4661.

Motion picture process patented (1864)

Louis Ducos du Hauron patented a process to take and project motion pictures; however, he never built the machine.

National Pig Day

Honors the pig as one of the most useful and intelligent domestic animals. Send an SASE for more information. *Sponsor:* Ellen Stanley, 7006 Miami Avenue, Lubbock, TX 79413; 806-792-5675.

Nebraska Admission Day

Nebraska became the 37th state of the U.S. in 1867. *Contact:* Nebraska Division of Tourism, P.O. Box 98913, Lincoln, NE 68509-8913; 402-471-3796; 800-228-4307.

Ohio Admission Day

Ohio became the 17th state of the U.S. in 1803. *Contact:* Ohio Division of Tourism, P.O. Box 1001, Columbus, OH 43211-0101; 614-466-8844; 800-282-5393.

Peace Corps founded (1961)
The Peace Corps was established by executive order of President John F. Kennedy. *Contact:* Peace Corps, 1990 K Street, Washington, DC 20526; 202-606-6000.

Portability Day
In 1993, toll-free (800) phone numbers became portable; that is, a company could keep the same 800 number even if it switched service providers.

Return Borrowed Books Week
Return any borrowed books to your friends and libraries during the first week in March. *Sponsor:* Prevention of Cruelty to Cartoonists, Al Kaelin, Secretary, 3119 Chadwick Drive, Los Angeles, CA 90032; 213-221-7909.

Saint David Feast Day
Patron saint of poets and Wales. Wear a leek on this day.

Universal Human Beings Week
The world is becoming a global village, and it is time for people to become universal human beings rather than members of one country or one group. Always celebrated the first 7 days in March. *Sponsor:* International Society of Friendship and Good Will. ✉

World Day of Prayer
Since 1887, on the first Friday in March, women all over the world have united for a day of informed prayer and prayerful action. In 1996, the Christian women of Haiti sponsor the following theme: God calls us to respond. *Sponsor:* Church Women United, Eleanor Dirrane, 475 Riverside Drive #812, New York, NY 10115; 212-870-2347; Fax: 212-870-2338.

Yellowstone National Park established (1872)
The first U.S. national park was established by Congress. *Contact:* Yellowstone National Park, P.O. Box 168, Yellowstone Park, WY 82190; 307-344-7381.

March 2

Cat in the Hat Day
On the birthday of Theodor Seuss Geisel (1904), we honor Dr. Seuss and all his wonderful stories. *Sponsor:* Open Horizons. ✉

Congress declares slave importation illegal (1807)

First antitrust law in the U.S. (1889)
The Kansas legislature passed the first U.S. antitrust law.

First flight of the Concorde (1969)

First non-stop flight around the world (1949)
Captain James Gallagher of the U.S. Air Force completed the first non-stop flight around the world (he refueled several times in mid-flight).

First school for the blind (1829)
The Perkins School for the Blind in Boston, Massachusetts, was the first in the U.S. Its original name was New England Asylum for the Blind.

Iditarod Day
The first Saturday in March is the first day of the Iditarod dog sled race that goes from Fairbanks to Nome, Alaska.

National Easter Seal Telethon
Held the first weekend in March, the telethon raises funds to provide rehabilitation and support services to 1 million disabled children and adults. It also promotes the society's mission to help people with disabilities. *Sponsor:* National Easter Seal Society, 230 W. Monroe #1800, Chicago, IL 60606-4802; 312-726-6200; 800-221-6827; Fax: 312-726-1494.

Puerto Rico Territory Day

In 1917, Puerto Rico became a territory of the U.S. *Contact:* Puerto Rico Tourism Corporation, 575 Fifth Avenue, 23rd Floor, New York, NY 10017; 212-599-6262; 800-223-6530; Fax: 212-818-1866.

Texas Independence Day

Texas declared its independence from Mexico in 1836. *Contact:* Texas Tourism Division, P.O. Box 12728, Austin, TX 78711; 512-462-9191; 800-888-8839; Fax: 512-320-9456.

Time magazine first published (1923)

Contact: Time magazine, Time-Life Building, Rockefeller Center, New York, NY 10020; 212-522-1212; 800-621-8200; Fax: 212-522-0325.

U.S. Court of Customs and Patent Appeals created (1929)

U.S. Department of Education created (1867)

Contact: U.S. Department of Education, 400 Maryland Avenue SW #2089, Washington, DC 20202; 202-401-1576; Fax: 202-272-5447.

March 3

AT&T incorporated (1885)

Contact: American Telephone & Telegraph, 32 Sixth Avenue, New York, NY 10013; 212-387-5400; Fax: 212-226-4935.

Federal Employees Recognition Week

By presidential proclamation, this is always celebrated the first full week in March.

First foreign aid bill passed by Congress (1812)

Congress approved an earthquake relief bill to aid Venezuelan victims.

First U.S. conscription act (1863)

First woman to practice before the Supreme Court (1879)

Belva Ann Lockwood was the first woman to practice before the U.S. Supreme Court. *Contact:* U.S. Supreme Court. ✉

Florida Admission Day

In 1845, Florida became the 27th state of the U.S. *Contact:* Florida Division of Tourism, Collins Building, 107 W. Gaines Street, Tallahassee, FL 32399-2000; 904-488-7999; Fax: 904-921-9169.

Help Someone See Week

Donate your old prescription glasses in order to improve the vision of poor people. Always celebrated during the first full week in March. *Sponsor:* Shane Hill Nursing Home, Dorothy Trisel, Activities Director, 10731 State Route 118, Rockford, OH 45882-0159; 419-363-2620.

I Want You to Be Happy Day

Treat others well even if you are not feeling happy. *Sponsor:* Harriet Grimes, P.O. Box 545, Winter Garden, FL 34777-0545; 407-656-3830.

Indian Appropriations Act passed (1885)

Made all Indians wards of the federal government. It also nullified all previous treaties with the Indians. *Contact:* Bureau of Indian Affairs, 1849 C Street NW #4160, Washington, DC 20245; 202-208-7163; Fax: 202-208-6334.

International Day of the Seal

A Congressional resolution founded this day to draw attention to the cruelty of seal hunts. Always celebrated on the first Sunday in March. *Sponsor:* Friends of the National Zoo, National Zoological Park, 3001 Connecticut Avenue NW, Washington, DC 20008; 202-673-4955; Fax: 202-673-4738.

Mount Rushmore Day

Mount Rushmore was dedicated on this day in 1933, and was completed October 31, 1941. *Contact:* Mount Rushmore National Monument, P.O. Box 268, Keystone, SD 57751; 605-574-2523.

National Aardvark Week

During the first week in March, work to enhance the image of the lowly aardvark. *Sponsor:* The Aardvark Group, Robert Bogart, President, P.O. Box 200, Parsippany, NJ 07054-0200; 201-729-4555.

National Anthem Day

In 1931, President Hoover signed a bill declaring "The Star-Spangled Banner" the U.S. national anthem.

National Camp Week

During the first full week in March, start looking at summer camps for your kids. Over 5,000,000 children attend summer camps each year. *Sponsor:* American Camping Association, 5000 State Road 67N, Martinsville, IN 46151-7902; 317-342-8456; Fax: 317-342-2065.

National Drug and Alcohol Awareness Week

Parents need to educate themselves with facts and preventive strategies to recognize, understand, and combat drug and alcohol abuse among teenagers. Theme: Prevention begins at home. Always the first full week in March. *Sponsor:* National PTA, 330 N. Wabash Avenue #2100, Chicago, IL 60611-3690; 312-670-6782; Fax: 312-670-6783.

National Lutheran School Week

The first full week in March draws attention to America's 2,000 Lutheran schools. *Sponsor:* School Services Unit, Lutheran Church–Missouri Synod, 1333 S. Kirkwood Road, Saint Louis, MO 63122-7295; 314-965-9000.

National Volunteers of America Week

An occasion to appreciate America's volunteers. Always celebrated the week of March 8th. *Sponsor:* Volunteers of America, Arthur Smith, Director, 3939 N. Causeway Boulevard, Metairie, LA 70002; 800-899-0089.

Party Party Day

An excuse to have a party once a month (when the day equals the month). *Sponsor:* Bonza Bottler Day.
✉

Saint Jonah Feast Day

Saint Jonah, the prophet who was swallowed by a whale, is patron saint of whales.

Save Your Vision Week

The first full week of March reminds people to take care of their eyes. For a free copy of *Teacher's Guide to Vision Problems*, send an SASE to the American Optometric Association. *Sponsor:* American Optometric Association, 243 N. Lindbergh Boulevard, St. Louis, MO 63141; 314-991-4100; Fax: 314-991-4101.

Severe Weather Awareness Week

Be more alert during the first week in March, which is traditionally a bad weather week.

TV Turn-Off Week

The first week in March encourages alternatives to watching TV, such as reading and talking. *Sponsor:* Plymouth Public Library, Friends of the Library, 132 South Street, Plymouth, MA 02360; 508-830-4250.

U.S. Department of the Interior created (1849)

Contact: Department of the Interior, 1849 C Street NW, Washington, DC 20240; 202-208-3171; Fax: 202-208-5048.

U.S. Forest Service established (1905)

Contact: U.S. Forest Service, 201 Fourteenth Street SW, Washington, DC 20250; 202-720-3935; Fax: 202-720-7729.

March 4

Downsizing Day

Also known as When Am I Going to Lose My Job Day. Always commemorated the first Monday in March, but it could happen at any time. Originated by the listeners of CFRB-AM. *Sponsor:* CFRB-AM, Ted Woloshyn, 2 St. Clair Avenue W, Toronto, Ontario M4V 1L6; 416-924-5711.

First cavalry unit under its own command (1833)

The First Regiment of Dragoons was the first U.S. cavalry unit under its own command.

First chartered railroad in the U.S. (1826)

The Granite Railway was chartered in Quincy, Massachusetts.

First meeting of Congress (1789)

The U.S. Congress met for the first time. The House of Representatives obtained a quorum on April 1st, the Senate on April 5th.

First tavern in America (1634)

The first tavern opened in Boston, Massachusetts.

First woman cabinet member (1933)

Frances Perkins was appointed Labor Secretary by Franklin Roosevelt. *Contact:* U.S. Department of Labor, 200 Constitution Avenue NW, Washington, DC 20210; 202-219-7316; Fax: 202-219-7312.

Football Coaches Day

On the birthday of Knute Rockne (1888), the great football coach of Notre Dame, we honor all football coaches.

National Procrastinators Week

Don't do it today if it can wait until tomorrow! Always celebrated the first full week in March. *Sponsor:* Procrastinators Club of America, Les Waas, President, P.O. Box 712, Bryn Athyn, PA 19009; 215-947-0500.

National Professional Pet Sitters Week

Do something special for a pet sitter this week. Always the week of March 6th (when the Professional Pet Sitter of the Year is announced). *Sponsor:* Pet Sitters International, Bill Foster, 418 E. King Street, King, NC 27021; 910-983-9222; Fax: 910-983-3755.

National School Breakfast Week

Celebrated the first full week in March; promotes a nutritious start to the school day. *Sponsor:* American School Food Service Association, 1600 Duke Street, 7th Floor, Alexandria, VA 22314; 703-739-3900; 800-877-8822; Fax: 703-739-3915.

Newspapers in Education Week

The first full week in March encourages the use of newspapers in classrooms. *Sponsor:* Newspaper Association of America, 11600 Sunrise Valley Drive, Reston, VA 22091; 703-648-1051.

People magazine first published (1974)

Mia Farrow was the first person to be featured on the cover of *People*.

✉ Addresses for frequently cited organizations are gathered on pages vii–viii.

Contact: People Weekly, 1271 Avenue of the Americas, New York, NY 10020-1303; 212-586-1212; 800-621-8200.

President-for-a-Day Day

In 1849, newly elected President Zachary Taylor was scheduled to take the oath of office. But because March 4th fell on a Sunday, he refused to take the oath. So, for one day, the President Pro Tempore, Missouri Senator David Rice Atchinson, assumed the office.

Pulaski Day

The first Monday in March is a holiday in Illinois, honoring Casimir Pulaski, Polish hero of the American Revolution. Pulaski was born in 1747 in Poland. Contact: Illinois Bureau of Tourism, 100 W. Randolph Street #3/400, Chicago, IL 60601; 312-814-4732; 800-223-0121; Fax: 312-814-6581.

Television Hall of Fame first established (1984)

The first people to be inducted into the TV Hall of Fame included Lucille Ball, Milton Berle, Paddy Chayefsky, Norman Lear, Edward R. Morrow, William S. Paley, and David Sarnoff. Other inductees include Johnny Carson and Mary Tyler Moore. Contact: Television Academy Hall of Fame, Acadamy of TV Arts and Sciences, 5220 Lankenshim Boulevard, North Hollywood, CA 91601; 818-953-7575; Fax: 818-761-2827.

U.S. Department of Labor created (1913)

Contact: U.S. Department of Labor, 200 Constitution Avenue NW, Washington, DC 20210; 202-219-9711; Fax: 202-219-8699.

Vermont Admission Day

In 1791 Vermont became the 14th state of the U.S. Contact: Vermont Department of Tourism, 134 State Street, Montpelier, VT 05602; 802-828-3236.

March 5

Crispus Attucks Day

Crispus Attucks was the first person to be killed during the Boston Massacre (1770). Crispus was possibly a runaway slave. Contact: Boston Visitors Bureau, P.O. Box 490, Boston, MA 02199; 617-536-4100; Fax: 617-424-7664.

Festival of Tobacco

In 1558, smoking tobacco was introduced in Europe by Francisco Fernandes, a Spanish physician. Sponsor: A Pilgrim's Almanac. ✉

First old age pension plans in the U.S. (1923)

Established by the states of Montana and Nevada.

First radio broadcast of a musical composition (1907)

Hall of Fame for Great Americans founded (1900)

Dedicated and opened to the public on May 30, 1901. It was the first hall of fame to open in the U.S. Contact: Hall of Fame for Great Americans, Bronx Community College, W. 181st Street & University Avenue, New York, NY 10451; 212-220-6003; 718-960-1114; Fax: 718-960-1120.

Iron Curtain named (1946)

During a speech at Westminster College, Winston Churchill first referred to an Iron Curtain separating eastern and western European countries.

National Sportsmanship Day

This day is designed to encourage athletes and others to discuss ethics, sportsmanship, and fair play on the field and in the classroom. More than 7,000 schools now participate in this day's activities on the first Tuesday in March. Sponsor: Institute for International Sports, P.O. Box 104, University of Rhode Island, Kingston, RI 02881; 401-792-4503; Fax: 401-792-4395.

Nuclear Non-Proliferation Treaty took effect (1970)

Sixty-one countries signed this treaty prohibiting the spread of nuclear weapons.

Purim (Feast of Lots)

Purim celebrates the intervention of Queen Esther to save the Jews in 6th Century B.C. Persia. It is celebrated with gifts, charity, and feasts. 1997: March 23; 1998: March 12.

Seed Moon

The full moon of March is the seed moon, symbolic of plants, spirituality, and the seed of success; also known as the Worm Moon or Sap Moon (in the American backwoods tradition).

Town Meeting Day

This is a Vermont state holiday; designed for holding town meetings and elections. *Contact:* Vermont State Government Info, State Administration Building, 133 State Street, Montpelier, VT 05633; 802-828-1110; Fax: 802-828-2327.

March 6

Census Bureau established by Congress (1902)

Contact: Bureau of the Census, 3 Silver Hill & Suitland Roads, Building 3, Suitland, MD 20746; 301-763-4040; Fax: 301-763-4191.

Fall of the Alamo (1836)

The Alamo in San Antonio, Texas, fell to the Mexican army. This was a major event in Texan independence. Remember the Alamo! *Contact:* Texas Tourism Division, P.O. Box 12728, Austin, TX 78711; 512-462-9191; 800-880-8839; Fax: 512-320-9456.

Frozen food first marketed (1930)

Clarence Birdseye marketed frozen food for the first time in Springfield, Massachusetts.

Michelangelo's Birthday

Michelangelo, who painted the Sistine Chapel and sculpted *David* and the *Pieta,* was born in Caprese, Italy, in 1475. He was perhaps the world's greatest artist.

Toronto's Birthday

Toronto was incorporated as a city in 1834. *Contact:* Toronto Visitors Association, 207 Queen's Quay W #590, Toronto, Ontario M5J 1A7; 416-203-2600; Fax: 416-867-3995.

March 7

American Negro Labor Congress organized (1925)

Burn Your Guitar Day

Celebrates the birthday of rock musician Jimi Hendrix. *Sponsor:* The Life of the Party. ✉

Corn Flakes's Birthday

Dr. John Kellogg first served corn flakes to his patients at the Kellogg Sanitarium in 1897. For the free kid's cookbook *Kellogg's Cereal Recipe Collection,* send a postcard to Department G9 at the following address. *Contact:* Kelloggs Foods, 1 Kellogg Square, Battle Creek, MI 49017; 616-961-2000; Fax: 616-961-2871.

Distinguished Service Medal Birthday

In 1918, President Wilson authorized a medal recognizing those who performed exceptionally meritorious service during the war.

First jazz record released (1917)

The Original Dixieland Band recorded the first jazz record for RCA Victor in Camden, New Jersey.

First trans-Atlantic radio-telephone conversation (1926)

Took place between London and New York City.

Legislative Action Day

The first Thursday in March is set aside to lobby federal legislators to let them know how much the meetings industry contributes to the national economy: $224 billion per year plus 3,000,000 jobs. *Sponsor:* Meeting Professionals International, 1950 Stemmons Freeway #5018, Dallas, TX 75207; 214-712-7700; Fax: 214-746-5248.

Monopoly Game Birthday

Monopoly was invented in 1933; it was mass-marketed by Parker Brothers in 1935. *Contact:* Parker Brothers, 50 Dunham Road, Beverly, MA 01915; 508-927-7600; Fax: 508-921-3066.

Salvadore Dali Museum opened (1982)

Contact: Salvadore Dali Museum, 1000 Third Street S, St. Petersburg, FL 33701; 813-823-3767.

"We Are the World" record released (1985)

The record "We Are the World" was released to provide relief to Africans suffering from famine.

World's Largest Concert

This concert kicks off Music in Our Schools Month on the first Thursday in March. It is broadcast on PBS stations nationally. Approximately 8 million people will participate. *Sponsor:* Music Educators National Conference, 1806 Robert Fulton Drive, Reston, VA 22091; 703-860-4000; 800-336-3768; Fax: 703-860-1531.

March 8

First dog license law (1894)

Issued in New York; a license cost $2.00.

International Women's Day

This day commemorates a demonstration by New York City women garment workers in 1857. *Sponsor:* United Nations. ✉

National Women's Get-Away Weekend

The second weekend in March is reserved for women to take some time away from home. *Sponsor: Country Inns* magazine, The Alden Group, 52 Vanderbilt Avenue, New York, NY 10017; 212-867-6400; Fax: 212-986-5988.

Saint John of God Feast Day

Patron saint of heart patients, hospitals, nurses, and the sick. He is also patron saint of booksellers and printers.

Stretch Your Legs Day

On the birthday of Cyd Charisse (1923), the great dancer and actress with the long, long legs, stretch your own legs in a dance of your own. Charisse was born as Tula Finklea in Amarillo, Texas. *Sponsor:* The Life of the Party. ✉

World Spaghetti Bridge Building Contest

The world record load is 388 pounds of spaghetti. It was suspended from a 1-meter bridge weighing less than 1$\frac{2}{3}$ lbs. This contest is held annually the second Friday in March. *Sponsor:* Okanagan University College, Garry Gaudet, 3333 College Way, Kelowna, British Columbia, V1V 1V7 Canada; 604-862-5662; Fax: 604-862-5476; e-mail: Gaudet@ okanagan.bc.ca.

March 9

Bang Clang Day

Celebrates the Battle of Hampton Roads (1862), the first battle between armored ships, the *Monitor* and the *Merrimac.*

Barbie's Birthday

Barbie still looks good, even though she is now well over 50 years old. *Contact:* Mattel Toys, 333 Continental Boulevard, El Segundo, CA 90245; 310-524-2000; 800-421-2887; Fax: 310-524-2179.

False Teeth Day

Charles Graham, a New York dentist, received a patent for false teeth on this date in 1822.

First Ford Mustang produced (1964)

Contact: Ford Motor Company, P.O. Box 1899, Dearborn, MI 48121; 313-322-3000.

First woman and Hispanic surgeon general (1990)

Antonia Novello was the first woman and first Hispanic surgeon general. *Contact:* Surgeon General's Office, Department of Health & Human Services, 200 Independence Avenue SW, Washington, DC 20201; 202-690-7000; Fax: 202-690-7203.

Mail box patented (1858)

Panic Day

A day to run around in circles shouting, "I can't take it any more!" *Sponsor:* Wellness Permission League. ✉

Saint Frances of Rome Feast Day

Considered a model for housewives and widows; the light of her guardian angel allowed her to see at night, so she is also a patron saint of motorists.

Score a Beautiful Babe Because You Have Money Day

Commemorates the day in 1995 when a listener of Camp Chaos won lots of money in a lottery and proceeded to get a date with a beautiful woman on the same day. *Sponsor:* Camp Chaos, ABC Radio Z Rock, Chaz Fernandez, 13725 Montfort Drive, Dallas, TX 75240; 214-991-9200.

March 10

Alexander Graham Bell Day (telephone invented)

In 1876, Alexander Graham Bell transmitted the first successful phone message when he said to his assistant, "Mr. Watson, come here!" Bell was born on March 3, 1847, in Scotland.

Deaf Awareness Week

Always celebrated the second full week in March.

First octuplets born (1967)

The first octuplets were born in Mexico.

First paper money issued by U.S. government (1862)

Featured Hamilton, Lincoln, and Liberty. Hamilton was on the $5.00 bill, Lincoln on the $10.00 bill, and Liberty on the $20.00 bill.

Girl Scouts Week

Celebrates the founding of the Girl Scouts in 1912. *Sponsor:* Girl Scouts of the USA, 420 Fifth Avenue, New York, NY 10018; 212-940-7500; Fax: 212-940-7859.

Harriet Tubman Day

Honors the 1913 death of Harriet Tubman, an American abolitionist and underground railroad leader.

Jerusalem temple rebuilt (515 B.C.)

Plant a Flower Day

Plant a flower on the second Sunday in March.

Salvation Army established in the U.S. (1880)

Contact: Salvation Army, 615 Slaters Lane, P.O. Box 269, Alexandria, VA 22313; 703-684-5500; Fax: 703-684-3478.

Uranus rings discovered (1977)

March 11

Champagne Music Day

On the birthday of Lawrence Welk, entertainer extraordinaire, we celebrate the music he was famous for.

Welk was born in 1903 in Strasburg, North Dakota.

Commonwealth Day (Canada)

Though not a public holiday, the second Monday in March celebrates Canada's membership in the British Commonwealth; also celebrated in other Commonwealth countries. *Contact:* Canadian Embassy, 501 Pennsylvania Avenue NW, Washington, DC 20001; 202-682-1740.

First public basketball game (1892)

Teachers challenged students in the first public basketball game; the students won. *Contact:* Basketball Hall of Fame, 1150 W. Columbus Avenue, P.O. Box 179, Springfield, MA 01101; 413-781-6500.

First rear-projection movie theater (1927)

The first rear-projection movie theater was built in New York City.

Human Services Day

On the anniversary of Whitney Young's death, we honor social workers. *Sponsor:* National Association of Social Workers, 750 First Street NE, Washington, DC 20002; 202-408-8600; Fax: 202-336-8310.

Johnny Appleseed Day

Johnny Appleseed planted apple trees all over the old Northwest

Territories; he died on this day in 1847.

Most Boring Films of the Year Awards

The awards are announced on the second Monday in March. *Sponsor:* The Boring Institute, Alan Caruba, Founder, P.O. Box 40, Maplewood, NJ 07040; 201-763-6392; Fax: 201-763-4287.

MTV Unplugged premiered (1992)

The first MTV *Unplugged* featured Eric Clapton. It aired in 1992. *Contact:* MTV, 1515 Broadway, 24th Floor, New York, NY 10036; 212-258-8000; Fax: 212-258-8100.

Paper invented

In 105 A.D., Ts'ai Lun of China invented paper. The first paper was created from mulberry leaves, bamboo, fish nets, and rags.

Save the Redwoods League founded (1918)

Contact: Save the Redwoods League, 114 Sansome Street #605, San Francisco, CA 94104; 415-362-2352; Fax: 415-362-7017.

March 12

Anti-Commercial Day

On an average day, Americans are exposed to more than 1,600 advertisements. Today you have permission to ignore all commercials and

advertisements. *Sponsor:* A Pilgrim's Almanac. ✉

Automatic telephone exchange patented (1889)

Almon Stronger of Kansas City patented the first automatic telephone exchange.

Coca-Cola first sold in bottles (1894)

For a free collection of Coca-Cola stickers featuring the Coca-Cola trademark in foreign languages, send a postcard to Coca-Cola Inc., Consumer Information Center, P.O. Box 1734, Atlanta, GA 30301. Ask for the Foreign Coca-Cola Stickers. *Contact:* Coca-Cola Inc., P.O. Box 1734, Atlanta, GA 30301; 404-676-2121; 800-438-2653; Fax: 404-676-6792.

Fireside Chat Day

President Franklin Roosevelt broadcast his first Sunday evening fireside radio chat in 1933.

First major U.S. department store opened (1877)

Founded by John Wanamaker of Philadelphia, Pennsylvania. *Contact:* John Wanamaker, Inc., 1300 Market Street, Philadelphia, PA 19107; 215-422-2000.

First steam engine used (1755)

Girl Scouts Day

Juliette Gordon Low founded the Girl Scouts in 1912 in Savannah,

✉ Addresses for frequently cited organizations are gathered on pages vii–viii.

MARCH **55**

Georgia. *Sponsor:* Girl Scouts of America, 420 Fifth Avenue, New York, NY 10018; 212-940-7500; Fax: 212-940-7859.

Hell's Angels Birthday
The Hell's Angels were created in 1948.

Parents without Partners Founder's Day (1957)
Contact: Parents without Partners, 401 N. Michigan Avenue, Chicago, IL 60611-4267; 312-644-6610; 800-637-7934.

Talk Mean to Your Spouse Day
On the birthday of playwright Edward Albee, author of *Who's Afraid of Virginia Woolf?*, you may speak meanly to your spouse for up to 32 seconds. Today only. Albee was born in 1928 in Washington, DC. *Sponsor:* The Life of the Party. ✉

U.S. Post Office established (1789)
Contact: U.S. Postal Service. ✉

March 13

Earmuffs Birthday
Chester Greenwood, a Farmington, Maine, teenager, patented earmuffs on this date in 1877.

First agricultural college in U.S. (1857)
Opened in East Lansing, Michigan. *Contact:* Michigan State University, John A. Hanna Building, East Lan-

sing, MI 48824; 517-355-1855; Fax: 517-336-2069.

Good Samaritan Involvement Day
This is the anniversary of the murder of Kitty Genovese in 1964; she was stabbed to death in front of her apartment as 38 neighbors just watched and listened. Get involved!

National Restaurant Association founded (1919)
Founded in Kansas City. *Contact:* National Restaurant Association, 1200 17th Street NW, Washington, DC 20003-2097; 202-331-5900; Fax: 202-331-2429.

Standard Time adopted in the U.S. (1884)

Strip tease first introduced (1894)
Introduced in Paris, France.

Tennessee prohibited the teaching of evolution (1925)
Contact: Tennessee Department of Tourism, P.O. Box 23170, Nashville, TN 37202-3170; 615-741-2158; 800-362-1971; Fax: 615-741-7225.

Uncle Sam Day
In 1852, the *New York Lantern* first featured the Uncle Sam character. Uncle Sam came to be a symbol of American patriotism.

Uranus discovered (1781)
English astronomer William Herschel discovered the planet Uranus.

March 14

Baseball Cap Birthday
The baseball cap was designed in 1860.

Celebrate Scientists Day
On the birthday of Albert Einstein, we honor all scientists. Einstein discovered the Special Theory of Relativity; he was born in 1879 in Ulm, Germany.

Cotton gin patented (1794)
Eli Whitney received a patent for the cotton gin.

First letter describing America mailed (1493)

First national bird reservation established (1903)

First town meeting in America (1743)
Held at Faneuil Hall in Boston, Massachusetts.

First transatlantic radio broadcast (1925)

First U.S. war bonds authorized (1812)
These bonds were sold to finance the War of 1812.

International Copyright Act approved (1891)

Moth-er Day
To make a big fuss over moth collecting and exhibits. *Sponsor:* Puns Corp. ✉

National Single Fathers Who Are Not Leeches on Society Day
This day was proposed by a listener of the Camp Chaos radio show to honor all those fathers who take responsibility for their own children. *Sponsor:* Camp Chaos, ABC Radio Z Rock, Chaz Fernandez, 13725 Montfort Drive, Dallas, TX 75240; 214-991-9200.

Waldorf Hotel opened (1893)
Contact: Waldorf-Astoria Hotel, 301 Park Avenue, New York, NY 10022; 212-355-3000; Fax: 212-758-9209.

World Championship Cutter Races
March 14 to 24. This western version of chariot racing is held every year at the Golden Spike Events Center. *Sponsor:* Ogden Visitors Bureau, Historic Union Station, 2501 Wall Avenue, Ogden, UT 84401; 801-627-8288; 800-255-8824; Fax: 801-399-0783.

March 15

American Legion founded (1919)
Founded in Paris, France. *Contact:* American Legion, P.O. Box 1055, Indianapolis, IN 46206; 317-630-1200; Fax: 317-630-1368.

Andrew Jackson Day (Tennessee)
A public holiday celebrating the birthday of our 7th president, Andrew Jackson. He was born in New Lancaster County, South Carolina in 1767. *Contact:* Tennessee Department of Tourism, P.O. Box 23170, Nashville, TN 37202-3170; 615-741-2185; 800-362-1971; Fax: 615-741-7225.

Buzzard's Day
This is the day that the turkey buzzards return to Hinckley, Ohio. *Sponsor:* Park Rangers, Hinckley, OH; 216-278-7618.

Californium created (1950)
Scientists at the University of California at Berkeley created californium, a radioactive element. *Contact:* University of California, Lawrence Radiation Laboratory, Berkeley, CA 94720; 510-642-6000; Fax: 510-643-8245.

Escalator patented (1892)
Jesse Reno of New York City patented the escalator. (See August 2nd.)

First American cardinal (1875)
John McCloskey of New York was appointed.

First Billboard record album chart (1945)
The King Cole Trio had the first #1 selling album. *Contact:* *Billboard* magazine, 1515 Broadway, 39th Floor, New York, NY 10036; 212-764-7300; Fax: 212-536-5358.

First black Archbishop (1988)
Eugene Marino of Atlanta, Georgia was appointed.

First black commissioned officer in the U.S. Navy
John Lee was assigned his first duty on this date in 1947. *Contact:* Department of the Navy, Pentagon Room #4E686, Washington, DC 20350; 703-695-0911.

First blood bank created (1937)

First Catholic nun in the U.S. (1729)
Sister Saint Stanilaus Hachard of the Ursuline Convent was the first nun in the U.S. She worked in New Orleans, Louisiana.

First Presidential press conference (1913)
Woodrow Wilson held the first open Presidential press conference.

First professional baseball team (1869)
The Cincinnati Red Stockings were the first professional baseball team. *Contact:* Cincinnati Reds, 100 Riverfront Stadium, Cincinnati, OH 45202; 513-421-4510; Fax: 513-421-7342.

First underseas national park (1960)
Biscayne National Underwater Park was the first; it opened near Key Largo, Florida. *Contact:* Biscayne National Underwater Park, P.O. Box 1369, Homestead, FL 33090-1369; 305-247-2044.

Ides of March
Julius Caesar was assassinated on this day in 44 B.C. Beware the Ides of March!

International Boss's Day Off
On the anniversary of the assassination of Julius Caesar, we recommend that all leaders stay home. Beware of assassins! And, of course, if the boss takes the day off, so can you! *Sponsor:* Open Horizons. ✉

Maine Admission Day
Maine was admitted as the 23rd state of the U.S. in 1820. *Contact:* Maine Publicity Bureau, Water Street, P.O. Box 230, Hallowell, ME 04347; 207-289-5711; 800-533-9595; Fax: 207-289-2861.

My Fair Lady premiered (1956)
My Fair Lady opened in New York City and went on to become one of the most successful musicals in modern theatre history.

True Confessions Day
Confession is good for the soul. *Sponsor:* Wellness Permission League. ✉

March 16

Black Press Day
In 1827, *Freedom's Journal*, the first black newspaper in the U.S., was published in New York City.

Curlew Day
Traditionally, this is the day that 500 long-billed curlew return to the Umatilla National Wildlife Refuge in Oregon. *Contact:* Umatilla National Forest, Ukiah, OR 97880.

Federal Trade Commission established (1915).
Contact: Federal Trade Commission, Pennsylvania Avenue & 6th Street NW, Washington, DC 20580; 202-326-2000; Fax: 202-326-2050.

First docking of an orbiting spacecraft (1966)
Gemini 8 docked with the *Agena*. *Contact:* NASA. ✉

First fertilizer law passed (1871)

First National Book Awards (1950)
Nelson Algren won the award in fiction for his novel *The Man with the Golden Arm.* Ralph L. Rusk won in nonfiction for his biography of Ralph Waldo Emerson. William Carlos Williams won in poetry for *Paterson: Book 3 and Selected Poems.* *Contact:* National Book Foundation, 260 Fifth Avenue #904, New York, NY 10001; 212-685-0261; Fax: 212-213-6570.

First radio station to feature country music (1922)
WSB Radio was the first to feature country music. *Contact:* WSB Radio, 1601 West Peachtree Street NE, Atlanta, GA 30309; 404-897-7500; Fax: 404-897-6211.

First woman pharmacist graduated (1883)
Susan Hayhurst was the first woman to become a certified pharmacist.

Freedom of Information Day
On the birthday of James Madison (1751), we honor his efforts and the continued efforts of many others who fight for freedom of in-

formation and a free press. *Sponsor:* American Library Association.

Goddard Day
In 1926, Robert Goddard developed the first liquid fuel powered rocket. *Contact:* NASA.

James Madison's Birthday
James Madison, the 4th President of the U.S., was born in 1751 in Port Conway, Virginia.

My Lai Massacre Anniversary (1968)
During the Vietnam War an American division killed 300 noncombatants.

Saint Urho's Day
This mythical saint drove the grasshoppers out of Finland. The local festival is always celebrated on the Saturday closest to the 16th of March. Hood River, Oregon, also has a local celebration honoring Saint Urho (for info, call 503-386-1802). *Sponsor:* St. Urho's Day Committee, P.O. Box 563, Finland, MN 55603; 218-353-7359.

West Point Military Academy authorized (1802)
Contact: West Point Military Academy, West Point, NY 10996; 914-938-4011; Fax: 914-938-3828.

March 17

American Chocolate Week
The third full week in March celebrates America's favorite flavor of everything. *Sponsor:* Chocolate Manufacturers Association, 7900 Westpark Drive #A-320, McLean, VA 22102; 703-790-5011.

Camp Fire Boys and Girls Founders Day
Mrs. Luther Gulick of Lake Sebago, Maine, founded the Camp Fire Girls in 1912. *Sponsor:* Camp Fire Boys and Girls, 4601 Madison Avenue, Kansas City, MO 64112, 816-756-1950; Fax: 816-756-0258.

Children and Hospitals Week
A campaign is held during the third full week in March to educate health care professionals, families, children, and the community-at-large about the special needs of children and families in health care settings. *Sponsor:* Association for the Care of Children's Health, 7910 Woodmont Avenue #300, Bethesda, MD 20814-3015; 301-654-6549; Fax: 301-986-4553.

Designated Driver St. Patrick's Day Campaign
When you go out partying today, make sure to have a friend who will be the designated driver and not drink. Drive safely. *Sponsor:* Mothers Against Drunk Driving, 511 E John Carpenter Frwy #700, Irving, TX 75062-8187; 214-744-6233.

Evacuation Day
This Boston holiday celebrates the evacuation of British troops in 1776. Actually, this holiday came about as a sneaky way for Boston's Irish politicians to celebrate Saint Patrick's Day as a legal day off from work. Let's have more Evacuation Days! *Contact:* Boston Visitors Bureau, P.O. Box 490, Boston, MA 02199; 617-536-4100; Fax: 617-424-7664.

First practical submarine demonstrated (1898)
John Holland demonstrated his sub off Staten Island, New York.

First ship to be named for a black naval officer (1972)
The *USS Jesse L. Brown* became the first ship to be named after a black naval officer. Brown was born on October 13, 1926, in Hattisburg, Mississippi, and was the first black American naval aviator. *Contact:* Department of the Navy, Pentagon Room #4E686, Washington, DC 20350; 703-695-0911.

First solar-powered satellite (1958)
The U.S. launched the first solar-powered satellite, *Vanguard I.* *Contact:* NASA.

First workable sidewheel steamboat (1811)

 Addresses for frequently cited organizations are gathered on pages vii–viii.

MARCH   **59**

National Agriculture Week

The week of the vernal equinox honors the people who grow our food and fiber. *Sponsor*: Agriculture Council of America, 927 15th Street NW #800, Washington, DC 20005; 202-682-9200; Fax: 202-289-6648.

National Gallery of Art founded (1941)

Contact: National Gallery of Art, 4th Street & Constitution Avenue, Washington, DC 20565; 202-737-4215; Fax: 202-842-2356.

National Poison Prevention Week

Spread the word about how to prevent poisonings, especially during the third full week in March. *Sponsor*: Poison Prevention Week Council, P.O. Box 1543, Washington, DC 20013; 301-504-0580.

Republic of Texas abolished slavery (1836)

Contact: Texas Tourism Division, P.O. Box 12728, Austin, TX 78711; 512-462-9191; 800-888-8839; Fax: 512-320-9456.

Saint Patrick's Day

Saint Patrick died on this date in 461. He is the patron saint of Ireland; this is a day to wear green or orange to show your Irish heart.

Small Family Farm Week

Celebrated the week of Spring.

Straw Hat Week

During the week of the vernal equinox, put away your winter hats and take your cool straw hats for spring and summer. *Sponsor*: Millinery Info Bureau, Casey Push, Executive Director, 302 West 12th Street, New York, NY 10014; 212-627-8333.

World's Shortest St. Patrick's Day Parade

Floats and bands march 97 feet down Buchanan Street in Maryville, Missouri. *Sponsor*: St. Patrick's Day Parade, Bruce Judd, Chair, 422 N. Buchanan Street, Maryville, MO 64468; 816-562-9965.

March 18

American Express founded (1850)

American Express was founded by Henry Wells and William Fargo. *Contact*: American Express Company, American Express Tower C, World Financial Center, New York; NY 10285; 212-640-2000; Fax: 212-767-2888.

Dangerous Dan's Annual Coffee Cup Washing

On the third Monday in March, join with Dangerous Dan in washing out your morning coffee cup at least once a year. *Sponsor*: Dan Jensen at WSYW-FM, Dangerous Dan's Morning Madness, 8203 Indy Court, Indianapolis, IN 46214; 317-271-9799.

First electric razor marketed (1931)

Schick began marketing the first electric razor.

First paper dress sold (1966)

Scott Paper sold the first paper dresses for $1.00 each. *Contact*: Scott Paper Company, Scott Plaza, Philadelphia, PA 19113; 215-522-5000; Fax: 215-422-6903.

Grover Cleveland's Birthday

The 22nd and 24th President of the U.S. was born in Caldwell, New Jersey in 1837.

Ham Radio Day

In 1909, Einar Dessau of Denmark was the first to broadcast over a ham radio.

National Free Paper Week

Free newspapers contribute to their communities by providing information and entertainment. Always celebrated the third Monday through Friday of March. *Sponsor*: Association of Free Community Papers, 401 N. Michigan Avenue, Chicago, IL 60611-4267; 312-644-6610.

National Manufacturing Week

During the annual convention of the National Association of Manufacturers, we celebrate what's new in manufacturing. The convention is held in Chicago, Illinois. *Sponsor:* National Association of Manufacturers, 1331 Pennsylvania Avenue NW #1500N, Washington, DC 20004; 202-637-3047; Fax: 202-637-3182.

North Atlantic Treaty ratified (1949)
Contact: NATO, 1110 Brussels, Belgium; 2-728-41-11; Fax: 2-728-41-17.

Poppin' Fresh Birthday
The Pillsbury Dough Boy was introduced in 1961. *Contact:* Pillsbury Company, 200 South 6th Street, Minneapolis, MN 55402; 612-330-4966; Fax: 612-330-5200.

Postal Workers Stress Syndrome Day
Commemorates the first strike by U.S. postal workers, which occurred in 1970 in New York City. Also known as I Have Postal Workers Stress Syndrome and Need the Day Off Day (as named by Bud

Spider of Clearfield, Pennsylvania). *Contact:* U.S. Postal Service. ✉

Space Walk Day
In 1965, USSR cosmonaut Aleksei Leonov was the first person to walk in space. *Contact:* NASA. ✉

Worst tornado in U.S. history (1925)
The Great Tri-State Tornado caused 695 deaths in Missouri, Illinois, and Indiana.

March 19

Avon Representative Day
Contact: Avon Products, 9 West 57th Street, New York, NY 10019; 212-546-6015; Fax: 212-546-6136.

First bank robbery in the U.S. (1831)
Edward Smith robbed $245,000 from the City Bank in New York City.

First lunar eclipse recorded (72 A.D.)
Ptolemy recorded the first eclipse of the moon.

First state to allow girls to compete with boys (1975)
Pennsylvania became the first state to allow girls to compete with boys in high school sports.

Saint Joseph's Feast Day
The foster father of Jesus is the patron saint of carpenters, engineers, house hunters, manual workers, bursars, fathers, social justice, the church, the poor, and the dying. He is also the patron saint of Palermo, Sicily.

Swallows Day
The swallows return to the San Juan Capistrano Mission in California on Saint Joseph's Feast Day. Traditionally, they leave on October 23. *Contact:* San Juan Capistrano Mission, San Juan Capistrano, CA; 715-493-1111.

U.S. Standard Time Act (1918)
Congress established the standard time zones.

March 20

Big Bird's Birthday
Contact: Sesame Street, Children's Television Network, 1 Lincoln Square Plaza, 3rd Floor, New York, NY 10023; 212-595-3456; Fax: 212-875-6106.

Earth Day
In 1979, children rang a bell at the United Nations at the moment of the Vernal Equinox. *Contact:* United Nations. ✉

Earth Month
The month between the first day of Spring and Earth Day. *Sponsor:* United Nations. ✉

First Day of Spring

Also known as the Vernal Equinox, Spring begins at 3:04 P.M., Eastern Standard Time.

First NCAA hockey championship won (1948)

The University of Michigan beat Dartmouth to win the first NCAA hockey championship. *Contact:* National Collegiate Athletic Association, 6201 College Boulevard, Overland Park, KS 66211; 913-339-1906; Fax: 913-339-1950.

First woman executed by electrocution (1899)

Martha M. Place of Brooklyn, New York was executed at Sing Sing Prison for the murder of her stepdaughter.

Great American Meatout

Kick the meat habit on the first day of Spring and explore a more wholesome, plant-based diet. *Sponsor:* Farm Animal Reform Movement, 10101 Ashburton Lane, Bethesda, MD 20817; 301-530-1737; 800-MEAT-OUT; Fax: 301-530-5747.

National Agriculture Day

The first day of Spring promotes American agriculture. *Sponsor:* Agri-

culture Council of America, 927 15th Street NW #800, Washington, DC 20005; 202-682-9200.

Photograph a Soup Can Day

Celebrates the first large pop art exhibition, which was held in 1962. *Sponsor:* The Life of the Party. ✉

Pigeons Day

On the first day of Spring, the pigeons return to the City/County Building in Fort Wayne, Indiana. *Sponsor:* WAJI Radio, Barb Richards, 347 W Berry #600, Fort Wayne, IN 46802; 219-423-3676.

Proposal Day

Celebrated twice-yearly, this day encourages men and women to propose marriage to their true loves. Today, night and day are of equal length, symbolizing that although men and women are different as night and day—they are equal! *Sponsor:* Lady, Lad, and Delia Company, John Michael O'Loughlin, 1333 W. Campbell #125, Richardson, TX 75080; 214-721-9975.

Shoe lasting machine patented (1883)

Black inventor Jan Ernst Matzeliger patented the shoe lasting machine.

Uncle Tom's Cabin published (1852)

Harriet Beecher Stowe's novel of slave oppression, *Uncle Tom's Cabin*, was published in Boston, Massachusetts.

March 21

Astrological New Year

The beginning of the astrological year begins with the first day of the sign of Aries.

Caldecott Medal Day

On the birthday of Randolph Caldecott, we celebrate all award-winning (as well as ordinary) illustrators of children's books. Caldecott, for whom the Caldecott Medal is named, was in 1846 in Chester, England.

Children's Poetry Day

First mutual fund in the U.S. (1924)

The Massachusetts Investors Trust was the first mutual fund in the U.S.; it was set up in Boston.

First professional club for women in the U.S.

The club, Sorosis, was founded in New York in 1868.

First U.S. naval officer commissioned

Hopley Yeaton was commissioned in 1791. *Contact:* Department of the Navy, Information Office, The Pentagon, Washington, DC 20350; 703-697-7391.

Fragrance Day

Celebrates the effects of perfumes and colognes on our lives. Formerly sponsored by Richard Falk, who died in 1994.

Indian New Year (Saka)

The official calendar of India celebrates its new year on March 22nd (21st on leap years). *Contact:* Government of India, Tourist Information Office, 30 Rockefeller Plaza #15, New York, NY 10112; 212-586-4901; Fax: 212-582-3274.

International Astrology Day

The day that starts the astrological year (first day of Aries). *Sponsor:* Association for Astrological Networking, 8306 Wilshire Boulevard #537, Beverly Hills, CA 90211.

International Day for the Elimination of Racism

First celebrated in 1966, this day commemorates the anniversary of the killing of 69 African demonstrators in Sharpeville, South Africa in 1960. *Sponsor:* United Nations. 🖂

International Flower Day

Bring bouquets of spring flowers into your home, business, school, or other places you frequent. *Sponsor:* All My Events. 🖂

Iranian New Year (Noruz)

The Iranian or Persian New Year is a national holiday in Iran and some other Middle East countries. Also known as the Baha'i New Year (Naw-Ruz). *Contact:* Islamic Republic of Iran, Mission to the United Nations, 622 Third Avenue, 33rd Floor, New York, NY 10017; 212-687-2020; Fax: 212-867-7086.

James T. Kirk Birthday

According to the official Star Trek biography, Captain James T. Kirk of the *Starship Enterprise* will be born in a small Iowa town in the year 2228. Riverside, Iowa, claims to be that town. *Contact:* Riverside Chamber of Commerce, P.O. Box 55, Riverside, IA 52327; 319-648-4808.

Johann Sebastian Bach's Birthday

One of the greatest classical composers, Bach was born in Eisenach, Germany in 1685.

Master Gardener Day

The first full day of Spring recognizes master gardeners. *Sponsor:* Master Gardener Program, Jim Arnold, 543 Wagner Street, Fort Wayne, IN 46805-4040; 219-426-9904.

Memory Day

To examine the use of memory aids throughout history. *Sponsor:* Puns Corp. 🖂

National Teenagers Day

To improve relationships between teenagers and adults. Formerly sponsored by M. J. Mamakos.

Sign of Aries

The astrological sign of Aries, the ram, runs from March 21st to April 19th. Aries people are bold, impulsive, and confident.

Street, Salt Lake City, UT 84150; 801-240-2531; Fax: 801-240-2033.

First steam fire engine (1841)
The first steam fire engine was tested in New York City.

Florida discovered (1512)
Florida was sighted by Juan Ponce de Leon, a Spanish explorer. *Contact:* Florida Division of Tourism, Collins Building, 107 W. Gaines Street, Tallahassee, FL 32399-2000; 904-488-7999; Fax: 904-921-9169.

Funky Winkerbean Birthday
The comic strip was first published on this date in 1972. *Sponsor:* Funky Winkerbean Comic Strip, Tom Batiuk, Creator, 2750 Substation Road, Medina, OH 44256; 216-722-8755.

Kerosene oil for lanterns patented (1855)

National Badminton Day
On the opening day of the U.S. National Championships, we salute the game of badminton. *Sponsor:* U.S. Badminton Association, One Olympic Plaza, Colorado Springs, CO 80909; 719-578-4808; Fax: 719-578-4507.

National Exchange Club Birthday
The first Exchange Club was formed in Detroit, Michigan, in 1911. *Sponsor:* The National Exchange Clubs, C. Neal Davis, 3050

Central Avenue, Toledo, OH 43606-1700; 419-535-3232; Fax: 419-535-1989.

U.S. Navy established (1794)
Contact: Department of the Navy, Pentagon, Room 4E686, Washington, DC 20350; 703-695-0911.

Urinal patented (1866)
Invented by Andrew Rankin.

World's worst aircraft disaster (1977)
A total of 582 people were killed when a Pan American 747 and a KLM 747 collided on the runway at the Santa Cruz de Tenerife airport in the Canary Islands. That's the highest number of people to die as the result of an aircraft accident in world history.

March 28

Beer Brewers Day
On the birthdays of Frederick Pabst (1836) and August Anheuser Busch Jr. (1899), we honor all great brewers.

Children's Picture Book Day
The first picture book for children was written by J. A. Comenius in 1592. *Sponsor:* Book Marketing Update. ✉

Czechoslovakian Teachers Day
Celebrates the birthday of Jan Amos Komensky (1592), a Moravian educational reformer. *Contact:*

Czech Republic Embassy, 3900 Spring of Freedom Street NW, Washington, DC 20008; 202-363-6315; Fax: 202-966-8540.

Eat an Eskimo Pie Day
Sponsor: The Life of the Party. ✉

First hospital ambulance service (1866)

First microfilm device introduced (1922)

Respect Your Cat Day
In 1384, King Richard II of England issued a royal edict condemning the eating of cats. Give your cat a little extra treat today! *Sponsor:* A Pilgrim's Almanac. ✉

Saint John Nepomucene Neumann Birthday
Bishop Neumann, the first U.S. male saint proclaimed by the Roman Catholic church, was born in Prachatice, Bohemia in 1811.

Three Mile Island nuclear power plant accident (1979)

A major accident occurred at the Three Mile Island nuclear power plant in Pennsylvania. This incident led to changes in the way nuclear plants are operated.

Washing machine patented (1797)

Nathan Briggs patented a version of the washing machine.

March 29

American Crossword Puzzle Tournament

March 29 to 31. Contestants must be the fastest and most accurate crossword puzzle solvers. The dates of the tournament change from year to year. *Sponsor:* American Crossword Puzzle Tournament, Will Shortz, Director, 55 Great Oak Lane, Pleasantville, NY 10570; 914-769-9128; Fax: 914-769-9128.

Coca-Cola's Birthday

Atlanta pharmacist, John Pemberton, concocted Coca-Cola on March 29th and introduced it to the public on May 8th, 1886. *Contact:* Coca-Cola, Inc, P.O. Box 1734, Atlanta, GA 30301; 404-676-2121; 800-438-2653; Fax: 404-676-6792.

John Tyler's Birthday

The 10th President of the U.S. was born in 1790 in Greenway, Virginia.

Knights of Columbus Founder's Day

Founded in 1882, The Knights of Columbus is a fraternal Catholic family service organization providing social services. *Sponsor:* Knights of Columbus, One Columbus Plaza, New Haven, CT 06510; 203-772-2130; Fax: 203-773-3000.

Know Your Stockbroker Day

On the day financier Michael Milken was indicted, take some extra time to know those who advise you on your investments. *Sponsor:* The Life of the Party.

National Teacher Appreciation Day

The Friday before Palm Sunday is reserved as a day for elementary and secondary students to show appreciation to their teachers. *Sponsor:* Joseph Kearley, 2129 Benbrook Drive, Carrollton, TX 75007; 214-245-6192.

23rd Amendment to the Constitution ratified (1961)

Gave D.C. citizens the right to vote in presidential elections.

Vietnam War: last U.S. troops left Vietnam (1973)

World Championship Snowmobile Hill Climb

This world championship event is held on the last weekend in March; snowmobiles try to ascend Snow King Mountain near Jackson Hole. *Sponsor:* Jackson Hole Snow Devils, Jackson Hole Chamber of Commerce, P.O. Box E, Jackson, WY 83001; 307-733-3316.

March 30

Egg incubator patented (1843)

First double-deck bridge opened (1909)

The Queensboro Bridge in New York City opened to traffic.

First passenger ship to circumnavigate the world

In 1923, the *Laconia* became the first passenger ship to sail around the world.

Genesis Awards Ceremony

Honors media portrayals of animal issues. The 1996 awards will be presented at the Beverly Hilton Hotel in Beverly Hills, California. *Sponsor:* The Ark Trust, 5461 Noble Avenue, Sherman Oaks, CA 91411; 818-786-9990.

✉ Addresses for frequently cited organizations are gathered on pages vii–viii.

MARCH 69

National Cherry Blossom Festival

For 2 weeks, beginning the Sunday before the 7th of April, Washington celebrates the National Cherry Blossom Festival. The cherry trees around the Tidal Basin were a gift from the people of Japan and planted in 1912. *Contact:* Washington, DC Visitors Bureau, 1212 New York Avenue NW #600, Washington, DC 20005; 202-789-7000; Fax: 202-789-7037.

National Doctors Day

On this date in 1842, Dr. Crawford Long of Jefferson, Georgia, first used ether to save a patient from discomfort during surgery. Today, give a red carnation to your doctor as a thanks for modern medicine.

Pencil with eraser patented (1853)

Hyman Lipman patented a pencil with eraser.

Starry Night

On the birthday of Vincent van Gogh, enjoy his most famous painting, *Starry Night.* Van Gogh was born in 1853 in the Netherlands.

March 31

Birth of the Symphony Day

Enjoy a symphony on the birthday of Franz Joseph Haydn, father of the symphony. Haydn was born in 1732 in Rohrau, Austria.

Bunsen Burner Day

On the birthday of Robert von Bunsen (1811), inventor of the Bunsen burner, we celebrate his simple device that allows chemists to efficiently control a gas flame.

Cottonseed hulling machine patented (1814)

John Lineback patented this machine.

Dateline NBC premiered (1992)

Contact: NBC-TV. ✉

Daylight savings time first observed in U.S. (1918)

Eiffel Tower's Birthday

Paris's best-known landmark was completed in 1889.

First black Roman Catholic cardinal (1960)

Laurian Rugambwa of Tanzania was the first black cardinal in the Roman Catholic church.

First black to hold heavyweight title (1878)

Jack Johnson became the first black to hold the heavyweight boxing title.

First black to vote in the U.S. (1870)

After the ratification of the 15th Amendment, Thomas Peterson Mundy of Perth Amboy, New Jersey, became the first black to vote in the U.S.

First dance marathon in the U.S. (1923)

The first dance marathon in the U.S. was held in New York City.

First town illuminated by electric lights (1880)

Wabash, Indiana, was the first town to be lit by electricity. *Contact:* Wabash Visitors Bureau, P.O. Box 371, Wabash, IN 46992; 219-563-1168; Fax: 219-563-6920.

Holy Week

March 31 to April 6. The week before Easter is known as Holy Week in many Christian churches.

I Think Therefore I Am Day

On the birthday of Rene Descartes, father of modern philosophy, we honor all great thinkers. Descartes was born in 1596 in Touraine, France.

National Farm Workers Day

On the birthday of Cesar Estrada Chavez, organizer of the National

Farm Workers Association, we honor all farm workers, especially migratory workers. Chavez was born in 1927 in Yuma, Arizona. Also known as Don't Buy Grapes Day.

Palm Sunday
On the Sunday before Easter, Jesus Christ entered Jerusalem in a triumphant parade.

Telugu New Year's Day
Celebrated on April 1st (March 31st on leap years), this is one of the new year's celebrated in India. *Contact:* Government of India, Tourist Information Office, 30 Rockefeller Plaza #15, New York, NY 10112; 212-586-4901; Fax: 212-582-3274.

V-8 engine introduced (1932)
Ford introduced the V-8 engine. *Contact:* Ford Motor Company, P.O. Box 1899, Dearborn, MI 48121; 313-332-3000; Fax: 313-845-8981.

Virgin Islands Transfer Day
Denmark transferred the Virgin Islands to the U.S. in 1917 for $25 million. *Contact:* Virgin Islands Tourism Department, 1270 Avenue of the Americas #2108, New York, NY 10020; 212-582-4520; 800-372-8784.

World Tobacco Spitting Championships
On Palm Sunday, the Calico ghost town outside Barstow hosts the World Tobacco Spitting Championships. *Sponsor:* Calico Hullabaloo, Calico Ghost Town Regional Parks, P.O. Box 638, Yermo, CA 92398; 619-254-2122.

APRIL

Actors Appreciation Month
Designed to further the appreciation of the acting profession.

Alcohol Awareness Month

Cancer Control Month
To educate people about the importance of early detection. Contact local chapters for more information. *Sponsor:* American Cancer Society, 1180 Avenue of the Americas, New York, NY 10036; 212-382-2169.

Child Abuse Prevention Month
Educates people about how to prevent child abuse. *Sponsor:* National Committee to Prevent Child Abuse, 332 S. Michigan Avenue #1600, Chicago, IL 60604-4357; 312-663-3520; Fax: 312-939-8962.

Confederate Heritage Month
Activities take place each week in April in Vicksburg, Mississippi. *Sponsor:* Vicksburg Visitors Bureau, P.O. Box 110, Vicksburg, MS 39181; 601-636-9421; 800-221-3536.

Dog Appreciation Month
April was declared Dog Appreciation Month in a 1994 *Outland* comic strip.

Fair Housing Month
By presidential proclamation.

Fresh Florida Tomato Month
They are versatile, nutritious, and delicious—celebrate Florida tomatoes. *Sponsor:* Florida Tomato Committee, Teri Cirelli-Pedersen, 49 East 21st Street, 8th Floor, New York, NY 10010; 212-420-8808; Fax: 212-254-2452.

Holy Humor Month
Lighthearted Christians can give parties and playshops to celebrate the resurrection of Jesus. Send for a copy of their catalog and *The Joyful Noiseletter.* *Sponsor:* Fellowship of Merry Christians, Cal Samra, Director, P.O. Box 895, Portage, MI 49081-0895; 616-324-0990; 800-877-2757.

Home Improvement Time
From April 1st to September 30th, encourage people to make their homes more livable and valuable. *Sponsor:* Home Improvement Time,

Air Force Academy, Colorado Springs, CO 80840; 719-472-1818; Fax: 719-472-3494.

April Fools' Day (All Fools' Day)

A time for jokes, pranks, and making fools of others or yourself. Also known as April Noddy Day, Gowkie Day, and Gowkin' Day.

Chicken Little Awards

On the first Monday in April, these awards are given to people who have scared large numbers of people with dubious scientific predictions, theories, or statements. *Sponsor:* National Anxiety Center, Alan Caruba, P.O. Box 40, Maplewood, NJ 07040; 201-763-6392; Fax: 201-763-4287.

Dollar sign ($) created (1778)

Oliver Pollock, a New Orleans businessman, created the dollar sign.

Firefighters Day

In 1853, Cincinnati became the first American city to pay its firefighters.

First accident insurance policy issued (1864)

The first accident insurance policy was printed in Hartford, Connecticut.

First bridge in the U.S. (1634)

The Massachusetts General Court authorized Israel Stoughton to build a bridge across the Neponset River, from Milton to Dorchester.

First treaty between Native Americans & colonists (1621)

First weather satellite launched (1960)

TIROS-1 was the first weather satellite launched. *Contact:* NASA. ✉

Internal combustion engine patented (1826)

Captain Sam Mory patented the first internal combustion engine.

National Laugh Week

Always the first 7 days in April.

National Radio Talk Show Host Day

Honors all radio talk show hosts. Take your favorite talk show host to dinner today; let him or her eat cake! *Sponsor:* WBVP-AM, The Dimitri Show, 1316 7th Avenue, Beaver Falls, PA 15010; 412-846-4100; Fax: 412-843-7771.

Publicity Stunt Week

Celebrated during the first 7 days of April. To show off the value of creating media events. Formerly sponsored by Richard Falk, who died in 1994.

Saint Stupid's Day

A San Francisco celebration of frivolity.

U.S. House of Representatives first meeting (1789)

First met on March 4th, but did not obtain a quorum until April 1st. The Senate obtained its quorum on April 5th. *Contact:* U.S. House of Representatives, Capitol Building, Washington, DC 20510; 202-224-3121.

April 2

First black coach to win NCAA basketball tourney

In 1984, John Thompson led Georgetown University basketball team to win the NCAA basketball tournament. *Contact:* Georgetown University, 37th & O Street NW, Washington, DC 20057; 202-687-3600.

First motion picture theater opened (1902)

The first movie theater opened in Los Angeles, California.

First White House Easter egg roll (1877)

First woman nominated for president of the U.S. (1870)

Victoria Woodhull was nominated for president of the U.S. by the National Radical Reformers party. She ran 4 other times with the Equal Rights Party.

Great Lovers Day
On Casanova's birthday (1725), we celebrate all great lovers (as well as ordinary lovers). Also the day the World Underwater Kiss Record was set (1980). *Sponsor:* Open Horizons. ✉

International Children's Book Day
On the birthday of Hans Christian Andersen, author of many fairy tales and children's stories, we celebrate children's literature. Anderson was born in 1805 in Odense, Denmark. *Sponsor:* International Reading Association, 800 Barksdale Road, P.O. Box 8139, Newark, DE 19714-8139; 302-731-1600; 800-336-READ; Fax: 302-731-1057.

National Ferret Day
Take your ferret for a walk today.

Pascua Florida Day
In 1512, Spanish explorer Juan Ponce de Leon landed near what is now Saint Augustine, Florida. *Contact:* Florida Division of Tourism, Collins Building, 107 W. Gaines Street, Tallahassee, FL 32399-2000; 904-488-7999; Fax: 904-921-9169.

Radar patented (1935)
Watson Watt patented radar.

Saint Francis of Paola Feast Day
Patron saint of seafarers, because many of his miracles involved the sea.

U.S. Mint established (1792)
The first U.S. Mint was built in Philadelphia, Pennsylvania. For a multimedia education program, The Money Story, send $4.50 to U.S. Mint, Attn: The Money Story, 633 Third Street NW #715, Washington, DC 20220; 202-874-6000; Fax: 202-874-6282.

Velcro's Birthday
Velcro was introduced in 1978.

April 3

American Circus Day
John Bill Ricketts organized the first American circus in Philadelphia, Pennsylvania in 1793.

Close Call Day
In 1989, a large asteroid came within 500,000 miles of Earth. In astronomical terms, that's a close call!

Don't Go to Work Unless It's Fun Day
Two-thirds of American workers are unhappy with their jobs. If you are one of them, today is a day to consider your alternatives. *Sponsor:* Frank Sanitate Associates, 1152 Camino Manadero, Santa Barbara, CA 93111-1063; 805-967-7899; Fax: 805-967-7303.

First stereo pop single released (1960)
RCA was the first to release a pop single in stereo.

Hare Moon
The full moon of April is the hare moon, symbolic of fertility, growth, and wisdom; also known as the pink moon or the sprouting grass moon.

Hat making machine patented (1866)
Rudolph Eickemeyer and G. Osterheld patented the hat shaping machine.

Pony Express service began (1860)
The Pony Express began postal service between St. Joseph, Missouri, and Sacramento, California.

Rip Van Winkle's Birthday
On the birthday of author Washington Irving, take a long, long nap. Irving, the creator of Rip Van Winkle and author of *The Legend of Sleepy Hollow*, was born in 1783 in New York City. *Sponsor:* The Life of the Party. ✉

Total eclipse of the moon

One of two total eclipses of the moon in 1996, this one will be visible in eastern North America. Watch for the total eclipse from 6:27 to 7:53 P.M. Eastern Standard Time.

Tweed Day

On the birthday of William "Boss" Tweed, we caution against political corruption. Boss Tweed was a political boss who bilked New York City out of millions of dollars.

April 4

Ballroom Dancing Day

We celebrate the birthday of Arthur Murray, famous ballroom dancing instructor, by going ballroom dancing. Dance up a storm! *Sponsor:* The Life of the Party. ✉

First electric power fueled by garbage (1972)

First Mexican-American elected mayor of a major city (1981)

Henry Cisneros was elected mayor of San Antonio, Texas. *Contact:* San Antonio Visitors Bureau, P.O. Box 2277, San Antonio, TX 78298; 210-270-8700; 800-447-3372; Fax: 210-270-8782.

First U.S. flag approved (1818)

In the Flag Act of 1918, Congress approved the stars and stripes flag.

First woman mayor elected in U.S. (1887)

Susanna Salter of Argonia, Kansas, was the first woman mayor in the U.S.

Hate Week

In Orwell's novel *1984*, Winston Smith started his journal on April 4, 1984; he began with the words, "Down with Big Brother."

Last Supper (Holy Thursday)

On the night before he died, Jesus Christ celebrated the Last Supper with his disciples. Also knowns as Maundy Thursday.

National Reading a Road Map Week

April 4 to 10. This week's motto is "Happiness is knowing how to read a road map." *Sponsor:* Rosalind Schilder, P.O. Box 708, Plymouth Meeting, PA 19462.

NATO founded (1949)

The North Atlantic Treaty Organization alliance was founded in Washington, DC. *Contact:* North Atlantic Treaty Organization, 1110 Brussels, Belgium; 2-728-41-11; Fax: 2-728-41-17.

Party Party Day

An excuse to have a party once a month (when the day equals the month). *Sponsor:* Bonza Bottler Day. ✉

Passover (Pesach)

April 4 to 11. Passover celebrates the exodus, the Jews' deliverance from slavery in Egypt. 1997: April 22 to 29; 1998: April 11 to 18.

Victims of Violence Holy Day

On the anniversary of the 1964 assassination of Dr. Martin Luther King, we take time out to show respect for everyone. *Sponsor:* Global Committee Commemorating Kingdom Respect Days, P.O. Box 21050, Chicago, IL 60621; 312-737-7328.

Vitamin C isolated (1932)

April 5

Alcohol-Free Weekend

First weekend in April. To focus attention on alcohol abuse, don't drink this weekend. *Sponsor:* National Council on Alcoholism and Drug Dependence, 12 West 21st Street, New York, NY 10010; 212-206-6770; Fax: 212-645-1690.

First woman at the North Pole (1971)

Mrs. Fran Phipps, wife of Canadian pilot Weldy Phipps, was the first woman to set foot at the North Pole.

Good Friday
On Good Friday, Jesus Christ was crucified; on Easter Sunday, he rose from the dead.

Lady Luck Day
This pagan festival of good luck honors Fortuna, goddess of good fortune. Fortuna is sometimes known as Lady Luck.

Plan Your Epitaph Day
On the same day as the Ching Ming Festival (Chinese festival of the dead), take time to think of the words you'd like to have on your tombstone. Plan your own epitaph, and make it great! *Sponsor:* Dead or Alive, Lance Hardie, P.O. Box 4595, Arcata, CA 95521; 707-822-6924.

Presidential Veto Day
President Washington cast the first presidential veto in 1792.

Red Nose Day USA
On the first Friday in April, wear a red nose to show your concern for saving children from sudden infant death syndrome. Contact SIDS to find out which local chapters are sponsoring events in your area. *Sponsor:* SIDS Alliance, Phipps Cohe, 1314 Bedford #210, Baltimore, MD 21208; 800-221-7437; Fax: 410-653-8709.

Saint Noah Feast Day
Noah survived the great flood by building his ark; he is patron saint of boat builders and sailors.

Saint Vincent Ferrer Feast Day
Patron saint of reconciliation (because of work he did in reconciling differences among various segments of the church); also a patron saint of builders.

Student Government Day
The first Friday in April is a Massachusetts holiday to recognize the value of student governments.

April 6

Animated Cartoon Birthday
The first animated cartoon was copyrighted in 1906.

First credit union law in the U.S. (1909)
St. Canadian Credit Union of Manchester, New Hampshire was chartered. *Contact:* Credit Union National Association, 5710 Mineral Point Road, P.O. Box 431, Madison, WI 53701; 608-231-4000; Fax: 608-231-4263.

First modern Olympic games opened (1896)
Opened in Athens, Greece. *Contact:* U.S. Olympic Committee. ✉

Mormon Church founded (1830)
Joseph Smith and Oliver Cowdery founded the Mormon Church in Fayette, New York. *Contact:* Church of Jesus Christ of Latter Day Saints, 50 E. North Temple Street, Salt Lake City, UT 84150; 801-240-2531; Fax: 801-240-2033.

North Pole reached (1909)
Matthew Henson and Robert Peary were the first people to reach the North Pole.

Remembrance Day
On the Saturday before Easter, remember your loved ones who have died. *Sponsor:* Happy Day Ministries, Mike Miller, 35 Hilcreek Boulevard, Charleston, SC 29412; 803-762-1585.

Sorry Charlie Day
The first Saturday in April is for those who, like Charlie Tuna, get turned down but never give up. Recognizes anyone who has been rejected and lived through it! For membership card and other info, send an SASE and $3.00 to Right Brain Publishing. *Sponsor:* Right Brain Publishing, Cathy Runyan, 7812 NW Hampton Road, Kansas City, MO 64152; 816-587-8687.

Tater Days
April 6 to 8. Celebrate the sweet potato during Benton's annual Tater Days. These are the country's oldest trade days, held annually since 1843. *Sponsor:* Benton Chamber of Commerce, 17 U.S. Highway 68 West, Benton, KY 42025; 502-527-7665; Fax: 502-527-2910.

Twinkies Day

In 1930, James Dewar invented the original junk food, Hostess Twinkies. *Contact:* Continental Baking Company, Hostess Division, 1034 Danforth Drive, Saint Louis, MO 63102; 314-982-4700; Fax: 314-982-2267.

April 7

Archeology Week

Celebrated the second full week in April. *Contact:* Archaeological Institute of America, 656 Beacon Street, Boston, MA 02215-2010; 617-353-9361; Fax: 617-353-6550.

Contract with America completed (1995)

On September 27, 1994, over 300 Republican congressional incumbents and challengers signed the Contract with America where they promised, if elected, to vote on 10 items within 100 days. On April 7, 1995, they fulfilled their promise. *Contact:* Republican National Committee, 310 First Street SE, Washington, DC 20003; 202-863-8500; Fax: 202-863-8820.

Easter Sunday

The holiest day of the Christian year, honors the Resurrection of Jesus Christ.

First radar signal bounced off the sun (1959)

I've Got the Blues Day

Celebrate the birthday of Billie Holiday by singing the blues. *Sponsor:* The Life of the Party. ✉

Matches invented (1827)

Invented by John Walker, an English chemist.

National Birthparents Week

Supports the rights of those who gave up their children for adoption. Always celebrated the week of the first Sunday in April. *Sponsor:* Concerned United Birthparents, Janet Fenton, 2000 Walker Street, Des Moines, IA 50317; 515-263-9558; 800-822-2777.

National Buildings Safety Week

The second week in April promotes building codes so all buildings will be safer. *Sponsor:* National Conference of States on Building Codes and Standards, 505 Hunt-

SAFETY COUNTS... One.. TWO.. THREE...

mar Park Drive #210, Herndon, VA 22070; 703-437-0100; Fax: 703-481-3596.

National Garden Week

The second full week in April honors America's gardeners. *Sponsor:* National Garden Bureau, Nona Wolfram-Koivula, 1311 Butterfield Road #310, Downers Grove, IL 60515.

National Medical Laboratory Week

The second week in April promotes the importance of lab technicians and pathologists in maintaining our health. *Sponsor:* American Society of Clinical Pathologists, 2100 W. Harrison Street, Chicago, IL 60612-3798; 312-738-4886; 800-621-4142.

No Housework Day

You don't have to carry out the trash, do dishes, make beds, etc. *Sponsor:* Wellness Permission League. ✉

Rough & Ready Secession Day

In 1850, due to a new tax levied on mining claims, the town of Rough and Ready, California briefly seceded from the U.S. They rejoined the union on July 4, 1850. *Sponsor:* Chamber of Commerce, Rough and Ready, CA 95975; 916-272-4320.

Saint John Baptist de la Salle Feast Day

Founder of the Christian Brothers, and patron saint of school teachers, especially teachers of boys.

Spring Forward Day

On the first Sunday in April, we set our clocks to daylight-savings time. Spring forward, fall back.

Television first demonstrated to the public (1927)

The image of Herbert Hoover, Secretary of Commerce, was transmitted long distance to an audience in New York City.

World Health Day

The World Health Organization was founded by the United Nations in 1948 to prevent disease. *Sponsor:* American Association for World Health, 1129 20th Street NW #400, Washington, DC 20036; 202-466-5883; Fax: 202-466-5896.

April 8

Behave Yourself Day

On the anniversary of the 1988 defrocking of Jimmy Swaggart, behave yourself. *Sponsor:* The Life of the Party. ✉

Buddha's Birthday

Buddha, the enlightened one, lived in India from 563 BC to 483 BC. This day, known as Hanamatsuri in Japan, is the most important Buddhist holiday. *Contact:* Buddhist Churches of America, 1710 Octavia Street, San Francisco, CA 94109-4341; 415-776-5600.

Easter Monday

In many countries, the Monday after Easter Sunday is an official bank holiday.

Egg Salad Week

The week after Easter is dedicated to the many delicious uses for all the Easter eggs that have been cooked, colored, hidden, and found. *Sponsor:* American Egg Board, 1460 Renaissance Drive, Park Ridge, IL 60068; 708-296-7044.

First synagogue founded in U.S. (1730)

Home Run Record Day

In 1974, Hank Aaron hit his 715th home run to break Babe Ruth's record.

Talking Book Week

The week following Easter honors those who help the visually impaired and physically disabled to read books and gain information. *Sponsor:* Audio Descriptive Network, Descriptavision, 115 Brenton Street, Richmond, VA 23222; 804-321-2063.

April 9

African Methodist Episcopal Church established (1816)

Rev. Richard Allen formed the first African Methodist Episcopal Church. *Contact:* African Methodist Episcopal Church, 1134 11th Street NW, Washington, DC 20001.

Astrodome's Birthday

The Houston Astrodome opened in 1965. *Contact:* Houston Astrodome, 8400 Kirby Drive, Houston, TX 77054; 713-799-9580.

Astronauts Day

The first 7 U.S. astronauts were selected in 1959. For a pass to watch a satellite launch, write to NASA Visitor Services, PA-PASS, Kennedy Space Center, Cape Canaveral, FL 32899. For updates on launches, call 407-867-4636. *Contact:* NASA. ✉

Civil War ended (1865)

General Robert E. Lee surrendered to General Ulysses S. Grant at Appomattox Court House in Virginia.

Dry milk patented (1872)

✉ Addresses for frequently cited organizations are gathered on pages vii–viii.

APRIL 79

First tax-supported public library (1833)

Established in Peterborough, New Hampshire. *Contact:* Peterborough Public Library, Peterborough, NH 03458.

Longest Word Day

The longest word (207,000 letters) was published in a science journal.

National Former Prisoners of War Recognition Day

TV Guide Birthday

TV Guide published its first issue in 1953. *Contact: TV Guide*, 100 Matsonford Road, P.O. Box 500, Radnor, PA 19088; 610-293-8500; 800-345-8500; Fax: 610-293-4849.

Winston Churchill Day

In 1963, Winston Churchill was made an honorary U.S. citizen.

April 10

Bataan Death March Anniversary

In 1942, the Japanese rounded up American and Filipino prisoners of war and marched them for 6 days with little more than one bowl of rice to eat. More than 5,200 Americans died on this march.

Commodore Perry Day

Celebrates the birthday (1794) of Commodore Matthew Perry, who negotiated the first treaty between the U.S. and Japan.

Encourage a Beginning Writer Day

On the birthday of newspaperman Joseph Pulitzer (1847), we honor all beginning writers. Formerly sponsored by Alice Lesch.

First American to circumnavigate the Earth (1790)

Robert Gray was first American to sail around the world. He left Boston in September 1787 and returned in April 1790.

First Arbor Day

Held in Nebraska in 1872; founded by J. Sterling Morton. Plant a tree today and another on National Arbor Day.

First full-length 3-D movie (1953)

Vincent Price starred in *The House of Wax.*

International Resistance Movement Day

In 1945, Buchenwald became the first Nazi concentration camp to be liberated by the Allies. More than 56,000 people died in Buchenwald alone. This day is also known as Buchenwald Liberation Day.

Prevent Cruelty to Animals Day

In 1866, the ASPCA was founded by Henry Bergh. *Sponsor:* ASPCA, 424 East 92nd Street, New York, NY 10128-6803; 212-876-7700; Fax: 212-876-9571.

Safety Pin Birthday

Walter Hunt of New York patented the safety pin in 1849.

Salvation Army Founder's Day

William Booth, founder of the Salvation Army, was born in 1829 in Nottingham, England. *Sponsor:* Salvation Army Headquarters, 615 Slaters Lane, P.O. Box 269, Alexandria, VA 22313; 703-684-5500; Fax: 703-684-3478.

Worst submarine disaster in U.S. history (1963)

The atomic-powered submarine *Thresher* sank in the north Atlantic Ocean in 1963. All 129 crew members were lost.

April 11

Barbershop Quartet Day

In 1938, The Society for the Preservation and Encouragement of Barbershop Quartet Singing in America was formed in Tulsa, Oklahoma. *Sponsor:* SPEBSQSA, Harmony Hall, 6315 Third Avenue, Kenosha, WI 53143-5199; 414-653-8440; Fax: 414-654-4048; e-mail: prspebsqa@aol.com.

Civil Rights Act of 1968 Anniversary

President Johnson signed the Civil Rights Act, providing greater protection of civil rights workers, anti-discrimination housing, and expanded rights for Native Americans.

First black to play major league baseball (1947)

Jackie Robinson of the Brooklyn Dodgers was the first black to play major league baseball. *Contact:* Major League Baseball. ✉

First building-and-loan mortgage (1831)

Comley Rich of Philadelphia, Pennsylvania, received the first mortgage.

First cigarette taxes (1921)

Iowa was the first state to tax cigarettes.

First Secretary of Health, Education and Welfare

Oveta Culp Hobby became the first HEW Secretary in 1953. *Contact:* Department of Health & Human Services, 200 Independence Avenue SW #348F, Washington, DC 20201; 202-245-2760; Fax: 202-245-0449.

Sexual harassment banned (1980)

EEO regulations banned sexual harassment of workers by supervisors. *Contact:* Equal Employment Opportunity Commission, 1801 L Street NW, Washington, DC 20507-0001; 202-663-4264.

Space: Don't Take It for Granted Week

In 1970, after an oxygen tank ruptured, *Apollo 13* astronauts Lovell, Haise, and Swigert spent 7 days in space wondering if they'd ever make it back home. They did. *Contact:* NASA. ✉

April 12

Anniversary of the Big Wind

In 1934, the highest-velocity natural wind (231 mph) occurred at Mount Washington in New Hampshire.

Billiards Day

In 1859, the first international billiards championship match was held in Detroit, Michigan.

Catcher's Mask Day

The catcher's mask was first used in a baseball game in 1877. The mask was patented on February 12, 1878.

Civil War started (1861)

The shelling of Fort Sumter in Charleston harbor started the Civil War.

Cosmonaut Day

In 1961, Russian Cosmonaut Yuri Gugarin became the first human in space. *Sponsor:* Space Center, P.O. Box 533, Alamogordo, NM 88310; 800-545-4021.

First black major league umpire (1966)

Emmett Ashford became the first black umpire to officiate a major league baseball game. *Contact:* Major League Baseball. ✉

First patent granted for an animal life form (1988)

Harvard was granted a patent for a genetically engineered mouse. *Contact:* Harvard University, 1350 Massachusetts Avenue, Cambridge, MA 02138; 617-495-1000; Fax: 617-495-5321.

First truancy law in the U.S. (1853)

First U.S. Senator to fly in space (1985)

Senator Jake Garn of Utah flew on the shuttle *Discovery.* *Contact:* NASA. ✉

National Tap Dance Party Day

On the birthday of Ann Miller, the 1950s actress who was famous for her tap dancing; throw a tap dance party. Miller was born Lucille Ann Collier in 1923 in Houston, Texas. *Sponsor:* The Life of the Party. ✉

Saint Zeno of Verona Feast Day

Legend says that Saint Zeno was stolen at birth by the devil, he is therefore considered a patron saint of babies.

Salk vaccine approved

The polio vaccine was developed by Dr. Jonas Salk, it was approved for use on this day in 1955.

Space shuttle Columbia first launched (1981)

Contact: NASA. ✉

Stupid Pet Tricks Day

Celebrate late night talk show host David Letterman's birthday by teaching your pet a stupid trick. Letterman was born in 1947 in Indianapolis, Indiana. *Sponsor:* The Life of the Party. ✉

World's Largest Trivia Contest

WWSP Radio hosts more than 11,000 contestants attempting to win the world's largest trivia contest. The exact dates change every year, but generally it's held the first weekend in April or the weekend after Easter. *Sponsor:* WWSP Radio, John Tracy, University of Wisconsin CAC #105, Stevens Point, WI 54481; 715-346-3755; Fax: 715-346-4012.

April 13

Air brake patented (1869)

George Westinghouse patented the first air brakes.

Dimestore Day

Celebrate Frank Woolworth's birthday by shopping for bargains. *Sponsor:* The Life of the Party. ✉

Edict of Nantes Anniversary (1598)

King Henry IV of France signed this edict; it was one of the first political acts to grant religious rights (in this case to the Huguenots).

First American to win Tchaikovsky Piano Contest (1958)

Van Cliburn won this contest in Moscow.

Great Chicago Flood (1992)

The Chicago River flooded the city's old tunnel system and basements.

Handel's Messiah premiered (1742)

Handel's *Messiah* was first performed publicly at the New Music Hall in Dublin, Ireland.

Metropolitan Museum of Art founded (1870)

Contact: Metropolitan Museum of Art, 1000 Fifth Avenue, New York, NY 10028-0198; 212-879-5500; Fax: 212-570-3879.

Pope visited synagogue (1986)

Pope John Paul II was the first Pope ever to visit a Jewish synagogue.

Silent Spring published (1962)

Rachel Carson's *Silent Spring* warned of ecological disaster if no action was taken. Take action today!

Solar New Year

This day is celebrated in many southeast Asian countries, and is known by different names: Baisakhi in India, Bangladesh, and Sri Lanka; Songkran in Thailand; Bun-Pi-Mai-Lao in Laos; Thingyan in Burma; and Bon Chol Chhnam in Cambodia.

Tamil New Year's Day

One of the local new years celebrated in India. *Contact:* Government of India, Tourist Information Office, 30 Rockefeller Plaza #15, New York, NY 10112; 212-586-4901; Fax: 212-582-3274.

Thomas Jefferson's Birthday

Thomas Jefferson was the third President of the U.S. He was born in Albermarle County, Virginia in 1743, and died on July 4, 1826. In addition to being a politician and leader, he was a writer, a musician, an inventor, and an architect.

World Catfish Festival

Celebrates the versatile catfish. Entertainment includes a catfish eating contest, crowning of the Catfish Queen, and lots more. *Sponsor:* Belzoni Chamber of Commerce, P.O. Box 268, Belzoni, MS 39038; 601-247-4838.

World Champion Pickled Quail Egg Eating Contest

Held on the first weekend in April (unless it conflicts with Easter), this contest determines who can eat the most pickled quail eggs in 60 seconds. *Sponsor:* Traders Village, Doug Beich, 2602 Mayfield Road, Grand Prairie, TX 75052; 214-647-2331; Fax: 214-647-8585.

World's Largest Hula Competition

The Merrie Monarch Festival begins on Easter, and ends the following Saturday with the World's Largest Hula Competition. *Sponsor:* Merrie Monarch Festival, Hawaii Naniloa Hotel, 93 Banyan Drive, Hilo, HI 96720; 808-935-9168.

April 14

Abraham Lincoln assassinated (1865)

President Lincoln was assassinated by John Wilkes Booth.

Boys and Girls Club Week

In April, 1860, the Dashaway Club was founded. It was one of the forerunners of the Boys and Girls Clubs of America. Celebrated during the third week in April. *Sponsor:* Boys & Girls Clubs of America, 1230 W. Peachtree Street NW, Atlanta, GA 30309; 404-815-5700; Fax: 404-815-5787.

The Boys in the Band opened (1968)

Matt Crowley's play about a group of gay men premiered in New York City.

Dungeons and Dragons game invented (1974)

Contact: TSR Inc., 201 Sheridan Springs Road, Lake Geneva, WI 53147; 414-248-3625; Fax: 414-248-0389.

First American abolition society (1775)

The Society for the Relief of Free Negroes Unlawfully Held in Bondage was founded in Philadelphia, Pennsylvania, by Benjamin Rush and Benjamin Franklin.

First American ace pilot (1918)

When he shot down his fifth German aircraft, Douglas Campbell became the first American pilot certified as an ace.

First commercial videotape recorder demonstrated (1956)

Ampex demonstrated the first video recorder. *Contact:* Ampex

Corporation, 401 Broadway Street, Redwood City, CA 94063; 415-367-2011; Fax: 415-367-2761.

First J. C. Penney store (1902)

The first J. C. Penney's opened in Kemmerer, Wyoming. *Contact:* J. C. Penney, 6501 Legacy Drive, Plano, TX 75024; 214-431-1000; 800-222-6161; Fax: 214-431-9543.

Grapes of Wrath published

John Steinbeck's novel was published in 1939.

National Coin Week

The third full week in April promotes the hobby of coin collecting as well as the numismatics who do the collecting. For a free coin collecting booklet, send a business-size SASE plus 2 first-class stamps to the following address. *Sponsor:* American Numismatic Association, 818 N. Cascade Avenue, Colorado Springs, CO 80903; 719-632-2646; Fax: 719-634-4085.

National Home Safety Week

Beginning on the second Sunday in April spend time during the week to make your home safer for you and your family. *Sponsor:* National Home Safety Business, 620 S. Sycamore Avenue #11, Lansing, MI 48933; 517-484-6041; Fax: 517-484-5034.

National Library Week

First observed in 1958, this week is a time to celebrate libraries and librarians as well as the pleasures of reading. *Sponsor:* American Library Association. ✉

National Public Safety Telecommunications Week
Celebrated the second full week in April.

National Week of the Ocean
During the third full week of April, recognize humanity's dependence on the ocean. *Sponsor:* National Week of the Ocean, Cynthia Hancock, P.O. Box 179, Fort Lauderdale, FL 33302; 305-462-5573; Fax: 305-463-9730.

National Wildlife Week
Celebrated the third full week in April. *Sponsor:* National Wildlife Federation, 1400 16th Street NW, Washington, DC 20036-2217; 202-797-6800; Fax: 202-797-6646.

Noah Webster's dictionary first published
Webster's *American Dictionary of the English Language* was published in 1828.

Pan American Day
This is the anniversary of the founding of the Pan American Union in 1912; celebrated since 1940.

Pan American Week
By presidential proclamation since 1940, the week of the 14th celebrates the founding of the Pan American Union.

Wuthering Heights premiered (1939)
This romantic film starring Laurence Olivier and Merle Oberon premiered in New York City.

April 15

Astronomy Week
To introduce everyone to the world of astronomy. *Sponsor:* Astronomical League, Gary Tomlinson, Coordinator, Chaffee Planetarium, 272 Pearl NW, Grand Rapids, MI 49504; 616-456-3977.

The Boston Marathon
One of the world's premier running events is held on the third Monday in April. *Sponsor:* Boston Athletic Association, P.O. Box 1994, Hopkinton, MA 01748; 617-236-1652.

Bottle opener invented (1738)

First American school for the deaf (1817)

General Electric incorporated (1892)
General Electric was formed by the merger of Edison Electric Light and other companies. *Contact:* General Electric, 3135 Easton Turnpike,

Fairfield, CT 06431; 216-266-4612; Fax: 216-266-4410.

Get That Stain Out Day
Celebrate the birthday of Heloise, provider of helpful hints, by getting out the stains in your clothes, carpets, sinks, and bathtubs. Heloise was born in 1951 in Waco, Texas. *Contact:* Heloise Syndicated Column, Heloise Cruse Evans, P.O. Box 795000, San Antonio, TX 78279.

Income Tax Pay Day
If your tax forms aren't on the way to the IRS, they're late. *Contact:* Internal Revenue Service. ✉

Ivory Soap Birthday
In 1878, Harley Procter of Procter & Gamble developed the floating soap, which became known as Ivory Soap. *Contact:* Procter & Gamble, 1 Procter & Gamble Plaza,

✉   Addresses for frequently cited organizations are gathered on pages vii–viii.

Cincinnati, OH 45202; 513-983-1100; Fax: 513-562-4500.

Leonardo da Vinci's Birthday
One of the Renaissance's greatest artists and thinkers, Leonardo da Vinci was born in Florence, Italy in 1452. In addition to painting the *Mona Lisa* and *The Last Supper*, he designed the first parachute.

McDonald's Birthday
The first McDonald's restaurant opened in Des Plaines, Illinois, in 1955. McDonald's has developed a series of programs to educate children about drug abuse, nutrition, fitness, safety, and self-esteem. For a free catalog, call 800-627-7646. *Contact:* McDonald's Corporation, 1 McDonald's Plaza, Oak Brook, IL 60521; 708-575-3000; Fax: 708-575-5700.

National Hostility Day
Paying taxes will bring out the worst even in a saint.

Patriot's Day
Massachusetts and Maine celebrate this holiday commemorating the 1775 Revolutionary War battles of Lexington and Concord. Celebrated the third Monday in April. *Contact:* Massachusetts Tourism Office, 100 Cambridge Street, 13th Floor, Boston, MA 02202; 617-727-3201; 800-447-6277; Fax: 617-727-6525.

Rubber Eraser Day
In 1770, Joseph Priestley discovered that a piece of rubber could erase pencil marks; he coined the term *eraser.*

San Francisco's Birthday
San Francisco was incorporated as a city in 1850. *Contact:* San Francisco Visitors Bureau, 900 Market Street, San Francisco, CA 94103; 415-974-6900.

Sinking of the Titanic
The luxury liner *Titanic* sank just past midnight in 1912; 1,500 people died in the tragedy.

April 16

Fibber McGee and Molly premiered (1935)
This radio comedy premiered on NBC. *Contact:* NBC. ✉

First auction (1864)
Took place in Austin, Nevada, with a sack of flour. *Contact:* Chamber of Commerce, P.O. Box 212, Austin, NV 89310; 702-964-2200.

First woman to fly across the English Channel (1912)
Harriet Quimby flew from Dover, England, to Hardelot, France.

Holocaust Remembrance Day (Yom Hashoah)
A day to remember the Holocaust; celebrated on the 27th day of Nissan in the Hebrew calendar, which, on April 10, 1945, was the day Allied troops liberated the first Nazi concentration camp. 1997: May 4; 1998: April 23. *Sponsor:* U.S. Holocaust Memorial Council, 100 Raoul Wallenberg Place SW, Washington, DC 20024; 202-488-0400.

Library Legislative Day
The Tuesday of National Library Week is a day for libraries to lobby congress on library-related issues. *Sponsor:* Special Libraries Association, 1700 18th Street NW, Washington, DC 20009; 202-234-4700.

Look-Alike Day
The third Tuesday of April celebrates individuals who are mistaken for someone else who is famous. *Sponsor:* WPXI-TV, Channel 11, Jack Etzel, Feature Reporter, 11 Television Hill, Pittsburgh, PA 15214; 412-237-4952; Fax: 412-237-4900.

National CPA's Goof-Off Day
Celebrated the first work day following April 15th, which is tax pay day. *Sponsor:* Joseph Kearley, CPA, 2129 Benbrook Drive, Carrollton, TX 75007; 214-245-6192.

National Stress Awareness Day
Stress is one of the major causes of illness. On the day after income taxes are due, we need a reminder to take a break from stress. *Sponsor:* The Health Resources Network, Morton C. Orman, 2936 E. Baltimore Street, Baltimore, MD 21224; 410-732-1900.

Natural Bridges National Monument established (1908)
Contact: Natural Bridges Monument, P.O. Box 1, Lake Powell, UT 84533; 801-259-5174.

Saint Benedict Joseph Labre Feast Day
He lived as a homeless hermit, and is considered a patron saint of tramps and the homeless.

Saint Bernadette Feast Day
A shepherdess who had many visions of the Virgin Mary, she is patron saint of shepherds. Her shrine in Lourdes, France, is a great place of healing. She died on this date in 1879.

Silent Movie Stars Day
On the birthday of Charlie Chaplin, the greatest silent movie star, celebrate by watching a silent movie. Chaplin was born in 1889 in London, England.

Slavery abolished in District of Columbia (1862)

Worst explosive disaster in U.S. history (1947)
A fire and resultant explosion on the French freighter *Grandcamp* destroyed most of Texas City, Texas. At least 516 people were killed.

Zoom lens patented (1947)

April 17

American Indian Week
Celebrated from the third Wednesday in April through Sunday, highlights the successes and challenges of Native Americans throughout the U.S. *Sponsor:* Indian Pueblo Cultural Center, 2401 12th Street NW, Albuquerque, NM 87102; 505-843-7270; Fax: 505-842-6959.

Bay of Pigs Invasion (1961)
U.S. trained Cuban exiles launched the Bay of Pigs invasion of Cuba in an attempt to overthrow dictator Fidel Castro. The invasion failed.

First commercial fishery (1629)

First horse imported to U.S. (1629)

First woman to fly solo around the world (1964)
Jerrie Mock of Columbus, Ohio, completed the first solo flight around the world.

Mustang's Birthday
The Ford Mustang was unveiled on this date in 1964. *Contact:* Ford Motor Company, P.O. Box 1899, Dearborn, MI 48121; 313-322-3000.

Night of a Thousand Stars
Celebrities read books at libraries around the country on the Wednesday of National Library Week. *Sponsor:* American Library Association. ✉

Pineapple cheese patented (1810)

Solidarity granted legal status (1989)
The Polish labor union was granted legal status; this led to the first non-communist government in the Eastern Bloc.

Thank Your School Librarian Day
Celebrate school librarians on the Wednesday of National Library Week. *Sponsor:* Carpe Libris, Judyth Lessee, P.O. Box 40503, Tucson, AZ 85717-0503; 520-318-2954; Fax: 520-795-6177; e-mail: rinophyl@rtd.com.

Verrazano Day
In 1524, Florentine explorer Giovanni Verrazano discovered New York harbor.

April 18

First country to adopt fingerprinting (1902)
Denmark was the first to adopt fingerprinting as a way to identify criminals.

First crossword puzzle book published (1924)
Simon & Schuster published the first crossword puzzle book. 40,000 copies were sold in 3 months. *Contact:* Simon & Schuster, 1230 Avenue of the Americas, New York, NY 10020; 212-698-7503; Fax: 212-698-7035.

First laundromat opened (1934)
A washeteria opened in Fort Worth, Texas.

First Walk/Don't Walk signs installed (1955)

International Special Librarians Day
Celebrated on the Thursday of National Library Week. *Sponsor:* Special Libraries Association, 1700 18th Street NW, Washington, DC 20009; 202-234-4700.

Junior Achievement incorporated (1921)
Founded to encourage young people to develop business skills. *Contact:* Junior Achievement, 1 Education Way, Colorado Springs, CO 80906; 719-540-8000; 800-843-6395; Fax: 719-540-9151.

Paul Revere's Ride (1775)

Pet Owners Independence Day
If you own a pet, take the day off. *Sponsor:* Wellness Permission League.

San Francisco Earthquake
This earthquake disaster occurred in 1906; it was the worst in U.S. history. More than 500 people died (many as a result of the fire that accompanied the quake). *Contact:* San Francisco Visitors Bureau, 900 Market Street, San Francisco, CA 94103; 415-974-6900.

Third World Day
The phrase "third world" was first used in 1955 when the president of Indonesia gave his opening address at the Bandung Conference of African and Asian nations.

Time Out Day
Take time out today to get to know someone new, read, play, visit family members, watch the sunset. Celebrated twice a year in April and October. *Sponsor:* All My Events.

April 19

First automobile built in U.S.
Brothers Charles and Frank Duryea built the first automobile in 1892. They drove it around Springfield, Massachusetts.

Gunslinger Day
Celebrate the birthday of actor Hugh O'Brian who played Wyatt Earp on the TV show *The Life and Legend of Wyatt Earp*. O'Brian was born Hugh Krampe in 1930 in Rochester, New York. *Sponsor:* The Life of the Party.

India launched its first satellite (1975)
India launched its first satellite atop a Soviet rocket. In 1980, India launched its first independent satellite. *Contact:* Republic of India Embassy, 2107 Massachusetts Avenue NW, Washington, DC 20008; 202-939-7000.

March for Parks
Held on the weekend of Earth Day, this nationwide event raises funds and awareness for local park programs. More than 1,000 communities participate in the walk. *Sponsor:* National Parks and Conservation Association, 1015 31st Street NW #400, Washington, DC 20007; 202-944-8530.

Addresses for frequently cited organizations are gathered on pages vii–viii.

Marry a Prince Day
In 1956, movie star Grace Kelly married Prince Rainier of Monaco.

Paper Money Day
The U.S. went off the gold standard in 1933.

Right Wing Extremists Day
Anniversary of the 1995 Oklahoma City federal office building bombing (the deadliest terrorist attack in U.S. history), the 1993 storming of the Branch Davidian compound in Waco, Texas, and the 1995 execution of Richard Wayce Snell, a white supremacist.

April 20

Astronomy Day
Celebrated on the Saturday nearest the first quarter moon between mid-April and mid-May. *Sponsor:* Astronomical League, Gary Tomlinson, Coordinator, Chaffee Planetarium, 272 Pearl NW, Grand Rapids, MI 49504; 616-456-3977.

Electron microscope first demonstrated by RCA (1940)

First Vice President to die in office (1812)
George Clinton, the fourth vice president of the U.S., died at the age of 73.

Historic Garden Week in Virginia
For a 200-page guidebook, send $3.00 to Historic Garden Week at the following address. This event has been celebrated since 1934 during the last week in April. *Sponsor:* Garden Club of Virginia, 12 E. Franklin Street, Richmond, VA 23219; 804-644-7776.

Hunger Clean Up
Celebrated the third Saturday in April. *Sponsor:* National Student Campaign Against Hunger & Homelessness, 29 Temple Place, 5th Floor, Boston, MA 02111; 617-292-4823.

Just Pray No: Worldwide Weekend of Prayer and Unity
During the third weekend in April, churches throughout the world hold prayer and educational sessions encouraging people to say no to drugs. *Sponsor:* Just Pray No, Steven Sherman, 124 Garfield Place, East Rockaway, NY 11518; 516-599-7399.

No State Mottoes Day
In 1977, the U.S. Supreme Court ruled that car owners did not have to display state mottos (such as New Hampshire's "Live Free or Die") on their license plates. *Contact:* U.S. Supreme Court. ✉

Radium discovery announced (1902)
French scientists Marie and Pierre Curie discovered radium.

Securities Fraud Day
In 1990, junk bond financier Michael Milken pled guilty to 6 felonies and paid $600 million in penalties to settle the largest securities fraud case in history.

Sign of Taurus
The astrological sign of Taurus the Bull runs from April 20th to May 20th. Taurans are patient, determined, and stubborn.

World Grits Day
Celebrated on the Saturday of the World Grits Festival in Saint George, South Carolina. *Sponsor:* World Grits Festival, P.O. Box 787, Saint George, SC 29477; 803-563-3255.

April 21

Alfred G. Packer Day
Celebrated since 1968; recognizes the only convicted cannibal in the U.S. *Sponsor:* University Memorial Center, Food Service Director, Campus Box 202, University of Colorado, Boulder, CO 80309; 303-492-8833; Fax: 303-492-4327.

American Home Week
This week is designed to make people more aware of their property rights; celebrated the third full week of April.

Big Brothers/Big Sisters Appreciation Week
Held the same week as National Volunteers Week; honors those who volunteer as Big Brothers and Big Sisters. *Sponsor:* Big Brothers/Big Sisters of America, 230 North 13th Street, Philadelphia, PA 19107; 215-567-7000; Fax: 215-567-0394.

Birthday of Rome
Rome was founded in 753 B.C.

Festival of Ridvan
April 21 to May 2. This annual Baha'i festival celebrates the 12 days in 1863 when the founder of the Baha'i faith, Baha'u'llah, proclaimed that he was God's messenger for this age. *Sponsor:* Baha'i National Center. ✉

First artificial heart implant (1982)
Dr. Michael E. DeBakey performed the first successful artificial heart implant in Houston, Texas.

Grange Week
The oldest organized agricultural movement in the U.S., the Grange was formed in 1867. Always the last full week in April. *Sponsor:* National Grange Headquarters, 1616 H Street NW, Washington, DC 20006; 202-628-3507; Fax: 202-347-1091.

Health Care for People Week
Single Payer Across the Nation, a nationwide coalition, collects signatures and organizes rallies and educational events. *Sponsor:* Single Payer Across the Nation, 312-409-3558.

Intergenerational Week
The last full week of April encourages interaction between the youngest and oldest people. *Sponsor:* Choo Choo Child Care Center, Anne L. Haas, P.O. Box 250, Williamsport, MD 21795; 301-582-4894; Fax: 301-582-4896.

Jewish Heritage Week
During the week of Israel's Independence Day (which changes from year to year according to the Jewish calendar), learn more about the importance of Jewish history. *Sponsor:* Jewish Community Relations Council, 711 Third Avenue, New York, NY 10017; 212-983-4800; Fax: 212-983-4084.

Kindergarten Day
Celebrates the birthday of Friedrich Froebel (1782), who began the first kindergarten in 1837.

National Crime Victim Rights Week
Co-sponsored by the National Organization for Victim Assistance; 202-232-NOVA. Usually the last full week in April. *Sponsor:* National Victim Center, 2111 Wilson Boulevard #300, Arlington, VA 22201; 703-276-2880; 800-239-3219; Fax: 703-276-2889.

National Earthquake Awareness Week
During the week of the birthday of Charles Francis Richter, inventor of the Richter scale, people are encouraged to become more aware of earthquake preparedness. Richter was born on April 26, 1900.

National Give-a-Sample Week
During the last full week in April, give out product samples to solicit consumers.

National Infant Immunization Week
Celebrated during the last full week in April. *Sponsor:* National Immunization Program, Eric Hoffman, 200 Independence Avenue SW #728E, Washington, DC 20201; 202-401-2305.

National Lingerie Week
The third full week in April promotes the pleasure and allure of lingerie. *Sponsor:* Intimate Apparel Council, The Bromley Group, 150 Fifth Avenue #510, New York, NY 10011; 212-807-0878; Fax: 212-675-3534.

National Organ and Tissue Donor Awareness Week
Always the third full week in April.

National Preschool Immunization Week
Always the last full week in April.

National Science and Technology Week
Sponsor: National Science Foundation, 4201 Wilson Boulevard #1245, Arlington, VA 22230; 703-306-1234; Fax: 703-306-0158; e-mail: info@nsf.gov.

National Student Leadership Week
The last week in April is designed to help high school students develop leadership skills.

National Volunteer Week
Designed to thank America's 80,000,000 volunteers. It is held the third or fourth week of April as long as it does not conflict with Easter. 1997: April 13 to 19; 1998: April 19 to 25. *Sponsor:* Points of Light Foundation, 1737 H Street NW, Washington, DC 20006; 202-223-9186; Fax: 202-223-9256.

National YWCA Week
The last full week in April promotes the YWCA nationwide.

Sponsor: YWCA of the USA, Jane Pinkerton, PR Director, 726 Broadway, New York, NY 10003; 212-614-2700; Fax: 212-677-9716.

Professional Secretaries Week
Thank secretaries for their contributions during the last full week in April. *Sponsor:* Professional Secretaries International, P.O. Box 20404, Kansas City, MO 64195-0404; 816-891-6600; Fax: 816-891-9118.

Reading Is Fun Week
The fourth week in April encourages children to read. *Sponsor:* Reading Is Fundamental, Ruth P. Graves, 600 Maryland Avenue SW #600, Washington, DC 20024; 202-287-3371; Fax: 202-287-3196.

Saint Beuno Feast Day
According to legend Saint Beuno brought his niece, Saint Winifred, back to life after she had been beheaded. Because of this legend, he is considered a patron saint of sick children.

San Jacinto Day
By winning the Battle of San Jacinto (1836), Texas gained independence from Mexico. *Contact:* Texas Tourism Division, P.O. Box 12728, Austin, TX 78711; 512-462-9191; 800-880-8839; Fax: 512-320-9456.

Sky Awareness Week
During the same time as National Science and Technology Week, take time to examine the sky. *Spon-*

sor: Think Weather, Inc., Barbara G. Levine, 1522 Baylor Avenue, Rockville, MD 20850; 301-762-7669; Fax: 301-762-7669; e-mail: fourclouds@aol.com.

Week of the Young Child
Promotes early childhood education. 1997: April 13 to 19. Call for future dates. *Sponsor:* National Association for the Education of Young Children, 1509 16th Street NW, Washington, DC 20036; 800-424-2460; Fax: 202-328-1846.

World Week for Animals in Labs
During the week of Earth Day, discourage the use of animals in scientific research and testing. *Sponsor:* In Defense of Animals, 816 W. Francisco Boulevard, San Rafael, CA 94901; 415-453-9984.

April 22

Barney Blake, Police Reporter premiered (1948)
Barney Blake was the first regularly scheduled television mystery series. *Contact:* NBC-TV. ✉

Be Careful What You Say Day
On the anniversary of the beginning of the McCarthy anti-Communist hearings (1954), be careful what you say; it may come back to haunt you. Also, campaign for the right of free speech; don't let anyone shut you up. *Sponsor:* The Life of the Party. ✉

Earth Day

First observed in 1970, Earth Day reminds us to handle our planet with care. *Sponsor:* Earth Day USA, P.O. Box 470, 2 Elm Street, Peterborough, NH 03458; 603-924-7720; Fax: 603-924-7855.

Fast Day

The fourth Monday in April is a day of fasting, prayer, and public humiliation in New Hampshire. Citizens of other states do not require these rites. *Contact:* New Hampshire Travel Office, 172 Pembroke Road, P.O. Box 1856, Concord, NH 03301; 603-271-2665; Fax: 603-271-2629.

First shot of the Spanish-American War (1898)

The *USS Nashville* captured a Spanish merchant ship off Key West, Florida.

Girl Scout Leader's Day

Honors the volunteer leaders who make Girl Scouts possible. *Sponsor:* Girl Scouts of the USA, 420 Fifth Avenue, New York, NY 10018; 212-940-7500; Fax: 212-940-7859.

In God We Trust Anniversary

The motto, In God We Trust, was first used on U.S. coins in 1864.

Oklahoma Land Rush Anniversary

The land rush began at noon in 1889. *Contact:* Oklahoma Tourism, P.O. Box 60789, Oklahoma City, OK 73146; 405-521-2409; 800-652-6552; Fax: 405-521-3089.

Saint Theodore of Sykeon Feast Day

Saint Theodore is patron saint for reconciling the unhappily married.

Sun Day

Promotes solar energy and the role the sun plays in ecology on earth. *Sponsor:* Public Citizen, 2000 P Street NW #650, Washington, DC 20036; 202-833-3000.

April 23

Albuquerque Founder's Day

Francisco Cuervo Valdez founded Albuquerque in 1706. *Contact:* Albuquerque Visitors Bureau, P.O. Box 26866, Albuquerque, NM 87125-6866; 505-842-9918; 800-733-9918; Fax: 505-247-9101.

American Academy of Arts and Letters founded (1904)

Contact: American Academy of Arts and Letters, 633 W. 155th Street, New York, NY 10032-7599; 212-368-5900.

Book Day and Lover's Day (Spain)

Because this is Saint George's Day and the anniversary of the death of Miguel de Cervantes (1714), people in Spain celebrate by giving a book and a red rose to someone they love. You can do the same.

First fast food restaurant in Beijing (1992)

McDonald's opened the first fast food restaurant in Beijing, China. *Contact:* McDonald's Corporation, 1 McDonald's Plaza, Oak Brook, IL 60521; 708-575-3000; Fax: 708-575-5700.

First movie premiere (1896)

Thomas Edison's movie premiere took place in New York City; he showed movies of ballet dancers, boxers, and ocean waves.

James Buchanan's Birthday

The 15th President of the U.S. was born in Cove Gap, Pennsylvania in 1791.

National Youth Service Day

Encourages young people to become actively involved in their communities. Generally held on the second to last Tuesday of April. *Sponsor:* Youth Service America, 1101 15th Street NW #200, Washington, DC 20005; 202-296-2992; Fax: 202-296-4030.

New Coke introduced (1985)

Coca-Cola announced it was changing the secret formula for Coke. *Contact:* Coca-Cola, Inc., P.O. Box 1734, Atlanta, GA 30301;

✉ Addresses for frequently cited organizations are gathered on pages vii–viii.

APRIL   91

404-676-2121; 800-438-2653; Fax: 404-676-6792.

No Smoking Ban Anniversary

The federal ban on smoking during domestic airline flights took effect in 1988. For a free No Smoking sign, send a postcard to American Lung Association, P.O. Box 596, New York, NY 10001. Ask for pamphlet #0121 Lungs at Work.

Saint George Feast Day

Patron saint of boy scouts, soldiers, butchers, armorers, and saddlers. Saint George is also patron saint of England, Venice, Genoa, Germany, Greece, Catalonia, and Portugal. He is also solicited for protection against skin diseases.

We All Grow Up Day

On the birthday of Shirley Temple Black, the famous child actress of the 1930s, remember that we all grow up. Shirley was born in 1928 in Santa Monica, California. *Sponsor:* The Life of the Party. ✉

William Shakespeare's Birthday

The world's greatest playwright was born on April 23, 1564, and died on April 23, 1616.

April 24

Ambivalence Day

Celebrate today by taking a stand, or not taking a stand, or staying in the middle. Oh, do whatever. *Sponsor:* The Life of the Party. ✉

Babylonian New Year

Begins the Nabonassar Era Year 2745 on April 25 (24th on leap years).

Change Your Batteries in Your Car Alarm Buzzer Day

Celebrated annually on the anniversary of the date that Tom and Ray decided to remind people to change the batteries in their car alarm remote control at least once a year. The first such day was in 1994. *Contact:* Car Talk, Tom and Ray Magliozzi, WBUR Radio, 630 Commonwealth Ave, Boston, MA 02215-2422; 617-353-2790.

China Space Day (1970)

The People's Republic of China launched its first satellite. *Contact:* People's Republic of China, Embassy, 2300 Connecticut Avenue NW, Washington, DC 20008; 202-328-2500.

Fathometer patented (1928)

First satellite relay of a TV signal (1962)

MIT relayed a television signal via satellite from Camp Parks, California, to Westford, Massachusetts. *Contact:* Massachusetts Institute of Technology, 77 Massachusetts Avenue, Cambridge, MA 02139; 617-253-1000; Fax: 617-253-8000.

Israel Independence Day (Yom Ha'atzma'ut)

The modern state of Israel was proclaimed on the 5th day of Iyar in the year 5708 of the Hebrew calen-

dar. *Contact:* Embassy of Israel, 3514 International Drive NW, Washington, DC 20008; 202-364-5500.

Library of Congress Birthday

Established by Congress in 1800; it is the largest library in the world. *Contact:* Library of Congress, 101 Independence Avenue SE, Washington, DC 20540-0001; 202-707-5000; Fax: 202-707-5844.

National TV Turn-Off Week

During this week, families take a No TV pledge to watch little or no TV from Wednesday, April 24, to Tuesday, April 30. More than 1,000,000 people participated in the 1995 event. *Sponsor:* TV Free America, 1322 18th Street NW #300, Washington, DC 20036; 202-887-0436; Fax: 202-887-0438; e-mail: tvfa@essential.org.

Oldest black medical association formed (1884)

The Medico-Chirurgical Society was formed in Washington, D.C.

Professional Secretaries Day

Show your appreciation of secretaries on the Wednesday during the last full week in April. *Sponsor:* Professional Secretaries International, 10502 NW Ambassador Drive, P.O. Box 20404, Kansas City, MO 64195-0404; 816-891-6600; Fax: 816-891-9118.

Read Me Day

On the last Wednesday in April, everyone is invited to read in schools. *Sponsor:* Book 'Em, Lee Fairbend, Director, 2012 21st Avenue S, Nashville, TN 37212; 615-834-7323; Fax: 615-790-0896.

Soda fountain patented (1833)

World YWCA Day
Celebrated on the last Wednesday in April. *Sponsor:* YWCA of the USA, 726 Broadway, New York, NY 10003; 212-614-2700; Fax: 212-677-9716.

April 25

Abortion first legalized (1967)
Colorado first legalized therapeutic abortions in the U.S.

Buddhist New Year
Buddha, the enlightened one, lived in India from 563 B.C. to 483 B.C. Some Buddhist sects celebrate his birthday on the eighth day of the fourth lunar month as their New Year's Day.

Cuckoo Day
In England, this is the traditional day honoring the cuckoo, which heralds the return of migratory birds from the south and, hence, the coming of summer.

First Memorial Day in U.S. (1866)
Held at Friendship Cemetery in Columbus, Mississippi, a year after the end of the Civil War. *Contact:* Columbus Visitors Bureau, P.O. Box 789, Columbus, MS 39703;

601-329-1191; 800-327-2686; Fax: 601-329-8969.

First seeing eye dog
His name was Buddy, and he was given to his owner, Morris Frank, in 1928.

First solar battery announced (1954)

First state to require license plates (1901)
New York was the first state to require car license plates; they cost $1.00.

Hubble space telescope deployed
Launched on April 12, 1990, this largest space telescope was deployed on April 25th. *Contact:* NASA. ✉

Integrated circuit patented (1961)
Robert Noyce patented the integrated circuit, the basis for electronics and computers.

Saint Lawrence Seaway opened to shipping (1959)
The first ships were allowed to enter the Seaway.

Saint Mark Feast Day
Author of one of the Gospels, patron saint of Venice, notaries, glaziers, and cattle breeders.

Take Our Daughters to Work Day
On the fourth Thursday in April, parents are encouraged to take their daughters to work with them. This day is designed to encourage girls to consider their career goals, problems, spirit, and dreams. *Sponsor:* Ms. Foundation for Women, 120 Wall Street, 33rd Floor, New York, NY 10005; 212-742-2300; 800-353-2525.

April 26

Ban on guns near schools overturned (1995)
The U.S. Supreme Court overturned the 1990 Gun-Free School Zones Act, a federal law that banned guns within 1,000 feet of schools. The Court said such laws are the province of the states. *Contact:* U.S. Supreme Court. ✉

Chernobyl nuclear reactor disaster (1986)
The worst nuclear accident to date. The reactor at the Chernobyl atomic power plant exploded.

First major league baseball team to have an organ
The Chicago Cubs installed an organ at Wrigley Field in 1941. Roy Nelson played the first pre-game

music program. *Contact:* Chicago Cubs Baseball Team, Wrigley Field, 1060 W. Addison Street, Chicago, IL 60613; 312-404-2827; Fax: 312-404-4111.

Hug an Australian Day
Show appreciation for the people from down under. *Sponsor:* Wellness Permission League. ✉

Largest bank robbery in the U.S. (1981)
The largest bank robbery thus far took place in Tucson, Arizona. $3,300,000 was stolen.

Milky Way Galaxy Birthday
Over 8 billion years ago, our galaxy came into being. *Sponsor:* A Pilgrim's Almanac. ✉

National Arbor Day
The last Friday in April recognizes the importance of trees. Plant a tree today! The National Arbor Day movement was founded by Edward Scanlon, editor of *Trees* magazine, following up on the work of J. Sterling Morton and Dr. Birdsey Northrup. *Sponsor:* National Arbor Day Committee, 640 Eagle Rock Avenue, West Orange, NJ 07052; 201-731-0594; Fax: 201-731-6020.

National Bird Day
On the birthday of American painter, John James Audubon, we honor all birds and ornithologists. Audubon was born in 1785 in Santo Domingo. His greatest work, *The Birds of America,* was completed in 1838. *Contact:* National Audubon Society, 700 Broadway, New York, NY 10003; 212-979-3000; Fax: 212-353-0508.

National Crayola Day
Near the birthday of Dan Crayola, inventor of crayons, do some coloring but don't color outside the lines. Celebrate this day on the last Friday in April. *Sponsor:* The Life of the Party. ✉

National Dream Hotline
The last weekend in April educates people about the significance and meaning of their dreams. By age 60, you will have slept 175,200 hours, dreamt for 87,000 hours, and will have had 197,100 dreams. *Sponsor:* School of Metaphysics, Barbara Cohen, Coordinator, HCR 1, Box 15, Windyville, MO 65783; 417-345-8411.

Richter Scale Day
Charles Richter developed the Richter Scale, which measures the magnitude of earthquakes.

April 27

First Social Security checks issued (1937)

Natural Law Day
In 1417, a chicken in Basel, Switzerland was burned at the stake for violating natural law by laying a brightly colored egg. *Sponsor:* A Pilgrim's Almanac. ✉

Saint Zita Feast Day
A servant herself, she is patron saint of maidservants; she is also invoked to help find lost keys.

South Africa's first non-racial election (1994)
Contact: Republic of South Africa Embassy, 3051 Massachusetts Avenue NW, Washington, DC 20008; 202-232-4400.

Ulysses Simpson Grant's Birthday
The 18th President of the U.S. was born in 1822 in Point Pleasant, Ohio.

WalkAmerica
Held on the last weekend in April, this is the largest walking event in the world with more than one million participants in 1,400 U.S. cities. WalkAmerica raises funds for preventing birth defects. *Sponsor:* March of Dimes Foundation, 1275 Mamaroneck Avenue, White Plains, NY 10605; 914-428-7100.

Wide World of Sports premiered (1961)
Contact: ABC-TV. ✉

World Championship Cow Chip Throw
Also known as cow pies or cow patties, cow chips are the tool of choice in this world championship

✉ Addresses for frequently cited organizations are gathered on pages vii–viii.

94 APRIL

throwing contest held on the fourth Saturday in April. *Sponsor:* Beaver Chamber of Commerce, 33 W. Second Street, P.O. Box 878, Beaver, OK 73932; 405-625-4726.

Worst maritime disaster in the U.S. (1865)

A boiler explosion on the steamboat Sultana caused the deaths of 1,547 people, mostly Union soldiers returning home after the Civil War. Most drowned in the Mississippi River a few miles upstream from Memphis, Tennessee.

Worthy Wage Day

Promotes action to secure better wages and working conditions for teachers and child care providers. Always celebrated on Thursday during the Week of the Young Child. *Sponsor:* Alliance of Early Childhood Professionals, Margaret Boyer, 310 East 38th Street #226A, Minneapolis, MN 55409; 612-823-5922; Fax: 612-824-0791.

April 28

Canada/U.S. Goodwill Week

Always celebrated the week of April 28th. The signing of the Rush-Bagot Treaty in 1817, limited armament buildups between the two countries. *Sponsor:* Kiwanis International. ✉

First successful parachute jump (1919)

Leslie Ervin made the first successful parachute jump.

First yellow fever vaccine (1932)

Great Poetry Reading Day

Read or write some great poetry today. *Sponsor:* Robert Stevens, Clio High School, One Mustang Drive, Clio, MI 48420.

James Monroe's Birthday

The 5th president of the U.S. was born in 1758 in Westmoreland County, Virginia.

Kiss Your Mate Day

When your someone special least expects it, kiss him or her. *Sponsor:* Alan W. Brue. ✉

Maryland Ratification Day

In 1788, Maryland became the 7th state to ratify the U.S. Constitution. Maryland was one of the orig-inal 13 states. *Contact:* Maryland Office of Tourism, 217 E. Redwood Street, 9th Floor, Baltimore, MD 21202; 410-333-6611; 800-543-1036; Fax: 410-333-6643.

Mutiny on the Bounty (1789)

Fletcher Christian led the famous naval mutiny against William Bligh.

National Kids Fitness Week

The week of May 4th teaches kids the importance of fitness. Formerly sponsored by Kraft Macaroni & Cheese.

Workers Memorial Day

Commemorates workers who were injured or killed on their jobs. Canadians celebrate the same day as the National Day of Mourning. *Sponsor:* AFL-CIO, 815 16th Street NW, Washington, DC 20000; 202-637-5010.

World's worst air show disaster (1988)

Three Italian Air Force jets collided over Ramstein Air Force Base in Germany and crashed into the crowd on the ground; 70 people were killed, including the pilots and many spectators.

April 29

Confederate Memorial Day

Celebrated on different days by various southern states. Alabama and Mississippi: the fourth Monday in April; Florida and Georgia: April 26; North and South Carolina: May 10; Virginia: the last Monday in May; Kentucky and Louisiana: June 3. All of these days commemorate those who fought and died for the South in the Civil War.

Dancers Day
Honors all dancers on the anniversary of the last Broadway performance of *Chorus Line* in 1990. *Sponsor:* The Life of the Party. ✉

First Broadway performance of Hair (1968)
The rock musical play *Hair* was controversial; it had been performed previously off-Broadway (premiering October 17, 1967).

Friendship Sees No Color Week
Celebrates non-racist friendships on the anniversary of the 1992 Los Angeles riots (April 29th). *Sponsor:* Brian Harris, P.O. Box 74, Stanton, CA 90680; 714-236-0805.

James Beard Awards Ceremony
Awards are given for books and articles on food and beverages, culinary videos, radio and TV cooking shows, restaurant design and graphics, chef, pastry chef, wine service, and new restaurant. *Sponsor:* The James Beard Foundation, 167 West 12th Street, New York, NY 10011; 212-675-4984; Fax: 212-645-1438.

Last Americans killed in action in Vietnam (1975)
The last 4 Americans killed in action in Vietnam were Lance Corporal Darwin Judge, Corporal Charles McMahon, Jr., Captain William Craig Nystul, and First Lieutenant Michael John Shea.

National Family Reading Week
Co-sponsored by Chrysler Learning Corporation, *Scholastic* magazine, American Federation of Teachers, and the Association for Supervision and Curriculum Development. *Sponsor:* Scholastic, Inc., 555 Broadway, New York, NY 10012; 212-343-6100.

Public Welfare Medal Award Ceremony
Carl Sagan received the 1994 medal. It is presented by the National Academy of Sciences during their annual meeting honoring extraordinary use of science for the public good. *Sponsor:* National Academy of Sciences, 2101 Constitution Avenue NW, Washington, DC 20418; 202-334-2446; Fax: 202-334-1597.

Rubber patented (1813)

Saint Catherine of Siena Feast Day
Patron saint of fire prevention; she is also patron saint of Italy.

Zipper's Birthday
Gideon Sundback of Hoboken, New Jersey, patented the zipper in 1913.

April 30

Beltane
Beltane (aka May Eve, Walpergis Night, Valborg) is a feast day in the old Wiccan religion where the god and goddess marry. It is also a spring festival for good crops and healthy animals.

First theatrical performance in North America (1598)
A Spanish comedy was performed on the banks of the Rio Grande near El Paso, Texas.

First toy advertised on television (1952)
Mr. Potato Head was the first toy to be advertised on TV.

George Washington inaugurated as president (1789)

George Washington was the first president of the U.S.

Hitler committed suicide (1945)

Adolf Hitler and his wife, Eva Braun, committed suicide in a Berlin bunker as the Russian troops approached the city.

International School Spirit Season

Build more school spirit from April 30 to September 30. *Sponsor:* Committee for More School Spirit, Jim Hawkins, P.O. Box 2652, San Diego, CA 92112-2652; 619-280-0999.

Leaders Are Readers Day

On the Tuesday of National Family Reading Week, school principals and other community leaders set an example by reading aloud to school children around the country. *Sponsor:* Scholastic, Inc., 555 Broadway, New York, NY 10012; 212-343-6100.

Louisiana Admission Day (1812)

The 18th state to be admitted to the union. *Contact:* Louisiana Office of Tourism, Capital Station, P.O. Box 94291, Baton Rouge, LA 70804-9291; 504-342-8119; 800-227-4386.

Mendelevium Day

Element 101, mendelevium, was discovered in 1955.

National Bandanna Day

On the birthday of country singer Willie Nelson, wear a bandana. Nelson was born in 1933 in Abbott, Texas. *Sponsor:* The Life of the Party.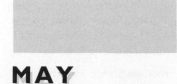

National Honesty Day

The motto for this day is "honesty is the best policy." *Sponsor:* The Book of Lies, M. Hirsh Goldberg, Author, 3103 Szold Drive, Baltimore, MD 21208; 410-339-7334. Home: 410-486-4150.

Organization of American States held first meeting (1948)

The first meeting was held in Bogota, Columbia. *Contact:* Organization of American States, 17th and Constitution Avenue NW, Washington, DC 20006; 202-458-3000; Fax: 202-458-3967.

Saint Adjutor Feast Day

A French crusader, Saint Adjutor once sprinkled holy water on a dangerous whirlpool in the Seine River, preventing drownings in the river. He is a patron saint of swimmers and yachtsmen; he is also invoked by those in danger of drowning.

U.S. Department of the Navy established (1798)

Contact: Department of the Navy, Pentagon, Room 4E686, Washington, DC 20350; 703-695-0911.

Wee Folk Day

In ancient times, people baked sweet breads on this day and left them out for the returning Wee Folk. If the breads were eaten, the family would have good fortune the rest of the year.

MAY

Asian/Pacific American Heritage Month

Better Sleep Month

Promotes the connection between quality beds and a good night's sleep. *Sponsor:* The Better Sleep Council, 333 Commerce Street, Alexandria, VA 22314; 703-683-8371; Fax: 703-683-4503.

Breathe Easy Month

Focuses attention on air pollution (indoor and outdoor) and second-hand smoke—and how they affect our lungs. *Sponsor:* American Lung Association, 1740 Broadway, New York, NY 10019-4374; 212-315-6473; 800-LUNG-USA; Fax: 212-315-8872.

Date Your Mate Month

Keep the romance sizzling in your relationship by making a date with your mate. *Sponsor:* Married Mistress Association, Rose Smith, President, P.O. Box 81064, Albuquerque, NM 87198-1064; 505-899-3121; Fax: 505-899-3120.

Electrical Safety Month

Family Support Month

Support families with children during divorces, separations, and custody issues. *Sponsor:* Children Hurt in Legal Disputes, Kathleen Quin, P.O. Box 241, Wilmette, IL 60091-0241.

Freedom Shrine Month

To rededicate America's Freedom Shrines. *Sponsor:* The National Exchange Clubs, C. Neal Davis, 3050 Central Avenue, Toledo, OH 43606-1700; 419-535-3232; Fax: 419-535-1989.

Fungal Infection Awareness Month

Fungus, yeast, and molds can cause skin infections. *Sponsor:* Mycology Institute, Dave Chapman, Ferguson Communication Group, 30 Lanidex Plaza W, Parsippany, NJ 07054; 201-884-2200; Fax: 201-884-2487.

Gazpacho Aficionado Time

During ripe tomato season, enjoy cold gazpacho soup.

Healthy Baby Month

Promotes reproductive health in men as well as a father's role in the health of the baby. *Sponsor:* Iowa Substance Abuse Info Center, Cedar Rapids Public Library, 500

1st Street SE, Cedar Rapids, IA 52401; 319-247-0614; 800-247-0614; Fax: 319-398-0408.

Iowa Tourism Month

Sponsor: Iowa Tourism Bureau, 200 E. Grand Avenue, Des Moines, IA 50309; 515-242-4705; 800-345-4692; Fax: 515-242-4749.

Labor History Month

May Is Better Hearing Month

To teach people about hearing loss. *Sponsor:* Texas Hearing Aid Association, 222 N. Riverside Drive, Fort Worth, TX 76111; 817-831-0592; Fax: 817-831-9875.

Melanoma/Skin Cancer Detection and Prevention Month

Each year 34,000 Americans get skin cancer; 7,200 die from it. Take time this month to have your skin checked out before exposing it to the hot rays of summer. *Sponsor:* American Academy of Dermatology, P.O. Box 4014, Schaumburg, IL 60168-4014; 708-330-0230; Fax: 708-330-0050.

Mental Health Month

To teach people about mental health. *Sponsor:* National Mental Health Association, 1021 Prince Street, Alexandria, VA 22314-2971; 703-684-7722; 800-969-6642; Fax: 703-684-5968.

Modern Dance Month

Two women responsible for the birth of modern dance, Isadora Duncan and Martha Graham, were born in May. Duncan: May 27, 1878; Graham: May 11, 1894.

The Month of Peace

Motorcycle Awareness Month

National Allergy and Asthma Awareness Month

Sponsor: Pharmacists Planning Services. ✉

National Amyotrophic Lateral Sclerosis Month

National Arthritis Month

Focuses awareness on the 100 different types of arthritis. *Sponsor:* Arthritis Foundation, Dennis Bowman, 1314 Spring Street NW, Atlanta, GA 30309; 404-872-7100.

National Asparagus Month
It's fresh, it's green, it's abundant! Nibble on a tender asparagus spear.

National Barbecue Month
Promotes the use of a barbecue grill early in the summer season. *Sponsor:* Barbecue Industry Association, DHM Group, Department B, P.O. Box 767, Holmdel, NJ 07733; 908-975-9675; Fax: 908-946-3343.

National Bike Month
Promotes bicycling and bike safety. Send for a catalog of low-cost brochures, videos, posters, and books. *Sponsor:* League of American Bicyclists, 190 W. Ostend Street #120, Baltimore, MD 21230; 410-539-3399.

National Birds of Prey Month

National Correct Posture Month
To remind people about the connection between correct posture and good health. *Sponsor:* American Chiropractic Association, 1701 Clarendon Boulevard, Arlington, VA 22209; 703-276-8800; Fax: 703-243-2593.

National Digestive Disease Awareness Month

National Duckling Month
To spread information and recipes about ducklings. Formerly sponsored by Concord Farms.

National Egg Month
Dedicated to the versatility, convenience, economy, and good nutri-

tion of the incredible edible egg. *Sponsor:* American Egg Board, 1460 Renaissance Drive, Park Ridge, IL 60068; 708-296-7044.

National Foster Care Month

National Guy Pride Month
In 1995, Dave Barry proclaimed May as National Guy Pride Month. This was one way to promote his book, *Dave Barry's Complete Guide to Guys.*

National Hamburger Month
Sponsor: White Castle Systems, 555 W. Goodale Street, Columbus, OH 43215-1171; 614-228-5781; Fax: 614-228-8841.

National High Blood Pressure Month
Promotes the treatment of high blood pressure. *Sponsor:* High Blood Pressure Education Program, National Heart, Lung, and Blood Institute, P.O. Box 30105, Bethesda, MD 20824-0105; 301-251-1222; Fax: 301-251-1223.

National Huntington's Disease Awareness Month

National Mime Month

National Photo Month
Promotes the importance of photography in documenting life's events. *Sponsor:* Photo Marketing Association, 3000 Picture Place, Jackson, MI 49201; 517-788-8100; Fax: 517-788-8371.

National Physical Fitness and Sports Month
To encourage fitness through sports. *Sponsor:* President's Council on Physical Fitness, 701 Pennsylvania Avenue NW #250, Washington, DC 20004; 202-272-3427; Fax: 202-504-2064.

National Salad Month
Sponsor: Association for Dressings and Sauces, 5775 Peachtree-Dunwoody Road #500, Atlanta, GA 30342; 404-252-3663; Fax: 404-252-0774.

National Senior Travel Month
Combines the spirit of Older Americans Month with National Tourism Week (first full week in May). Get out and travel no matter how old or young you might be! *Sponsor: New Choices* Magazine, 28 W. 23rd Street, New York, NY 10010; 212-366-8800; Fax: 212-366-8899.

National Sight-Saving Month
Watch out for hidden dangers at home during this month when more people are working in their yards and on home improvement projects. *Sponsor:* Prevent Blindness America. ✉

National Strawberry Month

Enjoy some California strawberries this month. *Sponsor:* California Strawberry Commission, P.O. Box 269, Watsonville, CA 95077-0269; 408-724-1301; Fax: 408-724-5973.

National Stroke Awareness Month

Strokes are the leading cause of disabilities in the U.S. *Sponsor:* American Heart Association, 7272 Greenville Avenue, Dallas, TX 75231-4596; 214-373-6300; 800-553-6321 (referral line for stroke survivors and their families); Fax: 214-706-1341.

National Tavern Month

National Trauma Awareness Month

National Tuberous Sclerosis Awareness Month

This disease strikes 1 in 5,500. *Sponsor:* National Tuberous Sclerosis Association, 8000 Corporate Drive #120, Landover, MD 20785; 800-225-6872; Fax: 301-459-0394.

Older Americans Month

First celebrated in 1963 as Senior Citizens Month; the name was changed in 1974.

Personal History Awareness Month

Educates people on the importance of compiling a personal history—for yourself as well as for your family. Formerly sponsored by Memories Plus.

Project Safe Baby Month

Encourages the proper use of child safety seats. *Sponsor:* Project Safe Baby Team, Golin/Harris Communications, 500 N. Michigan Avenue, Chicago, IL 60611; 312-836-7100.

REACT CB-Radio Month

Encourages the proper use of (emergency only) CB Channel 9. *Sponsor:* REACT, Inc., P.O. Box 998, Wichita, KS 67201; 316-263-2100; Fax: 316-263-2118.

Revise Your Work Schedule Month

Encourages the exploration of non-traditional work schedules that might better suit working individuals. *Sponsor:* Center for Worktime Options, Maggi Payment, 1043 University Avenue #192, San Diego, CA 92103; 619-232-0404.

Social Science Books Month

Read a book on politics, law, sociology, history, anthropology, psychology, or other social science. *Sponsor:* Book Marketing Update. ✉

Touring Theatre Month

Praises theatre companies bringing plays to the people. Formerly sponsored by Richard Falk, who died in 1994.

May 1

American Equal Rights Association founded (1866)

Devoted to equal rights for women and for Negroes. Lucretia Mott was the first president of the association.

Amtrak began service (1971)

The national railway passenger service began. *Contact:* Amtrak, 60 Massachusetts Avenue NE, Washington, DC 20002; 202-906-3000; 800-872-7245 (for tickets); Fax: 202-906-3865.

Batman's Birthday

The comic strip character *Batman* premiered in 1939; he was the first costumed crimefighter to use detective skills. *Contact:* DC Comics, 1325 6th Avenue, 27th Floor, New York, NY 10019; 212-636-5400; Fax: 212-636-5403.

Book Buddy Day

On the Wednesday of National Family Reading Week, read a book with someone. *Sponsor:* Scholastic, Inc., 555 Broadway, New York, NY 10012; 212-343-6100.

Cheerios' Birthday

The cereal was introduced in 1941. *Contact:* General Mills, 1 General Mills Boulevard, Minneapolis, MN 55426-1348; 612-540-2311; Fax: 612-540-4925.

Citizen Kane premiered (1941)

Orson Welles's greatest film premiered in New York City.

Empire State Building completed (1930)

Contact: Empire State Building, 5th Avenue and 34th Street, New York, NY 10118; 212-736-3100.

First adhesive postage stamps issued (1840)

Issued in England. *Contact:* U.S. Postal Service. ✉

First American to scale Mount Everest (1963)

James Whittaker of Redmond, Washington, was the first.

First newspaper ad in the U.S. (1704)

The *Boston News-letter* published the first.

First skyscraper began construction (1884)

Located in Chicago, Illinois, the Home Insurance Building was 10 stories.

First U.S. postcard issued (1872)

Contact: U.S. Postal Service. ✉

Law Day USA

To encourage respect for the law. *Sponsor:* American Bar Association, 750 N. Lake Shore Drive, Chicago, IL 60611; 312-988-5000; Fax: 312-988-6283.

Lei Day

Celebrated in Hawaii with a festival and lei making contests. *Contact:* Hawaii Visitors Bureau, 2270 Kalakaua Avenue #801, Honolulu, HI

96815; 808-923-1811; Fax: 808-922-8991.

May Day

Originates from a festival honoring Flora, the Roman goddess of spring; also traditionally a time to gather flowers and welcome warm weather. In the late 1800s, it also became a day to honor workers.

Mother Goose Day

To celebrate the poems of Mother Goose. *Sponsor:* Mother Goose Society, Gloria Delamar, President, 7303 Sharpless Road, Melrose Park, PA 19027; 215-782-1059.

National Anxiety Disorder Screening Day

Sponsor: National Mental Health Association, 1021 Prince Street, Alexandria, VA 22314-2971; 703-684-7722; 800-969-6642; Fax: 703-684-5968.

Pen-Friends Week International

The first 7 days in May encourage everyone to have at least one pen-friend in another country. *Sponsor:* International Society of Friendship and Good Will. ✉

U2 Day

In 1960, the Soviet Union shot down the American U2 spy plane piloted by Francis Gary Powers.

World's Largest Exercise Class (Project Aces)

Twenty million children from 47 countries around the world partici-

pate in this annual exercise class on the first Wednesday—All Children Exercising Simultaneously. For more info, send an SASE to Lenny Saunders, Valley View School, Montville, NJ 07045. *Sponsor:* Youth Fitness Coalition, Lenny Saunders, ACES Coordinator, Project ACES, P.O. Box 6452, Jersey City, NJ 07306-0452; 201-440-6345.

May 2

Good Housekeeping magazine first published (1885)

First published by Clara Bryan of Holyoke, Massachusetts. *Contact:* Good Housekeeping, 959 Eighth Street, New York, NY 10019-3737; 212-649-2264; Fax: 212-265-3307.

Make-a-Book Day

On the Thursday of National Family Reading Week, children create their own books. *Sponsor:* Scholastic, Inc., 555 Broadway, New York, NY 10012; 212-343-6100.

Martin Z. Mollusk Day

If Martin Z. Mollusk, a hermit crab, sees his shadow on the first Thursday in May, summer will come a week early. *Sponsor:* Martin Z. Mollusk Day, Mark Soifer, 9th Street & Asbury Avenue, Ocean City, NJ 08226; 609-399-6111.

National Day of Prayer

Since 1957; celebrated on the first Thursday in May.

✉ Addresses for frequently cited organizations are gathered on pages vii–viii.

MAY   101

Robert's Rules of Order Day

On the birthday of Henry Robert (1837), who wrote the parliamentary guide *Robert's Rules of Order,* follow all the rules. Or break them. Your choice.

Street Smart, Street Safe Day

On the first Thursday in May, take time to educate your family on how to prevent street crime. *Sponsor:* Cynthia Akerberg, 1424 Anthony Michael Drive, Lawrence, KS 66049; 913-841-0949.

Take a Baby to Lunch Day

Take a baby out to lunch on the birthday of Dr. Benjamin Spock, the authority on how to raise children. Spock was born in 1903 in New Haven, Connecticut. *Sponsor:* The Life of the Party. ✉

May 3

Faery Moon

The full moon of May is the faery moon, symbolic of faery power, love, romance, wisdom, and good health; also known as the flower moon.

The Fantasticks musical opened (1960)

First opened off Broadway on this day; it went on to become one of the longest running musicals on Broadway. As of this writing, the musical has had more than 14,500 performances.

First comic book published (1934)

Famous Funnies was the first comic book.

First state sales tax (1921)

West Virginia was the first state to impose a sales tax.

First woman director of the U.S. Mint (1933)

Nellie Ross headed the U.S. Mint. *Contact:* U.S. Mint, 633 Third Street NW #715, Washington, DC 20220; 202-874-6000; Fax: 202-874-6282.

International Hall of Fame Day

The Friday before the first full weekend honors every famous person in the world. *Sponsor:* Inventors Clubs of America, Alexander Marinaccio, P.O. Box 450261, Atlanta, GA 31145-0261; 404-938-5089; Fax: 404-355-8889.

International Tuba Day

Hard-working tuba players are honored on the first Friday in May. *Spon-*

sor: Music Department, Sy Brandon, Millersville University, Millersville, PA 17551; 717-872-3439.

Lumpy Rug Day

Shove unwelcome facts under the rug. *Sponsor:* Puns Corps. ✉

May Fellowship Day

The first Friday in May reminds us that women can support each other in their various roles. All have a place at the table. *Sponsor:* Church Women United, 475 Riverside Drive #812, New York, NY 10115; 212-870-2347; Fax: 212-870-2338.

National Public Radio Birthday

This noncommercial radio network began broadcasting in 1971. *Contact:* National Public Radio, 635 Massachusetts Avenue, Washington, DC 20001; 202-414-3232; Fax: 202-414-3329; World Wide Web: http://www.npr.org.

Put-a-Book-in-Your-Future Day

On the Friday of National Family Reading Week, make plans for your summer reading. *Sponsor:* Scholastic, Inc., 555 Broadway, New York, NY 10012; 212-343-6100.

Vesak Day (Singapore)

Commemorates the 3 most important events in the life of Lord Buddha: his birth, enlightenment, and death. Also known as Buddha Purnima, it is usually celebrated near the full moon in May. *Contact:* Singapore Tourist Promotion Board, 848 Wilshire Boulevard #510, Beverly Hills, CA 90211; 800-283-9595; Fax: 213-852-0129.

Washington, DC was incorporated as a city (1802)
The president appointed the mayor of this new city. *Contact:* Washington, DC Visitors Bureau, 1212 New York Avenue NW #600, Washington, DC 20005; 202-789-7000; Fax: 202-789-7037.

World Champion Junior Barrel Race
On the first weekend in May, world championship barrel races determine the best handler of horses among junior riders. The races are held at Josey's Ranch near Marshall, Texas. *Sponsor:* Chamber of Commerce, P.O. Box 520, Marshall, TX 75761; 903-935-7868.

World Championship Cribbage Tournament
Founded in 1972, this annual tournament is held at the Plumas County Fairgrounds on the first Friday and Saturday in May. The silver anniversary tournament will be held in 1996. *Sponsor:* World Championship Cribbage, Mike

Taborski, P.O. Box B, Quincy, CA 95971; 916-283-0800.

World Press Freedom Day
Commemorates the Windhoek Declaration on Promoting an Independent and Pluralistic African Press (adopted in 1991 by a U.N. seminar held in Windhoek, Namibia). *Sponsor:* United Nations. ✉

World's Only Thoroughbred Lobster Races at Lobster Down
Held on the first Friday night in May, Aiken also hosts the Oyster Parade at Mardi Claw. *Sponsor:* Chamber of Commerce, P.O. Box 892, Aiken, SC 29802; 803-641-1111.

May 4

Academy of Motion Picture Arts and Sciences founded (1927)
Contact: Academy of Motion Picture Arts and Sciences, 8949 Wilshire Boulevard, Beverly Hills, CA 90211; 310-247-3000; Fax: 310-859-9619.

Kent State Students Memorial Day
Honors all students killed in a fight for human rights, especially the 4 students killed at Kent State University in Kent, Ohio in 1970. *Contact:* Kent State University, Office

of Public Affairs, Kent, OH 44242; 216-672-2121.

Kentucky Derby Day
Since 1875, the Run for the Roses, the first race of horseracing's Triple Crown, has been run on the first Saturday in May. *Sponsor:* Kentucky Derby Museum, 704 Central Avenue, Louisville, KY 40208; 502-637-1111. For information, call 502-636-4400.

Long Necks Are Beautiful Day
On the birthday of Audrey Hepburn, celebrate all those who have beautiful necks (whether long or short). Hepburn was born in 1929, near Brussels, Belgium. *Sponsor:* The Life of the Party. ✉

Manhattan is bought for $24.00 in cloth and buttons
Dutch explorer Peter Minuit bought Manhattan Island in 1626.

Naked Day
Take a risk! Be as naked as you can be. *Sponsor:* Naked Day Committee, Kevin Eggers, P.O. Box 1551, Iowa City, IA 52244; 319-354-1132.

National Homebrew Day
On the first Saturday in May, hoist a couple of homemade beers to celebrate this offbeat hobby. *Sponsor:* American Homebrewers Association, P.O. Box 1679, Boulder, CO 80306-1679; 303-447-0816; Fax: 303-447-2825; e-mail: info@aob.org.

National Kids Fitness Day
To teach kids the importance of fitness. Formerly sponsored by Kraft Macaroni and Cheese.

National Weather Observer's Day
To honor people who watch and forecast the weather. *Sponsor:* Alan Brue. ✉

Relationship Renewal Day
Encourages the renewal and strengthening of relationships. *Sponsor:* Nondisposable Relationships, Peter Rosenzweig, Founder, 713 Golf Mill Professional Bldg., Niles, IL 60714; 708-297-5750.

Rhode Island Independence Day
The colony of Rhode Island declared its independence from Great Britain in 1776. *Contact:* Rhode Island Tourism Division, 7 Jackson Walkway, Providence, RI 02903; 401-277-2601; 800-556-2484; Fax: 401-277-2102.

May 5

American mainland attacked by the Japanese (1945)
A Japanese balloon bomb exploded at Gearhart Mountain, Oregon, killing a pregnant woman and 5 children who were picnicking. It was the only fatal attack of its kind during World War II.

American Wildflower Week
Promotes the appreciation of wildflowers; celebrated the first full week in May.

Be Kind to Animals Week
The first full week in May promotes kindness to animals. *Sponsor:* American Humane Association, 63 Inverness Drive E, Englewood, CO 80112; 303-792-9900; Fax: 303-792-5333.

California Raisin Week
Raisins are a fun and nutritious food. This week is celebrated the first full week in May.

Carnegie Hall opened (1891)
Contact: Carnegie Hall, 154 West 57th Street, New York, NY 10019; 212-247-7800.

Carpet Care Improvement Week
During the first full week in May, be sure to have your carpets cleaned. *Sponsor:* Carpet and Fabricare Institute, Roger Pierce, P.O. Box 149, Vancouver, WA 98666; 360-694-0048; 800-227-7389; Fax: 360-694-8401.

Cartoon Art Appreciation Week
The first full week in May celebrates America's native art form, cartoons! *Sponsor:* Cartoon Art Museum, Paola Stuff, 665 Third Street #505, San Francisco, CA 94107; 415-546-3922; Fax: 415-543-7790.

Cedar Pencil Week
The first week in May promotes cedar pencils, which are ecological because they are made from a renewable resource. For a copy of the education kit, "The Story of Pencils: Technology and Tradition," send $3.00 to the Incense Cedar Institute. *Sponsor:* Incense Cedar Institute, P.O. Box 7349, Stockton, CA 95267.

Cinco de Mayo
Mexican independence day, commemorating the Battle of Puebla (1862) when the Mexican army defeated Napoleon III's French army. Mexican-Americans celebrate this day with a cultural festival featuring parades, dancing, and food. *Contact:* Mexican Embassy, 1911 Pennsylvania Avenue NW, Washington, DC 20006; 202-728-1600.

Clean Air Week
The week of May 6th focuses on the connection between clean air and healthy people. *Sponsor:* American Lung Association, 1740 Broadway, New York, NY 10019-4374; 212-315-8700; Fax: 212-315-8872.

Conserve Water/ Detect-a-Leak Week
During the first full week in May, make an effort to conserve water.

Sponsor: American Leak Detection, S&S Public Relations, 400 Skokie Boulevard #200, Northbrook, IL 60062; 708-291-1616; Fax: 708-291-1758.

First American astronaut in space (1961)
Alan Shepard, Jr. became the first American in space. *Contact:* NASA. ✉

First perfect baseball game pitched (1904)
Cy Young pitched the first perfect game. *Contact:* Major League Baseball. ✉

First woman granted a U.S. patent
Mary Kies received her patent in 1809. *Contact:* Patent and Trademark Office, 211 Crystal Drive #700, Arlington, VA 20002; 703-305-4537; Fax: 703-305-6369.

Flexible Work Arrangements Week
During the first full week in May, encourage companies to use flex time arrangements at work. *Sponsor:* Center for Worktime Options, Maggi Payment, 1043 University Avenue #192, San Diego, CA 92103; 619-232-0404.

Goodwill Industries Week
Goodwill provides job training to people with disabilities and other special needs. Always the first full week in May. *Sponsor:* Goodwill Industries International, 9200 Wisconsin Avenue, Bethesda, MD 20814; 301-530-6500; Fax: 301-530-1516.

Ice: The Ultimate Disaster (2000)
In the novel *5/5/2000* by R. W. Noone, it is predicted that the ice buildup at the South Pole will tip the earth's axis, thus sending trillions of tons of ice and water sweeping over the planet.

Japanese Festival of Kites (Tango No Sekku)
Around 1200 B.C., the Chinese first used kites to communicate between various army units. Now kites are used only for fun. For a free kite catalog, write to: *Into the Wind* Catalog, 1408 Pearl Street, Boulder, CO 80302-5307.

National Bad Guy Day
Al Capone went to prison in 1932; celebrate the imprisonment of all deserving bad guys. *Sponsor:* The Life of the Party. ✉

National Correctional Officers Week
Celebrated the first full week in May.

National Drinking Water Week
Celebrated the first full week in May.

National Family Week
Honors the family; begins the first Sunday in May. Traditionally celebrated by many Christian churches.

National Pet Week
The first full week in May promotes veterinary services available for family pets. For a free *Traveling with Your Pet* brochure, send a business-size SASE to the following address. *Sponsor:* American Veterinary Medical Association, 1931 N. Meacham Road #100, Schaumburg, IL 60173-4360; 708-925-8070; Fax: 708-925-1329.

National Postcard Week
The first full week in May promotes collecting and using postcards. *Sponsor:* Postcard Historical Society, John McClintock, P.O. Box 1765, Manassas, VA 22110; 703-365-2757.

National Raisin Week
Celebrated the first full week in May.

National Self-Help Book Week

Read a self-help book, especially during the first full week in May. *Sponsor:* Deaconess Press, Robert Jackson, Consultant, 1555 Black Oaks Lane N, Plymouth, MN 55447; 612-375-0141.

National Suicide Prevention Week

Almost 30,000 Americans kill themselves every year. Suicide is the third leading cause of death among young people age 15 to 24. Be alert to warning signs of potential suicides. Celebrated the first week in May. *Sponsor:* American Association of Suicidology, Alan Berman, 4201 Connecticut Avenue NW #310, Washington, DC 20008; 202-237-2280; Fax: 202-237-2282.

National Tourism Week

The week starting with the first Sunday in May celebrates the tourism industry, the second largest employer in the U.S. *Sponsor:* Tourism Works for America Council, 1100 New York Avenue NW #450, Washington, DC 20005-3934; 202-408-8422; Fax: 202-408-1255; e-mail: ckeefe@tia.org.

O. Henry Pun-Off for the World Championship

An annual competition held on the first Sunday in May; crowns the world championship punner of the year. *Sponsor:* O. Henry Museum, Punsters United Nearly Yearly, 409 E. Fifth Street, Austin, TX 78701; 512-472-1903; Fax: 515-472-2174.

Party Party Day

An excuse to have a party once a month (when the day equals the month). *Sponsor:* Bonza Bottler Day. ✉

PTA Teacher Appreciation Week

During the first full week in May, the PTA says thank you to America's teachers. *Sponsor:* National PTA, 330 N. Wabash Avenue #2100, Chicago, IL 60611-3690; 312-670-6782; Fax: 312-670-6783.

Screwtop bottle with pourable lip patented (1936)

Singapore Caning Day

In 1994, Singapore officials caned American teenager Michael Fay for the crime of vandalism. He was struck by the cane 4 times. *Contact:* Republic of Singapore Embassy, 1824 R Street NW, Washington, DC 20009; 202-667-7555.

Women Journalists Day

On the birthday of Nelly Bly, once called the best reporter in America, all women journalists are honored. Bly was born in 1867 in Armstrong County, Pennsylvania.

May 6

4-minute mile broken (1954)

Roger Bannister ran the first mile in less than 4 minutes (3:59:04) during a track meet at Oxford, England.

American Lung Association first meeting (1904)

Contact: American Lung Association, 1740 Broadway, New York, NY 10019-4374; 212-315-8700; Fax: 212-315-8872.

Childcare Awareness Week

The first full week in May (Monday through Friday) honors all childcare providers. *Sponsor:* A Choice Nanny, 2126 W. Newport Pike #104, Wilmington, DE 19804; 302-995-1120.

English Chunnel opened (1994)

The tunnel under the English Channel runs between the United Kingdom and France.

First athletic club in the U.S.

The Olympic Club opened in 1860.

✉ Addresses for frequently cited organizations are gathered on pages vii–viii.

First major drawbridge accident (1853)

A New Haven Railroad train crashed through an open drawbridge and plunged into the Norwalk River; 46 people died.

Gillikins of Oz Day

Celebrates the birthday of L. Frank Baum, author of the *Wizard of Oz* books. *Sponsor:* International Wizard of Oz Club, Fred Meyer, 220 North 11th Street, Escanaba, MI 49829.

Great Lakes Awareness Day

The Monday of the first full week in May encourages more ecological use and preservation of the Great Lakes.

Hindenburg Disaster (1937)

The German dirigible crashed in Lakehurst, New Jersey, killing 36 of the 97 passengers.

Just Say No Week

Just say no to drugs during the second week of May—and for the rest of the year as well! *Sponsor:* Just Say No International, 2101 Webster Street #1300, Oakland, CA 94612; 800-258-2766; Fax: 510-451-9360.

The Martians Are Coming Day

Celebrate otherworldly creatures on the birthday of Orson Welles, the man who brought us the "War of the Worlds" broadcast. *Sponsor:* The Life of the Party. ✉

Melanoma Monday

Every year 34,000 Americans get skin cancer. Begin a habit on the first Monday of May of examining your skin for the early warning signs of skin cancer: new moles; changes in the size, color, shape, or texture of a mole; or unusual changes in your skin. *Sponsor:* American Academy of Dermatology, P.O. Box 4014, Schaumburg, IL 60168-4014; 708-330-0230; Fax: 708-330-0050.

National Herb Week

Monday through Sunday, ending with Mother's Day. Educates the public about how herbs and spices play a positive role in our lives. Eat some herbs this week. *Sponsor:* International Herb Growers and Marketers Association, 1202 Allanson Road, Mundelein, IL 60060; 708-949-4372; Fax: 708-566-4580.

National Nurses Week

To honor all nurses. *Sponsor:* American Nurses Association, 600 Maryland Avenue SW #100W, Washington, DC 20024-2571; 202-651-7000; 800-274-4262; Fax: 202-651-7001.

National Walking Week

Recently approved by both houses of Congress, always celebrated the first full week in May (from Monday to Sunday). *Sponsor: Prevention Magazine*, 33 E. Minor Street, Em-

maus, PA 18098; 215-967-5171; Fax: 215-967-8963.

Public Service Recognition Week

Founded in 1985, the first week (from Monday to Sunday) honors social workers, police officers, rangers, and other government workers. *Sponsor:* Public Employees Roundtable, P.O. Box 14270, Washington, DC 20044-4270; 202-927-5000; Fax: 202-927-5001.

Refrigerator patented (1851)

John Farrie patented a refrigeration machine.

Tax Freedom Day

In 1995, most Americans had to work until May 6th just to pay their tax bills. This day is calculated in the spring of each year by projecting the total taxes as a percentage of total national income. Chances are that the 1996 date will be later. *Sponsor:* Tax Foundation, 1250 H Street NW #750, Washington, DC 20005; 202-783-2760; Fax: 202-942-7676.

May 7

American Medical Association founded (1847)

The AMA was founded in Philadelphia, Pennsylvania. *Contact:* American Medical Association, 515 N.

State Street, 17th Floor, Chicago, IL 60610; 312-464-5000; Fax: 312-464-5839.

Beaufort Scale Day

Sir Francis Beaufort (born 1774) devised the Beaufort scale to describe wind velocities from 0 (calm) to 12 (hurricane force).

Beethoven's Ninth Symphony premiered (1824)

Ludwig von Beethoven premiered the symphony in Vienna, Austria.

Fire escape ladder patented (1878)

Black inventor J. R. Winters received a patent for the fire escape ladder.

First presidential inaugural ball (1789)

Held for President George Washington in New York City.

National Paste-Up Day

Honors people who paste up newspapers, magazines, books, and other printed materials. *Sponsor:* Foto News, Julie Sjuggerud, 805 E. Main Street, P.O. Box 606, Merrill, WI 54452; 715-536-7121.

National Teacher Day

On the Tuesday of the first full week in May, take time to honor the teachers of your children. *Sponsor:* National Education Association, 1201 16th Street NW, Washington, DC 20036; 202-822-7200.

Saint Notkar Balbulus Feast Day

Because he himself was a stammerer, he is a patron saint of stammering children. He is also a patron saint of musicians.

School Family Day

Recognizes the important role the family plays in the education of children. *Sponsor:* National Education Association.

May 8

Coca-Cola introduced (1886)

John Pemberton, Atlanta pharmacist, concocted Coca-Cola on March 29th and introduced it to the public on this day in 1886. *Contact:* Coca-Cola, Inc., P.O. Box 1734, Atlanta, GA 30301; 404-676-2121; 800-438-2653; Fax: 404-676-6792.

First automobile precurser patented in U.S. (1879)

First eye bank opened (1944)

First major train wreck (1842)

Fifty-three people were killed in the wreck, near Bellevue, France.

Harry S Truman's Birthday

Harry S Truman, the 33rd President of the U.S., was born 1884 near Lamar, Missouri. Truman Day is a public holiday in Missouri. *Contact:* Missouri Division of Tourism, P.O. Box 1055, Jefferson City, MO 65102; 314-751-4133.

Joan of Arc Day (France)

Saint Joan, born in 1412, is the patron saint of France. She was burned at the stake in 1431. The French celebrate this day to honor this hero and martyr. *Contact:* French Embassy, 4101 Reservoir Road NW, Washington, DC 20007; 202-944-6000.

National Receptionists Day

The second Wednesday of May celebrates receptionists, those who greet you at the door of businesses. *Sponsor:* National Receptionists Society, Jennifer Alexander, 51 Oakwood Trail, Sparta, NJ 07871; 201-729-1903.

National Third Shift Workers Day

The second Wednesday in May honors the much-forgotten folks on the night shift. *Sponsor:* Davis Community Hospital, Jeff Corbett, P.O. Box 1823, Statesville, NC 28687; 704-838-7105; Fax: 704-838-7111.

National Tourism Day

The Wednesday of the first full week in May promotes tourism, which is the second largest employer in the U.S.. Also known as National Tourist Appreciation Day. *Sponsor:* Tourism Works for America Council, Cathy Keefe, 1100 New York Avenue NW #450, Washington, DC 20005-3934; 202-408-8422; Fax: 202-408-1255; e-mail: ckeefe@tia.org.

No Socks Day

If you don't wear socks today, you'll feel a little freer. *Sponsor:* Wellness Permission League. ✉

Senior Citizens Day

Older Americans Month grew out of this day-long celebration.

V-E Day (1945)

Victory in Europe Day was when the German army surrendered, thus ending World War II.

World Red Cross Day

Celebrates the birthday of Red Cross founder, Jean Henry Dunant of Switzerland. *Sponsor:* American Red Cross Headquarters, 17th and D Streets, Washington, DC 20006-5399; 202-737-8300.

May 9

17th Amendment to the Constitution ratified (1913)

Called for the direct election of U.S. senators.

Dagwood's Birthday

In 1995, the *Blondie* comic strip wished Dagwood Bumstead a happy birthday. *Contact:* King Features Syndicate, 235 East 45th Street, New York, NY 10017; 212-682-5600.

Delivery Room Thursday

On May 11, 1995, TV viewers were treated to back-to-back births on *Friends* and *ER*. As a result, David Hiltbrand, TV critic for *People* magazine named that day Delivery Room Thursday, now celebrated on the 2nd Thursday of May. *Contact:* People Magazine, David Hiltbrand, TV Critic, 1271 Ave of Americas, New York, NY 10020-1303; 212-586-1212.

First American newspaper cartoon published (1754)

Published in the *Benjamin Franklin's Pennsylvania Gazette*.

First flight over the North Pole (1926)

Richard Byrd and Floyd Bennett made the first flight over the North Pole.

Hurray for Buttons Day

In 1247, the button hole was invented. *Sponsor:* A Pilgrim's Almanac. ✉

Lawn mower patented (1899)

Peter Pan Day

James Matthew Barrie, author of *Peter Pan* and other children's stories, was born in 1860 in Scotland. Let's all think happy thoughts and fly today!

Public sale of contraceptive pills approved (1960)

Contact: Food and Drug Administration, 5600 Fishers Lane #14-71, Rockville, MD 20857; 301-443-2410; Fax: 301-443-0755.

Tear the Tags Off the Mattress Day

Go ahead: under penalty of law, remove that tag! Go ahead: do it! *Sponsor:* The Life of the Party. ✉

Vast Wasteland Day

In 1961, FCC Chairman Newton Minow called television a vast wasteland.

May 10

First planetarium in the U.S. opened (1930)

Contact: Adler Planetarium, 1300 S. Lake Shore Drive, Chicago, IL 60605; 312-322-0304; Fax: 312-322-2257.

First woman to run for U.S. president (1872)

Victoria Woodhull, the first female presidential candidate, was born in 1838.

Golden Spike Day

In 1869, the first transcontinental railroad was completed at Promontory Point, Utah.

International Barbecue Festival

The barbecue capital of the world celebrates this international festival every year on the second Friday and Saturday of May. A cook-off determines the barbecue champion of the world. *Sponsor:* BBQ Festival, P.O. Box 434, Owensboro, KY 42302; 502-926-6938; 502-926-6938.

Mandela Inauguration Day

In 1994, long-time political prisoner Nelson Mandela, was inaugurated as the first black president of South Africa after winning the first free election in South Africa's history. *Contact:* Republic of South Africa Embassy, 3051 Massachusetts Avenue NW, Washington, DC 20008; 202-232-4400.

May 11

Budapest World's Fair

Begins on May 11 and ends on October 4, 1996.

Chair's Birthday

The chair was invented in 2181 B.C. Note: This date may well be facetious.

Computer core memory patented (1951)

Jay Forrester patented computer core memory.

Fire Insurance Day

The first U.S. fire insurance policy was issued in Philadelphia, Pennsylvania in 1752.

Glacier National Park established (1910)

Contact: Glacier National Park, West Glacier, MT 59936; 406-888-5441.

International Community Service Days

On the second weekend in May, people help each other fix up and beautify their own community. *Sponsor:* Sterling Community Service Foundation.

Jamestown Landing Day

The first permanent English settlement was established in 1607 in Jamestown, Virginia. *Contact:* Jamestown Yorktown Foundation, P.O. Box JF, Williamsburg, VA 23187; 804-253-4838.

Let's Go Fishing Day

On the Saturday before Mother's Day, take time out to go fishing.

Minnesota Admission Day

In 1858, Minnesota became the 32nd state. *Contact:* Minnesota Office of Tourism, 250 Skyway Level, 375 Jackson Street, Saint Paul, MN 55101; 612-296-5029; 800-657-3700; Fax: 612-296-7095.

National Bake Sale Day

Always on the second Saturday of May. Also National Garage Sale Day. *Sponsor:* All My Events. ✉

National Feminist Bookstore Week

Founded in 1995, celebrates feminist bookstores and draws attention to the importance of specialty, community, and independent bookstores. Celebrated from Saturday to Saturday, including Mother's Day. *Sponsor:* Feminist Bookstore Network, Carol Seajay, P.O. Box 882554, San Francisco, CA 94188; 415-626-1556.

Surrealistic Art Day

On the birthday of Salvador Dali, whose unusual art made him one of the leading figures of surrealism, celebrate modern art in all its forms. Dali was born in 1904 in Figueras, Spain.

Tubeless Tire Birthday

In 1947, B. F. Goodrich announced that it had developed a tubeless tire. *Contact:* B F. Goodrich, 3925 Embassy Parkway, Akron, OH 44333; 216-374-2000; Fax: 216-374-2333.

White Christmas in May

On the birthday of songwriter Irving Berlin, celebrate a white Christmas in May. Berlin was born Israel Isidore Baline in 1888 in Russia. *Sponsor:* The Life of the Party. ✉

May 12

Alcohol and Other Drug-Related Birth Defects Week

To show the connection between birth defects and chemical abuse. *Sponsor:* National Council on Alcoholism, 12 West 21st Street, New York, NY 10010; 212-206-6770; Fax: 212-645-1690.

Boycott Veal Day

This event is held on Mother's Day, and encourages people to stop eating veal. The production of veal involves cruelty to calves; also known as Veal Ban Action Day. *Sponsor:* Farm Animal Reform Movement, P.O. Box 30654, Bethesda, MD 20824; 301-530-1737; Fax: 301-530-5747.

Emergency Medical Services Week

Always the second full week in May.

First black to pitch a major league no-hitter (1955)

Chicago Cubs pitcher Sam Jones was the first black to pitch a no-hitter in major league baseball. *Contact:* Major League Baseball. ✉

Fractured English Day

On the birthday of Yogi Berra, baseball player and coach who was famous for fracturing the English language, it's okay to dangle modifiers and split infinitives. Berra was born in 1925 in St. Louis, Missouri.

Girls Incorporated Week

Formerly the Girls Clubs, Girls, Inc. focuses on the needs and rights of girls; celebrated during the week of the second Sunday. *Sponsor:* Girls Incorporated, 30 East 33rd Street, 7th Floor, New York, NY 10016; 212-689-3700; Fax: 212-683-1253.

Infant Mortality Awareness Day

Always celebrated on Mother's Day.

Kiwanis Prayer Week

The second full week in May promotes religion in Kiwanis hometowns. *Sponsor:* Kiwanis International. ✉

Limerick Day

Celebrates the birthday of Edward Lear (1812), whose *Book of Nonsense* popularized limericks.

Mother Ocean Day

On the same day as Mother's Day, cast a rose into the ocean as a symbol of appreciation for its many resources. *Sponsor:* National Week of the Ocean, Cynthia Hancock, P.O. Box 179, Fort Lauderdale, FL 33302; 305-462-5573; Fax: 305-463-9730.

Mother's Day

First observed on May 10, 1908 (in Philadelphia, Pennsylvania, and Grafton, West Virginia), the second Sunday in May honors all mothers. Anna Jarvis asked her church to hold a special service on the anniversary of her mother's death. *Contact:* International Mother's Day Shrine, Andrews Methodist Church, Grafton, WV 26354; 304-265-1177.

National Hamburger Week

Celebrated the second full week of May. *Sponsor:* White Castle Systems, 555 W. Goodale Street, Columbus, OH 43215-1171; 614-228-5781.

National Historic Preservation Week

The second full week of May spotlights historic preservation attempts everywhere. *Sponsor:* The National Trust for Historic Preservation, 1785 Massachusetts Avenue

✉ Addresses for frequently cited organizations are gathered on pages vii–viii.

MAY   111

NW, Washington, DC 20036; 202-673-4141; Fax: 202-673-4299.

National Hospital Week
The week of May 12th focuses attention on the contributions of hospitals. *Sponsor:* American Hospital Association, P.O. Box 1100, Sacramento, CA 95812-1100; 916-552-7504; 800-621-9212.

National Nurses Day
Florence Nightingale, founder of the nursing profession, was born in Florence, Italy in 1820. *Sponsor:* American Nurses Association, 600 Maryland Avenue SW #100W, Washington, DC 20024-2571; 202-651-7000; 800-274-4262; Fax: 202-651-7001.

National Nursing Home Week
Celebrated the week of the second Sunday in May, introduces people to the services of nursing homes. *Sponsor:* American Health Care Association, 1201 L Street NW, Washington, DC 20005; 202-842-4444; Fax: 202-842-3860.

National Osteoporosis Prevention Week
The week of Mother's Day is designed to help people suffering from excessive loss of bone tissue. *Sponsor:* National Osteoporosis Foundation, 1150 17th Street NW #500, Washington, DC 20036; 202-223-2226; 800-223-9994; Fax: 202-223-2237.

National Police Week
The week of the 15th honors America's law enforcement officers. *Sponsor:* National Association of Police Chiefs, 3801 Biscayne Boulevard, Miami, FL 33137; 305-573-0070; Fax: 305-573-9819.

National Safe Kids Week
Keep children safe by using child safety seats and smoke detectors; also teach them to ride bicycles safely. Always celebrated the second week of May. Safe Kids Week Hotline: 301-650-8296. Send $1.00 for *Safe Kids Are No Accident* booklet. *Sponsor:* National Safe Kids Campaign, 111 Michigan Avenue NW, Washington, DC 20010-2970; 202-939-4993; Fax: 301-650-8038.

National Stuttering Awareness Week
Celebrated the second full week of May. Send $3.00 for the book, *Self-Therapy for the Stutterer;* or send $1.00 for *Stuttering and Your Child: Questions*

and Answers. *Sponsor:* Stuttering Foundation of America, P.O. Box 11749, Memphis, TN 38111-0749; 800-992-9392; Fax: 901-452-3931.

National Transportation Week
Since 1957, celebrated the week with the third Friday in May. Also known as National Defense Transportation Week.

Prohibition of Spitting (1896)
The New York City Department of Health issued an ordinance that prohibited spitting on sidewalks.

Rural Life Sunday
Many churches celebrate this Sunday to recognize that the Earth first belongs to God. Humans have a responsibility to take care of the Earth and use it wisely. Also known as Rogation Sunday and Soil Stewardship Sunday.

Saint Pancras Feast Day
This 14-year-old Syrian orphan was martyred in 309 A.D. He is a patron saint of children, treaties, and oaths.

Small Business Week
The second full week in May honors small businesses. *Contact:* Small Business Administration, 409 Third Street SW, 7th Floor, Washington, DC 20416; 202-205-6606; 800-232-0082.

Universal Family Week
Since 1989, celebrated the second full week in May, highlights the

role of families in making the world a better place. *Sponsor:* International Society of Friendship and Good Will. ✉

Women's Hurricane Liberation Day

In 1978, the Department of Commerce officially announced that hurricanes would no longer be named after women only. *Contact:* Department of Commerce, 14th Street and Constitution Avenue, Washington, DC 20230; 202-482-2000; 800-424-5197; Fax: 202-482-3772.

Woodmen Rangers Day

The Woodmen Rangers were founded in 1903. *Contact:* Woodmen of the World, 1700 Farnam, Omaha, NE 68102; 402-271-7258; Fax: 402-271-7269.

May 13

Cold Feet Monday

On May 15, 1995, the lead characters in *The Fresh Prince of Bel Air* and *Murphy Brown* called their weddings off. David Hiltbrand, TV critic for *People* magazine, named it Cold Feet Monday. Now celebrated on the Monday after the second Thursday in May. *Contact: People* magazine, David Hiltbrand, TV Critic, 1271 Avenue of the Americas, New York, NY 10020-1303; 212-586-1212.

Daughter's Day of Rest

According to the *Sisters* TV show, daughters deserve a day to themselves to rest after visiting with their mothers on Mother's Day.

First air mail stamp in the U.S. (1918)

This air mail stamp was also the first to depict an airplane, and was the first stamp printed in two colors. *Contact:* U.S. Postal Service. ✉

First cross-country helicopter flight (1942)

First printing press in the U.S. patented (1821)

I Just Called to Say I Love You Day

On the birthday of Stevie Wonder, call someone you love and tell them so. Stevie Wonder was born in 1951 in Saginaw, Michigan. *Sponsor:* All My Events. ✉

Leprechaun Day

National Educational Bosses Week

The week after Teacher Appreciation Week recognizes the importance of those who support teachers: the office personnel and, especially, the top leaders (principals and superintendents). *Sponsor:* National Association of Educational Office Personnel, P.O. Box 12619, Wichita, KS 67277.

National Salvation Army Week

The second full week of May honors those who volunteer to help the needy. *Sponsor:* Salvation Army, 615 Slaters Lane, P.O. Box 269, Alexandria, VA 22313; 703-684-5500; Fax: 703-684-3478.

Our Lady of Fatima Day

In 1917, Mary first appeared as the Virgin of the Rosary to 3 shepherd children in Fatima, Portugal. *Contact:* Portuguese National Tourist Office, 590 Fifth Avenue, 4th Floor, New York, NY 10036-4704; 212-354-4403; 800-767-8842; Fax: 212-764-6137.

Saint Lawrence Seaway Act Anniversary (1954)

President Eisenhower signed the act establishing the Saint Lawrence Seaway between the U.S. and Canada. The Seaway allows ocean-going vessels to travel the Great Lakes.

U.S.-Mexico War declared (1846)

May 14

Condensed milk patented (1853)

Gail Borden applied for a patent for condensed milk. *Contact:* Borden, Inc., 180 E. Broad Street, Columbus, OH 43215; 614-225-4000; Fax: 614-225-3382.

First smallpox vaccination (1796)
Edward Jenner, an English physician, administered the first smallpox vaccination.

Lewis and Clark Expedition began (1804)
Lewis and Clark took off from Saint Louis, Missouri, on their cross-country exploration.

Skylab (first U.S. manned space station) launched (1973)
Contact: NASA. ✉

Star Wars Day
Celebrate the birthday of George Lucas, who brought us the *Star Wars* trilogy, by working to establish a true human presence in space. Lucas was born in 1944 in Modesto, California, a town he immortalized in *American Graffiti*. *Sponsor*: The Life of the Party. ✉

Stars and Stripes Forever Day
In 1897, John Philip Sousa's march was performed for the first time.

U.S. Department of Health and Human Services inaugurated (1980)
Contact: Department of Health and Human Services, 200 Independence Avenue SW, Washington, DC 20201-0001; 202-245-7000; Fax: 202-245-7203.

Underground America Day
Founded in 1964, this day encourages people to build their homes underground (as a way to help turn America green again). Such homes are fire safe, silent, and easy to maintain. *Sponsor*: Malcolm Wells, Architect, 673 Satucket Road, Brewster, MA 02631; 508-896-6850; Fax: 508-896-5116.

Women's Auxiliary Army Corps created (1942)
The WAACs were created by an act of Congress to allow women to serve in a noncombatant capacity. *Contact*: Department of the Army, Pentagon, Washington, DC 20310; 703-695-5135; Fax: 703-614-8533.

May 15

Cape Cod Discovery Day
In 1602, the English navigator Bartholomew Gosnold discovered Cape Cod. *Sponsor*: Cape Cod Chamber of Commerce, Routes 6 & 132, P.O. Box 16, Hyannis, MA 02601-0016; 508-362-3225; Fax: 508-362-3698.

First female U.S. generals appointed (1970)
President Nixon appointed Elizabeth Hoisington and Anna Mae Mays.

First oceanarium opened (1937)

First regularly scheduled air mail in U.S. (1918)
Service was between New York and Washington, DC, with a stop in Philadelphia, Pennsylvania. *Contact*: U.S. Postal Service. ✉

International Day of Families
Declared in 1993 by the U.N. General Assembly. *Sponsor*: United Nations. ✉

National Employee Health and Fitness Day
The third Wednesday in May encourages workplace fitness programs. *Sponsor*: National Association of Governors, Councils on Physical Fitness, 201 S. Capitol Avenue #560, Indianapolis, IN 46225; 317-237-5630.

Never Turn Your Back on the Ocean Day
Why? Because it might be waving at you.

Nylons Day
Nylon stockings went on sale nationally in 1940. *Contact*: E. I. duPont de Nemours and Company, 1007 Market Street, Wilmington, DE 19898; 302-774-1000.

Peace Officers Memorial Day
Honors police officers killed in the line of duty. *Sponsor*: National Association of Police Chiefs, 3801 Biscayne Boulevard, Miami, FL 33137; 305-573-0070; Fax: 305-573-9819.

Saint Isidore the Farmer Feast Day
Patron saint of farmers, laborers, and rural communities.

✉ Addresses for frequently cited organizations are gathered on pages vii–viii.

Stewardess Day

In 1930, Ellen Church became the first airline stewardess. She flew on a United Airlines flight between San Francisco, California, and Cheyenne, Wyoming.

Working Solo Day

Celebrates the most dynamic sector of the small business market: individuals who are working as independent entrepreneurs. Working Solo is a registered trademark of Terri Lonier. *Sponsor:* Portico Press, Terri Lonier, P.O. Box 190, New Paltz, New York 12561; 914-255-7165; Fax: 914-255-2116; e-mail: lonier@aol.com.

May 16

Academy Awards Birthday

The first Oscars were presented at the Hollywood Roosevelt Hotel in 1929. *Wings* won for best movie; Janet Gaynor won for best actress; Emil Jannings won for best actor. *Contact:* Academy of Motion Picture Arts and Sciences, 8949 Wilshire Boulevard, Beverly Hills, CA 90211; 310-247-3000; Fax: 310-859-9619.

Ascension Thursday

The day Jesus Christ ascended into heaven (40 days after Easter).

Biographers Day

In 1763, James Boswell first met Samuel Johnson, the subject of his famous biography. Read or write a biography today.

Celebrated Jumping Frog of Calaveras County

Recreating the famous frog jumping contest described by Mark Twain, this jubilee features frog jumping contests on Friday, Saturday, and Sunday of the third weekend in May. *Sponsor:* Calaveras County Fair, Angels Camp Chamber of Commerce, P.O. Box 489, Angels Camp, CA 95222; 209-736-2561; Fax: 209-736-2476.

Don't Light My Fire Day

On this date in 1988, cigarettes were declared to be addictive. *Sponsor:* The Life of the Party. ✉

First woman to scale Mount Everest (1975)

Junko Tabei, a Japanese climber, was the first woman to scale Mount Everest. On September 29, 1988, Stacy Allison became the first American woman to climb Mount Everest.

Food stamps introduced (1939)

Mississippi River steamboat service began (1817)

The trip from New Orleans, Louisiana, to Louisville, Kentucky, took 25 days.

Nickel's Birthday

The U.S. nickel was first coined in 1866.

Saint Brendan the Navigator Feast Day

This Irish monk is considered a patron saint of sailors. He is rumored to have traveled to North America long before Columbus or Lief Erickson.

Saint John of Nepomuk Feast Day

Patron saint of discretion, Bohemia, Czechoslovakia, bridges, running water, and silence.

Spending Freedom Day

Since the U.S. government has been spending more money than it receives through taxes, Spending Freedom Day is celebrated about 10 days after Tax Freedom Day. *Sponsor:* Tax Foundation, 1250 H Street NW #750, Washington, DC 20005; 202-783-2760; Fax: 202-942-7676.

Table Knife Birthday
In 1639, French Cardinal Richelieu invented the table knife by ordering that any knives at his table be rounded off at the tip.

Wear Purple for Peace Day
According to The Moderns, this is the First Intergallactic Holiday. The Moderns believe it is essential to work for peace if we hope to be contacted by the people of outer space. *Sponsor:* The Moderns, Jon E. Mod, 4915 Eighth Avenue, Kenosha, WI 53140; 414-653-0230.

May 17

Brown vs Board of Education Anniversary (1954)
The Supreme Court outlawed segregated schools, saying that segregation solely on the basis of race denied black children equal educational opportunities. *Contact:* U.S. Supreme Court. ✉

First Kentucky Derby run (1875)
Aristides became the first horse to win the Kentucky Derby at Churchill Downs. *Contact:* Kentucky Derby Museum, 704 Central Avenue, Louisville, KY 40208; 502-637-1111.

First platinum album on day of release (1975)
Elton John's *Captain Fantastic and the Brown Dirt Cowboy* sold 1 million copies in one day in 1975.

First sports event televised (1939)
NBC broadcast a basketball game between Princeton and Columbia. *Contact:* NBC-TV. ✉

First state to ban sex discrimination (1971)
Washington was the first state to ban sex discrimination.

First Wild West Show (1883)
Buffalo Bill Cody presented the first wild west show in Omaha, Nebraska.

International Pickle Week
Take a crunchy bite out of the world's funniest food during the last two weekends in May (Friday to Monday). *Sponsor:* Pickle Packers International, DHM Group, Department P, P.O. Box 767, Holmdel, NJ 07733; 908-975-9675; Fax: 908-946-3343.

National Memo Day
Write a memo against memos. Take a memo. Post a memo. Formerly sponsored by KMJI Radio on the third Friday of May.

National Morel Hunting Championships
This annual celebration, held the weekend after Mother's Day, crowns the national champion mushroom hunter. *Contact:* Mushroom Festival Committee, P.O. Box 5, Boyne City, MI 49712.

New York Stock Exchange established (1792)
The largest stock exchange in the U.S. began as a simple meeting of brokers under a tree on Wall Street. *Contact:* New York Stock Exchange, 11 Wall Street, New York, NY 10005; 212-656-3000; Fax: 212-656-5725.

Rubber Band Birthday
The rubber band was patented in 1845.

Saint Madron Feast Day
Saint Madron's chapel in Cornwall, England, has been associated with miraculous cures from pain; Saint Madron is considered a patron saint of cures from pain.

Walk for the Cure
This national walk event in over 80 cities raises funds for diabetes research and prevention. While this event is recommended to be held on the third weekend in March, some cities hold it on other weekends. *Sponsor:* Juvenile Diabetes Foundation, 120 Wall Street, New York, NY 10005; 212-785-9500.

World Champion Lutefisk Eating Contest

On the weekend nearest the 17th, Viking Fest sponsors a contest to determine the world champion lutefisk eater. *Sponsor:* Viking Fest, Poulsbo, WA; 206-697-2011.

World Telecommunications Day

This day celebrates the electronic age of communications. *Sponsor:* United Nations. ✉

May 18

Armed Forces Day

Since 1950, this day has been celebrated on the third Saturday in May.

Blow Your Top Day

On the anniversary of the eruption of Mount Saint Helens, you also have the right to blow your top—as long as you do it with style and grace. *Sponsor:* The Life of the Party. ✉

First lawn mower ad (1831)

Edwin Budding built the first lawn mower.

First state to make school attendance mandatory

In 1852, Massachusetts passed a law requiring all school age children to attend school.

First woman to break the sound barrier (1953)

Jacqueline Cochran broke the sound barrier as she flew an F-86 over the California desert near Rogers Dry Lake.

Head Start's Birthday

Head Start is designed to help underprivileged children get a head start in school. Call 1-800-27-START for a brochure on volunteer opportunities. *Contact:* Department of Education, 400 Maryland Avenue SW #2089, Washington, DC 20202; 202-401-1576; Fax: 202-272-5447.

Herb Day

The third Saturday in May is set aside to learn more about herbs: how to grow them, how to use them, and why to use them.

International Migratory Bird Day

On the third Saturday in May, take the time to learn more about migratory birds and how you can help them. Also take a hike to bird watch.

International Museum Day

Celebrate the role of the world's museums in furthering human understanding. *Sponsor:* American Association of Museums, 1225 Eye Street NW #200, Washington, DC 20005; 202-289-1818; Fax: 202-289-6578.

Islamic New Year (Muharram)

At sundown, year 1417 of the Islamic Era begins. This day commemorates Prophet Muhammad's flight from Mecca to Medina (the Hegira), the first major event in the development of Islam. 1997: May 8; 1998: April 27.

Kids Helping Kids Day

Celebrated on the third Saturday in May. *Sponsor:* All My Events. ✉

Montreal's Birthday

The Canadian city was founded in 1642. *Contact:* Montreal Tourism Bureau, 1555 Peel Street #600, Montreal, Quebec H3A 1X6 Canada; 514-844-5400; Fax: 514-844-5757.

National Defense Transportation Day

Celebrated since 1957 by presidential proclamation on the third Friday in May.

National Pike Festival

During the third weekend in May, communities along the National Pike (U.S. 40 from Baltimore, Maryland, to Wheeling, West Virginia) celebrate the longest festival in the world. U.S. 40 was the first national road and the first to receive federal funds. *Sponsor:* Washington

County Tourism, 1826-C Dual Highway, Hagerstown, MD 21740; 800-228-7829; Fax: 301-791-2601.

Preakness Stakes
Since 1873, the second horse race of the Triple Crown is held on the third Saturday in May. *Sponsor:* Maryland Jockey Club, Plimico Race Course, Baltimore, MD 21215; 410-542-9400.

Tennessee Valley Authority created (1933)
Contact: Tennessee Valley Authority, 400 W. Summit Hill Drive, Knoxville, TN 37902; 615-632-8063; Fax: 615-632-6634.

Visit Your Relatives Day
Renew family ties. *Sponsor:* Ann Chase Moeller, P.O. Box 71, Clio, MI 48420; 810-687-0423.

World Champion Pickle Juice Drinking Contest
On the third weekend in May, Atkins hosts two world champion events: pickle juice drinking and pickle eating. Atkins is the home of the fried dill pickle. *Sponsor:* Pickle Fest, Brian Miller, 611 N. Church, Atkins, AR 72823; 501-641-2785.

World Championship Steak Cook-Off
Founded in 1989, this cook-off awards prizes for showmanship, best looking rig, and best-tasting steak. Always held on the third Saturday in May. *Sponsor:* Magnolia

Blossom Festival, Ray Sullivent, 420 E. Main, Magnolia, AR 71753; 501-234-6122; 501-234-4352.

May 19

Boys Clubs of America Birthday
The forerunner of the Boys Clubs, the Federated Boys' Clubs, was organized in 1906. *Sponsor:* Boys and Girls Clubs of America, 1230 W. Peachtree Street NW, Atlanta, GA 30309; 404-815-5700; Fax: 404-815-5787.

Circus Day
The first Ringling Brothers circus was performed in 1884. *Contact:* Ringling Brothers Circus, 8607 Westwood Center Drive, Vienna, VA 22182; 703-448-4000; Fax: 703-448-4100.

Dow Jones industrial average first hit 2500 (1989)
Contact: Dow Jones & Company, 200 Liberty Street, New York, NY

10281; 212-416-2000; 800-831-1234; Fax: 212-416-2658.

First department store opened (1848)

First federation of American colonies (1643)
Representatives from the colonies of Connecticut, Massachusetts Bay, New Haven, and Plymouth met in Boston to form the United Colonies of New England.

First fingerprint conviction (1911)
In New York, a burglar named Crispey was sentenced to 6 months.

First woman to fly solo across the Atlantic Ocean
In 1932, Amelia Earhart became the first woman to fly solo across the Atlantic Ocean, from Newfoundland to Londonderry, Ireland.

Fish Culture Hall of Fame Day
New members are inducted into the Fish Culture Hall of Fame on the third Sunday in May. *Sponsor:* Fish Culture Hall of Fame, D. C. Booth Fish Hatchery, 423 Hatchery Circle, Spearfish, SD 57783; 605-642-7730; Fax: 605-642-2336.

Malcolm X's Birthday
Malcolm X, a black nationalist and activist, was born in Omaha, Nebraska, in 1925.

May Ray Day

Enjoy the sunny days to come. Also honors people named Ray (it's the birthday of the sponsor's brother Ray). *Sponsor:* The Fifth Wheel Tavern, Richard Ankli, 639 Fifth Street, Ann Arbor, MI 48103; e-mail: rankli@umich.edu.

Mufflers Day

According to Tim "The Tool Man" Taylor of the TV sitcom *Home Improvement*, the Sunday after Mother's Day is Mufflers Day (in honor of all those men who forgot to buy something nice for their wives on Mother's Day).

National Bike to Work Week

During the week in May with the third Tuesday, ride your bike to work every day and save gas, get healthy, and enjoy the scenery. *Sponsor:* League of American Bicyclists, 190 W. Ostend Street #120, Baltimore, MD 21230; 410-539-3399.

National Cellular Phone Safety Week

Celebrated the third full week of May.

National Safe Boating Week

The week before Memorial Day is devoted to promoting water safety while boating. *Sponsor:* National Safe Boating Council, U.S. Coast Guard Headquarters, 2100 Second Street SW, Washington, DC 20593; 202-267-1060; 800-368-5647.

National Senior Smile Week

The third week in May promotes dental care for older people. Formerly sponsored by the American Dental Association (312-440-2500).

National Surgical Technologist Week

Always celebrated the week beginning with the third Sunday in May. *Sponsor:* Association of Surgical Technology, 7108-C South Alton Way, Englewood, CO 80112; 303-694-9130.

News Services Week

This week celebrates the week that the Associated Press (22nd) and United Press International (24th) were founded. *Sponsor:* Open Horizons. ✉

North American Air Defense Command established (1958)

The North American Air Defense Command, a joint U.S./Canadian effort, was formally organized.

Peace Day: Discovering Our Common Ground

Sponsored by the Peace Day Project, the third Sunday in May is designed to bring awareness to our common need for peace.

Pneumatic hammer invented (1892)

Charles Brady King of Detroit, Michigan invented the pneumatic hammer.

Public Relations Week

To honor PR people nationwide, and the causes that they promote. Formerly sponsored during the last week in May by Richard Falk, who died in 1994.

Saint Ivo Feast Day

A lawyer himself, Saint Ivo is patron saint of lawyers.

St. Louis Walk of Fame Induction Ceremony

Features celebrities who have lived in St. Louis, including T. S. Eliot, Chuck Berry, Josephine Baker, William Burroughs, Scott Joplin, Masters and Johnson, Stan Musial, Tina Turner, Miles Davis, and others. *Sponsor:* Blueberry Hill, Joe Edwards, 6504 Delmar, St. Louis, MO 63130; 314-727-0880; Fax: 314-727-1288.

Salvation Army Advisory Organizations Sunday

The last day of National Salvation Army Week honors all those who help the Salvation Army in its work for the needy. *Sponsor:* Salvation Army, 615 Slaters Lane, P.O. Box

✉ Addresses for frequently cited organizations are gathered on pages vii–viii.

269, Alexandria, VA 22313; 703-684-5500; Fax: 703-684-3478.

World Trade Week
Celebrated since 1948 by presidential proclamation, the third week in May is designed to encourage world trade.

World's Largest Foot Race
From the bay side of San Francisco to the breakers at Ocean Beach, this 7.5 mile race attracts 100,000 runners every year on the third Sunday in May. It is the world's largest foot race. *Sponsor: Examiner* Bay to Breakers Race, P.O. Box 429200, San Francisco, CA 94142; 415-808-5000, ext. 2222.

Youngest doctor in the world (1995)
Balamurali Ambati, age 17, graduated from Mount Sinai Medical School. He is the youngest known medical doctor in the world. *Contact:* Mount Sinai Medical School, 1 Gustave L. Levy Place, New York, NY 10029; 212-241-6500; Fax: 212-831-1816.

May 20

Are You Somebody? Day
Honors all of us who are good but not yet "somebody." Celebrate you for who you are. Make a list of what you do, what you have done, and what you want to do. Build your self-esteem at the end of the

school year. *Sponsor:* All My Events.
✉

Clothes Dryer's Birthday
George Sampson patented the clothes dryer in 1892.

Eliza Doolittle Day
Promotes speaking one's native language with proper precision; also to honor the heroine of *Pygmalion*, Bernard Shaw's play.

First railroad timetable published (1830)
The Baltimore American published the first railroad timetable to appear in a newspaper.

First school maintained by community taxes (1639)
The city council of Dorchester, Massachusetts, established the first school funded by community taxes.

First working helicopter demonstrated (1940)
Igor Sikorsky invented the helicopter.

Homestead Act signed (1862)
The Homestead Act opened up many more lands for settling.

Lafayette Day (Massachusetts)
Honors the revolutionary hero, the Marquis de Lafayette. *Contact:* Massachusetts Tourism Office, 100 Cambridge Street, 13th Floor, Boston, MA 02202; 617-727-3201; 800-447-6277; Fax: 617-727-6525.

Lindbergh Flight Days
May 20 to 21. Lindbergh ended the first solo airplane flight across the Atlantic Ocean in 1927.

Mecklenburg Independence Day
Commemorates the first signing of a declaration of independence in America. The citizens of Mecklenburg County, North Carolina, signed this declaration in 1775.

National Park Week
During the week before Memorial Day, celebrate our national parks.

Poppy Week
Each year during the week before Memorial Day, the American Legion Auxiliary collects contributions to help hospitalized veterans of wars with their personal needs. *Sponsor:* American Legion Auxiliary, P.O. Box 1055, Indianapolis, IN 46206; 317-635-8411.

Regular transatlantic air service began (1939)
The Pan American Yankee Clipper took off from Port Washington, New York, for Europe.

Right and Left Shoes Day
In 1310, shoes were made for both the right and left feet (the first time since the fall of the Roman Empire).

Show Your Navel Day
Celebrate Cher's birthday by showing your navel. Cherilyn Sarkisian

was born in 1946 in El Centro, California. *Sponsor:* The Life of the Party. ✉

Victoria Day (Canada)
The Monday before the 25th of May is the official holiday commemorating the birthday of Queen Victoria (May 24, 1819). *Contact:* Canadian Embassy, 501 Pennsylvania Avenue NW, Washington, DC 20001; 202-682-1740.

Weights and Measures Day
The International Bureau of Weights and Measures was established in 1875.

World Champion Woodchopper Festival
Lumberjacks from around the world compete for the title of world champion in cross-cut sawing, power sawing, and horizontal and vertical woodchopping. Always held the week before Memorial Day. *Sponsor:* Webster County Woodchopping Festival, John Reed, Webster Springs, WV; 304-847-2454; 800-336-7009 (Pocahontas County Tourism Commission).

May 21

American Red Cross founded (1881)
Clara Barton founded the American Red Cross. *Contact:* American Red Cross Headquarters, 8111 Gatehouse Road, Falls Church, VA

22042; 703-206-6000; Fax: 703-206-7507.

First Democratic National Convention (1832)
Held in Baltimore, Maryland in 1832. *Contact:* Democratic National Committee, 420 S. Capitol Street SE, Washington, DC 20003-4095; 202-863-8000; Fax: 202-863-8081.

First nuclear fusion bomb (1956)
Detonated at Bikini Atoll in the Pacific Ocean, it was also the first airborne hydrogen bomb to be exploded.

First woman to graduate from U.S. service academy
Jean Marie Butler of Treichers, Pennsylvania, graduated from the Coast Guard Academy of New London, Connecticut, in 1980. *Contact:* Coast Guard Academy, 15 Mohegan Avenue, New London, CT 06320-4195; 203-444-8294; Fax: 203-444-8288.

Greek Philosopher's Day
Plato, one of the great Greek philosophers and author of *The Republic* and other books, was born in 429 B.C.

National Bike to Work Day
On the third Tuesday in May, ride your bike to work and save gas, get healthy, and enjoy the scenery. *Sponsor:* League of American Bicyclists, 190 W. Ostend Street #120,

Baltimore, MD 21230; 410-539-3399.

National Waitresses Day
Appreciate those who wait on you. Also known as Waitrons Day. *Sponsor:* Gaylord Ward, 1505 E. Bristol Road, Burton, MI 48529-2214.

Oldest radio station west of the Mississippi River
KFKA-AM was licensed in 1921. *Contact:* KFKA Radio, Mike Rice of Colorado A.M., 820 11th Avenue, Greeley, CO 80631; 970-356-1310.

Sign of Gemini
The astrological sign of Gemini, the twins, runs from May 21st to June 20th. Geminis are ambitious, alert, and intelligent.

May 22

Associated Press incorporated (1900)
AP was incorporated in New York City in 1900. *Contact:* Associated Press, 50 Rockefeller Plaza, New

York, NY 10020; 212-621-1500; Fax: 212-621-1679.

Atlas Day
The first modern atlas was published in Belgium by Abraham Ortelius in 1570.

First life insurance policy in the U.S. (1761)
Issued in Philadelphia, Pennsylvania.

First operational jet fighter (1943)
A test flight of the German Me262 jet fighter was made on this date in 1943. It was the only operational jet during World War II.

First public motion picture show (1891)
Thomas Edison showed a visiting women's club a movie of a bowler.

First revolving restaurant dedicated (1961)
The Top of the Needle restaurant in the Space Needle of Seattle, Washington, was the first revolving restaurant.

First use of a lucky rabbit's foot (600 B.C.)

First wagon train leaves on Oregon Trail (1843)
The first wagon train left Independence, Missouri. 300 men, 150 women, and about 500 children were part of the wagon train.

First woman to reach the North Pole
Anne Bancroft reached the North Pole in 1986.

Great Train Robbery occurred (1868)
Seven members of the Reno gang held up a train near Marshfield, Indiana, and made off with $96,000 in cash, bonds, and gold.

Mister Rogers' Neighborhood premiered (1967)

Mysteries Are Marvelous Day
On the birthday (1859) of Sir Arthur Conan Doyle, author of the Sherlock Holmes mysteries, we celebrate all mysteries, crime novels, and books about police and detective work. *Sponsor*: Book Marketing Update. ✉

National Maritime Day
Celebrates the first Atlantic crossing by a steamship. *The Savannah* sailed from Savannah, Georgia to Liverpool, England in 1819.

Saint Rita Feast Day
Patron saint of marital problems, parenthood, and desperate causes.

Skyscraper building system patented (1888)
Considered the father of the skyscraper, Leroy Buffington patented the system for building skyscrapers.

Toothpaste tube invented (1892)
Dr. Sheffield invented the toothpaste tube.

May 23
Bifocals Birthday
In 1875, Benjamin Franklin announced that he had invented bifocals.

Brown Bag It
On the fourth Thursday in May, workers brown bag their lunch and donate the money they saved to the National Head Injury Foundation for people who have sustained traumatic brain injuries. *Sponsor*: National Head Injury Foundation, Barbara Green, Washington, DC; 202-296-6443.

Canadian Mounties established (1873)
The Northwest Mounted Police force was established in Canada. *Contact*: Canadian Embassy, 501 Pennsylvania Avenue NW, Washington, DC 20001; 202-682-1740.

Chestertown Tea Party
In 1774, a few months after the Boston Tea Party, the residents of Chestertown, Maryland, held their own tea party by throwing tea onboard the *Geddes* into the Chester River. Chestertown celebrates the event on the Saturday before Memorial Day. *Sponsor*: Chestertown Tea Party Festival, Kent County Chamber of Commerce, P.O. Box 146, 400 S. Cross Street, Chestertown, MD 21620; 410-778-0416; Fax: 410-778-0416.

Cliff's Notes first used in schools (1953)

Contact: Cliff' Notes, Inc., 4851 South 16th Street, Lincoln, NE 68512; 402-423-5050; 800-228-4078; Fax: 402-423-9254.

Declaration of the Bab

In 1844, the Bab announced that he was herald of a new messenger of God. *Sponsor:* Baha'i National Center. ✉

Don't Rob a Bank Day

On the anniversary of the 1934 shooting deaths of Bonnie and Clyde, reconsider any desire you might have to rob a bank. It's not worth it.

Linnaeus Day

This day celebrates the birthday of Carolus Linnaeus, the Swedish naturalist who is known as the father of biology. He was born Carl von Linne in 1707.

New York Public Library Birthday

The New York Public Library was incorporated in 1895. *Contact:* New York Public Library, 5th Avenue and 42nd Street, New York, NY 10018; 212-930-0800; Fax: 212-921-2546.

South Carolina Ratification Day

In 1788, South Carolina became the 8th state to ratify the U.S. Constitution. *Contact:* South Carolina Tourism Division, P.O. Box 71, Columbia, SC 29202; 803-734-0264; 800-346-3634; Fax: 803-734-0133.

May 24

Alchemy Day

This is the feast day of Hermes Trismegistus, one of the great alchemists who might have discovered a way to turn lead into gold. Alchemists were the first chemists.

Blowing in the Wind Day

On Bob Dylan's birthday, look for the answers—they are blowing in the wind. Robert Zimmerman was born in 1941 in Duluth, Minnesota. *Sponsor:* The Life of the Party. ✉

Brooklyn Bridge opened (1883)

Have I got a bridge for you? You can buy it cheap.

Designated Driver Memorial Day Weekend Campaign

When you go out partying this weekend, make sure to have one friend who will be the designated driver and not drink. Drive safely. *Sponsor:* Mothers Against Drunk Driving, 511 E. John Carpenter Freeway #700, Irving, TX 75062-8187; 214-744-6233.

First automobile repair shop opened (1899)

The first automobile repair shop opened in Boston, Massachusetts.

First night Major League baseball game (1935)

The Cincinnati Reds defeated the Philadelphia Phillies 2-1 in the first baseball game to be played at night (played in Cincinnati, Ohio). *Contact:* Cincinnati Reds, 100 Riverfront Stadium, Cincinnati, OH 45202; 513-421-4510; Fax: 513-421-7342.

First passenger railroad service in the U.S.

In 1830, passenger railroad service was established between Baltimore and Elliott's Mills, Maryland.

First telegraph line in America opened (1844)

Samuel F. B. Morse opened the first telegraph line between Washington, DC and Baltimore, Maryland.

"Mary Had a Little Lamb" was written (1830)

National Death Busters Day

Celebrated on the Friday before Memorial Day. Let's have no traffic fatalities on this weekend. *Sponsor:* Joseph Kearley, 2129 Benbrook Drive, Carrollton, TX 75007.

Shavuot (Feast of Weeks)

Celebrates the day Moses received the Torah from God on Mount Sinai. 1997: June 11; 1998: May 31.

United Press International formed (1958)

United Press and International News Service merged in 1958. *Contact:* United Press International, 1400 Eye Street NW #800, Washington, DC 20005; 202-898-8000; 800-777-5532; Fax: 202-789-2362.

World Championship Old-Time Piano Playing Contest

Held annually the weekend of Memorial Day, this contest features piano-playing contests in ragtime, honky-tonk, and other old-time music. *Sponsor:* Old Time Music Preservation Association, Judy Leschewski, P.O. Box 4714, Decatur, IL 62525; 217-428-2403.

World's worst soccer disaster (1964)

Over 300 soccer fans were killed and 500 injured in Lima, Peru, when fans rioted after an unpopular ruling by a referee in a game between Peru and Argentina.

May 25

African Liberation Day

Honors the anniversary of the formation of the Organization of African Unity in 1963 in Addis Ababa, Ethiopia. Also known as African Freedom Day.

American Japan Week

Encourages cultural exchange between Japan and the U.S. Every year a different city hosts special events in celebrating this week (usually held the week of Memorial Day). *Sponsor:* Boston Visitors Bureau, Prudential Towers #400, P.O. Box 990468, Boston, MA 02199; 617-536-4100; Fax: 617-424-7664.

Babe Ruth hit his 714th home run (1935)

Babe Ruth hit his last home run for the Boston Braves.

BobFest (in honor of Bob, the Ultimate Okay Guy)

Held every Memorial Day weekend in Vail, Colorado, home of the Bob Bridge. *Sponsor:* BobFest, Vail, CO; 800-775-8245.

First doctor to have office hours in space (1973)

Joseph Kerwin, Paul Weitz, and Pete Conrad, Jr. went into space on *Skylab* 2. *Contact:* NASA. ✉

First Roman Catholic priest ordained in U.S. (1793)

Father Stephen Theodore Badin was ordained in Baltimore, Maryland.

Gateway Arch dedicated (1968)

Dedicated in St. Louis, Missouri. The arch is as tall as it is wide.

Hands Across America Anniversary (1986)

Over 7,000,000 people participated in Hands Across America by holding hands to bring attention to the plight of the hungry and the homeless in America.

National Missing Children's Day

Teaches kids safety skills and reminds all of us about missing children. *Sponsor:* Child Find of America, 7 Innis Avenue, P.O. Box 277, New Paltz, NY 12561-0277; 914-255-1848; 800-I-AM-LOST; Fax: 914-255-5706.

National Tap Dance Day

Celebrates the birthday of Bill Bojangles Robinson, the king of tap dancers. Robinson was born in 1878 in Richmond, Virginia.

Self-Reliance Day

Commemorates the birthday of Ralph Waldo Emerson (1803), who wrote *Self-Reliance.* It is a day to rely on yourself in whatever you do.

Star Wars premiered (1977)

Week of Solidarity with the Peoples of All Colonial Territories

Recognizes those fighting for freedom, independence, and human rights. *Sponsor:* United Nations. ✉

World Champion Cross-Country Kinetic Sculpture Race

Billed as the greatest race on earth, the World Champion Great Arcata to Ferndale Cross-Country Kinetic Sculpture Race tests the left brain (technical design), right brain (artistic design), and bodies (racing) of all competitors. *Sponsor:* 707-725-3851.

World's Largest Nonmotorized Parade

On the Saturday of Mule Days (right before Memorial Day), Bishop hosts the Mule Parade, the world's largest nonmotorized parade, with more than 250 entries. *Sponsor:* Mule Days, P.O. Box 815, Bishop, CA 93514; 619-872-4263.

Worst domestic air disaster (1979)

An American Airlines DC-10 crashed at O'Hare Airport in Chicago, Illinois; 275 people died. *Contact:* American Airlines, P.O. Box 619616, Dallas, TX 75261; 817-963-1234.

May 26

Actors' Equity Association organized (1913)

Contact: Actors' Equity Association, 165 West 46th Street, New York, NY 10036-2598; 212-869-8530; Fax: 212-719-9815.

Archaeological Institute of America founded (1906)

Contact: Archaeological Institute of America, 656 Beacon Street, Boston, MA 02215-2010; 617-353-9361; Fax: 617-353-6550.

Celebrity Marriage Day

In 1994, Lisa Marie Presley and Michael Jackson got married in the Dominican Republic.

Dow Jones Industrial Average Birthday

In 1896, the Dow Jones average first appeared in the *Wall Street Journal*. *Contact:* Dow Jones and Company, 200 Liberty Street, New York, NY 10281; 212-416-2000; 800-831-1234; Fax: 212-416-2658.

First legal casinos in the eastern U.S. opened

Opened in 1978 in Atlantic City, New Jersey. *Contact:* Atlantic City Visitors Bureau, 2314 Pacific Avenue, Atlantic City, NJ 08401; 609-348-7100; 800-262-7395; Fax: 609-345-3685.

Human Fly Day

George Willig, the Human Fly, climbed the outside of the 110-story World Trade Center in 1977. *Contact:* World Trade Center, Tower 2, West and Church Streets, New York, NY 10048; 212-466-7377.

Indianapolis 500

The first Indianapolis 500 took place in 1911. It is always held the Sunday before Memorial Day; it is the world's largest single-day sporting event. *Sponsor:* Indianapolis 500 Speedway, 4790 West 16th Street, Indianapolis, IN 46224; 317-248-6750.

Pentecost Sunday

On Pentecost Sunday, the Holy Spirit came down and inspired the Apostles of Jesus Christ. Pentecost Sunday is held 50 days after Easter, 10 days after Ascension Thursday. Also known as Whitsunday.

Put Up Your Dukes Day

On the birthday of John Wayne, the Duke, stand up for what you believe in. Wayne, whose name was Marion Michael Morrison, was born in 1907 in Winterset, Iowa. *Sponsor:* The Life of the Party. ✉

Ski to Sea Relay Race

On the Sunday of Memorial Day weekend, one of the world's most unusual relay races takes place as competitors start by cross-country skiing at the top of Mount Baker and go 85 miles skiing, biking, running, canoeing, and sailing to Bellingham, Washington. *Sponsor:* Bellingham Chamber of Commerce, P.O. Box 958, Bellingham, WA 98227; 360-734-1330; Fax: 360-734-1332.

May 27

First American execution of a witch (1647)
The first recorded execution of a witch (by hanging) in America took place in Massachusetts.

First black light sold (1961)

Golden Gate Bridge opened (1937)

Masking tape patented (1930)
Developed in 1925, masking tape was patented in 1930. *Contact:* 3M Company, 3M Center, Maplewood, MN 55144; 612-733-1110; 800-362-3456; Fax: 612-736-3094.

Memorial Day
First celebrated in 1868 as Decoration Day, Memorial Day is a time for Americans to honor all citizens killed in wars. Traditionally, this holiday was celebrated on May 30th but it is now celebrated on the last Monday in May.

Modern Dance Day
On the birthday of Isadora Duncan, the free-spirited dancer who is often known as the founder of modern dance, let's all get out and dance. Duncan was born in 1878 in San Francisco, California.

National Frozen Yogurt Week
Celebrated from Memorial Day to the first Sunday in June. *Sponsor:* TCBY, S&S Public Relations, 40 Skokie Boulevard #430, Northbrook, IL 60062-1617; 708-291-1616; Fax: 708-291-1758.

No Pesticides Day
On the birthday of Rachel Carson, author of *Silent Spring* and other environmental books deploring the use of pesticides, don't use any pesticides in your garden. Rachel Carson was born in 1907 near Springdale, Pennslyvania.

Pop-up toaster patented (1919)
Charles Strite of Stillwater, Minnesota, invented the toaster.

Sinking of the Bismarck
In 1941, the "unsinkable" German battleship *Bismarck* sank off the coast of France; 2,300 lives were lost.

Three Little Pigs premiered (1933)
Contact: Walt Disney Company. ✉

World Championship Flat Water Canoe Race
Runs along the Susquehanna River from Cooperstown, New York, 70 miles to Bainbridge, New York. It is always held on Memorial Day. *Sponsor:* General Clinton Canoe Regatta, Bainbridge, NY; 607-967-8700.

May 28

Ashura (Day of Fasting)
On the 10th day of the 1st month of the Islamic Lunar Calendar, Muslims celebrate the day that Noah left the ark after the great flood and the time when Moses led the Jews out of Egypt. This day of fasting is the main festival of the Shi'ite sect.

Athlete of the Century Day
James Thorpe was one of America's greatest athletes. Besides winning the pentathlon and decathlon at the 1912 Olympics, he also played professional baseball and football. Thorpe, an American Indian, was born in 1888 near Prague, Oklahoma.

First color movie released (1929)
The first talking movie to be released in color was *On with the Show.* It opened in New York City.

First whooping crane born in captivity (1975)

National Geography Bee Finals
The national competition for those who know geography is held on

the last Tuesday and Wednesday of May. *Sponsor:* National Geographic Society, 1145 Seventeenth Street NW, Washington, DC 20036; 202-828-6659.

Saint Bernard of Montjoux Feast Day

Patron saint of mountain climbers and skiers. He is also patron saint of travelers in the Alps.

Sierra Club founded (1892)

The Sierra Club, which is devoted to conservation of nature, was organized in San Francisco, California. *Contact:* Sierra Club, 730 Polk Street, San Francisco, CA 94109; 415-776-2211; Fax: 415-776-0350.

Slugs Return from Capistrano

It is a little-known fact that slugs return from Capistrano to our gardens and lawns on this date. *Sponsor:* Wellness Permission League. ✉

Spy Novels Are Splendid Day

On the birthday (1908) of Ian Fleming, creator of *James Bond* spy novels, we celebrate all spy and adventure novels. *Sponsor:* Book Marketing Update. ✉

U.S. Custom Court created (1926)

Wonder Girl of the Air Day

In 1930, English aviator Amy Johnson completed the first solo airplane flight from England to Australia. She had started the trip

23 days earlier on May 5th. Because of this feat and others, she was known as the wonder girl of the air.

May 29

Baha'u'llah Ascension Day

Baha'u'llah, prophet-founder of the Baha'i faith, died in 1892. *Sponsor:* Baha'i National Center. ✉

Entertain the Troops Day

Celebrate Bob Hope's birthday by taking a few military people out to lunch. Hope was born in England as Leslie Townes in 1903. *Sponsor:* The Life of the Party. ✉

First climbers to reach the top of Mount Everest

In 1953, Edmund Hillary and Tensing Norkay were the first to climb Mt. Everest.

John Fitzgerald Kennedy's Birthday

The 35th president of the U.S. was born in Brookline, Massachusetts in 1917.

National Senior Health and Fitness Day

The last Wednesday in May promotes exercise and fitness among older adults. *Sponsor:* Mature Market Resource Center, 621 E. Park Avenue, Libertyville, IL 60048; 708-816-8660; 800-828-8226; Fax: 708-816-8662.

National Spelling Bee Finals

Held on the Wednesday and Thursday after Memorial Day, to determine the best speller in the land. *Sponsor:* National Spelling Bee, Scripps-Howard, P.O. Box 5380, Cincinnati, OH 45201; 513-977-3028.

Rhode Island Ratification Day

In 1790, Rhode Island was the 13th state to ratify the U.S. Constitution. *Contact:* Rhode Island Tourism Division, 7 Jackson Walkway, Providence, RI 02903; 401-277-2601; 800-556-2484; Fax: 401-277-2102.

Truth in Lending Act signed (1968)

"White Christmas" recorded (1942)

"White Christmas" is the biggest-selling single ever recorded with over 40 million copies sold. Bing Crosby recorded the song, which was written by Irving Berlin.

Wisconsin Admission Day

Wisconsin became the 30th state in 1848. *Contact:* Wisconsin Division of Tourism, 123 W. Washington Street, P.O. Box 7970, Madison, WI 53707; 608-266-7621; 800-432-8747; Fax: 608-266-3403.

May 30

Compact disc introduced (1981)

First American daily newspaper published (1783)
The *Pennsylvania Evening Post* was published by Benjamin Towner of Philadelphia, Pennsylvania.

First automobile accident (1896)
Occurred In New York City when Henry Wells, a Massachusetts driver, hit bicyclist Evylyn Thomas. Wells wasn't hurt, but Thomas had a fractured leg.

Ice cream freezer patented (1848)
William G. Young patented the first ice cream freezer.

Lincoln Memorial dedicated (1922)

Loomis Day
Another punny day, this day honors Mahlon Loomis, who received a patent on wireless telegraphy in 1872, many years before Marconi. *Sponsor:* Puns Corp. ✉

Memorial Day (traditional)
A day to honor our dead, especially those killed in wars.

Saint Ferdinand Feast Day
Saint Ferdinand III of Castile, a warrior king, is a patron saint of engineers, rulers, governors, magistrates, prisoners, the poor, and Seville, Spain.

Saint Joan of Arc Feast Day
Born in 1412, she is the patron saint of France. She was burned at the stake on this date in 1431. On May 16, 1920, she was canonized a saint by the Roman Catholic church.

May 31

American Poetry Day
Celebrates the birthday of Walt Whitman (1819); also honors all poets and poetry lovers. *Sponsor:* Book Marketing Update. ✉

Copyright Day
The first U.S. copyright law was passed in 1790. *Sponsor:* Book Marketing Update. ✉

Feast of the Visitation of Mary
Celebrates the time when the virgin Mary visited her cousin Elizabeth to announce the coming birth of Jesus.

First electric railway opened (1879)
Opened at the Berlin Trades Exposition.

First official bicycle race (1868)

Johnstown Flood (1889)
The most disastrous flood in U.S. history occurred at Johnstown, Pennsylvania in 1889. More than 2,200 people died as a result of the flood, which was caused by a burst dam.

Make My Day Day
Celebrate the birthday of Clint Eastwood, star of the Dirty Harry movies, many spaghetti westerns, and *Unforgiven*. He was also mayor of Carmel, California. Eastwood was born in 1930 in San Francisco, California. *Sponsor:* The Life of the Party. ✉

National Biplane Expo
This is the world's largest biplane expo. *Sponsor:* Bartlesville Chamber of Commerce, P.O. Box 2366, Bartlesville, OK 74005; 800-364-8708. Charles Harris, organizer; 918-622-8400.

Take This Job and Shove It Day
On the birthday of Johnny Paycheck, don't take any lip from your boss. Paycheck was born in 1941 in Greenfield, Ohio. *Sponsor:* All My Events. ✉

World No-Tobacco Day
Sponsor: American Association for World Health, 1129 20th Street NW #400, Washington, DC 20036; 202-466-5883; Fax: 206-466-5896.

JUNE

American Rivers Month
To promote the enjoyment of America's rivers. *Sponsor:* American Rivers, Inc., Randy Showstack, 801 Pennsylvania Avenue SE #400, Washington, DC 20003; 202-547-6900; Fax: 202-543-6142.

Black Music Month
This month is kicked off by the annual conference of the International Association of African American Music.

Cancer in the Sun Month
To warn people about the dangers of skin cancer caused by overexposure to the sun. *Sponsor:* Pharmacists Planning Services. ✉

Fiction Is Fun Month
Read a good book of fiction this month. *Sponsor:* Book Marketing Update. ✉

Fireworks Safety Month
Get ready for the 4th! Be careful when watching or using fireworks. *Sponsor:* Prevent Blindness America. ✉

Fresh Fruits and Vegetables Month
Promotes the consumption of fruits and veggies. *Sponsor:* United Fresh Fruits and Vegetables Association, 727 N. Washington Street, Alexandria, VA 22314; 703-836-3410; Fax: 703-836-7745.

Gay Pride Month

Hurricane Season
Hurricane season runs from June 1 to November 30 in the east; from June 1 to October 31 in the west. *Contact:* National Oceanic and Atmospheric Administration, Washington Science Center, Building 5, 6010 Executive Boulevard, Rockville, MD 20852; 202-482-6090; Fax: 202-482-3154.

June Dairy Month
Since 1937, dairy farmers have celebrated in June. *Sponsor:* American Dairy Association, 10255 W. Higgins Road #900, Rosemont, IL 60018-5616; 708-803-2000.

June Is Turkey Lovers Month
Sponsor: National Turkey Federation, 11319 Sunset Hills Road, Reston, VA 22090-5227; 703-435-7206.

National Accordion Awareness Month
Celebrates the accordion's storied past as well as its influence on today's music. *Sponsor:* Those Darn Accordions!, Tom Torriglia, 2269 Chestnut Street #183, San Francisco, CA 94123; 415-346-5862; e-mail: tommy@crl.com.

National Adopt a Cat Month
Adopt cats from animal shelters. Also known as Adopt a Shelter Cat Month. *Sponsor:* ASPCA, 424 East 92nd Street, New York, NY 10128; 212-876-7700.

National Dream Work Month
Learn more about yourself through your dreams. *Sponsor:* Jean Benedict Raffa, 17 S. Osceola Avenue, Orlando, FL 32801; 407-426-7077; Fax: 407-649-8601.

National Drive Safe Month
Encourages safe driving among teenagers. Formerly sponsored by DriveSafe, Inc.

National Forest System Month

National Frozen Yogurt Month
Sponsor: TCBY, S&S Public Relations, 40 Skokie Boulevard #430, Northbrook, IL 60062-1617; 708-291-1616; Fax: 708-291-1758.

National Iced Tea Month
Sponsor: Tea Council of the USA, 230 Park Avenue, New York, NY 10169; 212-697-8658; Fax: 212-986-6998.

National Lesbian and Gay Book Month
Founded in 1992 to celebrate authors, publishers, and sellers of gay and lesbian books. Send for a promotional kit. *Sponsor:* The Publishing Triangle, Michele Karlsberg,

Publicity, 47 Dongan Hills Ave., 1st Floor, Staten Island, NY 10306; 718-351-9599.

National Pest Control Month
Thanks to the exterminators who work to get rid of disease-carrying pests in buildings. *Sponsor:* Orkin Pest Control, 2170 Piedmont Road NE, Atlanta, GA 30324; 404-888-2000; Fax: 404-888-2730.

National Rose Month
It's the peak season for America's favorite flower. *Sponsor:* Roses, Inc., Jim Krone, P.O. Box 99, Haslett, MI 48840; 517-339-9544; Fax: 517-339-3760.

National Scleroderma Awareness Month
To increase public knowledge of this disease. *Sponsor:* United Scleroderma Foundation, P.O. Box 399, Watsonville, CA 95077-0399; 408-728-2202; 800-722-4673.

Own Your Share of America Month
Encourages people to invest in American stocks. NAIC offers brochures, flyers, posters, banners, flags, bumper stickers, pins, and buttons to promote personal investing. *Sponsor:* National Association of Investors Clubs, P.O. Box 220, Royal Oak, MI 48068; 810-583-6242; Fax: 810-583-4880; e-mail: 76703.4372@compuserve.com.

Portable Computer Month
Promotes portable computing. Formerly sponsored by Panasonic.

Supreme Court Month of Tough Decisions
The Supreme Court has made some of its toughest and most controversial decisions during the month of June, including decisions on flag burning, hate crimes, prayers in schools, criminal rights, the draft, and the death penalty. *Contact:* U.S. Supreme Court. ✉

Surimi Seafood Month
Get acquainted with imitation crab, lobster, and other surimi seafood products. *Sponsor:* Surimi Seafood Education Center, 1525 Wilson Boulevard #500, Arlington, VA 22209.

Tony Award Month
The Tonys are given for best broadway plays, actors, etc. *Sponsor:* League of New York Theaters and Producers, New York, NY; 212-764-1122.

Youth Suicide Prevention Month

Zoo and Aquarium Month
Visit your local zoo or aquarium! Also known as ZAM! *Sponsor:* American Zoo and Aquarium Association, 7970 Old Georgetown Road, Bethesda, MD 20814; 301-907-7777; Fax: 301-907-2950.

June I

Cable News Network debuts (1980)
CNN provides round-the-clock newscasts on cable TV. *Contact:* Cable News Network, 100 International Boulevard, 1 CNN Center, Atlanta, GA 30303; 404-827-1500; Fax: 404-827-1593.

Don't Give Up the Ship Day
During the war of 1812, Captain James Lawrence of the U.S. frigate *Chesapeake* gave the U.S. Navy its motto when he uttered these words as he lay dying, "Don't give up the ship." *Contact:* Department of the Navy, Information Office, Pentagon Room 4E686, Washington, DC 20350; 703-697-7391.

Free Fishing Days
Many states offer free fishing (without a license) during the first weekend of June.

International Children's Day

Celebrated in the People's Republic of China, Poland, Germany, Russia, and other countries.

Up with Kids!

International Volunteers Week

During the first 7 days of June, thank volunteers and encourage people to serve their communities. *Sponsor:* International Society of Friendship and Good Will. ✉

June Bug Day

This is a local celebration in Arkansas, but there is no reason why the rest of us can't also celebrate June bugs on the first Saturday in June. *Sponsor:* June Bug Days, Brenda Scrimager, 9417 Geyer Springs Road, Little Rock, AR 72209; 510-570-4149.

Kentucky Admission Day

Kentucky became the 15th state on June 1, 1792. *Contact:* Kentucky Department of Travel, P.O. Box 2011, Frankfort, KY 40602-2011; 502-564-4930; 800-225-8747; Fax: 502-564-6100.

Marilyn Monroe's Birthday

Born in 1926 in Los Angeles, California, Monroe was an icon of the movie industry. She had something special—setting her apart from other actresses.

Mead Moon

The full moon of June is the mead moon, symbolic of love, romance, marriage, career, success, abundance, and good health. Also known as the hot moon, rose moon, or strawberry moon.

National Trails Day

The first Saturday in June celebrates the anniversary of the National Trail System Act, which built hiking and biking trails over former railroad rights-of-way. For a free copy of the Day Hiker's Checklist, call L. L. Bean at 800-221-4221. *Sponsor:* American Hiking Society, David Lillard, P.O. Box 20160, Washington, DC 20041-2160; 703-255-9304.

Saint Justin Feast Day

Patron saint of philosophers and apologists.

Superman's Birthday

The first issue of *Superman*, by Jerry Siegel, was published in 1938. *Contact:* DC Comics, 1325 Sixth Avenue, 27th Floor, New York, NY 10019; 212-636-5400; Fax: 212-636-5430.

Tennessee Admission Day

Tennessee became the 16th state on June 1, 1796. *Contact:* Tennessee Department of Tourism, P.O. Box 23170, Nashville, TN 37202-3170; 615-741-2158; 800-362-1971; Fax: 615-741-7225.

World Champion Rubber Duckie Races

Call for firm dates in the spring. *Sponsor:* Great Napa Valley Duck Race, Downtown Merchants Association, Napa, CA 94559; 707-257-0322.

World's Largest Garage Sale

Over 12,000 people attend this annual event on the first Saturday in June. People in Duncan, Oklahoma also claim to hold the World's Largest Garage Sale on the first weekend in August. *Sponsor:* City of South Bend, 501 W. South Street, South Bend, IN 46601; 219-235-9951.

June 2

American Indian Citizenship Day

Congress granted American Indians U.S. citizenship in 1924.

Dinosaur Day

Dinosaurs ruled the earth for millions of years but died out about 67 million years ago. *Sponsor:* A Pilgrim's Almanac. ✉

✉ Addresses for frequently cited organizations are gathered on pages vii–viii.

First major circus in the U.S. (1835)

P. T. Barnum ran the first major 3-ring circus.

First President to marry while in office (1886)

President Grover Cleveland married Frances Folsom, becoming the only President to marry at the White House while in office.

First state to prohibit alcoholic drinks (1851)

Maine was the first state to ban alcohol.

International Mothers' Peace Day

Celebrated on the first Sunday in June, this day was founded in 1872 by Julia Ward Howe to give mothers a voice in world events. *Sponsor:* Mothers' Peace Day Committee, Jeanne Schramm, P.O. Box 102, West Liberty, WV 26074; 304-336-7159; Fax: 304-336-8186; e-mail: schramm@w15vax.wvnet.edu.

International PBX Telecommunications Week

Starting on the first Sunday in June, honors switchboard operators for making businesses run smoothly. *Sponsor:* International PBX/Telecommunicators, Mary Bohl, 2505 Paul Street, Eau Claire, WI 54701; 715-839-6075.

Lyme Disease Awareness Week

Always the first full week in June.

National Cancer Survivors Day

Always the first Sunday in June, NCSD is the world's largest cancer survivor event with over 600 officially recognized local events. They provide an extensive Celebration Planning Guide for anyone wanting to take part. *Sponsor:* National Cancer Survivors Day Foundation, P.O. Box 682285, Franklin, TN 37068-2285; 615-794-3006; Fax: 615-794-0179.

National Dry Land Canoe Races

Always the first weekend in June. Two-person teams vie to see who can run the fastest while carrying canoes 8 city blocks in Truro, Iowa. *Sponsor:* Madison County Visitors Bureau, 73 Jefferson, Winterset, IA 50273; 515-462-1185.

National Fragrance Week

Theme: Mystery is in the air. Always celebrated the first full week in June. *Sponsor:* The Fragrance Foundation, 145 East 32nd Street, New York, NY 10016-6002; 212-725-2755; Fax: 212-779-9058.

National Frozen Yogurt Day

Celebrated the first Sunday in June. *Sponsor:* TCBY, S&S Public Relations, 40 Skokie Boulevard #430, Northbrook, IL 60062-1617; 708-291-1616; Fax: 708-291-1758.

Radio patented in the U.S. (1896)

Guglielmo Marconi patented his radio.

State Parks Open House Day

Wisconsin offers free fishing and free admission to state parks on the first Sunday in June. *Sponsor:* Wisconsin Bureau of Parks and Recreation, P.O. Box 7921, Madison, WI 53707; 608-266-2621.

Teacher Thank You Week

During the first full week in June, thank the teacher who influenced you or helped give you a direction in life. *Sponsor:* Lake Superior State University, 1000 College Drive, Sault St. Marie, MI 49783; 906-635-2315.

Teacher's Day

The first Sunday in June is celebrated in Massachusetts in honor of teachers.

Trinity Sunday

On the Sunday after Pentecost, Christians celebrate the Holy Trinity, the three divine persons in one God: the Father, the Son, and the Holy Spirit.

June 3

Brain Tumor Awareness Week

Brain tumors strike more than 40,000 people every year in the U.S. Always celebrated the first full week in June. *Sponsor:* American Brain Tumor Association, 2720 River Road, Des Plaines, IL 60018; 708-827-9910; Fax: 708-827-9918; e-mail: ABTA@aol.com.

Casey at the Bat first published (1888)

The famous poem *Casey at the Bat*, written by Ernest Thayer, was first printed in the *San Francisco Examiner*. *Contact: San Francisco Examiner*, 110 Fifth Street, San Francisco, CA 94103-2972; 415-777-2424.

First American to walk in space (1965)

Gemini 4 astronaut Edward White was the first American to walk in space. *Contact:* NASA. ✉

First tattoo performed (208 B.C.)

First woman rabbi in the U.S. (1972)

Sally Jan Priesand of New York City was ordained as a rabbi.

First woman to graduate at the top of her West Point class

In 1995, Rebecca Marier became the first woman in the 193-year history of the West Point Military Academy to graduate at the top of her class. *Contact:* West Point Military Academy, West Point, NY 10996; 914-938-4011; Fax: 914-938-3828.

Jack Jouett's Ride (1781)

Jack Jouett began a 45-mile ride to warn Thomas Jefferson and other American patriots that the British were coming. For want of a Longfellow to celebrate his ride, he would be as famous as Paul Revere.

Jefferson Davis's Birthday

The only president of the Confederate States of America, was born in Christian County, Kentucky in 1808. His birthday is a public holiday in Florida, South Carolina, Alabama, Mississippi, Kentucky, and Louisiana.

Love Conquers All Day

In 1937, the Duke of Windsor married divorcee Wallis Warfield Simpson. He gave up the crown of England so he could marry her (at the time, he was known as King Edward VIII).

National Bathroom Reading Week

During the first full week, promote reading in bathrooms. *Sponsor:* Red-Letter Press, Jack Kreismer, President, P.O. Box 393, Saddle River, NJ 07458; 201-818-8951; Fax: 201-652-5469.

National Fishing Week

The first full week in June promotes the sport of fishing. *Sponsor:* American Sport Fishing Association, Ms. Brandon Miner, 1033 N. Fairfax Street #200, Alexandria, VA 22314-1540; 703-684-3201; Fax: 703-519-1872.

Repeat Day

Today, learn a new word by repeating it as often as possible while using it in different sentences. This day was founded by Danny Rubalcaba, a Gransby, Connecticut, fifth grader. *Contact:* Hartford Courant, Kenton Robinson, Features Writer, 285 Broad Street, Hartford, CT 06115; 203-241-3947.

June 4

First free flight by a woman (1784)

Marie Thible of Lyons, France made the first balloon flight by a woman.

International Day of Innocent Children Victims of Aggression

This day has been recognized since 1983. *Sponsor:* United Nations. ✉

Pulitzer Prizes first awarded (1917)

Prizes are awarded for journalistic and book writing achievements.

Roquefort cheese first discovered (1070)

The cheese was discovered in a cave.

Shopping cart invented (1937)
Sylvan Goldman of Oklahoma City invented the shopping cart.

Socrates's Birthday
One of the world's greatest philosophers was born in 470 B.C.

Tiananmen Square Massacre (1989)
Chinese troops fired upon demonstrating students occupying this Beijing square. Several hundred protesters died, ending hope of political change.

June 5

AIDS Birthday
The first case of AIDS was reported on this date in 1981.

First balloon flight (1783)
The Montgolfier brothers of Annonay, France, were the first to demonstrate a hot air balloon flight; it was the first sustained flight of any human-made object.

Saint Boniface of Mainz Feast Day
Patron saint of Germany, Prussia, and brewers.

Women's Bureau established by Congress (1920)
Established to promote the welfare of wage-earning women. *Contact:* Department of Labor, Women's Bureau, Room S3002, 200 Constitution Avenue NW, Washington, DC 20210; 202-219-6611; Fax: 202-219-7312.

World Environment Day
Celebrates the anniversary of the U.N. Conference on the Human Environment (1972). *Sponsor:* United Nations. ✉

Youngest college graduate (1994)
Michael Kearney, age 10, graduated from the University of South Alabama with a bachelor's degree in anthropology. His ambition at the time was to become a TV game show host. *Contact:* University of South Alabama, 207 University Boulevard, Mobile, AL 36688; 205-460-6101.

June 6

20/20 premiered
The TV news magazine premiered in 1978. *Contact:* ABC-TV. ✉

Career Nurse Assistants Day
On the first Thursday in June, thank people who make life easier for both nurses and patients. *Sponsor:* Career Nurse Assistants Programs, Genevieve Gipson, Coordinator, 3577 Easton Road, Norton, OH 44203-5661; 216-825-9342.

Chrysler Corporation founded (1925)
Walter Percy Chrysler founded Chrysler Corporation. *Contact:* Chrysler Corporation, 12000 Chrysler Drive, Detroit, MI 48288; 313-956-5741; Fax: 313-956-3747.

D-Day Anniversary
Commemorates the anniversary of the 1944 Allied invasion of Europe during World War II.

Digestive Processes Day
In 1822, U.S. Army surgeon William Beaumont had the chance to observe the digestive processes of Canadian fur trapper Alexis St. Martin, who had been gut shot. Beaumont's observations gave medical science a better understanding of how digestion works.

First drive-in movie theater opened (1933)
Opened in Camden, New Jersey; the first movie shown was *Wife Beware* starring Adolph Menjou.

First transatlantic trip by rowboat (1896)
George Harbo and Frank Samuelson rowed an 18-foot boat across the Atlantic Ocean in 56 days.

National Patriots Month

June 6 to July 4. Begins on Nathan Hale's birthday (1755) and ends on Independence Day. *Sponsor:* Patriots' Club of America, Jack Coulter, 316 SE 2nd Street, Fort Meade, FL 33841.

National Sure You Can Travel Day

Encourages people with disabilities to get out and travel.

National Yo-Yo Day

Celebrates the birthday of Donald Duncan, the man who made yo-yo a household word. *Contact:* Duncan Toy Company, Flambeau Products Corporation, P.O. Box 5067, Columbus, IN 47202; 812-372-4899; Fax: 812-379-9707.

Party Party Day

An excuse to have a party once a month (when the day equals the month). *Sponsor:* Bonza Bottler Day. ✉

Proposition 13 Anniversary (1978)

California voters cut property taxes, beginning a taxpayer revolt.

Securities and Exchange Commission established (1934)

Contact: Securities and Exchange Commission, 450 Fifth Street NW, Washington DC 20549; 202-272-2650; Fax: 202-272-7050.

Susan B. Anthony Fined for Voting Anniversary (1872)

Fined for trying to vote in a local election when women were excluded from voting. She never paid the fine. She was fined again later for trying to vote in the presidential elections. Again, she never paid.

YMCA founded (1844)

Founded in London; the first YMCA in the U.S. was founded in Boston, Massachusetts in 1851. *Contact:* YMCA of the USA, U.S. National Council, 101 N. Wacker Drive, Chicago, IL 60606-7386; 312-977-0031; 800-872-9622; Fax: 312-977-9063.

June 7

Biggest single military explosion (1917)

The British detonated 1 million tons of Ammonal in tunnels 100 feet below the German lines near Ypres, Belgium. It was the largest single military explosion using conventional ordnance (before the atomic bomb).

Donut Days

In commemoration of the donuts served to World War I doughboys, the Salvation Army collects donations from individuals and gives them a paper donut in return. This fundraising event has been going on since 1938 on the first Friday and Saturday of June. *Sponsor:* The Salvation Army, 5040 N. Pulaski, Chicago, IL 60630; 312-725-1100; Fax: 312-725-2822.

Most Boring Day of the Year

Do something today to make this boring day memorable. *Sponsor:* Open Horizons. ✉

Vatican City became an independent country (1929)

With the signing of the Lateran Treaty, Vatican City became a sovereign state. Italy formally recognized Vatican City on February 11, 1929. *Contact:* Apostolic Nunciature, 3339 Massachusetts Avenue NW, Washington, DC 20008; 202-333-7121.

June 8

American Architecture Day

We honor all American architects on the birthday of Frank Lloyd Wright (1867). Born in Richland Center, Wisconsin, he was probably the greatest American architect.

Belmont Stakes

Since 1867, the third race of horceracing's Triple Crown is held on the fifth Saturday after the Kentucky Derby. It is held at the Belmont Park Racetrack. *Sponsor:* New York Racing Association, P.O. Box 90, Jamaica, NY 11417; 718-641-4700; Fax: 718-488-6044.

Death of Prophet Mohammed (632)

Mohammed, founder of the Islamic faith, died in 632.

First public award to a woman in America (1697)

After escaping capture by Indians who had killed her baby and others, Hannah Duston killed and scalped 10 Indians. Six weeks after her escape, her husband was awarded (on her behalf) 25 pounds for her efforts.

First stolen car (1896)

Ice Cream USA Birthday

Ice cream was first sold in the U.S. on this date in 1786.

Largest flower ever to bloom (1937)

A giant Sumatran calla lily (measuring 8 1/2 feet high and 4 feet in diameter) bloomed at the New York Botanical Gardens. However, its distinctive fragrance, like that of a rotting corpse, drove people out of doors.

NFL and AFL merge

The merger, announced in 1966, took effect in 1970. *Contact:* National Football League. ✉

State Park Week

During the week including the second and third Saturdays in June, celebrate and enjoy state parks. *Sponsor:* Iowa Department of Natural Resources, Steve Pennington, Wallace State Office Building, Des Moines, IA 50319-0034; 515-281-5145.

Vacuum cleaner patented (1869)

Ives McGaffey of Chicago patented the vacuum cleaner.

World's Largest Strawberry Shortcake

On the Saturday of the first weekend in June (Friday through Sunday), the Lebanon Strawberry Festival serves the world's largest shortcake free to all who attend. *Sponsor:* Lebanon Strawberry Festival, 1040 Park Street, Lebanon, OR 97355; 503-258-7164; Fax: 503-258-7166.

World's longest breakfast table

Hosted by Kellogg, Ralston Foods, and Post Division of Kraft General Foods in the cereal capital of the world, Battle Creek, Michigan. Always held on the morning of the second Saturday in June. *Sponsor:* Cereal Festival, Battle Creek Visitors Bureau, 34 W. Jackson Street #4-B, Battle Creek, MI 49017; 616-962-2240; 800-397-2240.

June 9

Boxing Hall of Fame induction ceremonies

Opened in 1990, this hall of fame has already inducted 152 boxers. Their annual induction ceremonies are held on the Sunday of the second weekend in June. *Sponsor:* International Boxing Hall of Fame, 1 Hall of Fame Drive, Canastota, NY 13032; 315-697-7095.

Children's Sunday

In many Christian churches children are the focus on the second Sunday in June.

Corpus Christi

On the Sunday after Trinity Sunday, Catholics commemorate the establishment of the sacrament of the Holy Eucharist. In the U.S., this day is celebrated on the Sunday after Trinity Sunday; in other parts of the world, on the Thursday after Trinity Sunday.

Donald Duck's Birthday

Donald Duck was born in 1934. Disney was his proud father. *Contact:* Walt Disney Company. ✉

First American book to be copyrighted (1790)

John Barry's *Philadelphia Spelling Book* was the first book to be copyrighted in America.

First dime novel published (1860)

The first dime novel, *Malaeska: The Indian Wife of the White Hunter,* was published.

Mormons accept black men for priesthood (1978)

The 148-year-old ban against black men in the Mormon priesthood ended. *Contact:* Church of Jesus Christ of Latter-Day Saints, 50 E. North Temple Street, Salt Lake City, UT 84150; 801-240-2531; Fax: 801-240-2033.

National Flag Week

Always celebrated the week of the 14th.

National Hug Holiday Week

Hug your family, friends, and associates; held the week of the second Sunday in June. Your daily hug prescription: 4 hugs for survival, 8 hugs for maintenance, 12 hugs for growth. Get your hugs today! *Sponsor:* Hugs for Health Foundation, Jo Lindberg, P.O. Box 1704, Tustin, CA 92681; 714-832-4847.

National Men's Health Week

Celebrated from the second Sunday in June until Father's Day. For a free 48-page booklet, *Guide to a Man's Life,* call 800-955-2002. *Sponsor:* Men's Health Magazine, 33 E. Minor Street, Emmaus, PA 18098; 610-967-5171.

National Women in Agriculture Day

Race Unity Day

On the second Sunday in June, work to create an atmosphere of better understanding for all races. *Sponsor:* Baha'i National Center, 1320 Nineteenth Street NW #701, Washington, DC 20036; 202-833-8990.

Writers Rights Day

Promotes better compensation and contracts for professional writers. *Sponsor:* National Writers Union, 873 Broadway #203, New York, NY 10003; 212-254-0279; Fax: 212-254-0673.

June 10

Alcoholics Anonymous founded (1935)

William Wilson and Robert Smith founded Alcoholics Anonymous in Akron, Ohio. *Contact:* Alcoholics Anonymous, 475 Riverside Drive, New York, NY 10115; 212-870-3400; Fax: 212-870-3003.

Ballpoint Pen's Birthday

Lasalo Biro of Budapest, Hungary, patented the ballpoint pen in 1943.

Bureau of the Budget established

Congress established the Bureau of the Budget and the office of the Comptroller General in 1921. *Contact:* Office of Management & Budget, 725 17th Street NW, Washington, DC 20503; 202-395-3000; Fax: 202-395-3746.

Comstock Lode Discovery Day

In 1859, Peter O'Riley and Patrick McLaughlin discovered the Comstock Lode near Virginia City, Nevada. It was the richest mining discovery in U.S. history.

Federal Power Commission created (1920)

The Water Power Act created the Federal Power Commission to regulate power plants. *Contact:* Department of Energy, 1000 Independence Avenue SW, Washington, DC 20585; 202-586-5000; Fax: 202-586-4073.

First drive-through restaurant opened (1952)

First incorporation law in the U.S. (1837)
Connecticut passed the first general incorporation law in the U.S.

First mint in America (1652)
John Hull opened the first mint.

First steamboat to navigate the open seas (1809)
The steamboat *Phoenix* took 13 days to sail from Philadelphia, Pennsylvania, to New York City.

First tornado ever recorded (1682)
Occurred near New Haven, Connecticut.

Lidice Memorial Day
In 1942, Nazi troops shot all male inhabitants of the Czech village of Lidice, destroyed the village, and deported the women and children to Germany. Also known as the Rape of Lidice.

Mourn for Your Money Day
In 1943, tax withholding became law. Also known as W-2 Day. *Sponsor:* The Life of the Party. ✉

National Dog Bite Prevention Week
More than 2 million dog bites are reported every year. For free information about dog bite prevention and responsible pet ownership, send a business-size SASE to the following address. Always celebrated during the second week in June. *Sponsor:* Humane Society of the U.S., 2100 L Street NW, Washington, DC 20037-1525.

National Little League Baseball Week
Celebrated since 1959 during the week of the second Monday in June. *Sponsor:* Little League Baseball, P.O. Box 3485, S. Williamsport, PA 17701; 717-326-1921; Fax: 717-326-1074.

Pediatric and Adolescent AIDS Awareness Week
Celebrated the week of the second Monday in June.

Six-Day War ended (1967)
Israel and Syria agreed to a cease fire, ending the Six-Day War that saw Israel capture the Sinai Peninsula, the West Bank, and the Golan Heights. *Contact:* Israeli Embassy, 3514 International Drive NW, Washington, DC 20008; 202-364-5500.

U.S. Capital Day
In 1793, Philadelphia ceased to be the capital of the U.S. when all federal government offices moved to Washington, DC. *Contact:* Washington, DC Visitors Bureau, 1212 New York Avenue NW #600, Washington, DC 20005; 202-789-7000; Fax: 202-789-7037.

Where the Wild Things Are Day
On the birthday of Maurice Sendak, author and illustrator of *Where the Wild Things Are,* we celebrate all author/illustrators of children's books. Sendak was born in 1928 in Brooklyn, New York. *Sponsor:* Book Marketing Update. ✉

Window envelope patented (1902)
A. F. Callahan of Chicago patented the window envelope.

World's largest motion picture premiere (1995)
Walt Disney Pictures presented the free premiere of *Pocahontas* on 4 giant screens (8 stories tall) in New York's Central Park. 100,000 people attended. *Contact:* Walt Disney Pictures. ✉

June 11

Dirty Book Day
The Postmaster General banned *Lady Chatterly's Lover* from the U.S.

mail. *Sponsor:* The Life of the Party. ✉

First black to be ordained a Mormon priest (1978)
Joseph Freeman Jr. became the first black to be ordained as a priest in the Church of Jesus Christ of Latter-day Saints. *Contact:* Church of Jesus Christ of Latter-Day Saints, 50 E. North Temple Street, Salt Lake City, UT 84150; 801-240-2531; Fax: 801-240-2033.

First recipient of Distinguished Flying Cross
In recognition of his solo flight across the Atlantic Ocean, Charles Lindbergh was awarded the first Distinguished Flying Cross in 1927.

First Triple Crown winner (1919)
Sir Barton became the first horse to win the Triple Crown of horceracing: the Kentucky Derby, Preakness, and Belmont Stakes.

Franklin stove invented (1742)
Benjamin Franklin invented the Franklin stove.

King Kamehameha I Day
This Hawaiian state holiday honors King Kamehameha, who was responsible for uniting the Hawaiian Islands. *Contact:* Hawaii Visitors Bureau, 2270 Kalakaua Avenue #801, Honolulu, HI 96815; 808-923-1811; Fax: 808-922-8991.

June 12

Baseball Hall of Fame dedicated (1939)
On the anniversary of the first baseball game played in America (1839), the Baseball Hall of Fame was dedicated. For a Hall of Fame decal, send $1.00 to Decal Offer at the following address. *Contact:* National Baseball Hall of Fame, P.O. Box 590, Cooperstown, NY 13326; 607-547-9988.

First girls to play in Little League baseball game
Girls were first allowed to play Little League baseball in 1974. *Contact:* Little League Baseball, P.O. Box 3485, S. Williamsport, PA 17701; 717-326-1921; Fax: 717-326-1074.

First human blood transfusion (1767)
Dr. Jean Baptiste Denys performed the first blood transfusion.

First human-powered flight across English Channel
Bryan Allen flew the *Gossamer Albatross* across the English Channel in 1979.

George Herbert Walker Bush's Birthday
The 41st President of the U.S. was born in Milton, Massachusetts, in 1924.

Interracial Marriage Day
Celebrates the anniversary of the *Loving v. Virginia Supreme Court* decision (1967). This decision overturned state laws prohibiting interracial marriages. *Contact:* U.S. Supreme Court. ✉

Spousal Abuse Day
On the anniversary of the 1994 murders of Nicole Brown Simpson and Ronald Goldman, be alert to signs of spousal abuse among your friends. Stop it before it goes too far.

June 13

Beyond the Solar System Day
The U.S. space probe *Pioneer 10,* which was launched on March 2, 1972, became the first spacecraft to leave the solar system when it crossed Neptune's orbit in 1983. *Contact:* NASA. ✉

Cigarette company found guilty for death of smoker
In 1988, the Liggett Group was the first tobacco company to be found responsible for the death of a smoker. *Contact:* Liggett Group, Inc., 300 N. Duke Street, Durham, NC 27701; 919-683-9000; Fax: 919-683-5573.

First nudist colony (1930)

Homeowner's Loan Act passed (1933)
The Federal Savings and Loan Association was established.

Kitchen Klutzes of America Day

To celebrate the not-so-accomplished cook.

Miranda Decision Anniversary

In 1966, the U.S. Supreme Court ruled in *Miranda v Arizona* that suspects had to be informed of their rights before being questioned by police. *Contact:* U.S. Supreme Court. ✉

Saint Anthony of Padua Feast Day

Patron saint of the poor, the illiterate, young lovers, barren women, lost articles, and careless people. Also patron saint of Portugal and Brazil. He died in 1231.

U.S. Department of Labor created (1888)

Congress created the forerunner of the Department of Labor. *Contact:* Department of Labor, Public Affairs Department #S1032, 200 Constitution Avenue NW, Washington, DC 20210; 202-219-9711; Fax: 202-219-8699.

June 14

Bunsen burner invented (1847)

Robert von Bunsen invented the Bunsen burner. His simple invention allows a chemist to control a gas flame efficiently.

Canadian parliament first meeting (1841)

Contact: Canadian Embassy, 501 Pennsylvania Avenue NW, Washington, DC 20001; 202-682-1740.

Casual Day

On the Friday before the summer solstice, people go to work dressed casually (in exchange for a contribution to United Celebral Palsy). 500,000 workers participated in the 1995 celebration and raised $3,000,000. *Sponsor:* United Cerebral Palsy Association, 1660 L Street NW #700, Washington, DC 20036; 800-872-5827; Fax: 202-776-0414.

Dollars Against Diabetes Days

DAD's Days, celebrated the weekend of Father's Day, raises money for diabetes research. *Sponsor:* AFL-CIO, Building and Construction Trades, 815 16th Street NW, Washington, DC 20006; 202-637-5000; Fax: 202-659-5559.

Family History Day

A time to share family stories with other family members. *Sponsor:* Wellness Permission League. ✉

First breach of promise suit (1623)

Greville Pooley sued Cicely Jordan for breach of promise in Charles City, Virginia.

First non-stop transatlantic flight (1919)

The first non-stop transatlantic flight was made by Captain John Alcock and Lieutenant Arthur Brown.

First President broadcast on radio (1922)

President Harding was heard on radio when the dedication of the Francis Scott Key Memorial in Baltimore, Maryland, was broadcast by WEAR.

Flag Day

In 1777, the Continental Congress resolved that the Stars and Stripes flag would be the national flag of the U.S. For a free booklet on how to handle and display flags, write to the VFW at the following address

(ask for the U.S. Flag Folders). *Contact:* VFW National Headquarters, Education Department, 34th and Broadway, Kansas City, MO 64111.

Own Your Share of America Day

To encourage people to invest in American stocks. Send for a free 20-page brochure on how to invest in common stocks. Celebrated on the 15th, if a workday; or on the nearest workday. *Sponsor:* National Association of Investors Clubs, P.O. Box 220, Royal Oak, MI 48068; 810-583-6242; Fax: 810-583-4880; e-mail: 76703.4372@compuserve.com.

U.S. Army established (1775)

Congress established the first U.S. military service. *Contact:* Department of the Army, Pentagon SAPA-CR, Room 3E718, Washington, DC 20310; 703-695-0363; Fax: 703-693-5737.

Univac Computer Birthday

The world's first commercial computer was demonstrated in Philadelphia, Pennsylvania in 1951.

June 15

12th Amendment to the Constitution ratified (1804)

Changed the way the president and vice president are selected by electors.

Arkansas Admission Day

The 25th state was admitted to the U.S. in 1836. *Contact:* Arkansas Department of Tourism, 1 Capital Mall, Little Rock, AR 72201; 501-682-1081; 800-872-1259; Fax: 501-682-1364.

Billy the Kid Tombstone Race

On the Saturday in the second weekend of June, the Old Fort Days Celebrations include many festivities including the world's richest tombstone race. Competitors must run an obstacle course carrying an 80 lb. tombstone. *Sponsor:* Old Fort Days Celebration, De Baca County Chamber of Commerce, P.O. Box 28, Fort Sumter, NM 88119; 505-355-7705.

Birthday of Plastic

John Wesley Hyatt invented the first plastic, celluloid, in 1869.

Cork-centered baseball patented (1909)

Espionage Act passed (1917)

Made it illegal to spy against the U.S.

First black to graduate from West Point (1877)

Henry Flipper graduated in 1877. *Contact:* U.S. Military Academy, West Point, NY 10996; 914-938-4011; Fax: 914-938-3828.

First fatal aviation accident (1785)

Jean Pilatre de Rozier died in a balloon fire over the English Channel.

Justice for Janitors Day

Encourages governments to focus on raising revenues rather than cutting vital services such as janitors. *Sponsor:* SEIU, 1313 L Street NW, Washington, DC 20005; 202-898-3200.

Kid's Fishing Day

Many local parks and lakes sponsor a kid's fishing day (with contests and prizes) on the second or third Saturday of June.

Magna Carta Day

In Runnymede, England, King John signed the Magna Carta in 1215. This first charter of English liberties was the basis for American democratic thought. *Contact:* United Kingdom Embassy, 3100 Massachusetts Avenue NW, Washington, DC 20008; 202-462-1340.

National Electricity Day

In 1752, Benjamin Franklin flew a kite to prove that lightning is electricity.

National Hollerin' Contest

The old-time way to communicate without technology, give a shout on the third Saturday in June. *Sponsor:* National Hollerin' Contest, Volunteer Fire Department, P.O.

✉ Addresses for frequently cited organizations are gathered on pages vii–viii.

Box 332, Spivey's Corner, NC 28335; 919-567-2156.

National Skillet Throwing Contest

Contestants throw cast-iron skillets as far as they can in this national contest held at Macksburk, Iowa, on the third Saturday in June. *Sponsor:* Madison County Visitors Bureau, 73 Jefferson, Winterset, IA 50273; 515-462-1185.

National Soccer Hall of Fame induction ceremonies

Induction ceremonies are usually held the second weekend in June. Call to confirm dates. *Sponsor:* National Soccer Hall of Fame, 5-11 Ford Avenue, Oneonta, NY 13820; 607-432-3351.

Process for strengthening rubber patented (1844)

Charles Goodyear patented a process for vulcanizing or strengthening rubber (so it won't stick in hot weather). *Contact:* Goodyear Tire & Rubber, 1144 E. Market Street, Akron, OH 44316; 216-796-2121; Fax: 216-796-2222.

World Juggling Day

Celebrate the art of juggling on the Saturday nearest June 19, the founding date of the International Jugglers Association. *Sponsor:* International Jugglers Association, P.O. Box 443, Davidson, NC 28036; 704-892-2244; Fax: 704-892-2499.

June 16

Bloomsday

James Joyce's *Ulysses,* the best known stream of consciousness novel, recounted the events of a single day (June 16, 1904) in the lives of three Dubliners: Leopold and Molly Bloom, and Stephen Dedalus.

Day of the African Child

Anniversary of the 1976 student uprising in Soweto. *Sponsor:* UN Center Against Apartheid, United Nations. ✉

Father's Day

First celebrated in Spokane, Washington in 1910, Father's Day was made a national holiday in 1966. Always celebrated on the third Sunday in June.

Federal Deposit Insurance Corporation established

The Banking Act of 1933 was passed by Congress; it established the Federal Bank Deposit Insurance Corporation, which insures deposits in banks. *Contact:* Federal Deposit Insurance Corp., 550 17th Street NW, Washington, DC 20429; 202-393-8400; Fax: 202-347-2775.

First major rock 'n' roll festival (1967)

50,000 people attended The Monterey International Pop Festival. Among the performers were Janis Joplin, Jimi Hendrix, The Who, Otis Redding, The Byrds, Jefferson Airplane, the Grateful Dead, and The Mamas and the Papas.

First squeeze play in baseball (1894)

On a bunt with 2 out, George Case of Yale scored from third base in the first squeeze play ever. *Contact:* Major League Baseball. ✉

First sustained helicopter flight (1922)

Took place in College Park, Maryland.

First woman in space (1963)

Soviet Cosmonaut Valentina Tereshkova was the first woman in space. *Contact:* NASA. ✉

Ford Motor Company incorporated (1903)

Contact: Ford Motor Company, American Road, Dearborn, MI 48121-0000; 313-332-3000; Fax: 313-845-8981.

The International Day of Solidarity with the Struggling People of South Africa

This is now a day of celebration rather than a day of remembrance. Also known as Soweto Day. *Sponsor:* United Nations. ✉

Ladies' Day Anniversary

The first Ladies' Day was hosted by the New York Gothams in 1883. *Contact:* Major League Baseball. ✉

National Housing Week

The third week in June (Sunday to Sunday) recognizes construction workers and other people who build homes.

National Morticians' Day

Honors all morticians and other people who work in the dead and gone industry. It is celebrated on the anniversary of the death of the founder's mother.

Orange Band Memorial Day

In 1987, Orange Band, the last dusky seaside sparrow, died in captivity at Walt Disney World.

Psycho, the movie, premiered (1960)

Alfred Hitchcock's thriller opened in New York City.

June 17

Bunker Hill Day

The Battle of Bunker Hill was fought in 1775.

Bureau of Indian Affairs established (1824)

Contact: Bureau of Indian Affairs, Public Affairs Office, Mail Stop 1340 - MIB, Washington, DC 20240; 202-219-4150; Fax: 202-208-3711.

First person killed in a railroad accident (1831)

When the boiler exploded on the first passenger locomotive in the U.S., the fireman was killed.

First woman to fly across the Atlantic Ocean

In 1928, Amelia Earhart flew from Newfoundland to Wales in 21 hours. In 1932, she became the first woman to fly solo across the Atlantic Ocean.

Good Roads Day

The first Good Roads Day was introduced in 1913.

International Violin Day

On the birthday of violinist and composer Igor Stravinsky, listen to some classical music. Stravinsky was born in 1882 in Russia. *Sponsor:* The Life of the Party. ✉

Naked body first used as a stage costume (1969)

The Broadway musical *Oh! Calcutta!* was the first Broadway production to use the naked human body as a stage costume.

National Old-Time Fiddlers Contest

On the Monday through Saturday following Father's Day, fiddlers from around the country gather at Weiser for this national contest. *Sponsor:* Weiser Chamber of Commerce, 8 E. Idaho Street, Weiser, ID 83672; 208-549-0452.

Republican Party held its first convention (1856)

The GOP held its first national convention in Philadelphia. *Contact:* Republican Party, 310 First Street SE, Washington, DC 20003; 202-863-8500; Fax: 202-863-8820.

Sweden-America Day

The first Swedish immigrants to the U.S. began their trip in Kalmar and landed in Wilmington, Delaware. *Contact:* Kingdom of Sweden Embassy, 600 New Hampshire Avenue NW, Washington, DC 20037; 202-944-5600.

Watergate Day

The Watergate burglary that brought down Nixon occurred in 1972.

White Bronco Day

In 1994, TV audiences watched in stunned silence as Los Angeles police followed O. J. Simpson on a low-speed chase over the freeways of Los Angeles. Simpson had been accused of murdering his ex-wife, Nicole, and her friend Ron Goldman.

June 18

Battle of Waterloo

Napoleon met his Waterloo in 1815.

Children's carriage patented (1889)

Black inventor W. H. Richardson patented the children's carriage.

Count Your $$ Day

Count your money on the birthday of money management writer Sylvia Porter. She was born in 1913 in Patchogue, New York. *Sponsor:* The Life of the Party. ✉

Ellery Queen mystery radio show premiered (1939)

First American woman in space (1983)

Dr. Sally Ride was the first American woman to travel in space (aboard the space shuttle *Challenger*). *Contact:* NASA. ✉

First bicycle traffic court (1936)

First genetically engineered vaccine announced (1981)

Designed to prevent hoof and mouth disease.

International Declaration of Human Rights adopted (1948)

Contact: United Nations. ✉

National Splurge Day

Go ahead, have some fun today. Don't worry about the cost. *Sponsor:* All My Events. ✉

No Headline Day

Every day 40,000 people die of starvation; yet this news makes no headlines. Why not? *Sponsor:* A Pilgrim's Almanac. ✉

Salt II Strategic Arms Limitation Treaty signed (1979)

President Jimmy Carter and Soviet President Leonid Brezhnev signed this treaty in Vienna, Austria.

War of 1812 declared

Because of repeated violations of American rights to the sea, and the incitement of Indians on the frontier, the U.S. declared war against Great Britain.

June 19

Federal Communications Commission created (1934)

Contact: Federal Communication Commission, 1919 M Street NW, Washington, DC 20554; 202-632-7000; Fax: 202-653-5402.

First baseball game played under Cartwright Rules

Played in Hoboken, New Jersey, in 1846. *Contact:* Major League Baseball. ✉

First married couple executed in the U.S. (1953)

Julius and Ethel Rosenberg were executed at Sing Sing Prison in Ossining, New York for spying.

First movie of the sun taken (1934)

Taken at the University of Michigan. *Contact:* University of Michigan, 530 Thompson Avenue, Ann Arbor, MI 58109; 313-764-1817.

Garfield the Cat's Birthday

Created by Jim Davis; the cartoon strip first appeared in 1978. *Sponsor:* Paws Incorporated, Kim Campbell, PR Director, 5440 E. County Road 450N, Albany, IN 47320-9728; 317-287-2364; Fax: 317-287-2329.

I've Got a Secret debut (1952)

Garry Moore was host of this TV game show with celebrity panelists. *Contact:* CBS-TV. ✉

Juneteenth

Celebrates the day that Union General Granger declared slaves free in Texas in 1865. Also known as Emancipation Day, this day is now celebrated as a black freedom festival.

June 20

Ancient Greek New Year

Ed Sullivan Show premiered (1948)

One of the longest-running variety shows in TV history. *Contact:* CBS-TV. ✉

First bank chartered by Congress (1863)

Congress chartered the National Bank of Philadelphia, Pennsylvania.

First honeymoon in a balloon (1909)

First native African to graduate from U.S. college
In 1901, Charlotte Manye of South Africa became the first native African to graduate from a U.S. university.

First Ph.D. in science awarded to a woman (1895)
Caroline Baldwin earned a doctorate degree in science from Cornell University. *Contact:* Cornell University, Ithaca, NY 14853; 607-255-4144; Fax: 607-255-9346.

First wedding performed over the radio
A sailor on the *USS Birmingham* and his bride in Detroit, Michigan were married over the radio.

Great Seal of the U.S. adopted (1782)
Congress adopted the design for the Great Seal of the U.S.

Guam American Day
In 1898, the Spanish commander of Guam surrendered to Captain Glass of the *USS Charleston* during the Spanish-American War. *Contact:* Guam Visitors Bureau, 1150 Mauna Village Parkway, Alameda, CA 94501; 800-228-4826.

Lighten Up America Day
At noon on the first day of summer, lighten up. Do something outrageously silly. *Sponsor:* C. W. Metcalf, Addison Wesley, Route 128, Reading, MA 01867; 617-944-3700; 800-447-2226; Fax: 617-944-9338.

Longest Day of the Year

National Bald Eagle Day
In 1982, Congress chose the bald eagle as our national symbol.

Noxema skin cream got its name (1914)
Noxema got its name because it knocks out eczema (knocks eczema).

Summer Solstice
Summer begins at 10:24 P.M., Eastern Standard Time.

West Virginia Admission Day
In 1863, West Virginia became the 35th state of the U.S. *Contact:* West Virginia Tourism Authority, 252 B George Street, Beckley, WV 25801; 304-256-6702; 800-225-5982.

June 21

First long-playing record produced (1948)
Peter Goldmark of CBS demonstrated the first successful commercial long-playing record. RCA demonstrated a 33⅓ rpm record on September 18, 1931.

Flag-Burning Day
In 1989, the Supreme Court ruled that the First Amendment protected flag-burning as a form of political protest. This day comes 1 week after Flag Day. *Contact:* U.S. Supreme Court. ✉

International Flower Day
Bring bouquets of summer flowers into your home, business, school, or other places you frequent. *Sponsor:* All My Events. ✉

International Knock-Knock Man Day
Always celebrated on the third Thursday in June. *Sponsor:* Camp Chaos, ABC Radio Z Rock, Chaz Fernandez, 13725 Montfort Drive, Dallas, TX 75240; 214-991-9200.

New Hampshire Ratification Day
In 1788, New Hampshire became the 9th state to ratify the U.S. Constitution. *Contact:* New Hampshire Travel Office, 172 Pembroke Road, P.O. Box 1856, Concord, NH 03301; 603-271-2665; Fax: 603-271-2629.

Reaper patented (1834)
Cyrus McCormick patented his reaping machine.

Saint Alban Feast Day
Saint Alban, a Roman soldier, was beheaded for harboring a priest refuge. He became Britain's first martyr. He is considered the patron saint of refugees.

✉ Addresses for frequently cited organizations are gathered on pages vii–viii.

Saint Aloysius Gonzaga
Feast Day
He died at the age of 23, and is considered patron saint of youth and teenagers.

Sign of Cancer
Cancer the crab runs from June 21st to July 22nd. Cancer people are moody, sensitive, and impressionable.

Tough Decisions Week
During the third week in June, the Supreme Court has made some of its toughest and most controversial decisions, including decisions on flag burning (1989), hate crimes (1992), prayers in schools (1962), the draft (1981), and the death penalty (1972). *Contact:* U.S. Supreme Court. ✉

U.S. Constitution
took effect (1788)

World Sauntering Day
On the third Friday in June, saunter along the world's longest front porch at the Grand Hotel on Mackinac Island. *Sponsor:* Grand Hotel, Mackinac Island, MI 49757; 906-847-3331; 800-334-7263; Fax: 906-847-3259.

June 22

Cross Burning Day
In 1992, the Supreme Court ruled that hate-crime laws violated the right of free speech. Hate-crime laws banned such acts as cross burning and other expressions of racial bias. *Contact:* U.S. Supreme Court. ✉

Cuyahoga River
burned (1969)
In downtown Cleveland, Ohio, the Cuyahoga River burned. Actually, it was the oil and other scum on it that burned. A concerted effort was launched to clean up the river. *Contact:* Cleveland Visitors Bureau, 50 Public Square #3100, Cleveland, OH 44113; 216-621-4110; 800-321-1001; Fax: 216-621-5967.

Doughnuts Day
On the day that doughnuts were invented (1847), eat lots of them.

First automobile race in the world (1894)
This race took place between Paris and Rouen in France.

GI Bill of Rights
signed (1944)
Provided educational and other benefits for returning World War II veterans.

Saint Thomas More
Feast Day
Patron saint of lawyers.

U.S. Department of Justice
created (1870)
Congress created the Department of Justice headed by the Attorney General. *Contact:* Department of Justice, 10th Street and Constitution Avenue, Washington, DC 20530; 202-514-2000; Fax: 202-633-4371.

June 23

Amateur Radio Week
The week ends with the 4th weekend and spotlights amateur radio operators. More than 650,000 Americans are ham radio operators. *Sponsor:* American Radio Relay League, 225 Main Street, Newington, CT 06111; 203-666-1541; 800-326-3942; Fax: 203-665-7531; e-mail: 215-5052@mci.com.

American Women
Athletes Week
Celebrates the accomplishments of all women athletes, especially Olympic track star, Wilma Rudolph (born on the 23rd) and Babe Didrikson Zaharias (born on the 26th).

Bobbitt entered the English language (1993)
John Wayne Bobbitt met his Waterloo when his wife cut off his male appendage and threw it away. Don't let anyone bobbitt you.

Carpenter Ant
Awareness Week
The last full week in June promotes getting rid of wood-destroying carpenter ants. *Sponsor:* Batzner Pest Management, 16700 W. Victor Road, New Berlin, WI 53151; 414-797-4177; 800-878-2110 (WI); Fax: 414-797-4166.

Cosmic Patience Day
In 1974, the first extraterrestrial message was sent from Earth into space. How long will we have to wait for an answer? *Sponsor:* A Pilgrim's Almanac.

First animated feature filmed in CinemaScope
In 1955, Walt Disney's *Lady and the Tramp* opened in theaters. *Contact:* Walt Disney Company.

First black presidential candidate
The Kentucky delegation to the 1888 Republican convention gave abolitionist Frederick Douglass 1 vote as they placed his name in nomination for president.

First job discrimination victory for transsexual
In 1992, pilot Jessica Hearns was reinstated by Continental Airlines after having a sex-change operation. *Contact:* Continental Airlines, 2929 Allen Parkway #1501, Houston, TX 77019; 713-834-5000; Fax: 713-523-4085.

First round-the-world flight in a single-engine
In 1931, Wiley Post and Harold Gatty took off from New York City on the first round-the-world flight in a single-engine plane.

Gay Pride Week
The week of June 27th is celebrated with Gay Pride parades in New York, San Francisco, and elsewhere.

International Sit on the Front Pew Sunday
On the 4th Sunday in June, show your pastor that you really want to hear his or her sermon by sitting up front. *Sponsor:* KJIL Radio, Don Hughes, General Manager, P.O. Box 991, Meade, KS 67864; 316-873-2991; Fax: 316-873-2755.

Midsummer Eve
Celebrated in Scandinavian countries on Saint John's Eve.

National Ducks and Wetlands Day
Proclaimed by the president to be celebrated on the last Sunday in June.

National Forgiveness Day
The goal of this day is to eliminate hurt, anger, resentment, bitterness, hatred, and rage in our world. Always celebrated the 4th Sunday in June. *Sponsor:* Center for Awesome Love, Robert and Mary Lynne Moyers, 1014 McKinley Street, Fremont, OH 43420; 419-355-0810.

National Sheriff's Week
Always celebrated the last full week in June.

Saxophone patented (1846)
Antoine Joseph (Adolphe) Sax patented the saxophone.

Triumph over Adversity Day
The birthday of Olympic track star Wilma Rudolph; born in Saint Bethlehem, Tennessee in 1940. She wore a leg brace due to polio until age 12; at age 20, she became the first American woman to receive 3 Olympic gold medals—for running!

Typewriter patented (1868)
Christopher Sholes received a patent for the typewriter in 1868.

June 24

Berlin airlift began (1948)
The Soviet Union blockaded West Berlin; for 321 days the Western nations conducted an airlift to get supplies into West Berlin.

Celebration of the Senses
Enjoy all 5 senses and the 6th if you can. *Sponsor:* Wellness Permission League.

First sighting of North America by European (1497)
Englishman John Cabot made the first recorded sighting of North America.

Flying Saucer Day

Flying saucers were first sighted by Kenneth Arnold, near Washington's Cascade Mountains in 1947.

Midsummer Day

This day is celebrated in the Scandinavian countries on the feast day of Saint John the Baptist.

Newfoundland Discovery Day

Newfoundland was discovered by John Cabot in 1497.

Resurrection City shut down (1968)

Resurrection City, the shantytown built as part of the Poor People's March on Washington, DC, was shut down by the government.

Saint John the Baptist Feast Day

Patron saint of Macau and Florence, Italy (San Giovanni Battista). .

Think Your Way to Health Day

On the birthday of Norman Cousins (1915), laugh your way to a healthier mind and body. *Sponsor:* The Life of the Party. ✉

June 25

Custer's Last Stand

In 1876, General Custer and 200 other men were killed after attacking a Sioux camp near the Little Big Horn. It was the last great Indian victory.

First color TV broadcast (1951)

CBS broadcast the first color TV program. *Contact:* CBS-TV. ✉

Korean War Remembrance Day

In 1950, North Korea invaded South Korea. The U.S. became involved on June 30th.

Leon Day

Leon Day (noel spelled backwards) is 6 months from Christmas; today we celebrate anyone named Leon. It is also a day to receive rather than give a gift.

Male-Only Draft Day

In 1981, the U.S. Supreme Court ruled that it was constitutional to draft only men for military service. *Contact:* U.S. Supreme Court. ✉

National Columnist's Day

The 4th Tuesday in June honors local and national syndicated newspaper columnists. *Sponsor:* Gloucester County Times, Jim Six, Columnist, 309 S. Broad Street, Woodbury, NJ 08096; 609-845-3300; Fax: 609-845-5480.

No Prayers in School Day

In 1962, the U.S. Supreme Court banned official prayers in public schools. *Contact:* U.S. Supreme Court. ✉

Tennis shoe designed (1947)

Virginia Ratification Day

Virginia became the 10th state to ratify the U.S. Constitution in 1788. *Contact:* Virginia Division of Tourism, 1629 K Street NW, Washington, DC 20006; 202-659-5523; 800-847-4882; Fax: 202-659-8646.

June 26

Babe Didrikson Zaharias's Birthday

Because she excelled at so many sports (All-American in basketball, Olympic medals in track and field, professional golfer), Babe was named the woman athlete of the first half of the 20th century; she was born in 1914 in Port Arthur, Texas.

Bicycle patented (1918)

William Clarkson, Jr. of New York patented a modern version of the bicycle. For a free bicycle safety pamphlet, write to Aetna Life & Casualty, Consumer Information Department, 151 Farmington Avenue, Hartford CT 06156.

Federal Credit Union Act signed (1934)

Allowed credit unions to be formed anywhere in the U.S. *Contact:* Credit Union National Association, 5710 Mineral Point Road,

P.O. Box 431, Madison, WI 53701;
608-231-4000; Fax: 608-231-4263.

First movie theater opened (1896)

The first movie theater in the U.S. offered 10-cent movies.

Good Earth Day

On the birthday of Pearl Buck, author of *The Good Earth*, celebrate the earth. Take time today to go outside and enjoy the good earth. Buck was born in 1892 in Hillsboro, West Virginia. *Sponsor:* The Life of the Party. ✉

International Day Against Drug Abuse and Illicit Trafficking

Since 1987, this day has been celebrated by the United Nations. *Sponsor:* United Nations. ✉

New York Daily News first published (1919)

Contact: New York Daily News, Communications Department, 220 East 42nd Street, New York, NY 10017-5858; 212-210-2100; Fax: 212-661-4675.

Saint Lawrence Seaway officially opened (1959)

The seaway allows ocean-going vessels to travel the Great Lakes.

United Nations Charter signed (1945)

Fifty nations signed the Charter. *Contact:* United Nations. ✉

World's tallest structure opened (1976)

The CN Tower, the world's tallest self-supporting structure, opened. *Contact:* CN Tower, 301 Front Street West, Toronto, Ontario, M5V 2T6 Canada; 416-360-8500.

June 27

First pen with truly erasable ink (1978)

"Happy Birthday to You" Birthday

The most popular song in the world was first published in 1924. Mildred Hill composed the tune. Patty Hill wrote the lyrics. Mildred was born in 1859.

Helen Keller's Birthday

Blind and deaf from the age of 18 months, Keller overcame her handicaps and became an outspoken advocate for the blind; she was born in 1880 in Tuscumbia, Alabama. *Sponsor:* Helen Keller International, 90 Washington Street, 15th Floor, New York, NY 10006; 212-943-0890; Fax: 212-943-1220.

National Fink Day

Celebrate finks and people named Fink.

Stonewall Inn Incident (1969)

Patrons of the Stonewall Inn, a gay bar, fought with police during a raid. This incident is considered a landmark of the modern gay rights movement.

World Championship Seed-Spitting Contest

On the last Thursday, Friday, and Saturday in June, the world champion seed-spitter is determined. *Sponsor:* Luling Watermelon Thump Association, P.O. Box 710, Luling, TX 78648; 210-875-3214.

June 28

Clara Maass Day

Honors the birthday of Clara Louise Maass (1876), a nurse who gave her life during the yellow fever experiments of 1901. *Sponsor:* Clara Maass Foundation, 1 Clara Maass Drive, Belleville, NJ 07109; 201-450-2277; Fax: 201-450-0181.

First dog show (1859)
The first dog show was held in Newcastle, England.

First human to receive a baboon liver transplant
In 1992, the first animal liver transplant occurred at the University of Pittsburgh.

Monday Holiday Law Anniversary
The Monday Holiday Law was signed in 1968.

National Sobriety Checkpoint Week
During the week of July 4th, don't drink and drive. *Sponsor:* Mothers Against Drunk Driving, 511 E. John Carpenter Frwy #700, Irving, TX 75062-8187; 214-744-6233.

U.S. Air Force Academy went coed (1976)
The Coast Guard Academy went coed at the same time. *Contact:* U.S. Air Force Academy, Colorado Springs, CO 80840; 719-472-1818; Fax: 719-472-3494.

World War I (beginning and ending)
On June 28, 1914, Archduke Ferdinand of Austria was assassinated in Sarajevo, Bosnia, thus starting World War I (the war was actually declared on July 28, 1914). On June 28, 1919, the Treaty of Ver-sailles was signed, thus officially ending World War I.

June 29

Biggest All Night Gospel Singing in the World
Over 10,000 people sing gospel tunes all night at Memorial Field in Bonifay, Florida. Always the Saturday before July 4th. *Sponsor:* Bonifay Kiwanis Club, Rickey Callahan, P.O. Box 425, Bonifay, FL 32425; 904-547-3613; Fax: 904-547-9223.

Death penalty banned as cruel and unusual punishment
In 1972, the U.S. Supreme Court banned the death penalty; it was rescinded in 1976 and capital punishment was allowed for crimes of murder. *Contact:* U.S. Supreme Court. ✉

First 1st National Bank opened (1863)
Opened in Davenport, Iowa.

First person to high-jump 7 feet
Charlie Dumas high-jumped 7 feet 5/8 inches at the 1956 Olympic trials.

First remote control for a TV (1964)

First transcontinental auto race finished (1909)
A Ford factory team won the first transcontinental auto race, which ran between New York and Seattle; it took 28 days.

Interstate Highway System approved (1956)
Congress passed the Federal Highway Act, authorizing construction of the Interstate Highway System. *Contact:* Department of Transportation, Federal Highway Administration, 400 7th Street SW #4218, Washington, DC 20590; 202-366-0660; Fax: 202-366-3235.

Runic New Year
In the Wicca religion, this day marks the beginning of Feoh, the half-month of wealth and success.

Saints Peter and Paul Feast Day
Saint Peter is patron saint of longevity (the doorkeeper of heaven,) fishermen, the Catholic Church, and the papacy. Both Saint Peter and Saint Paul are also considered patrons of good weather.

World Championship Rotary Tiller Race
During their annual Purple Hull Pea Festival on the last Saturday in June, Emerson hosts this race and many other events. Founded in 1990. *Sponsor:* Purple Hull Pea Festival,

✉ Addresses for frequently cited organizations are gathered on pages vii–viii.

150   JUNE

P.O. Box 1, Emerson, AR 71740;
501-547-3349; 501-547-2220.

June 30

26th Amendment to the Constitution ratified (1971)
Gave all persons over the age of 18 the right to vote.

Feast of the Hunter's Moon
On the full moon nearest the summer solstice, the goddess and god of the hunt are honored. With the aid of the full moon, it is easier to hunt summer game animals.

First people to die in space (1971)
Cosmonauts G. T. Dobrovolsky, V. I. Patsayev, and V. N. Volkov died during re-entry after a 24-day mission in space. *Contact:* NASA. ✉

First plastic laminated car (1953)
GM's Corvette was the first plastic laminated car. *Contact:* General Motors, 3044 W Grand Avenue, Detroit, MI 48202-0000; 313-556-5000; Fax: 313-556-5108.

First woman to graduate from law school (1870)
Ada Kepley graduated from the Union College of Law in Chicago, Illinois.

Gone with the Wind published
Margaret Mitchell's novel was published in 1936.

Guiding Light premiered (1952)
The longest running soap opera on TV, also the longest running TV series. *Contact:* CBS-TV. ✉

Log Cabin Day
The last Sunday in June is celebrated in Michigan by visiting more than 50 log cabins and homes open for tours, festivals, and special activities. Send for a free brochure from the Society. Most events are free and open to the public. *Sponsor:* Log Cabin Society of Michigan, 3503 Edwards Road, Sodus, MI 49126; 616-944-5719; Fax: 616-944-5719.

Meteorite Day
In 1908 a large meteorite crashed in central Siberia, causing the most powerful explosion in human history.

Niagara Falls first crossed on tightrope (1859)
Emile Blondin, a French acrobat, was the first person to cross Niagara Falls on a tightrope.

Pure Food and Drug Act becomes law (1906)
The Pure Food and Drug Act and the Meat Inspection Act were enacted. *Contact:* Food and Drug Administration, 5600 Fishers Lane #14-71, Rockville, MD 20857; 301-443-2410; Fax: 301-443-0755.

Transistors demonstrated (1948)
Transistors were invented by 3 Bell Laboratory scientists.

JULY

Hitchhiking Month
Promotes hitchhiking. Formerly sponsored by Richard Falk, who died in 1994.

Minority Tourism Month
Encourages minorities to travel. *Sponsor:* Greater New Orleans Black Tourism Network, 1520 Sugar Bowl Drive, New Orleans, LA 70112; 800-725-5652.

National Anti-Boredom Month
Designed to help people avoid boredom, because boredom can lead to depression, addiction, and other self-defeating behavior. Send $3.00 to receive their guide, *Beating Boredom. Sponsor:* The Boring Institute, Alan Caruba, Founder, P.O. Box 40, Maplewood, NJ 07040; 201-763-6392; Fax: 201-763-4287.

National Baked Bean Month
Sponsor: Michigan Bean Commission, 1031 South US 27, St. Johns, MI 48879; 517-224-1361; Fax: 517-224-6374.

National Eye Exam Month
Get your eyes examined this month. Sometimes also held in August. *Sponsor:* Prevent Blindness America. ✉

National Hot Dog Month

To encourage the consumption of hot dogs. *Sponsor:* American Meat Institute, P.O. Box 3556, Washington, DC 20007; 703-841-2400.

National Ice Cream Month

Promotes America's favorite dessert, ice cream. *Sponsor:* International Ice Cream Association, 1250 H Street NW #900, Washington, DC 20005; 202-737-4332; Fax: 202-331-7820.

National July Belongs to Blueberries Month

Promotes the peak month for blueberries. *Sponsor:* North American Blueberry Council, P.O. Box 1036, Folsom, CA 95630; 916-985-6644; Fax: 916-985-0666.

National Lamb and Wool Month

National Peach Month

National Picnic Month

To increase appreciation of picnics and picnic foods. Formerly sponsored by Campbell Soup Company.

National Purposeful Parenting Month

Tell your children you love them. Do this often. *Sponsor:* Parenting without Pressure. ✉

National Recreation and Parks Month

To invite community participation in America's parks. *Sponsor:* National Recreation and Park Association, 2775 S. Quincy Street #300, Arlington, VA 22206; 703-820-4940; Fax: 703-671-6772.

National Tennis Month

Tennis magazine encourages everybody to learn tennis. *Sponsor: Tennis* Magazine, Marilyn Wilkes, 5520 Park Avenue, P.O. Box 395, Trumbull, CT 06611-0395; 203-373-7120; Fax: 203-371-2127.

Sports and Recreation Books Month

Read a book on sports, recreation, exercise, hunting, fishing, hiking, biking, sailing, or games. *Sponsor:* Book Marketing Update. ✉

July 1

Bureau of Internal Revenue established (1867)

The IRS was established by an act of Congress to collect taxes. Also on this day in 1862, President Lincoln signed a law establishing an income tax. *Contact:* Internal Revenue Service. ✉

Canada Day

Formerly known as Dominion Day, this holiday celebrates Canada's confederation in 1867. When July 1st falls on a Sunday, the legal holiday is celebrated on the following Monday. *Contact:* Canadian Embassy, 501 Pennsylvania Avenue NW, Washington, DC 10001; 202-682-1740.

Court TV premiered (1991)

Contact: Courtroom Television Network, 600 Third Avenue, 2nd Floor, New York, NY 10016; 212-973-2800; Fax: 212-973-3355.

First adhesive U.S. postage stamp (1847)

Contact: U.S. Postal Service. ✉

First class postage drops from 3 cents to 2 cents

This was a first for the U.S. Postal Service; postage actually dropped by a penny in 1919. *Contact:* U.S. Postal Service. ✉

First nude scene in a movie (1915)

Actress Annette Kellerman stripped in the movie, *Daughter of the Gods.*

First search and rescue satellite launched (1982)

Kosmos 1383 was launched by the Soviet Union in cooperation with the U.S. and France. It was the first satellite equipped to pick up distress signals from planes and ships. *Contact:* NASA. ✉

First zoo in the U.S. (1874)
Opened in Philadelphia, Pennsylvania.

Man Watchers' Compliment Week
Men aren't used to being complimented, say something nice during the first full week of July (starting on the first Monday). *Sponsor:* Man Watchers International, Suzy Mallery, 12021 Wilshire Boulevard #371, Los Angeles, CA 90049; 310-826-9101; e-mail: Smallery@aol.com.

National Youth Sports Program Day

Nuclear Non-Proliferation Treaty signed (1968)
Sixty-one countries signed this treaty that prohibits the spread of nuclear weapons.

Payroll income tax withholding began (1943)
Contact: Internal Revenue Service. ✉

Sunglasses Birthday
Invented in China in 1200 to conceal the eyes of judges while sitting in court. Only in the 1930s were tinted glasses used to cut the glare of the sun.

Vitamins first described (1911)
Casimir Funk, a Polish biochemist, first used the word vitamins.

Zip Code's Birthday
The U.S. Post Office began the Zone Improvement Program on this date in 1963. *Contact:* U.S. Postal Service. ✉

July 2

Civil Rights Act of 1964 Anniversary
Forbids racial discrimination in public places and in employment; also set up the Equal Employment Opportunity Commission. *Contact:* Equal Employment Opportunity Commission, 1801 L Street NW,

Washington, DC 20507; 202-663-4900; 800-669-3362; Fax: 202-663-4912.

First flight of a zeppelin (1900)

National Literacy Day
Celebrated by presidential proclamation, encourages more people to read. For more information on literacy programs, call the National Literacy Hotline at 800-228-8813.

Salvation Army established (1865)
William Booth founded the Salvation Army in London, England. *Contact:* Salvation Army Headquarters, 615 Slaters Lane, P.O. Box 269, Alexandria, VA 22313; 703-684-5500; Fax: 703-684-3478.

Sherman Antitrust Act passed by Congress (1890)
Designed to break up monopolies.

U.S. Army Air Corps created (1926)
Contact: Department of the Army, Pentagon SAPA-CR, Room 3E718, Washington, DC 20310; 703-695-0363; Fax: 703-693-5737.

Voting Rights Act became law (1964)
Signed by President Johnson, the law prohibits discrimination on the basis of race in public accommodations, voter registration, union

July 3

Air Conditioning Appreciation Days
From July 3rd to August 15th, the Dog Days, we should be glad to have the comforts of air conditioning. *Sponsor:* Air Conditioning and Refrigeration Institute, 4301 N. Fairfax Drive #425, Arlington, VA 22203; 703-524-8800; Fax: 703-528-3816; Web home page: http://www.ari.org.

Birthday of the Automobile
Karl Benz drove the first automobile in the world in Mannheim, Germany in 1886.

Compliment Your Mirror Day
Compliment your mirror on what a wonderful owner it has. *Sponsor:* Puns Corp. ✉

Dog Days
July 3 to August 15. The ancients believed Sirius (star) caused hot,

DOG DAYS OF SUMMER

sultry weather, they sacrificed a dog at the beginning of the hot, sultry time to appease the rage of Sirius.

First American bank opened (1819)
The Bank for Savings in New York City opened.

First hot-air balloon travellers to cross Atlantic
In 1987, Richard Branson and Per Lindstrand became the first to cross the Atlantic Ocean in a hot-air balloon going from east to west.

Idaho Admission Day
In 1890, Idaho became the 43rd state of the U.S. *Contact:* Idaho Travel Council, 700 W. State Street, 2nd Floor, Boise, ID 83720; 208-334-2470; 800-635-7820; Fax: 208-334-2631.

Let Freedom Ring Day

Saint Thomas Feast Day
Patron saint of doubters and doubting Thomases (as a result of the story in the Bible where he doubted that Jesus had risen from the dead until he had seen him himself and touched his wounds).

Stay Out of the Sun Day
Sponsor: Wellness Permission League. ✉

U.S. Veterans Administration created (1930)
Contact: Department of Veterans Affairs, 810 Vermont Avenue NW,

Washington, DC 20420; 202-535-8300; Fax: 202-233-2807.

Women admitted to Jaycees (1984)
The Supreme Court ruled that state laws may force the Jaycees (and other all-male organizations) to admit women as full members with the same status as men. *Contact:* U.S. Supreme Court. ✉

World's Oldest Rodeo
Billed as the world's oldest rodeo (it began in 1888); it's held on July 4th weekend. *Sponsor:* Prescott Frontier Days, Chamber of Commerce, P.O. Box 1147, Prescott, AZ 86302; 520-445-2000; 800-358-1888; Fax: 520-445-0068.

July 4

"America the Beautiful" published (1895)
The original poem for this song was written by Katherine Lee Bates on July 22, 1893.

American Redneck Day
Celebrates the work-hard, play-hard spirit of the rural working class. *Sponsor:* American Redneck Trading Post, Ed Mason, 317 Fowell Road, Centreville, MD 21617; 410-758-0777.

American Top 40 first aired (1970)

membership, employment, and publicly owned or operated facilities.

Calvin Coolidge's Birthday
The 30th President of the U.S. was born in 1872 in Plymouth, Vermont.

Freedom Week
Celebrate freedom and liberty during the week of July 4–10. *Sponsor:* International Society of Friendship and Good Will. ✉

Independence Day
The Declaration of Independence was proclaimed in 1776; also known as the 4th of July.

National Country Music Day
A day for those who love to listen to America's favorite music. *Sponsor:* Alan W. Brue. ✉

National Toe Jam Day
This is 1 day of the year when you are almost certain to see your neighbor's bare feet—on the beach or at a picnic. Take a good look.

Sponsor: KCAQ-FM, The Woody Show, Jewel Langway, Producer, 1701 Pacific Avenue #270, Oxnard, CA 93033; 805-483-1000; Fax: 805-483-6555.

West Point Military Academy opened (1802)
Contact: West Point Military Academy, West Point, NY 10996; 914-938-4011; Fax: 914-938-3828.

World's Greatest Lizard Race
Sponsor: Lovington Chamber of Commerce, P.O. Box 1347, Lovington, NM 88260; 505-396-5311.

Yankee Doodle Dandy Day
Celebrate the birthday of George M. Cohan, the popular songwriter who wrote many patriotic songs, including "You're a Grand Old Flag," "Give My Regards to Broadway," and "The Yankee Doodle Boy." He was born in 1878 in Providence, Rhode Island.

July 5

Birthday of the Bikini
In 1946, the bikini was first shown in Paris. It was designed by Louis Reard and named after the Bikini Atoll, where an American atom bomb had been detonated on July 1st.

First black male tennis player to win at Wimbledon
In 1975, Arthur Ashe won the men's singles championship.

First travel agency (1841)
The Thomas Cook Travel service was started in 1841; it was recently bought by American Express Travel.

National Labor Relations Act signed (1935)
Guaranteed workers the right to organize and bargain collectively. *Contact:* National Labor Relations Board, 1717 Pennsylvania Avenue NW, Washington, DC 20570; 202-606-8438; Fax: 202-606-8243.

Phineas T. Barnum Birthday
The Greatest Showman Who Ever Lived was born in 1810.

Workaholics Day
Salute those too busy to take time out to give themselves a pat on the back for a job well done. *Sponsor:* Workman Publishing Company, 708 Broadway, New York, NY 10003; 800-722-7202.

World Championship Timber Carnival
This annual event is held on the weekend of the 4th, and determines

✉ Addresses for frequently cited organizations are gathered on pages vii–viii.

JULY   155

the world champion loggers and lumberjacks. *Sponsor:* Albany Visitors Association, 300 Second Avenue SW, Albany, OR 97321; 503-928-0911; 800-526-2256; Fax: 503-926-1500.

July 6

Beatrix Potter's Birthday
Author of the many tales of Peter Rabbit, she is a most beloved children's author. One of the early self-publishing success stories, she was born in 1866 in London, England. *Sponsor:* Book Marketing Update. ✉

First all-star baseball game (1933)
The game was played in Chicago; the American League won. *Contact:* Major League Baseball. ✉

First all-talking motion picture (1928)
The Lights of New York was presented in New York City.

First black U.S. attorney (1961)
Cecil Poole was sworn in as a U.S. attorney for Northern California.

First crossing of the Atlantic Ocean by an airship
In 1919, a British dirigible became the first airship to cross the Atlantic Ocean.

International Cherry Pit Spitting Contest
Held on the first Saturday in July to determine the world champion cherry pit spitter. *Sponsor:* Tree-Mendus Fruit Farm, Herb Teichman, 351 East Eureka Road, Eau Claire, MI 49111; 616-782-7101.

National Air Traffic Control Day

National Nude Weekend
The weekend after July 4th promotes acceptance of the naked human body. *Sponsor:* The Naturist Society, P.O. Box 132, Oshkosh, WI 54902; 414-231-9950; 800-558-8250; Fax: 414-231-9977.

Rabies vaccine first tested (1885)
Louis Pasteur tested the vaccine on a boy bitten by rabid dog.

Republican Party formed (1854)
The Grand Old Party was formally organized in Jackson, Michigan. *Contact:* Republican Party, 310 First Street SE, Washington, DC 20003; 202-863-8500; Fax: 202-863-8820.

Saint Maria Goretti Feast Day
She died while resisting an attempted rape when she was 12 years old, and is considered a model and patron saint of young girls.

World's Largest Salmon Barbecue
Over 5,000 pounds of fresh salmon are barbecued at Noyo Harbor in Fort Bragg on the first Saturday in July. *Sponsor:* World's Largest Salmon Barbecue, Michele White, P.O. Box 68, Fort Bragg, CA 95437; 707-964-6598.

World's Most Unusual Heat Wave (1949)
The central coast of Portugal experienced a 2-minute heat wave that sent temperatures soaring to 158 degrees Fahrenheit.

July 7

Be Nice to New Jersey Week
The first full week in July recognizes the assets of the state most maligned by comedians. Formerly sponsored by Lone Star Publications.

Chocolate Day
Chocolate was introduced in Europe in 1550.

First American woman executed for a crime (1865)
Mary Surratt, owner of the boarding house where John Wilkes Booth stayed while planning Lincoln's assassination, was hanged for her part in the alleged conspiracy.

Mother Cabrini Canonization (first American saint)

In 1946, Mother Frances Xavier Cabrini was the first American to be canonized. Her feast day is November 13th.

Music for Life Week

The first full week in July encourages the use of music to soothe, heal, nurture, and inspire. *Sponsor:* Music for Life, Ann Fabe Isaacs, 8080 Springvalley Drive, Cincinnati, OH 45236-1395; 513-631-1777.

National Awareness Week for Lifesaving Techniques

According to presidential proclamation, this week is celebrated the first full week in July.

National Canned Luncheon Meat Week

The first week in July celebrates canned luncheon meats; it's kicked off with a festival in Austin, Minnesota, the canned meat capital of the world. *Sponsor:* Canned Food Information Council, Golin/Harris Communications, 500 N. Michigan Avenue #200, Chicago, IL 60611; 312-836-7279; Fax: 312-836-7170.

National Therapeutic Recreation Week

The second week in July promotes a leisure lifestyle for people with limitations. *Sponsor:* National Therapeutic Recreation Society, 2775 S. Quincy Street #300, Arlington, VA 22206; 703-578-5548; Fax: 703-671-6772.

Party Party Day

An excuse to have a party once a month (when the day equals the month). *Sponsor:* Bonza Bottler Day.

Special Recreation Week

From the Sunday after July 4th to the following Sunday, this week promotes the rights, needs, and aspirations of people with disabilities. Write for information including a Suggested Day and Week Activity Guide, Credo, and Special Recreation Planner. *Sponsor:* Special Recreation, Inc., John Nesbitt, President, 362 Koser Avenue, Iowa City, IA 52246; 319-337-7578.

Travelers checks patented (1891)

July 8

First American passport issued (1796)

Issued by the U.S. State Department. *Contact:* Passport Service, Department of State, 1425 K Street NW, Washington, DC 20524; 202-647-0518.

First woman to ride a horse across the U.S. (1911)

Nan Jane Aspinwall rode from San Francisco, California, to New York City, starting on September 1, 1910, and ending on July 8, 1911.

First Ziegfeld Follies (1907)

Showman Florenz Ziegfeld produced his first Follies on the roof of the New York Theater.

Ice Cream Sundae Birthday

Edward Berner of Two Rivers, Wisconsin, served the first ice cream sundae in 1881. *Contact:* Two Rivers Historical Society, 1622 Jefferson Street, Two Rivers, WI 54241; 414-793-2490.

National TV Sports Day
Celebrate the birthday of Roone Arledge, TV sports executive, by watching your favorite sport on TV. Arledge was born in Forest Hills, New York in 1931. *Sponsor:* The Life of the Party. ✉

Nude Recreation Week
Begins on the Monday before the second full weekend in July (Monday through Sunday); celebrates the naked human body. People have the right to enjoy recreation, clothed or not, at their own option. *Sponsor:* The Naturist Society, P.O. Box 132, Oshkosh, WI 54902; 414-231-9950; 800-558-8250; Fax: 414-231-9977.

Wall Street Journal first published (1889)
The first issue was a 4-page afternoon daily. *Contact: Wall Street Journal,* 200 Liberty Street, New York, NY 10281; 212-416-2000; Fax: 212-416-2658.

July 9

14th Amendment to the Constitution ratified (1868)
Defines U.S. citizenship and protections, including due process; it was declared in effect on July 28, 1868.

American Bandstand debuts (1956)
Dick Clark first hosted *Bandstand* on WFIL-TV in Philadelphia, Pennslyvania.

Armenian New Year
The Armenian Era, an old way of measuring time, began in 552.

Baseball All-Star Game
The annual baseball all-star game is always held on the second Tuesday in July. *Contact:* Major League Baseball. ✉

Corncob pipe invented (1869)

Cost of Government Day
Around July 10th (the date changes each year), the cost of government, if figured as a percentage of the gross national product, has been paid for. The rest of the year can be devoted to all the other things we want. *Sponsor:* Americans for Tax Reform Foundation, 1320 18th Street NW #200, Washington, DC 20036; 202-785-0202; Fax: 202-785-0261.

Donut cutter invented (1872)
John Blondel of Maine invented the donut cutter.

First open heart surgery without anesthesia
in 1893, black physician Dr. Daniel Hale Williams performed the world's first successful open heart surgery without using anesthesia.

Nobelium announced
The discovery of element 102 was announced in 1957.

Religious Tolerance Day
Also known as the Martyrdom of the Bab. In 1850, Mirza Ali Muhammad, the prophet of the Baha'i faith, was executed by a firing squad in Tabriz, Iran. In commemoration, learn to tolerate the religious beliefs of other people. *Sponsor:* Baha'i National Center. ✉

U.S. National Debt Day
In 1795 James Swan paid off the U.S. national debt of $2 million.

Worst railroad disaster in U.S. history (1918)
101 people were killed when 2 trains collided near Nashville, Tennessee.

July 10

Clerihew Day
Celebrate the birthday of Edmund Clerihew Bentley (1875), inventor of the clerihew, which is a humorous verse form consisting of 2 rhyming couplets of unequal length.

Color movies first demonstrated (1928)

George Eastman demonstrated his invention. *Contact:* Eastman Kodak Co., 343 State Street, Rochester, NY 14653; 716-724-4000; 800-242-2424; Fax: 716-724-0663.

First elected president of the Russian republic

In 1991, Boris Yeltsin took office as the first elected president of the Russian republic.

Lady Godiva Day

Around 1040, Lady Godiva rode horseback through Coventry while naked. According to legend, she rode as part of a bargain to get her husband Leofric, Earl of Mercia, to ease taxes on the people of Coventry.

National Sporting Goods Week

Held the same time as the NSGA World Sports Expo trade show. *Sponsor:* National Sporting Goods Association, 1699 Wall Street, Mount Prospect, IL 60056-5780; 708-439-4000; Fax: 708-439-0111.

Sinking of the Rainbow Warrior

In 1985, the environmental protest ship *Rainbow Warrior* was blown up and sunk in the harbor of Auckland, New Zealand; it had been scheduled to leave on a trip to protest French nuclear tests in the South Pacific. *Contact:* Greenpeace, 1436 U Street NW, Washington, DC 20009; 202-462-1177.

Telstar launched (1962)

Owned by AT&T, it was the world's first privately owned satellite; also the first satellite to relay TV signals across the Atlantic Ocean. *Contact:* NASA. ✉

Wyoming Admission Day

In 1890, Wyoming became the 44th state of the U.S. *Contact:* Wyoming Division of Tourism, I-25 and College Drive, Cheyenne, WY 82002; 307-777-7777; 800-225-5996; Fax: 307-777-6904.

July 11

Bowdler's Day

Celebrates the birthday of Thomas Bowdler (1754), an Englishman who tried to censor Shakespeare by removing all the so-called indecent words from his plays. The word "bowdlerize," meaning to expurge self-righteously, is derived from his name.

Day of the Five Billion Anniversary

In 1987, the 5 billionth inhabitant of this planet Earth was born. *Sponsor:* The UN Fund for Population, Department of Public Information, 1st Avenue and 42nd Street, New York, NY 10017; 212-963-1234; Fax: 212-963-4879. Also contact Zero Population Growth, 1400 16th Street NW #320, Washington, DC 20036; 202-332-2200; Fax: 202-332-2302.

Diplomatic relations with Vietnam normalized

In 1995, President Clinton announced the normalization of full diplomatic relations with Vietnam. *Contact:* Socialist Republic of Vietnam, Mission to the United Nations, 20 Waterside Plaza, New York, NY 10010; 212-679-3779; Fax: 212-686-8534.

First major league pitcher to strike out 4,000

Nolan Ryan of the Texas Rangers struck out his 4,000 batter in 1985. *Contact:* Major League Baseball. ✉

John Quincy Adams's Birthday

The 6th president of the U.S. was born in Braintree, Massachusetts in 1767. He was the son of John Adams, 2nd president of the U.S. He is the only president to have a father who was also president.

Marine Corps created (1798)

Contact: U.S. Marine Corps, 2 Navy Annex, Washington, DC 20380; 703-614-2500; Fax: 703-697-7246.

Napalm first used (1945)

The U.S. Army used napalm on Japanese forces on the island of Luzon in the Philippines.

National Cheer Up the Lonely Day

Cheer up the lonely in hospitals and nursing homes by visiting them.

Saint Alexis Feast Day
Patron saint of beggars.

Saint Benedict Feast Day
Benedictine monks operate many schools, and Saint Benedict is considered a patron saint of schoolchildren; also patron saint of Europe, farmworkers, coppersmiths, and the dying.

Skylab returned to Earth (1979)
Skylab, the abandoned space station, fell from orbit and burned up in the atmosphere, showering debris all over the Indian Ocean and Australia. *Contact:* NASA. ✉

Vegetarian Food Day
Commemorates Theano, wife of the Greek philosopher Phythagoras, who was known as a patroness of vegetarianism.

World Population Day
The anniversary of 5 billion people highlights the problems of overpopulation. World population will have increased to 6.2 billion people by the end of this century. *Sponsor:* United Nations. ✉

July 12

Alimony Equality Day
In 1981, for the first time, a woman was ordered to pay alimony to her husband.

Different Colored Eyes Day
Celebrates the variety of eye and skin colors in the world.

Eat Your Jell-O Day
On the birthday of comedian Bill Cosby, star of many Jello commercials, eat your Jell-O. Cosby was born in 1938 in Philadelphia, Pennsylvania. *Sponsor:* The Life of the Party. ✉

Minimum Wage Day
In 1933, Congress passed the first national minimum wage law ($.40 per hour). *Contact:* Department of Labor, Public Affairs, Room S1032, 200 Constitution Avenue NW, Washington, DC 20210; 202-219-9711; Fax: 202-219-8699.

National Book Store Weekend
Visit a bookstore the second full weekend of July and buy some good books for yourself and your friends. *Sponsor:* All My Events. ✉

Simplicity Day
On the birthday of Henry David Thoreau (1817), we get back to basics by following his advice: "Simplify, simplify, simplify!" *Sponsor:* Open Horizons. ✉

World Moose Dropping Toss Championship
Held during the second weekend in July. *Sponsor:* Talkeetna Moose Dropping Festival, Talkeetna His-

torical Society, P.O. Box 76, Talkeetna, AK 99676; 907-733-2487.

July 13

First black inducted into Tennis Hall of Fame
In 1985, Arthur Ashe was inducted into the International Tennis Hall of Fame. *Contact:* International Tennis Hall of Fame, Newport Casino, 194 Bellevue Avenue, Newport, RI 02840; 401-849-3990; 800-457-1144.

International Puzzle Day
On the birthday of Erno Rubik (1944), inventor of Rubik's Cube, we celebrate and enjoy all puzzles. *Sponsor:* Open Horizons. ✉

July 14

Bastille Day
The French independence day celebrates the fall of the Bastille prison, which marked the beginning of the French Revolution in 1789. *Contact:* French Embassy, 4101 Reservoir Road NW, Washington, DC 20007; 202-944-6000.

Captive Nations Week
Since 1959, celebrated the second full week in July.

Face on Mars Day (1965)
Mariner 4 flew by Mars taking pictures that revealed something that looked like a human face. *Mariner 4*

was launched on November 28, 1964. *Contact:* NASA. ✉

First public demonstration of refrigerated ice

George W. Carver National Monument dedicated (1951)

Contact: George Washington Carver, National Monument, P.O. Box 38, Diamond, MO 64840; 417-325-4151.

Gerald Rudolph Ford's Birthday

The 38th President of the U.S. was born in Omaha, Nebraska in 1913. He was the first President to serve without having been chosen in a national election.

International Obscurity Day

Celebrate this day on the birthday of Ingmar Bergman, director of many avant-garde films; he was born in 1918 in Uppsala, Sweden. *Sponsor:* The Life of the Party. ✉

Saint Camillus de Lellis Feast Day

Because she pioneered modern nursing practices (such as providing patients with fresh air and good diets), she is patron saint of nurses.

Space Week

Celebrates the first landing of human beings on the moon on July 20, 1969. *Contact:* NASA. ✉

Special Recreation Day

The second Sunday of Special Recreation Week promotes the recreation rights, needs, and aspirations of people with disabilities, including all age groups with all levels of disabilities in community, residential, and institutional settings. *Sponsor:* Special Recreation, Inc., John Nesbitt, President, 362 Koser Avenue, Iowa City, IA 52246; 319-337-7578.

Tape measure invented (1868)

Alvin Fellows of New Haven, Connecticut, invented the tape measure.

World Mashed Potato Wrestling Championship

During the third full week in July (Sunday to Sunday), the Maine Potato Blossom Festival features mashed potato wrestling and other events to celebrate the potato. *Sponsor:* Maine Potato Blossom Festival, Chamber of Commerce, 121 Main Street, Fort Fairfield, ME 04742; 207-472-3802; Fax: 207-472-3810.

July 15

Boeing Company founded (1916)

William Boeing founded Pacific Aero Products, later to become Boeing, in Seattle, Washington. *Contact:* Boeing Company, P.O. Box 3707, Seattle, WA 98124; 206-655-2121; Fax: 206-237-3491.

Crisis of Confidence Day

In 1979, President Jimmy Carter delivered his so-called malaise speech in which he decried the crisis of confidence he saw occurring in the U.S. That speech spelled doom for his 1980 re-election bid.

First baseball no-hitter pitched (1876)

Saint Louis's Washington Bradley pitched the first no-hitter. *Contact:* Major League Baseball. ✉

Health warnings on cigarette packages required

In 1965, Congress passed a law requiring all cigarette packages to carry a health warning.

Olympic New Year

Saint Swithun's Day

An old English belief says that if it rains today, it will rain for the next 40 days.

July 16

Atomic Bomb Day

The first atomic bomb, nicknamed Fat Boy, was detonated at Alamagordo Air Base, New Mexico in 1945.

District of Columbia Day

In 1790, DC was established as the new seat of government for the U.S. *Contact:* Washington DC Visitors Bureau, 1212 New York Avenue NW #600, Washington, DC 20005; 202-789-7000; Fax: 202-789-7037.

First parking meters installed (1935)

Installed in Oklahoma City, Oklahoma. *Contact:* Oklahoma City Visitors Bureau, 123 Park Avenue, Oklahoma City, OK 73102; 405-297-8906; 800-225-5652; Fax: 405-297-8916.

First rear admiral in the U.S. Navy (1862)

David Farragut was appointed the first rear admiral in the U.S. Navy. *Contact:* Department of the Navy, Pentagon Room #4E686, Washington, DC 20350; 703-695-0911.

SpaceWeek International

Encourages space programs around the world, especially from July 16–24 of every year. *Sponsor:* Spaceweek International Association, 1110 NASA Road 1, Houston, TX 77058.

July 17

Disneyland Birthday

Disneyland was founded in 1955. *Contact:* Walt Disney Productions, 1313 S. Harbor Boulevard, Anaheim, CA 92802; 714-999-4565.

First city to be lit by atomic energy (1955)

Arco, Idaho, was the first city in the world to be lighted by atomic energy. Arco celebrates Atomic Days on the third weekend in July. *Contact:* Lost River Valleys Chamber of Commerce, P.O. Box 837, Arco, ID 83213; 208-527-8294.

First spaceship hookup between U.S. and U.S.S.R.

Spaceships from the U.S. and U.S.S.R. linked up in 1975 (Apollo and Soyuz). *Contact:* NASA. ✉

Spain ceded Florida to the U.S. (1821)

Contact: Florida Division of Tourism, Collins Building, 107 W. Gaines Street, Tallahassee, FL 32399-2000; 904-488-7999; Fax: 904-921-9169.

Spanish-American War ended (1898)

Spain surrendered to the U.S. in Santiago, Cuba.

Stealth bomber first test flight (1989)

The B-2 stealth bomber took its first test flight at Edwards Air Force Base in California.

Wrong Way Corrigan Day

In 1938, Douglas Corrigan took off from Brooklyn, New York, saying he was heading for Los Angeles, California, but he landed in Ireland a little over 28 hours later. Also known as Compass Day.

July 18

First baseball player to get 4,000 hits

Ty Cobb got his 4,000 hit in 1927. *Contact:* Major League Baseball. ✉

First perfect 10 scored in the Olympics (1976)

Gymnast Nadia Comaneci from Romania scored the first perfect 10. *Contact:* U.S. Olympic Committee. ✉

India Space Day

In 1980, India launched its first independent satellite, *Rohini 1*. *Contact:* Republic of India Embassy, 2107 Massachusetts Avenue NW, Washington, DC 20008; 202-939-7000.

Perfect Family Day

On Harriet Nelson's birthday, spend time with your family. A perfect family is simply a family that cares about each other. *Sponsor:* The Life of the Party. ✉

Senator Edward Kennedy met his Chappaquiddick

In 1969, Senator Edward Kennedy had an accident, driving his car off a bridge on Chappaquiddick Island. Mary Jo Kopechne, a passenger in the car, died.

✉ Addresses for frequently cited organizations are gathered on pages vii–viii.

Voting by secret ballot introduced in Britain (1872)

World's oldest woman to give birth (1994)
Rosanna Della Corte, a 62-year-old Italian woman, gave birth to a healthy son, Riccardo. Her egg was artificially inseminated by the sperm of her 63-year-old husband, Mauro.

July 19

Bloomer Day
In 1848, at the first Women's Rights Convention in Seneca, New York, Amelia Bloomer introduced the first liberating dress for women: loose fitting trousers. Mrs. Bloomer didn't actually wear them until 3 years later.

First in-flight movie shown (1961)

First personal ad looking for a spouse (1695)

First woman vice presidential candidate chosen (1984)
Geraldine Ferraro, a Democratic representative from New York, was chosen as the vice presidential candidate.

Flight Attendant Safety Professionals Day

Franco-Prussian War began (1870)

Largest armored car robbery in the U.S. (1984)
Members of the white supremacist group, The Order, held up a Brinks truck outside Ukiah, California; they got away with over $3.6 million. *Contact:* Ukiah Chamber of Commerce, 495 E. Perkins Street, Ukiah, CA 95482; 707-462-4705.

Summer Olympics
The 1996 Summer Olympics will be held from July 19 to August 4 in Atlanta, Georgia. *Sponsor:* U.S. Olympic Committee. ✉ Atlanta, Georgia. 404-224-1996.

V for Victory sign introduced (1941)
Sir Winston Churchill introduced the V for Victory hand signal as part of his campaign to liberate Europe from the Nazis.

Women's Convention Anniversary (1848)
The first Seneca Falls convention was held to draft the Declaration of Sentiments; called for immediate citizen rights for all women. *Contact:* National Women's Hall of Fame, 76 Fall Street, Seneca Falls, NY 13148; 315-368-8060.

July 20

Creative Ice Cream Flavor Day
Invent your own flavor. Formerly sponsored by Cool Temptations.

First admission fee charged for a baseball game (1859)

First Billboard singles chart (1940)
The first #1 single was Tommy Dorsey's and Frank Sinatra's "I'll Never Smile Again." *Contact: Billboard* magazine, 1515 Broadway, 39th Floor, New York, NY 10036; 212-764-7300; Fax: 212-536-5358.

First black female tennis player to win Wimbledon (1957)
Althea Gibson was the first black tennis player to win the women's singles championship at Wimbledon.

First U.S. spacecraft on Mars (1976)
Viking I, made the first successful landing on Mars; it was launched on August 20, 1975. *Contact:* NASA. ✉

Moon Day (first landing on the moon, 1969)
Celebrates the anniversary of the first landing on the Moon; Neil Armstrong and Edwin Aldrin were the first people to walk on the moon. *Contact:* NASA. ✉

National Nap Day

On the birthday of the founder, Jeff Gould, everyone should take some time off to take a nap. *Sponsor:* WSN-AM Gould Morning, Jeff Gould, 1704 S. Cleveland Avenue, Sioux Falls, SD 57103; 605-335-6500.

Riot Act Anniversary

In 1715, the English Riot Act, which prohibited assemblages of more than 12 people, took effect. If more than 12 people assembled, they were read the Riot Act which called upon them to depart.

Saint Margaret of Antioch Feast Day

Just before she died she promised that anyone who prayed to her would be sure of a safe delivery; she is patron saint of safe childbirth and births in general.

Saint Wilgefortis Feast Day

Also known as Saint Uncumber, Saint Wilgefortis is patron saint of unhappy marriages. In England, she is prayed to by women who want to rid themselves of troublesome husbands.

Space Exploration Day

Commemorates the first human landing on the Moon in 1969. *Contact:* NASA. ✉

Vamp Day

On the birthday of the original movie sex queen, Theda Bara, have a little fun. *Sponsor:* The Life of the Party. ✉

Women's Auxiliary Army Corps began training (1942)

The first unit of the WACs began basic training at Fort Des Moines, Iowa. *Contact:* Department of the Army, Public Affairs, Pentagon, Washington, DC 20310; 703-695-5135; Fax: 703-614-8533.

July 21

First daily black newspaper published (1864)

The *New Orleans Tribune* was published in both English and French.

First robot homicide

On this date in 1984, a robot accidentally crushed a worker in a Jackson, Michigan, auto plant.

Invite an Alien to Live with You Day

On the birthday of Robin Williams, the alien Mork of *Mork and Mindy*, invite an alien to live with you or, at the very least, invite a stranger to lunch. Williams was born in Chicago, Illinois in 1952. *Sponsor:* The Life of the Party ✉

Jesse James's first train robbery (1873)

He held up the Rock Island Express near Adair, Iowa.

National Ice Cream Day (aka Sundae Sunday)

Enjoy an ice cream sundae on the third Sunday in July. *Sponsor:* International Ice Cream Association, 1250 H Street NW #900, Washington, DC 20005; 202-737-4332; Fax: 202-331-7820.

National Women's Hall of Fame dedicated (1979)

Honors women important to America's history. *Contact:* National Women's Hall of Fame, 76 Fall Street, Seneca, NY 13148; 315-568-8060.

Take a Monkey to Lunch Day

On the anniversary of the 1925 conviction of John Scopes for teaching evolution, take an evolved monkey to lunch. The famous Monkey Trial, with Clarence Darrow and William Jennings Bryan as the opposing lawyers, lasted from July 10 to July 21, 1925. *Sponsor:* The Life of the Party. ✉

July 22

Biggest mass wedding in history (1982)

Reverend Sun Myung Moon married 2,200 couples in New York City.

Cleveland's Birthday

Cleveland was founded by General Moses Cleaveland in 1796. *Contact:* Cleveland Visitors Bureau, 50 Public Square #3100, Cleveland, OH 44113; 216-621-4110; 800-321-1001; Fax: 216-621-5967.

First solo flight around the world completed (1933)
Wiley Post completed this flight in 7 days, 18 hours, 45 minutes.

International Childbirth Education Awareness Day
Call to confirm the date for this event, it is subject to change in 1996. *Sponsor:* International Childbirth Education Association, P.O. Box 20048, Minneapolis, MN 55420; 612-854-8660; Fax: 612-854-8772.

Rat Catchers Day
Celebrates the anniversary of the Pied Piper of Hamelin who piped away the town's rats in 1376. When the town refused to pay him for his services, he piped away the town's children as well. Always pay the piper!

Saint Mary Magdalene Feast Day
Patron saint of penitent sinners and repentant prostitutes; also patron saint of the contemplative life.

Sony Walkman Birthday
The Walkman first went on sale in 1979. *Contact:* Sony Corporation of America, 1 Sony Drive, Park Ridge, NJ 07656; 201-930-1000; 800-222-7669.

Spooner's Day
Celebrates the birthday of William Spooner (1844), whose many misstatements created spoonerisms.

Summer Leisure Day
Take some time today to play. Sit back and relax. Enjoy. *Sponsor:* A Pilgrim's Almanac. ✉

The bases are loaded...two outs and here comes...

July 23

First Miss America to resign (1984)
After *Penthouse* magazine published nude photos of her, Vanessa Williams resigned her title.

First non-Caucasian in space (1980)
Lieutenant Colonel Pham Tuan of Vietnam was launched into space on board *Salyut 6,* a Russian spacecraft. *Contact:* NASA. ✉

First U.S. swimming school (1827)
The school opened in Boston, Massachusetts.

Ice cream cone invented (1904)
According to some legends, the world's first ice cream cone was served by Charles Menches at the St. Louis World Fair in 1904. See Ice Cream Cone Birthday for another account.

Private Eye Day
On the birthday of Raymond Chandler (1888), creator of Philip Marlowe, we honor all private eyes. *Sponsor:* Book Marketing Update. ✉

Saint Bridget of Sweden Feast Day
Because she often worked with the sick, she is patron saint of healers; also patron saint of Sweden and scholars. She is also known as Saint Birgit or Saint Birgitta.

Saint Phocas Feast Day
A market gardener of ancient Turkey, Saint Phocas is patron saint of market gardeners; also patron saint of sailors.

Sign of Leo
The astrological sign of Leo the lion runs from July 23rd to August 22nd. Leo people are noble, generous, and enthusiastic.

Typewriter forerunner patented (1829)

William Burt of Vernon, Michigan, received the first patent for a typographer, the machine that came before the modern typewriter.

July 24

Bolivar Day

This Venezuelan holiday celebrates the birthday (1783) of Simon Bolivar, South America's liberator. Bolivar is known as the father of 5 countries: Venezuela, Ecuador, Colombia, Peru, and Bolivia. *Contact:* Venezuelan Embassy, 1099 30th Street NW, Washington, DC 20007; 202-342-2214.

Detroit's Birthday

In 1701, the French explorer Antoine de la Mothe Cadillac landed at the present day site of Detroit and founded Fort Detroit. *Contact:* Detroit Visitors Bureau, 100 Renaissance Center #1950, Detroit, MI 48243-1056; 313-259-4333; 800-225-5389; Fax: 313-259-7583.

First copyright law instituted (1793)

Instituted in France.

First guided missile ship launched (1956)

First national convention of the People's Party

In 1896, the Populists held their first convention in St. Louis, Missouri.

The party nominated William Jennings Bryan for president. *Contact:* St. Louis Visitors Commission, 10 S. Broadway #1000, St. Louis, MO 63102; 314-992-0606; 800-325-7962; Fax: 314-421-0039.

First successful lung removal operation (1933)

Dr. W. F. Reinhoff, Jr. performed this operation in Baltimore, Maryland.

First underwater nuclear test (1946)

The U.S. conducted the first underwater test of an atomic bomb at Bikini Atoll in the Pacific Ocean.

Instant Coffee Birthday

Instant coffee was invented in 1938.

Kitchen Debate Day

In 1959, Vice President Richard Nixon engaged in a "kitchen debate" with Nikita Khrushchev of the Soviet Union.

Pioneer Day

In 1847, Brigham Young and the Mormans founded the first settlement in Utah. This is a public holiday in Utah. *Contact:* Utah Travel Council, Council Hall, Capital Mall, Salt Lake City, UT 84114; 801-538-1030; Fax: 801-538-1399.

Public Opinion Day

The first public opinion poll in the U.S. was published by the *Harrisburg Pennsylvanian* and the *Raleigh Star*. It predicted the winner of the 1824 election.

Tennessee Readmission Day

In 1866, Tennessee became the first Confederate state to be readmitted to the U.S. after the Civil War. *Contact:* Tennessee Department of Tourism, P.O. Box 23170, Nashville, TN 37202-3170; 615-741-2158; 800-362-1971; Fax: 615-741-7225.

Women Aviators Day

On the birthday of Amelia Earhart, the first woman to fly solo across the Atlantic and the Pacific Oceans, all women pilots are honored. Earhart was born in 1897 in Atchison, Kansas. In 1937, her plane disappeared over the Pacific Ocean.

July 25

First General of the Army (1866)

Ulysses S. Grant was the first officer to hold the rank of General of the Army.

First international overseas airplane flight

In 1909, French aviator Louis Bleriot flew from Calais, France, to Dover, England, across the English Channel. He made the flight in 37 minutes.

First steam locomotive (1814)

George Stephenson of England tested his first steam locomotive.

First woman to walk in space (1984)

Cosmonaut Svetlana Savitskaya was the first. *Contact:* NASA. ✉

Great Texas Mosquito Festival

During the Great Texas Mosquito Festival, held on the last Thursday through Saturday in July, Willie Man Chew, the world's largest mosquito, helps people to celebrate nature's biting insect. *Sponsor:* Parks and Recreation Department, City of Clute, P.O. Box 997, Clute, TX 77531; 409-265-8392; Fax: 409-265-8767.

International Brick and Rolling Pin Throw

July 25 to 27. Men and women from Stroud, England; Stroud, Canada; Stroud, Australia; and Stroud, Oklahoma, attempt to out-throw each other in this international competition. *Sponsor:* Stroud Chamber of Commerce, 216 W. Main Street, P.O. Box 633, Stroud, OK 74079; 918-968-3321.

Israel and Jordan sign a peace treaty (1994)

46 years of war ended when Israeli Prime Minister Yitzhak Rabin and Jordan's King Hussein signed a peace agreement at the White House.

Lowest temperature ever recorded (1983)

The lowest natural temperature (–129 degrees) was recorded in Antarctica.

Merry-Go-Round Birthday

In 1871, the merry-go-round was invented by William Schneider of Davenport, Iowa.

Puerto Rico Constitution Day

In 1952, the Puerto Rican constitution was proclaimed, thus manking Puerto Rico a self-governing commonwealth. This day is also known as Occupation Day or Commonwealth Day. *Contact:* Puerto Rico Tourism Corporation, 575 Fifth Avenue, 23rd Floor, New York, NY 10017; 212-599-6262; 800-223-6530; Fax: 212-818-1866.

Rain of Black Worms

In 1872, one of the most unusual rains in history occurred as thousands of black worms rained from the sky over Bucharest, Rumania.

Saint Christopher Feast Day

Because of a legend that he helped Jesus cross a stream, St. Christopher is known as the patron saint of travelers. A St. Christopher medal is protects people from danger while traveling; also patron saint of bachelors, bus drivers, and truck drivers.

Saint James the Greater Feast Day

Patron saint of rheumatism; Santiago (his name in Spanish) is also patron saint of Spain.

Test Tube Baby Birthday

In 1978, Louise Joy Brown of Oldham, England, was the first test-tube baby conceived outside her mother's womb.

Tisha B'Av (Fast of Ab)

This Jewish holiday commemorates the destruction of the first (586 B.C.) and second (70 A.D.) Temples in Jerusalem. Always on the 9th day of Ab in the Jewish calendar (varies from year to year on the standard calendar).

Wyoming Territory Day

In 1868, the U.S. Congress created the Wyoming Territory. *Contact:* Wyoming Division of Tourism, I-25 and College Drive, Cheyenne, WY 82002; 307-777-7777; 800-225-5996; Fax: 307-777-6904.

July 26

Americans with Disabilities Act signed (1990)

President Bush signed this act. *Contact:* National Council on Disability,

1331 F Street NW, Washington, DC 20004; 202-272-2004; Fax: 202-272-2022.

Brave New World Day
On the birthday of Aldous Huxley, author of *Brave New World* and other books, we look forward with some trepidation to the future. Huxley was born in 1894 in Godalming, England.

FBI forerunner created (1908)
Attorney General Charles Bonaparte created an investigative agency that was the forerunner of the Federal Bureau of Investigations. *Contact:* Federal Bureau of Investigations, 10th Street and Pennsylvania Ave, Washington, DC 20535-0001; 202-324-3000; Fax: 202-324-4705.

First Postmaster General (1775)
Benjamin Franklin was the first Postmaster General. *Contact:* U.S. Postal Service. ✉

National 2001 Day
On the birthday of Stanley Kubrick, producer of *2001*, take time to prepare for the next millenium. Kubrick was born in 1928 in Bronx, New York. *Sponsor:* The Life of the Party. ✉

National Security Act signed (1947)
President Harry Truman signed the National Security Act, which created the Department of Defense, Joint Chiefs of Staff, Central Intelligence Agency, and National Security Council.

New York Ratification Day
New York became the 11th state to ratify the U.S. Constitution in 1788. *Contact:* New York State Tourism Division, One Commerce Plaza, Albany, NY 12245; 518-474-4116; 800-847-4862; Fax: 518-486-6416.

Saint Joachim and Anne Feast Day
The parents of Mary, mother of Jesus. As such, they are the patron saints of grandparents. Anne is also patron saint of pregnant women and women in labor.

U.S. armed forces integrated (1946)
President Truman signed an order that called for the desegregation of all U.S. armed forces.

July 27

57 Varieties Day
H. J. Heinz Company, maker of catsup with at least 57 varieties of tomatoes, was incorporated in 1900. *Contact:* H. J. Heinz Company, 600 Grant Street, 60th Floor, Pittsburgh, PA 15219; 412-456-5700; Fax: 412-456-6128.

All in the Family Day
Celebrate the birthday of Norman Lear, producer of the TV show, *All in the Family*. He was born in 1922 in New Haven, Connecticut. *Sponsor:* All My Events. ✉

Bugs Bunny's Birthday
In 1940, Bugs made his debut in the short animated feature, *A Wild Hare*.

Coconut oil refining process patented (1880)
Black inventor A. P. Abourne was awarded a patent for refining coconut oil.

First airplane flown for the U.S. Army (1909)
Orville Wright flew the army's first plane for 1 hour and 12 minutes.

First person to die of Legionnaire's Disease (1976)
Ray Brennan, an Air Force veteran, died of Legionnaire's Disease.

First underwater telegraph cable crosses Atlantic (1866)

The laying of the cable between the U.S. and Europe was completed by Cyrus Field.

Insulin discovered (1921)

Frederick Banting, a Canadian doctor, discovered insulin.

Korean War ended (1953)

The Korean War Armistice was signed at Panmunjom, ending 3 years of fighting.

National Scottish Fiddling Championships

During the last weekend in July, the Virginia Scottish Games features, among many other events, the National Scottish Fiddling Championships. *Sponsor:* Virginia Scottish Games, Alexandria Visitors Bureau, 221 King Street, Alexandria, VA 22314-3209; 703-838-4200; 800-388-9119; Fax: 703-838-4383.

Public Lands Appreciation Day

On the last Saturday in July, PLAD encourages people to participate in making public lands more accessible while still conserving their natural state. *Sponsor:* Times Mirror Magazines, Conservation Council, 1705 DeSales Street NW, Washington, DC 20036; Fax: 202-467-4858.

Saint Pantaleone Feast Day

Patron saint of trousers, doctors, and Venice. Because the war cry of

Venice was "Plant the lion," Pantaleone became a patron saint of Venice. The citizens of Venice wore distinctive trousers known as pantaloons.

Take Your House Plants for a Walk Day

Sponsor: Wellness Permission League. ✉

U.S. Department of State established (1789)

The Department of Foreign Affairs (later known as the Department of State) was the first presidential cabinet department established by Congress. *Contact:* Department of State, 2201 C Street NW, Room 6800, Washington, DC 20520; 202-647-6575; Fax: 202-647-5939.

World's Biggest Bagel Breakfast

At Bagelfest enjoy free bagels and toppings, a bagel buggy derby, and other festivities. On the last Saturday in July, enjoy the world's biggest bagel breakfast. *Sponsor:* Bagelfest, Mattoon Chamber of Commerce, 1701 Wabash, Mattoon, IL 61938; 217-235-5661.

World's Largest Egg Contest

The Central Maine Egg Festival also features a quiche contest, egg toss, egglympics, and plenty of eggs. *Sponsor:* Central Maine Egg Festival, P.O. Box 82, Pittsfield, ME 04967; 207-487-5416.

July 28

Coffee rationing ended (1943)

During World War II, President Roosevelt announced that coffee rationing was no longer in effect.

Comedy Celebration Day

Say thank you to San Francisco for the many comics who started out there. A local celebration is held every year on the last Sunday in July. *Sponsor:* Jose Simon, Executive Producer, 468 Dellbrook Avenue, San Francisco, CA 94131; 415-566-3042; Fax: 415-564-4904.

First Asian-Americans in Congress (1959)

Hawaii elected the first Chinese-American to the U.S. Senate (Senator Hiram Fong), and the first Japanese-American to the House of Representatives (Representative Daniel Inouye).

First railway mail car begins operation (1862)

Hamburger Day

In 1900, Louis Lassing of New Haven, Connecticut created the first hamburger. Some people, however, say the hamburger was introduced at the Louisiana Purchase Exposition on April 30, 1904. And Seymour, Wisconsin, claims it was by Charlie Nagreen in 1889.

Marry a Millionaire Day

Celebrate the birthday of the wife of both John F. Kennedy and Aristotle Onassis, Jacqueline Lee Bouvier Kennedy Onassis, she married rich and lived well. Born in 1929, she died on May 19, 1994. *Sponsor:* The Life of the Party. ✉

Miami's Birthday

In 1898, Miami, Florida was incorporated as a city. *Contact:* Miami Visitors Bureau, 701 Brickell Avenue #2700, Miami, FL 33131; 305-539-3000; 800-933-8448; Fax: 305-539-3113.

Most expensive movie ever made opened (1995)

Waterworld, starring Kevin Costner, cost almost $200 million to make. Beset by crew injuries, tsunami warnings, a sinking set, a dispute between Kevin Costner and Kevin Reynolds, the director, this movie went well over its $100 million budget. *Contact:* Universal Pictures, 3900 Lankenshim Boulevard, Universal City, CA 91608; 818-777-1000; Fax: 818-777-6431.

Singing Telegram Birthday

The first singing telegram was sent to Rudy Vallee in 1933 on his 32nd birthday.

July 29

First transcontinental airmail flight (1920)

From New York to San Francisco. *Contact:* U.S. Postal Service. ✉

First transcontinental telephone link (1914)

Established between New York and San Francisco.

Friday Night Videos premiered (1983)

NBC's Friday night music video program, *Friday Night Videos,* premiered. *Contact:* NBC-TV. ✉

International Atomic Energy Agency established (1957)

Contact: International Atomic Energy Agency, 1 UN Plaza, Room DC1-1155, New York, NY 10017; 212-963-6011; Fax: 212-751-4117.

Most kisses in a single movie (1926)

The movie, *Don Juan,* included 127 kisses.

NASA created (1958)

President Eisenhower signed the National Aeronautics and Space Act. For free booklets on the space program, write NASA, Public Affairs Office, John F. Kennedy Space Center, Cape Canaveral, FL 32899. *Contact:* NASA. ✉

Saint Martha Feast Day

As sister of Lazarus and hostess to Jesus, Martha is patron saint of cooks, servants, innkeepers, housewives, and lay sisters.

July 30

Baltimore's Birthday

Baltimore, Maryland was founded in 1729. *Contact:* Baltimore Visitors Bureau, 100 Light Street, 12th Floor, Baltimore, MD 21202; 410-659-7300; 800-343-3468; Fax: 410-727-2308.

Body Builders Day

On the birthday of strongman and movie star Arnold Schwarzenegger, take time to exercise. Arnold was born in 1947 in Graz, Austria. *Sponsor:* The Life of the Party. ✉

Corn Moon

The full moon of July is known as the corn moon by the Zuni Indians because it comes about the time the corn ripens. It is also known as the hay moon, buck moon, or thunder moon.

First legislative assembly in the U.S. (1619)

The House of Burgesses, convened in Jamestown, Virginia.

Guru Purnima Celebration

On the first full moon in July, Hindus honor all religious teachers; also known as the Day of Fullness.

Herb Moon

The full moon of July is the herb moon, symbolic of herb harvest, magical potency, health, success, and strength.

Medicare Birthday

In 1965, President Johnson signed the Medicare bill, which became effective in 1966.

WAVES created (1942)

President Roosevelt signed a bill creating the women's navy auxiliary, the WAVES. *Contact:* Department of the Navy, Information Office, Pentagon; Washington, DC 20350; 703-697-7391.

July 31

First U.S. government building

Construction of the U.S. Mint began in 1792. *Contact:* U.S. Mint, 633 Third Street NW #715, Washington, DC 20220; 202-874-6000; Fax: 202-874-6282.

Make a Budget Day

On the birthday of economist Milton Freidman, check out your personal finances. Make a budget. Spend wisely. Freidman was born in 1912 in Brooklyn, New York. *Sponsor:* The Life of the Party. ✉

Shredded Wheat Birthday

Henry Perky patented shredded wheat in 1893. *Contact:* Nabisco Brands, Inc., 100 Deforest Avenue,

East Hanover, NJ 07936; 201-503-2000; 800-622-4726; Fax: 201-503-2202.

Strategic Arms Reduction Treaty signed (1991)

President Bush and Soviet president Gorbachev signed this treaty.

TV Network Buyout Day

In 1995, Disney merged with Capital Cities/ABC. A day later, Westinghouse bought CBS.

U.S. Patent Office opened (1790)

The first patent was granted to Samuel Hopkins, inventor of a method for making potash. *Contact:* Patent and Trademark Office, 211 Crystal Drive #700, Arlington, VA 20002; 703-305-4537; Fax: 703-305-6369.

AUGUST

American Artists Appreciation Month

Celebrates the roles of artists, musicians, and writers in American life. Formerly sponsored by American Artists Studio.

Architecture Month

Breastfeeding Month

Fall of Empires Month

On August 6, 1806, the Holy Roman Empire ceased to exist. On August 13, 1521, the Aztec Empire fell. On August 29, 1533, the Inca Empire fell. On August 14, 1945, Japan surrendered. On August 24, 410, Rome fell to the Visigoths.

Foot Health Month

Spread the word about healthy feet and how a podiatrist can help. *Sponsor:* Dr. Scholl's, Andy Horrow, Porter Novelli, 303 E. Wacker Drive #1214, Chicago, IL 60601; 312-856-8826.

National Canning Month

August is the month to can and preserve vegetables and fruits for the winter.

National Catfish Month

Promotes the benefits of eating genuine U.S. farm-raised catfish. *Sponsor:* Loyal Order of Catfish Lovers, Golin/Harris Communications, 666 Third Avenue, New York, NY 10017; 212-692-2680; Fax: 212-769-1776.

National Golf Month

Promotes family participation in the sport of golf; millions of dollars have been raised for charities since the beginning of this industry-wide promotion in 1952. *Sponsor:* Professional Golfers Association, 100 Avenue of the Champions, Palm

✉ Addresses for frequently cited organizations are gathered on pages vii–viii.

AUGUST   171

Beach Gardens, FL 33418; 407-624-8400; Fax: 407-624-8448.

National HAIRitage Month
Salutes all those who work in the hair care industry. *Sponsor:* All My Events. ✉

National Parks Month
Sponsor: National Parks and Conservation, 1776 Massachusetts Ave. NW #200, Washington, DC 20036; 202-223-6722; Fax: 202-659-0650.

National Sandwich Month

National Water Quality Month
To spotlight the importance of quality water. *Sponsor:* Culligan International, One Culligan Parkway, Northbrook, IL 60062; 708-205-6000.

Psychic Month
To recognize the power of psychics and the good they do. Formerly sponsored by Richard Falk, who died in 1994.

Romance Awareness Month
Make romance an important part of your daily life by identifying what your partner considers to be romantic; spotlights ideas for new romantic adventures! *Sponsor:* Celebrate Romance, Eileen Buchheim, 5199 E, Pacific Coast Hwy #303A, Long Beach, CA 90804-3398; 714-459-7620; 800-368-7978.

Science, Medicine, and Technology Books Month
Read a good book on math, medicine, health, computers, electronics, technology, engineering, biology, physics, chemistry, astronomy, and other sciences. *Sponsor:* Book Marketing Update. ✉

August 1

Atomic Energy Commission established (1946)
Contact: Office of Nuclear Energy, Room 5A-115, 1000 Independence Avenue SW, Washington, DC 20585; 202-586-6450; Fax: 202-586-8353.

Cable cars successfully tested (1873)
Andrew Hallide tested the San Francisco cable cars.

Chopsticks song was written (1877)

Colorado Admission Day
In 1876, Colorado became the 38th state of the U.S. The public holiday, Colorado Day, is celebrated on the first Monday in August. *Contact:* Colorado Tourism Board, 1625 Broadway #1700, Denver, CO 80238; 303-592-5510; 800-433-2526.

EAA International Fly-In
During the week that ends with the first Wednesday in August, the Experimental Aircraft Association hosts the world's largest annual aviation event. Held at the Wittman Regional Airport, over 850,000 people attend. *Sponsor:* Experimental Aircraft Association, P.O. Box 3086, Oshkosh, WI 54903-3086; 414-426-4800; Fax: 414-426-6560.

Emancipation of 500 Anniversary
In 1791, Robert Carter III, a major Virginia plantation owner, issued a deed of emancipation freeing his 500 slaves. It was the largest private emancipation proclamation in U.S. history.

Festival of Green Corn
Native Americans celebrate this festival to thank the Corn Grandmother for the bounty of their harvest.

First atomic bomb plant
The Oak Ridge plant was the first to manufacture the enriched uranium required to build atomic bombs. *Contact:* Oak Ridge National Laboratory, P.O. Box 2009,

Oak Ridge, TN 37831-2009; 615-574-0733; Fax: 615-574-0334.

First black tennis player named to U.S. Davis Cup

In 1964, Arthur Ashe became the first black on the U.S. Davis Cup tennis team.

First U.S. census completed (1790)

When the census was completed, America had about 4,000,000 people. *Contact:* Bureau of the Census, 3 Silver Hill and Suitland Roads, Building 3, Suitland, MD 20746; 301-763-4040; Fax: 301-763-4191.

Helsinki Human Rights Day

The Helsinki Accords were signed in 1975. Prior to this, 35 countries had met in Helsinki, Finland, to make agreements on human rights and security.

International Clown Week

The first 7 days in August promote the fun and charitable activities that clowns offer. *Sponsor:* International Clowns of America, Thomas Oswald, P.O. Box 306, Two Harbors, MN 55616; 218-834-8415; Home phone: 218-834-6406.

MTV's Birthday

The rock music video channel began in 1981. The first video aired was the Buggles' "Video Killed the Radio Star." Other videos featured in the first hour were by Pat Benatar, Rod Stewart, The Who, The Pretenders, Styx, and others. *Contact:* MTV (Music Television), 1515 Broadway, 24th Floor, New York, NY 10036; 212-258-8000; Fax: 212-258-8100.

National Polka Festival

On the first weekend in August, from Thursday through Sunday, people dance the polka to the top polka bands in the country. The event is held under a large tent at Hunter Mountain. *Sponsor:* Hunter Mountain Festivals, Hunter, NY 12442; 518-263-3800.

NORAD created (1957)

Canada and the U.S. agreed to form NORAD, the North American Air Defense Command.

Oxygen isolated from air (1774)

British scientist Joseph Priestley first isolated oxygen from air.

Rounds Resounding Day

Join the world in harmony by singing contrapuntal American folksongs. *Sponsor:* Rounds Resounding Society, Gloria T. Delamar, President, 7303 Sharpless Road, Melrose Park, PA 19126; 215-782-1059.

Saint Alphonsus Liguori Feast Day

Patron saint of theologians and vocations.

Simplify Your Life Week

During the first 7 days of August, do something to make your life simpler, more organized, less complicated, less cluttered. *Sponsor:* International Society of Friendship and Good Will. ✉

U.S. Customs began (1789)

Contact: U.S. Customs Service, 1301 Constitution Ave NW #3422, Washington, DC 20229; 202-622-2000; Fax: 202-633-7645.

Woman Astronomers Day

Maria Mitchell was the first female professional astronomer, first American woman to become a professor of astronomy, and first woman to be elected to the American Academy of Arts and Sciences. She was born in Nantucket, Massachusetts in 1918.

August 2

Escalator patented (1892)

Charles Wheeler patented the first practical moving staircase.

Freight elevator invented (1743)

Gambling Is Dangerous Day

In 1876, Wild Bill Hickok was shot while playing poker in Deadwood, South Dakota. *Sponsor:* Open Horizons. ✉

Hatch Act signed (1939)

This act prohibited government workers from taking an active part in any political campaigns.

International Championship Burro Race

During Leadville's Boom Days Celebration on the first weekend in August, these burro races are held. *Sponsor:* Leadville Boom Days Celebration, Chamber of Commerce, P.O. Box 861, Leadville, CO 80461; 719-486-3900; 800-933-3901.

Police Car Owners of America National Convention

Founded in 1992, this annual convention features a parade and display of police cars, from vintage to modern. *Sponsor:* Eureka Springs Chamber of Commerce, P.O. Box 551, Eureka Springs, AR 72632; 501-253-8737.

Signing of the Declaration of Independence (1776)

Touch of Class Day

Celebrate the birthday of Myrna Loy, a movie actress with a lot of class. She was born in 1905 near Helena, Montana. *Sponsor:* The Life of the Party. ✉

World Freefall Convention

The world convention for skydivers is held on the first full week in August (from Friday through Sunday). *Sponsor:* World Freefall Convention, Rob Ebbing, 1515 Kentucky, Quincy, IL 62301; 217-222-5867; Fax: 217-222-5867.

August 3

American Canoe Association founded (1880)

Contact: American Canoe Association, 7432 Alban Station Boulevard #B226, Springfield, VA 22150; 703-451-0141; Fax: 703-451-2245.

Crop Day

The first Saturday in August recognizes when cotton was king of all crops in the South. *Sponsor:* Leflore County Chamber of Commerce, P.O. Box 848, Greenwood, MS 38930-0848; 601-453-4152; Fax: 601-453-8003.

First crop dusting from an airplane (1921)

John Macready used an airplane to dust a 6-acre grove in Troy, Ohio.

First vessel to sail under the North Pole (1958)

The submarine *Nautilus* passed under the North Pole.

National Basketball Association formed (1949)

Contact: National Basketball Association, 645 Fifth Avenue, 15th Floor, New York, NY 10022; 212-826-7000; Fax: 212-826-0579.

New Worlds Day

Christopher Columbus set sail from Palos, Spain in 1492. While in search of China, he discovered the new worlds of the Western Hemisphere.

Prime Time Live premiered (1989)

Contact: ABC-TV. ✉

August 4

American Family Day

Michigan and Arizona observe this on the first Sunday in August.

Celebration of Peace Day

Formerly sponsored by National Peace Day Celebrations, the first Sunday in August is now celebrated in many local communities. Dedicated to learning about justice and peace and to celebrating life.

Champagne invented (1693)

Dom Perignon invented champagne.

Chicago's Birthday

In 1830, the city of Chicago was designed. *Contact:* Chicago Visitors Bureau, 2301 S. Lake Shore Drive, Chicago, IL 60616; 312-567-8500; Fax: 312-567-8537.

Coast Guard Day

The Coast Guard was founded in 1790 as the Revenue Cutter Service. *Contact:* U.S. Coast Guard, 2100 Second Street SW, Washington, DC 20593; 202-267-2229.

First federal income tax collected (1862)

Contact: Internal Revenue Service. ✉

Freedom of the Press Day

Recognizes the 1735 acquittal of John Peter Zenger, publisher of the *New York Weekly Journal,* on a charge of seditious libel. This victory established freedom of the press in the U.S.

Friendship Day

The first Sunday in August is designed to help people keep their friendships in constant repair. A congressional resolution in 1935 created this day. Send an SASE for information. *Sponsor:* The Best to You, Linda Gorin, 7920 Silverton Avenue #F, San Diego, CA 92126; 619-578-2740; Fax: 619-578-0138.

National Psychiatric Technician Week

The first full week in August honors technicians who care for psychiatric patients. *Sponsor:* Lakeshore Mental Health Institute, Ellen Adcock, 5908 Lyons View Drive, Knoxville, TN 37919; 615-584-1561; Fax: 615-450-5231.

Saint John Vianney Feast Day

Patron saint of priests.

Twins Day

During the first weekend in August, the only city named after twins (early settlers Aaron and Moses Wilcox) celebrates twins. *Sponsor:* Twins Day Festival, Twinsburg Chamber of Commerce, P.O. Box 29, Twinsburg, OH 44087; 216-425-3652.

U.S. Department of Energy created (1977)

President Carter signed the Energy Organization Act. The Department officially opened for business on October 1, 1977. *Contact:* Department of Energy, 1000 Independence Avenue SW, Washington, DC 20585; 202-586-5000; Fax: 202-586-4073.

August 5

American Bandstand made its network debut (1957

Dick Clark hosted the first *American Bandstand* show on ABC-TV. *Contact:* ABC-TV. ✉

Boxing Hall of Fame inducted first boxers (1954)

Among the first boxers inducted were John L. Sullivan, Jack Johnson, Jack Dempsey, Gentleman Jim Corbett, Joe Louis, and Henry Armstrong.

Damn the Torpedoes, Full Speed Ahead Day

In 1864, these immortal words were uttered by Admiral David Farragut as he led union ships into Mobile Bay during the Civil War.

Federal Income Tax Birthday

In 1861, President Abraham Lincoln signed into law the first income tax. The first federal income tax was collected on August 4, 1862. *Contact:* Internal Revenue Service. ✉

First English colony in North America founded

English navigator Humphrey Gilbert claimed Newfoundland for England in 1583.

Goodbye, Norma Jean

In 1962, Marilyn Monroe (born Norma Jean Mortenson) died, an apparent suicide.

Little Orphan Annie's Birthday

In 1924, Harold Gray's *Little Orphan Annie* comic strip premiered in the *New York Daily News. Contact:* New York Daily News, 220 East 42nd Street, New York, NY 10017-5858; 212-210-2100; Fax: 212-661-4675.

National Failures Day

National Mustard Day

Honors the condiment of kings. The Mount Horeb Mustard Museum contains the world's largest collection of prepared mustards and mustard memorabilia. *Sponsor:* Mount Horeb Mustard Museum, Barry M. Levenson, 109 E. Main

Street, Mount Horeb, WI 53572;
608-437-3986.

National Smile Week

Wear a smile, create happiness for
you and the receiver during the first
full week in August (Monday
through Sunday). *Sponsor:* Heloise
Syndicated Column, Heloise
Cruse Evans, P.O. Box 795000, San
Antonio, TX 78279.

Nuclear Test Ban Treaty signed (1963)

Banned nuclear tests in the atmosphere, in space, and under water.

Saint Afra Feast Day

A daughter of Saint Hilaria, Saint
Afra became a prostitute who was
converted and later burned to death
for her faith. She is considered a patron saint of fallen women.

Spectrum of a comet ob-served for first time (1864)

Observed by Giovanni Donati.

Take a Walk on the Moon Day

On the birthday of Neil Armstrong,
the first man to walk on the moon,

get ready to take your own walk on
the moon. Armstrong was born in
1930 in Wapakoneta, Ohio. *Sponsor:*
The Life of the Party. ✉

Traffic Lights Birthday

In 1914, the first electric traffic lights
were installed in Cleveland, Ohio.
Contact: Cleveland Visitors Bureau,
50 Public Square #3100, Cleveland,
OH 44113; 216-621-4110; 800-
321-1001; Fax: 216-621-5967.

World's largest hamburger served (1989)

Cooked and served at the Outagamie County Fair in Seymour,
Wisconsin; it weighed 5,520
pounds and was 21 feet in diameter.
Seymour now sponsors the World's
Best Hamburger Cook-Off. *Sponsor:* Outagamie County Fair, Seymour Chamber of Commerce, P.O.
Box 95, Seymour, WI 54165; 414-
833-6969.

World's tallest cake completed (1990)

Baked and served at the Shiawassee
County Fair in Corunna, Michigan,
the cake was 101 feet tall. *Sponsor:*
Shiawassee County Fair, 2900 E.
Hibbard Road, Corunna, MI
48817; 517-743-2223.

August 6

Electric Chair Day

In 1890, the electric chair was used
for the first time to execute con-

victed murderer William Kemmler
at Auburn State Prison in New York.

First American woman to swim the English Channel (1926)

Gertrude Ederle of New York was
the first American women to swim
the English Channel. It took her
14.5 hours.

Hiroshima Day

In 1945, the first atomic bomb to
be dropped on a populated area exploded on Hiroshima, Japan. More
than 140,000 people were killed.

Holy Roman Empire ceased (1806)

When Emperor Francis I abdicated
the throne, the Holy Roman Empire ceased to exist.

Intertribal Indian Ceremonial

On Tuesday to Sunday of the second weekend in August, the country's largest and oldest (since 1922)
all-Indian ceremony takes place at
Red Rock State Park near Gallup,
New Mexico. More than 50 tribes
participate. Saturday features the
only all-Indian, non-mechanized
parade in the U.S. The 1996 ceremonial will be the 75th annual
event. *Sponsor:* Intertribal Indian
Ceremonial Association, P.O. Box
1, Church Rock, NM 87311; 800-
233-4528; Fax: 505-722-5158.

National Gossip Day

On the birthday of gossip columnist Louella Parson, take time to

catch up on the latest gossip in your neighborhood. *Sponsor:* The Life of the Party. ✉

National Night Out

The first Tuesday in August encourages police and communities to work together to reduce crime. *Sponsor:* National Association of Town Watch, 7 Wynnewood Road #215, P.O. Box 303, Wynnewood, PA 19096; 610-649-7055; 800-648-3688; Fax: 610-649-5456.

Peace Day

Commemorates the day the first atomic bomb was dropped on a city. Work for peace on this day so nothing like that ever happens again.

Transfiguration of the Lord

On Mount Tabor, Jesus appeared in all his divine splendor before 3 of his disciples: Peter, James, and John.

Voting Rights Act became law (1965)

President Johnson signed the Voting Rights Act.

August 7

First photo of Earth from space (1959)

Explorer 6 was launched; it sent back the first photograph from space. *Contact:* NASA. ✉

Gulf of Tonkin Resolution (Vietnam War started)

In 1964, Congress authorized President Johnson to wage war in Vietnam. The resolution was the result of an attack on U.S. destroyers by North Vietnamese torpedo boats in the Gulf of Tonkin several days earlier.

Name of Jesus Feast Day

National Lighthouse Day

National Psychiatric Technician Appreciation Day

On the Wednesday of the first full week in August show appreciation to those technicians who care for psychiatric patients. *Sponsor:* Lakeshore Mental Health Institute, Ellen Adcock, 5908 Lyons View Drive, Knoxville, TN 37919; 615-584-1561; Fax: 615-450-5231.

Purple Heart Birthday

In 1782, George Washington established the Order of the Purple Heart at Newburgh, New York. The Purple Heart recognizes merit in enlisted soldiers who have been wounded.

Revolving door patented (1888)

Theophilus Van Kannel of Philadelphia, Pennsylvania, patented the revolving door.

Tightrope Walking Day

In 1974, Philippe Petit, a French stuntman, walked a tightrope strung between the 2 towers of the World Trade Center in New York City.

U.S. War Department established (1789)

Congress established the Department of War, predecessor to the Department of Defense. *Contact:* Department of Defense, Public Affairs, Pentagon, Room 2E-800, Washington, DC 20310; 703-697-9312; Fax: 703-695-1149.

August 8

America's Oldest Baby Parade

Ocean City's annual baby parade has been held since the turn of the century. Take your baby for a stroll on the second Thursday in August. *Sponsor:* Ocean City Visitors Bureau, P.O. Box 157, Ocean City, NJ 08226; 609-399-0272; 800-232-2465; Fax: 609-398-3932.

First savings and loan (1933)

The First Federal Savings and Loan Association of Miami, Florida, was the first.

First silent mammoth whistle (50,000 B.C.)

According to a *Far Side* cartoon by Gary Larson, Gak Eisenberg invented the first and only silent mammoth whistle in 50,000 B.C. In the cartoon, Gak was crushed by a stampede of woolly mammoths. *Contact:* Universal Press Syndicate, Gary Larson of The Far Side, 4900 Main Street, 9th Floor, Kansas City, MO 64112; 816-932-6600; 800-255-6734.

Grand American World Trapshooting Tournament

August 8 to 17. Held since 1899, this is the world's largest trapshooting event. The dates change every year, so call to confirm future years. *Sponsor:* Amateur Trapshooting Association, 601 W. National Road, Vandalia, OH 45377; 513-275-7788; Fax: 513-898-5472.

Mimeograph machine patented (1876)

Thomas Edison patented the mimeograph machine.

Odie's Birthday

Odie the dog, Garfield's best friend, first appeared in 1978. *Contact:* Garfield the Cat, United Features Syndicate, 200 Park Avenue, 6th Floor, New York, NY 10166; 212-692-3700; Fax: 212-692-3758.

Omak Stampede Suicide Hill Race

Each day of the Stampede, riders race on horseback down an almost vertical slope. It looks like an impossible ride, yet dozens of riders do it every year during the second weekend in August. *Sponsor:* Omak Visitors Bureau, Route 2, Box 5200, Omak, WA 98841; 800-225-6625.

Party Party Day

An excuse to have a party once a month (when the day equals the month). *Sponsor:* Bonza Bottler Day. ✉

Saint Dominic Feast Day

Patron saint of astronomers.

Sneak Zucchini onto Your Neighbor's Porch Night

To get rid of extra zucchini, give it to your neighbors at night. *Sponsor:* Wellness Permission League. ✉

Swim Day

On the birthday of Esther Williams, professional swimmer and actress, everyone should go out for a swim during the dog days of summer. Williams was born in 1923 in Los Angeles, California. *Sponsor:* The Life of the Party. ✉

August 9

Betty Boop's Birthday

In 1930, a forerunner of Betty Boop, a cartoon character created by Max Fleischer, made her debut in the animated short *Dizzy Dishes*.

Birthday of the Prophet Muhammad (Milad-an-Nabi)

The founder of Islam was born in 570 in Mecca, Saudi Arabia. In many Middle Eastern countries, Muhammad's birthday is celebrated on the 12th day of the 3rd month of the Islamic lunar calendar (1996: July 29; 1997: July 18).

International Day of Solidarity with the Struggle of the Women of South Africa and Namibia

Sponsor: United Nations. ✉

First ship to carry the American flag around world

Returning to Boston, Massachusetts in 1790 after a 3-year voyage, *Columbia* became the first ship to carry the American flag around the world.

International Heroes Week

August 9 to 16. Honors all the women in the world who have played a role in shaping the lives of everyone today. *Sponsor:* All My Events. ✉

Isaac Walton Day

Isaac Walton (born in 1593) wrote *The Complete Angler,* one of the first books about fishing.

Moment of Silence

Observe a moment of silence to mourn for the victims of the atomic bombing of Nagasaki, Japan in 1945.

Mosquito Awareness Weekend

During the second weekend in August, the World Championship Mosquito Calling Contest and the World Championship Mosquito Cook-Off and Recipe Contest are held. Also includes a blood-sucking contest, swatting contest, and mosquito trapping demonstrations. *Sponsor:* Crowley's Ridge State Park, Mosquito Awareness Weekend, P.O. Box 97, Walcott, AR 72474; 501-573-6751.

Presidential Resignation Anniversary (1974)

President Richard Nixon was the first president of the U.S. to resign his office. And, we hope, the last.

Smokey the Bear's Birthday

Born in 1944, Smokey is the spokesbear for forest fire prevention. Send birthday cards to Smokey Bear Headquarters, Room 1163, MRC 402, Washington DC 20252. *Contact:* Smithsonian Institution, Office of Elementary Education, Arts and Industry Building #1163, Washington, DC 20560.

Thoreau's Walden published (1854)

Henry David Thoreau of Concord, Massachusetts, self-published his classic book, *Walden.* In it, he wrote about his experiences in self-sufficiency while living in a small cabin by Walden Pond outside Concord.

Webster-Ashburton Treaty signed (1842)

This treaty resolved a border dispute between the U.S. and Canada.

August 10

Candid Camera premiered (1948)

Allen Funt's show made its debut on ABC-TV; it was originally called *Candid Microphone. Contact:* ABC-TV. ✉

Certified Registered Nurse Anesthetist Week

Held during their annual convention, recognizes the work of certified registered nurse anesthetists. *Sponsor:* American Association of Nurse Anesthetists, 222 S. Prospect Avenue, Park Ridge, IL 60068-4001; 708-692-7050; Fax: 708-692-6968.

E Pluribus Unum became the U.S. motto (1776)

Family Volleyball Day

YMCA launched the game of volleyball over 100 years ago. This day is celebrated on the second Saturday in August. *Sponsor:* YMCA of the USA, 101 N. Wacker Drive, Chicago, IL 60606-7386; 312-977-0031; 800-872-9622; Fax: 312-977-9063.

First electric streetcar commercially operated (1885)

It was designed by Leo Daft and opened in Baltimore, Maryland.

First human-made object recovered from space

In 1960, an ejected space capsule from *Discoverer 13* was recovered when it returned from orbit. *Contact:* NASA. ✉

Herbert Clark Hoover's Birthday

The 31st President of the U.S. was born in West Branch, Iowa in 1874. Hoover was the first President born west of the Mississippi River.

International Soap Box Derby

Since 1938, this derby has determined the world champion soap box derby driver. The actual race is always held on the Saturday of the first full week in August. *Sponsor:* All-American Soap Box Derby, Jeff Iula, P.O. Box 7233, Derby Downs,

Akron, OH 44306; 216-733-8723; Fax: 216-733-1370.

Middle Children's Day
On the second Saturday in August, pay attention to your middle children. Give them some attention, too! *Sponsor:* Mid-Kid Company, 402 Oak Avenue, Seabring, FL 33870; 813-385-7386.

Missouri Admission Day
In 1821, Missouri became the 24th state admitted to the U.S. *Contact:* Missouri Division of Tourism, P.O. Box 1055, Jefferson City, MO 65102; 314-751-4133.

National Hobo Convention
Hoboes from all over the U.S. meet each year at this convention on the second Saturday in August. *Sponsor:* Britt Chamber of Commerce, P.O. Box 63, Britt, IA 50423; 515-843-3867.

Saint Laurence Feast Day
Patron saint of cooks, brewers, confectioners, cutlers, armorers, schoolboys, students, washerwomen, and glaziers. His patronage of cooks is based on the legend that he was martyred by being roasted alive on a grid.

Smithsonian Museum chartered by Congress (1846)
English scientist Joseph Smithson's $500,000 bequest helped establish this museum. For a free quarterly teaching guide, *Art to Zoo,* contact OESE, Smithsonian Institution, Arts and Industry Building #1163, MRC 402, Washington, DC 20560; 202-357-2425. You may also request a free copy of the *Smithsonian Resource Guide for Teachers,* which lists more than 500 educational books, videos, newsletters, and teaching guides available from the Smithsonian. *Contact:* Smithsonian Museum, 900 Jefferson Drive SW #2410, Washington, DC 20560; 202-357-2700; Fax: 202-786-2515.

U.S. Department of Defense renamed (1949)
The National Military Establishment was renamed the Department of Defense. *Contact:* Department of Defense, Public Affairs, Pentagon, Room 2E-800, Washington, DC 20310; 703-697-9312; Fax: 703-695-1149.

World Championship Spike-Driving Contest
Held on the second Saturday in August at Promontory Summit, where the transcontinental railroad was completed. *Sponsor:* Railroaders Festival, Golden Spike Historic Site, P.O. Box 897, Brigham City, UT 84302; 801-471-2209; Fax: 801-471-2341. For info, call the Utah Travel Council at 800-200-1160.

World Whimmy Diddle Competition
What's a whimmy diddle? Find out by attending this annual world championship competition held on the second Saturday in August. *Sponsor:* Southern Highland Handicraft Guild, Milepost 382, Blue Ridge Parkway, Box 9545, Asheville, NC 28815; 704-298-7928; Fax: 704-298-7962.

August 11

Alcatraz's Birthday
The island prison in San Francisco Bay received its first prisoners in 1934. Alcatraz is no longer a prison, but was (and probably still is) the best known American prison.

Annual Medical Check-Up Day
Visit your doctor today and have a medical check-up.

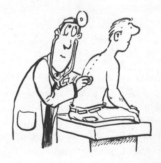

Daughter's Day
On the second Sunday in August, celebrate your female children. Formerly sponsored by American Artists Studio.

Don't Wait . . .
Celebrate! Week

The second full week in August encourages frequent spontaneous festivities that acknowledge small but significant accomplishments such as team wins, good grades, completed projects, new neighbors, balanced checkbooks, and so on. *Sponsor:* Celebration Creations, Patty Sachs, 73-729 Manzanita Court, Palm Desert, CA 92260; 619-341-2066; Fax: 619-341-2066.

Electric light bulb socket with pull chain (1896)

Patented by Harvey Hubbell.

Explore Your Roots Day

Celebrates the 1921 birthday of Alex Haley, author of the Pulitzer Prize-winning novel *Roots,* which was the basis for the first major mini-series. Use this day to explore your own family roots.

Family Day

The family is the best place to teach values and beliefs; always celebrated on the second Sunday in August. *Sponsor:* Kiwanis International. ✉

First successful silver mill in U.S. (1860)

The mill opened near Virginia City, Nevada.

Mall of America opened (1992)

The largest shopping center in the U.S. opened in Bloomington, Minnesota. It also features the largest indoor theme park, Knott's Camp Snoopy. *Contact:* Bloomington Visitors Bureau, 1550 East 79th Street #450, Bloomington, MN 55425; 612-858-8500; Fax: 612-858-8854. Visitors bureau: 800-346-4289. Mall phone: 612-883-8800.

Meteor Shower Night

Sometime around the 11th of August, give or take a day, the earth passes closest to the Perseid meteor belt; and there is a greater chance of seeing falling stars or meteor showers. Also known as the Night of the Shooting Stars.

National Apple Week

The Beatles proclaimed this week in 1965 when they released their first records on the Apple label (1965).

National Recreational Scuba Diving Week

A time to promote scuba diving to the general public. Celebrated the second or third week of August. *Sponsor:* PADI, John Nesbit, 1251 E. Dyer Road #100, Santa Ana, CA 92705-5605; 714-540-7234; Fax: 714-540-2609.

Presidential Joke Day

In 1984, President Reagan tested his mike by saying, "I just signed legislation outlawing Russia forever. We begin bombing in 5 minutes." His joking remarks were picked up by live TV cameras.

Saint Clare of Assisi Feast Day

This friend of Saint Francis is patron saint of television. When she was too sick to attend mass, the Holy Spirit lit up a wall in her bedroom so she could watch the mass. She is also patron saint of embroiderers and is invoked against sore throats.

SOS signal first used by an American ship (1909)

The *Arapahoe* was the first American ship to send the SOS distress signal, as it floundered off the coast of Cape Hatteras, North Carolina.

Umpire Appreciation Day

Three cheers for umpires, the hardest working professionals in baseball. Always celebrated the second Sunday in August.

Watts Riots Anniversary (1965)

One of our nation's largest racial riots began. It ended about a week later; 34 people were killed and thousands were injured.

August 12

First successful communications balloon satellite (1960)

Echo 1, was launched from Cape Canaveral, Florida.

First use of disinfectant in surgery

Dr. Joseph Lister was the first surgeon to use disinfectant in surgery.

Get a Tan Day

On the birthday of actor George Hamilton, who is known for his tan, attempt to get your own tan. Hamilton was born in 1939 in Memphis, Tennessee. *Sponsor:* The Life of the Party. ✉

Hawaii annexed to the U.S. (1898)

The U.S. formally annexed the kingdom of Hawaii. *Contact:* Hawaii Visitors Bureau, 2270 Kalakaua Avenue #801, Honolulu, HI 96815; 808-923-1811; Fax: 808-923-0678.

King Philip's War, first Indian war, ended (1676)

The first war between American Indians and white settlers ended. King Philip was killed by a member of his own troops, thus ending the war.

Last American ground troops leave Vietnam (1972)

Sewing machine patented (1851)

Isaac Singer patented the first sewing machine with a rocking treadle.

Soviet Union's first hydrogen bomb

In 1953, the Soviet Union conducted its first test of the hydrogen bomb.

Victory Day (Rhode Island)

This public holiday commemorates the end of the first war between Indians and the colonists in 1676. *Contact:* Rhode Island Tourism Division, 7 Jackson Walkway, Providence, RI 02903; 401-277-2601; 800-556-2484; Fax: 401-277-2102.

Weird Contest Week

Why should the people of Ocean City be the only ones to enjoy such contests as artistic pie eating, french fry sculpting, wet t-shirt throwing, and animal impersonations? Why not celebrate this third week of August in your own home town? *Sponsor:* City of Ocean City, Mark Soifer, PR Director, City Hall, Ocean City, NJ 08226; 609-399-0272; Fax: 609-399-0374.

World's worst single aircraft disaster (1985)

Japan Air Lines Boeing 747 crashed into a mountain, killing 520 passengers and crew.

August 13

Bambi's Birthday

The animated movie *Bambi* premiered at Radio City Music Hall in New York City in 1934. *Contact:* Walt Disney Company. ✉

Cowardly Lion Day

Celebrate the birthday of Bert Lahr, the cowardly lion in the movie *The Wizard of Oz*. *Sponsor:* The Life of the Party. ✉

Eyeglasses invented (1287)

Fall of the Aztec Empire

In 1521, the Spanish conqueror Hernando Cortez captured Mexico City from the Aztecs; it was the beginning of the end for the Aztec Empire.

First 2-way telephone conversation via satellite

With the help of *Echo 1*, the first phone conversation via satellite took place in 1960.

First bus line in U.S. (1914)

Carl Wickman started Greyhound in Hibbing, Minnesota. *Contact:* Greyhound Lines, 15110 N. Dallas Parkway, Dallas, TX 75248; 214-715-7000; Fax: 214-419-3994.

First coin-operated telephone patented (1889)

William Gray of Hartford, Connecticut, patented the first coin-operated telephone.

First country music record to sell a million (1924)

Vernon Dalhart's "The Prisoner's Song" was the first million-seller country music record.

First roller derby (1935)

Len Seltzer promoted the first roller derby in Chicago Stadium.

First woman to enroll at the Citadel (1995)

Shannon Faulkner began her first full day on campus at The Citadel, formerly a men-only military academy in Charleston, South Carolina. Less than a week later, she dropped out because the stress and isolation was ruining her health. *Contact*: The Citadel, Charleston, SC 29409; 803-953-5000; Fax: 803-792-7084.

International Lefthanders Day

Acknowledges the special needs and frustrations of lefthanders. Also celebrate some of history's greatest lefthanders: Jimi Hendrix, Picasso, Alexander the Great, Michelangelo, Babe Ruth, and Leonardo da Vinci. *Sponsor*: Lefthanders International, Dean R. Campbell, President, P.O. Box 8249, Topeka, KS 66608-0249; 913-234-2177.

Li'l Abner's Birthday

The *Li'l Abner* cartoon strip, created by Al Capp, premiered in 1934.

August 14

Atlantic Charter issued (1941)

Issued by President Roosevelt and Prime Minister Winston Churchill, renounced aggression as a policy of government.

International Gourmet Day

On the birthday of Julia Child, we celebrate all gourmets and gourmet chefs. Julia Child was born in 1912 in Pasadena, California. *Sponsor*: All My Events.

Liberty Tree Day

A Massachusetts state holiday. *Contact*: Massachusetts Tourism Office, 100 Cambridge Street, 13th Floor, Boston, MA 02202; 617-727-3201; 800-447-6277; Fax: 617-727-6525.

National Senior Citizens Day

The Social Security Act was passed in 1935.

Official end of American combat in Indochina (1973)

The U.S. ceased bombing Cambodia, thus ending 12 years of American combat involvement in Indochina.

Oregon Territory Day

In 1848, the Oregon Territory was established. *Contact*: Oregon Tourism Division, 775 Summer Street NE, Salem, OR 97310; 503-986-0000; 800-547-7842; Fax: 503-986-0001.

Saint Maximilian Kolbe Feast Day

A modern-day saint in Nazi Poland, patron saint of political prisoners.

Social Security Birthday

The Social Security Act was approved by Congress in 1935.

V-J Day (Victory in Japan, 1945)

President Truman announced that Japan had surrendered in World War II. The official surrender signing took place on September 2.

Whiffle Ball Birthday

In 1953, David Mullany, Sr. invented the ball for his 13-year-old son.

August 15

Assumption of the Virgin Mary

Celebrates Mary's assumption into Heaven. Also known as the Dormition of the Virgin Mary.

Chauvin Day

Honors Nicholas Chauvin, a soldier so blindly devoted to Emperor Napoleon that his name became a word: "chauvinism," which means an absurd attachment to a cause. Napoleon was born on this date in 1769.

✉ Addresses for frequently cited organizations are gathered on pages vii–viii.

AUGUST   183

National Relaxation Day

This is the day to totally relax. Do not contact the sponsor of this day. He does not provide any collateral materials. *Sponsor:* Sean Moeller, 12079 Belann Court, P.O. Box 71, Clio, MI 48420; 810-687-0423.

Panama Canal opened to traffic (1914)

Transcontinental railroad completed (1870)

Some history books say that the transcontinental railroad was completed in Promontory Point, Utah in 1869, but it was actually completed almost a year later just outside the town of Strasburg, Colorado. *Contact:* Strasburg Business Association, P.O. Box 535, Strasburg, CO 80136; 303-622-4218.

Wizard of Oz premiered (1939)

The movie *The Wizard of Oz* premiered at Grauman's Chinese Theater.

Woodstock Rock 'n' Roll Festival (1969)

August 15 to 17. The most famous rock 'n' roll festival rocked the world in 1969. It was actually held near Bethel, New York.

August 16

Bennington Battle Day (Vermont)

In 1777, the American rebels won the Battle of Bennington. This day is a public holiday in Vermont. *Contact:* Vermont Department of Tourism, 134 State Street, Montpelier, VT 05602; 802-828-3236.

Elvis International Tribute Week

The week of August 16 celebrates Elvis, the King. In memory of Elvis, the city of Memphis sponsors over 35 events during this week. For a free brochure, call 800-238-2000. *Contact:* Graceland, P.O. Box 16508, Memphis, TN 38186-0508; 901-332-3322.

Elvis Presley Commemoration Day

At age 42, Elvis Presley died at Graceland Mansion in Memphis, Tennessee. Elvis died for the first time in 1977. He has been sighted many times since then. *Sponsor:* Elvis Presley Birthplace, 306 Elvis Presley Drive, P.O. Box 1339, Tupelo, MS 38802; 601-841-1245.

Harmonic Convergence Anniversary (1987)

People gathered at 20 sites around the world to greet the New Age.

Joe Miller's Joke Day

The English comic actor died in 1738. He inspired the first book of jokes, *Joe Miller's Jests.*

Klondike Gold Discovery Day

George Carmack discovered gold in 1896 at Bonanza Creek in the Yukon. This day is celebrated as a holiday in the Yukon Territory on the Monday nearest the 16th.

Material Girls Day

On the birthday of singer/actress Madonna Ciccone, be a material girl (or guy). Madonna was born in 1958 in Bay City, Michigan. *Sponsor:* The Life of the Party. ✉

Sports Illustrated first published (1954)

Contact: Sports Illustrated, Time and Life Building, Rockefeller Center, New York, NY 10020; 212-522-1212; 800-541-1000; Fax: 212-977-4540.

True Love Forever Day

In 1965, Francesca and Robert, the main characters of *The Bridges of Madison County,* first met. Coincidentally, the novel first appeared on the *New York Times* bestseller list on this same date in 1992. *Contact:* Warner Books, 1271 Avenue of the Americas, New York, NY 10020; 212-522-7974.

World's oldest continuous rodeo

Begun in 1884 and held on the third full weekend in August, this rodeo is the oldest continuous rodeo in the world. Among other competitions, it features bull riding, calf roping, and barrel racing. *Sponsor:* Payson Rodeo, Chamber of Commerce, P.O. Box 1380, Payson, AZ 85547; 520-474-4515; 800-672-9766; Fax: 520-474-8812.

August 17

Cat Nights begin
Shortly after Dog Days end, Cat Nights begin.

Come Up and See Me Sometime Day
On her birthday, celebrate the immortal words of Mae West, one of the original movie sex goddesses. *Sponsor:* The Life of the Party. ✉

First air mail in the U.S. (1859)
The first airmail took off from Lafayette, Indiana, in a balloon. *Contact:* U.S. Postal Service. ✉

First steamboat trip in America (1807)
Robert Fulton's *Clermont* went from New York City to Albany, New York. John Fitch demonstrated an earlier version of the steamboat on August 22, 1787.

First transatlantic balloon crossing (1978)
The *Double Eagle II* landed in Miserey, France. Balloonists Maxie Anderson, Ben Abruzzo, and Larry Newman made the trip in 137 hours and 3 minutes.

National Golf Day
Amateur golfers try to beat the professional scores at a PGA tournament on the third Saturday in August. *Contact:* Professional Golfers Association, 100 Avenue of the Champions, Palm Beach Garde, FL 33418; 407-624-8400; Fax: 407-624-8448.

National Hippie Day
On the Saturday nearest August 15 to 17 (Woodstock Weekend), celebrate the tie-dye culture of the 60's. Give out flowers, throw a love-in or mazola party, wear a head band, and string some love beads. *Sponsor:* The Life of the Party. ✉

National Homeless Animals Day
Due to overpopulation, over 12 million cats and dogs are killed each year at animal shelters. Here's the solution: spay or neuter your pets! Always held on the third Saturday in August. *Sponsor:* International Society for Animal Rights, 421 S. State Street, Clarks Summit, PA 18411; 717-586-2200; Fax: 717-586-9580.

Natural Chimneys Jousting Tournament
Held since 1821, this jousting tournament is the oldest continuously held sporting event in the U.S. Always held on the third Saturday in August. *Sponsor:* Natural Chimneys Regional Park, Upper Valley Regional Parks, P.O. Box 478, Grottoes, VA 24441; 703-350-2510.

August 18

19th amendment to the Constitution ratified (1920)
Gave women the right to vote.

Bad Poetry Day
This day is a celebration of really bad poetry. Write some yourself. *Sponsor:* Wellness Permission League. ✉

First black graduate of University of Mississippi (1963)
James Meredith was the first. *Contact:* University of Mississippi, Oxford, MS 38677; 601-232-7211; Fax: 601-232-5093.

First English child born in North America (1587)
Virginia Dare was born to Ellinor and Ananias Dare on Roanoke Island.

Lolita published (1958)
The sexy novel was written by Vladimir Nabokov.

Parsi New Year's Day

Celebrated on August 23 (April 22nd on leap years), this is one of the local new years celebrated in India. *Contact:* Government of India, Tourist Information Office, 30 Rockefeller Plaza #15, New York, NY 10112; 212-586-4901; Fax: 212-582-3274.

Vietnam Conflict began (1945)

Just a few days after the Japanese surrendered, Communist guerrila leader Ho Chi Minh led a successful coup. In response, the French parachuted into Vietnam to fight the coup. *Contact:* Socialist Republic of Vietnam, Mission to the United Nations, 20 Waterside Plaza, New York, NY 10010; 212-679-3779; Fax: 212-686-8534.

August 23

Birth Control Birthday

In 2032 B.C., Egyptians introduced the first birth control method other than the rhythm method. They altered the pH of the vagina by inserting crocodile dung and honey, making it too acid for sperm to survive.

First girl to play in Little League World Series

Victoria Brucker of San Pedro, California, played in 1989. *Contact:* Little League Baseball, P.O. Box 3485, South Williamsport, PA 17701; 717-326-1921; Fax: 717-326-1074.

First human-powered flight (1977)

Bryan Allen won the Kremer Prize for the first human-powered flight as he pedalled the Gossamer Condor for at least a mile at Schafter, California.

First National Women's Rights Convention (1850)

August 23 to 24. The first national women's rights convention was held in Worcester, Massachusetts. It attracted 1,000 people. *Contact:* Worcester County Visitors Bureau, 33 Waldo Street, Worcester, MA 01608; 508-753-2920; Fax: 508-754-8560.

Gasoline Alley Birthday

The comic strip by Frank King first appeared in the *Chicago Tribune* in 1919.

Great American Duck Race

The fourth weekend in August features the world's richest duck races as well as Great American Duck Queen Ball, Best Dressed Duck contest, the World's Richest Tortilla Toss, an outhouse race, and the Tournament of Ducks Parade. *Sponsor:* Deming Chamber of Commerce, P.O. Box 8, Deming, NM 88031; 505-546-2674; 800-848-4955; Fax: 505-546-9569.

Hug Your Boyfriend or Girlfriend Day

Take the time today to appreciate your soulmate in a healthy relationship. *Sponsor:* Sharkbait Press, Marcus Meleton Jr, P.O. Box 11300, Costa Mesa, CA 92627; 714-645-0139.

Sacco-Vanzetti Memorial Day

In 1927, Nicola Sacco and Bartolomeo Vanzetti, immigrant laborers, were electrocuted for a payroll robbery they did not commit. Fifty years later, in 1977, Governor Dukakis declared this day a memorial day for these victims of prejudice.

Sign of Virgo

The astrological sign of Virgo the virgin runs from August 23rd to September 22nd. Virgo people are intellectual, methodical, and placid.

Singing in the Rain Day

On the birthday of Gene Kelley, a great movie star and dancer, sing and dance in the rain. Kelley was born in 1912 in Pittsburgh, Pennsylvania. *Sponsor:* The Life of the Party. ✉

August 24

Fall of Rome (410)

The Visigoths invaded and sacked Rome, ending the Roman Empire in the west.

✉ Addresses for frequently cited organizations are gathered on pages vii–viii.

First black delegate to the U.N.

In 1950, Edith Sampson was named the first U.S. black alternate delegate to the U.N.

First woman to fly non-stop across the U.S. (1932)

Amelia Earhart flew from Los Angeles to Newark in 19+ hours.

France became a nuclear power (1968)

France exploded a hydrogen bomb in the South Pacific. It became the fifth nation to have the bomb. *Contact:* French Embassy, 4101 Reservoir Road NW, Washington, DC 20007; 202-944-6000.

Saint Bartholomew Feast Day

Patron saint of plasterers. If his feast day is fair and clear, a prosperous autumn is almost certain.

Vesuvius Day

In 79 A.D., Mount Vesuvius erupted, burying the resort town of Pompeii, Italy. 20,000 people died. Pompeii is now one of the richest archaeological digs. Even bread has been found buried in ovens.

Waffle iron patented (1869)

Washington, D.C. invaded (1814)

Our nation's capital was invaded for the first and only time during the War of 1812. British troops took control of the city, burned many public buildings, and left a day later. *Contact:* Washington, DC Visitors Bureau, 1212 New York Avenue NW #600, Washington, DC 20005; 202-789-7000; Fax: 202-789-7037.

Windows 95 Birthday

This day in 1995 was the official launch date for Windows 95, the new computer operating system from Microsoft. *Sponsor:* Microsoft Corporation, 1 Microsoft Way, Redmond, WA 98052; 206-882-8080; 800-426-9400; Fax: 206-936-7329; e-mail: info@microsoft.com.

August 25

007 Day

On the birthday of Sean Connery, the best of all the actors in the James Bond movie series, do a little spying of your own. Connery was born in 1930 in Edinburgh, Scotland. *Sponsor:* The Life of the Party. ✉

Be Kind to Humankind Week

Celebrated the last 7 days in August, includes separate special days (see specific days). *Sponsor:* Lorraine Jara, P.O. Box 586, Island Heights, NJ 08732; 908-270-6112.

First person to swim English Channel (1875)

Matthew Webb swam from Dover, England, to Calais, France, in 22 hours.

First seeding machine patented (1840)

Joseph Gibbons of Adrian, Michigan, patented the first seeding machine.

Gas Mask Day

In 291 B.C. China, poison gas was first used in warfare, hundreds of years before the gas mask was invented. *Sponsor:* A Pilgrim's Almanac. ✉

Hauling Grass World Championship Grass Drags

Held the fourth weekend in August, this race determines the world champion of snowmobile drag racing on grass. *Sponsor:* Eagle River Derby Races, P.O. Box 1447, Eagle River, WI 54521; 715-479-4424; Fax: 715-479-9711.

Healthy Lifestyle Day
In 1995, over 30,000 people in Singapore set a record for the world's largest exercise workout as they celebrated Healthy Lifestyle Day. *Contact:* Republic of Singapore Embassy, 1824 R Street NW, Washington, DC 20009; 202-667-7555.

Kiss and Make Up Day
A day to mend your relationships. *Sponsor:* Jay Inc, Jacqueline Millgate, 170 Linden Oaks Drive, Rochester, NY 14625; 716-264-3600.

National Park Service Anniversary
In 1916, the Park Service was established under the Department of Interior. *Contact:* National Park Service, 1849 C Street NW #3424, Washington, DC 20240-0001; 202-208-7394; Fax: 202-343-7520.

National Religious Software Week
The last full week in August recognizes the role that software plays in studying the Bible. *Sponsor:* Zondervan Publishing House, Jonathan Petersen, 5300 Patterson Avenue SE, Grand Rapids, MI 49530; 616-698-3417; Fax: 616-698-3439.

Paris Liberation Day
In 1944, during World War II, Paris was liberated from Nazi occupation. *Contact:* French Embassy, 4101 Reservoir Boulevard NW, Washington, DC 20007; 202-944-6000.

Sacrifice Our Wants for Others Needs Sunday
Do like it says. Always celebrated on the Sunday of the last 7 days in August. *Sponsor:* Lorraine Jara (see previous address).

Sleeping Car Porters Union organized (1925)
A. Phillip Randolph organized the Sleeping Car Porters Union.

Society for Investigation of Unexplained founded (1965)

August 26

Cannon was first used in battle (1346)
Edward III of England defeated Philip VI of France at Crecy.

First roller coaster built in America (1929)

First televised baseball games (1939)
WXBS televised 2 games between the Cincinnati Reds and the Brooklyn Dodgers. *Contact:* Major League Baseball. ✉

International Hockey Hall of Fame opened (1961)
Opened in Toronto, Ontario. *Contact:* International Hockey Hall of Fame, Exhibition Place, Toronto, Ontario M6K 3C3 Canada; 416-595-1345.

Krakatoa Eruption Anniversary
The Indonesian volcano erupted in 1883. The resulting tidal waves killed over 36,000 people. Because of dust hurled into the atmosphere, weather worldwide was affected for many years. This was the biggest explosion in human history.

Make Your Own Luck Day
Take control of your destiny by creating your own opportunities! *Sponsor:* J. Richard Falls, P.O. Box 165090, Irving, TX 75016-5090; 214-252-9026.

Motorist Consideration Monday
Let other people merge, signal when passing, and lay off the horn. Always celebrated on the Monday of the last 7 days in August. *Sponsor:* Lorraine Jara (see previous address).

Saint Augustine of Canterbury Feast Day

The first archbishop of Canterbury. He died on May 26, 604.

Toilet Paper Birthday

Invented by the Chinese in 580, but it took another 1000 years to reach the West. Toilet paper was first sold on a roll in 1871. *Sponsor:* A Pilgrim's Almanac. ✉

Women's Equality Day

In 1920, the 19th Amendment was certified, giving women the right to vote. Secretary of State Bainbridge Colby signed the amendment into law, it was ratified 8 days earlier.

August 27

Beauty Is in the Eye of the Beholder Day

Celebrates the birthday (1850 in Ireland) of Margaret Hungerford who, in one of her popular novels, gave us the saying that beauty is in the eye of the beholder. *Sponsor:* The Dutchess Who Wasn't Day, Peggy Shirley, 1261 Quail Run, Columbia SC 29206; 803-782-0560.

Cherokee National Holiday

Celebrates the establishment of the Cherokee Nation (on September 6, 1839, the Cherokee Nation signed its constitution). Always celebrated the Thursday through Sunday before Labor Day. *Sponsor:* Cherokee Tribal Office, P.O. Box 948, Tahlaquah, OK 74465-0948; 918-456-0671.

First play performed in North American colonies

In 1655, *Ye Bare and Ye Cubb* was performed in Acomac, Virginia.

First solo sea voyage around the world (1966)

Sir Francis Chichester began the first solo sea voyage around the world.

First successful oil well drilled (1859)

The first commercially successful oil well was drilled near Titusville, Pennsylvania, by Edwin Drake.

Guinness Book of World Records first published

Came off the bindery in 1955; since then, over 70 million copies have been sold, more than any other book but the Bible.

Kellogg-Briand Pact signed (1928)

This pact, which was signed in Paris, France, renounced war as an instrument of foreign policy. It provided for peaceful resolutions to disputes.

Lyndon Baines Johnson's Birthday

The 36th President of the U.S. was born in 1908, near Stonewall, Texas. He succeeded to the presidency after the assassination of John F. Kennedy in Dallas, Texas, on November 22, 1963. Johnson's birthday is a Texas holiday.

Saint Monica Feast Day

The mother of Saint Augustine, she is patron saint of married women and mothers, especially mothers of difficult children.

Tarzan's Birthday

In 1912, the first Tarzan story by Edgar Rice Burroughs appeared in a magazine.

Touch a Heart Tuesday

Do something special for the ones you love and depend upon. Always celebrated on the Tuesday of the last 7 days of August. *Sponsor:* Lorraine Jara (see previous address).

August 28

Barley Moon

The full moon of August is the barley moon, symbolic of harvest, agriculture, bounty, fertility, marriage, and good health. It is associated with grain goddesses and sun gods. It is also known as the sturgeon moon in the American backwoods tradition.

Dream Day

Celebrates the anniversary of Martin Luther King's "I-Have-A-Dream" speech made in 1963. *Sponsor:* Global Committee Commemorating Kingdom Respect Days, P.O.

Box 21050, Chicago, IL 60621;
312-737-7328.

First horse to break 2-minute mile (1897)

First radio commercial (1922)
Aired on WEAF in New York City;
it was a 10-minute ad for a real estate company. Cost: $100.00.

Largest single demonstration in U.S. history
In 1963, the March on Washington for Jobs and Freedom was the largest single demonstration every held in the U.S. During this event, Martin Luther King gave his famous "I-Have-A-Dream" speech.

Saint Augustine of Hippo Feast Day
Patron saint of printers, theologians, and brewers.

United Parcel Service started (1907)
UPS was started by teenagers Jim Casey and Claude Ryan in Seattle, Washington. *Contact:* United Parcel Service, 400 Perimeter Center Terrace N, Atlanta, GA 30346; 404-913-6000; Fax: 404-913-6137.

Willing to Lend a Hand Wednesday
The smallest good deed is greater than the largest good intention. Always celebrated on the Wednesday of the last 7 days in August. *Sponsor:* Lorraine Jara (see previous address).

August 29

According to Hoyle Day
Edmond Hoyle's *Short Treatise* on the game of whist was published in 1742.

Chop suey invented (1896)
The chef of the Chinese ambassador introduced chop suey in New York City.

Fall of the Incan Empire
In 1533, the Spanish executed Atahualpa, the last Incan King. That was the beginning of the end for the Incan Empire.

More Herbs, Less Salt Day
For better health, cut down on salt and eat more herbs. *Sponsor:* Wellness Permission League. ✉

National Plastic Surgery Day
On the birthday of rock star Michael Jackson, consider what you can do to make yourself look better. Jackson was born in 1958 in Gary, Indiana. *Sponsor:* The Life of the Party. ✉

Pretty Woman Day
In 1964, Roy Orbison released the recording of the song "Pretty Woman."

Soviet Communist Party suspended (1991)
Communist Party activities were suspended by the Soviet parliament. *Contact:* Russian Federation Embassy, 1125 16th Street NW, Washington, DC 20036; 202-628-7551.

Thoughtful Thursday
Not a big deal, but try to make someone else's life easier. Always celebrated on the Thursday of the last 7 days in August. *Sponsor:* Lorraine Jara (see previous address).

August 30

Alexandrian New Year
The first day of the month of Thoth was the beginning of the new year in the Greco-Egyptian calendar of ancient Alexandria.

Favors Granted Friday
Do something special for others. Always celebrated on the Friday of the last 7 days in August. *Sponsor:* Lorraine Jara (see previous address).

First black American astronaut (1983)

Lt. Col. Guion Bluford, Jr., flew on the shuttle *Challenger. Contact:* NASA. ✉

First recorded observation of a comet hitting sun

First White House presidential baby (1893)

Mrs. Grover Cleveland gave birth to a baby girl named Ester, becoming the first wife of a president to give birth in the White House.

International Red Telephone Day

The hot line telephone was installed between Russia and the U.S. in 1963. *Sponsor:* The Life of the Party. ✉

International Strange Music Weekend

August 30 to 31. People play music on strange instruments, ranging from vacuum cleaners to stethoscopes, washing machines to other household appliances. Also includes an exhibit of the Strange Music Hall of Fame. Call to verify dates which change from year to year. *Sponsor:* Carter Caves State Resort Park, John Tierney, Route 5, Box 1120, Olive Hill, KY 41164; 606-286-4411.

National Hard Crab Derby

Since 1947, the hard crab derby races are held on Saturday after-noon before Labor Day. Other events in the derby are held from Friday evening through Sunday—including the crab picking contest and the crowning of the Miss Crustacean beauty queen. *Sponsor:* Derby and Fair Association, Crisfield Chamber of Commerce, P.O. Box 292, Crisfield, MD 21817; 800-782-3913.

Saint Fiacre Feast Day

A gardener himself, he is patron saint of gardeners; also patron saint of cab drivers (because the first cabs in France were based at Hotel Saint-Fiacre) and hosiers.

Saint Rose of Lima Feast Day

The first saint of the Western Hemisphere is patron saint of the Americas. Because of her name, she is also patron saint of florists and gardeners. She is also patron saint of Peru, the Philippines, and India.

August 31

Capital Day

The Saturday before Labor Day honors people who save and invest their money. *Sponsor:* Albert L. Maguire, 1094 Maple Street, Arroyo Grande, CA 93420; 805-489-2645.

First U.S. tennis championships (1881)

Played in Newport, Rhodes Island. *Contact:* Tennis Hall of Fame, New-port Casino, 194 Bellevue Avenue, Newport, RI 02840; 401-849-3990; 800-457-1144.

Kinetoscope patented (1887)

Thomas Edison patented the kinetoscope, the forerunner of the movie projector.

National Neighborhood Day

On the last Saturday in August, arrange a block party with your neighbors.

Saint Raymond Nonnatus Feast Day

Since Raymond was born by Caesarean section, he is patron saint of childbirth, pregnant women, midwives, and children.

Solidarity Labor Union formed (1980)

The Solidarity Labor Union was formed in Gdansk, Poland.

Speak Kind Words Saturday

Keep your words soft and sweet because you may have to eat them. Always celebrated on the Saturday of the week of August 25 to 31. *Sponsor:* Lorraine Jara (see previous address).

U.S. Department of Housing and Urban Development established (1965)

Contact: U.S. Department of Housing and Urban Development, 451 7th Street SW, Washington, DC 20410; 202-708-0980; Fax: 202-619-8153.

World Championship Barbecue Goat Cook-Off

The 23rd annual cook-off will be held over Labor Day weekend in 1996. *Sponsor:* Brady Chamber of Commerce, 101 E. First Street, Brady, TX 76825; 915-597-3491; Fax: 915-597-2420.

SEPTEMBER

Adult Literacy Awareness Month

American Newspaper Month

Celebrates American newspapers. *USA Today* began publishing on the 15th and the *New York Times* on the 18th. Newspaper Carrier Day is the 4th. The first American newspaper was published on September 25th, and the first daily on September 21st. *Sponsor:* Book Marketing Update. ✉

Baby Safety Month

Promotes the safety of baby products. For a free copy of the brochure *Safe and Sound for Baby,* send an SASE to JPMA. *Sponsor:* Juvenile

Products Manufacturers Association, P.O. Box 955, Marlton, NJ 08053; 609-985-2878; Fax: 609-986-3238.

Be Kind to Editors and Writers Month

A time for editors and writers to observe the Golden Rule. Formerly sponsored by Lone Star Publications.

Board and Care Recognition Month

Celebrated in New Jersey and gives credit to the people who operate board and care facilities. *Sponsor:* Board and Care Governor's Association, Nancy Heydt, MCDSS, P.O. Box 3000, Freehold, NJ 07728.

Childhood Cancer Month

Children's Books Month

Read and enjoy books for and about children, parents, and other members of a family. *Sponsor:* Book Marketing Update. ✉

Children's Eye Health and Safety Month

Sponsor: Prevent Blindness America. ✉

Classical Music Month

First celebrated in 1994 after Congress passed a resolution designating September as Classical Music Month. *Sponsor:* Classical Music Coalition, National Association of Recording Merchandisers.

Emergency Care Month

Great American Breakfast Club

From September 1st to November 30th, celebrate the first meal of the day with bacon and sausage. *Sponsor:* National Pork Producers Council, P.O. Box 10383, Des Moines, IA 50306; 515-223-2600; 800-456-7675; Fax: 515-223-2646.

Hand-Craft Soap Month

Educates others about the benefits of using hand-crafted soap, also encourages people to take soap-making classes. *Sponsor:* Valley Hills Press, Elaine C. White, 1864 Ridgeland Drive, Starkville, MS 39759; 601-323-7100; Fax: 601-323-7100.

International Cooperation in Learning Month

International Gay Square Dance Month

Celebrates the joy of square dancing. *Sponsor:* International Association of Gay Square Dance Clubs, P.O. Box 15428, Crystal City, VA 22215-0428; 800-835-6462.

International Solar Month

International Visitors Month

Jazz Month

Library Card Sign-up Month

Libraries encourage children to get library cards. *Sponsor:* American Library Association. ✉

✉   Addresses for frequently cited organizations are gathered on pages vii–viii.

Marriage Health Month

Work to improve your marriage this month. For a free quiz on the health status of your marriage, write to the following address. *Sponsor:* Monogamous Male Association, Rose Smith, P.O. Box 81064, Albuquerque, NM 87198-1064; 505-899-3121; Fax: 505-899-3120.

National Alcohol and Drug Treatment Month

National Beach Clean Up Month

More than 158,000 volunteers have taken part in cleaning up 4,500 miles of shoreline in 32 states. 1993 searchers collected nearly 3.2 million pounds of debris and garbage. *Sponsor:* Center for Marine Conservation.

National Chicken Month

Promotes the health benefits of eating chicken. For promotional items featuring chicken, write to National Chicken Month, P.O. Box 5817, Columbia, SC 29250; 803-254-8158; Fax: 803-252-2016. *Sponsor:* National Broiler Council, 1155 15th Street NW #614, Washington, DC 20005; 202-296-2622; Fax: 202-293-4005.

National Cholesterol Education and Awareness Month

Educates people on how to reduce their cholesterol levels. *Sponsor:* Cholesterol Council of America,

P.O. Box 1336, Sausalito, CA 94966; 800-523-2222.

National Courtesy Month

Go ahead: Increase civility in American life. *Sponsor:* Tom Danaher, P.O. Box 1778, Las Vegas, NV 89125; 702-386-9115.

National Honey Month

Sponsor: National Honey Board, 421-21st Avenue #203, Longmont, CO 80501-1421; 303-776-2337; 800-553-7162; Fax: 303-776-1177.

National Ice Cream Sandwich Month

National Literacy Month

40 million Americans are functionally illiterate. For more information on literacy, contact the Literacy Volunteers of America at 315-445-8000.

National Mind Mapping Month

Increase creativity through mind mapping, a visual outline technique for organizing information and generating ideas. *Sponsor:* The Innovative Thinking Network, Joyce Wycoff, 101 E. Victoria #33, Santa Barbara, CA 93101; 805-963-9151; e-mail: staff@thinksmart.com.

National Piano Month

Celebrate our favorite musical instrument, the piano. *Sponsor:* National Piano Foundation, Brenda Dillon, 4020 McEwen #105, Dallas, TX 75244-5019; 214-247-1414; Fax: 214-490-4219.

National Rice Month

Sponsor: USA Rice Council, P.O. Box 740121, Houston, TX 77274; 713-270-6699; Fax: 713-270-9021.

National School Success Month

Help parents encourage their children to do better in school. *Sponsor:* Parenting without Pressure. ✉

National Sewing Month

National Spina Bifida Awareness Month

Organic Harvest Month

Sponsor: Committee for Sustainable Agriculture, P.O. Box 838, San Martin, CA 95046-0838; 408-778-7366; Fax: 408-778-7186. *Co-Sponsor:* Organic Foods Production Association of North America, P.O. Box 1078, Greenfield, MA 01301; 413-774-7511. Write to the co-sponsor for information on merchandising materials.

Pleasure Your Mate Month
Take time to show appreciation and love to your mate. *Sponsor:* MFCC, Donald Etkes, 112 Harvard Avenue #148, Claremont, CA 91711; 909-981-7333.

Potato Bread Month

Project Aware Month
Encourages environmental protection of water areas. *Sponsor:* Professional Association of Diving Instructors, 1251 E. Dyer Road #100, Santa Ana, CA 92705-5605; 714-540-7234; Fax: 714-540-2617.

PTA Membership Enrollment Month
Participate in Parent/Teacher Associations. *Sponsor:* Texas PTA, 408 West 11th Street, Austin, TX 78701; 512-476-6769.

Sea Cadet Month
Teaches youths (ages 11 to 17) leadership and self-appreciation. The Naval Sea Cadet Corps was established on September 10th. *Sponsor:* Naval Sea Cadet Corps, 2300 Wilson Boulevard, Arlington, VA 22201; 703-243-6910; Fax: 703-243-3985.

Self-Improvement Month
Improve yourself. *Sponsor:* International Society of Friendship and Good Will. ✉

Southern Gospel Music Month
Sponsor: Southern Gospel Music Guild, One Riverfront Plaza #1710, Louisville KY 40202; 502-587-9653; Fax: 502-587-6153.

Stop the Violence and Save Our Kids Month
Work with others to tackle the problems of drugs, gangs, violence, and vandalism that plague the youth of America. *Sponsor:* Tune, Inc., Paul Bernstein, 748 Miller Drive SE, P.O. Box 5000, Leesburg, VA 22075.

Women of Achievement Month
Honors women who make a contribution to their companies, their environment, and their families. For a free 80-page booklet, *Women of Courage,* write to Nestle USA, Public Affairs Department, 800 N. Brand Boulevard, Glendale, CA *Sponsor:* Women's News, 33 Halstead Avenue, P.O. Box 829, Harrison, NY 10528; 914-835-5400; Fax: 914-835-5718.

September 1

Chicken Boy's Birthday
Chicken Boy is the famous statue of a boy with a chicken head featured in the *Chicken Boy Catalog for a Better World. Sponsor:* Future Studio, Amy Inouye, P.O. Box 292000, Los Angeles, CA 90029; 213-660-0620; 800-422-0505; Fax: 213-660-2571.

Child Injury Prevention Week
Held on the first 7 days in September. *Sponsor:* Safety by Design, P.O. Box 4312, Great Neck, NY 11023; 516-488-5395.

Emma M. Nutt Day
In 1878, Emma M. Nutt became the first woman telephone operator.

First African-American U.S. Senator born
Hiram Revels was born in 1822.

Golden Gloves Boxing Day
Celebrate the birthday of heavyweight boxing champion Rocky Marciano by attending at least 1 prize fight today. *Sponsor:* The Life of the Party. ✉

Martin Kane, Private Eye premiered (1951)
Martin Kane was the first successful crime drama series on TV. *Contact:* NBC-TV. ✉

Mental Health Workers Week
The week of the first Monday in September honors all those who work in the mental health profession. *Sponsor:* American Association of Psychiatric Technicians, P.O. Box 14014, Phoenix, AZ 85063; 602-873-1890; 800-391-7589; Fax: 602-873-4616.

Muscular Dystrophy Association Labor Day Telethon

Jerry Lewis made this Labor Day telethon famous. Broadcast by 200 stations, this telethon raises money for research and treatment of muscular dystrophy and 40 other neuromuscular diseases that affect more than a million Americans. *Sponsor:* Muscular Dystrophy Association, 3300 E. Sunrise Drive, Tucson, AZ 85718-3208; 602-529-2000; Fax: 602-529-5300.

National Championship Chuckwagon Races

Founded in 1986 and held on the Sunday and Monday of Labor Day weekend, these races determine the national championship for chuckwagon racers. *Sponsor:* National Chuckwagon Races, Dan Eoff, Route 6, Box 143, Clinton, AR 72031; 501-745-8407.

National Financial Services Week

During the week of Labor Day, take time to thank financial people in all businesses. *Sponsor:* Tuality Community Hospitals, Joyce Curran, P.O. Box 309, Hillsboro, OR 97123; 503-681-1111.

National Oral Hygiene Week

Take good care of your teeth, especially during the first 7 days of September. *Sponsor:* Dr George Meining,

P.O. Box 10, Ojai, CA 93023; 805-646-2865.

National Religious Reference Books Week

The first full week in September celebrates concordances, dictionaries, atlases, commentaries, and other reference books useful in biblical studies. *Sponsor:* Zondervan Publishing House, Jonathan Petersen, 5300 Patterson Avenue SE, Grand Rapids, MI 49530; 616-698-3417; Fax: 616-698-3439.

National Spanish Green Olive Week

Celebrated the first full week in September.

National Wilderness Week

Celebrated the first full week in September.

Rock and Roll Hall of Fame opened (1995)

The world's first museum dedicated to rock music opened. *Contact:* Rock and Roll Hall of Fame Museum, 1 T Plaza, Cleveland, OH 44114; 216-781-7625; 800-282-5393.

Saint Giles Feast Day

A hermit who took nourishment by suckling a hind, Saint Giles is patron saint of breast feeding and nursing mothers; also patron saint of the physically disabled, beggars, blacksmiths, woods and forests, and Edinburgh, Scotland.

Self-University Week

Education is a lifelong pursuit. Learning is the lifeblood of democracy and the key to living life to its fullest. Celebrated the first 7 days in September. *Sponsor:* Autodidactic Press, Nancy Hayes, P.O. Box 872749, Wasilla, AK 99687; 907-376-2932.

September 2

Anthracite Coal Miners Day

The Anthracite Miners Memorial Statue is located in Shenandoah. This special day is always held on Labor Day. *Sponsor:* Shenandoah Chamber of Commerce, P.O. Box 187, Shenandoah, PA 17976-0187; 800-755-1942.

Bowling shirt is designed (1921)

Calendar Adjustment Day

Great Britain and its colonies adjusted their calendar so the day following September 2nd became September 14, 1752. It then matched the Gregorian calendar. Most other countries had made the adjustment in 1582.

First half-hour network news show (1963)
When the *CBS Evening News* expanded from 15 minutes to 30 minutes, it became the first nightly half-hour network news show. Walter Cronkite was the anchor. *Contact:* CBS-TV. ✉

First non-stop flight from Europe to the U.S.
Aboard the *Question Mark,* Captain Dieudonne Coste and Maurice Bellonte of France flew from east to west, landing in Valley Stream, New York on September 2, 1930.

Full Employment Week
The week of Labor Day recognizes that Americans want work.

Labor Day
Since 1894, this national holiday honors working people and labor unions. Held on the first Monday in September, Labor Day is the unofficial end of summer. The first Labor Day parade was held on September 5, 1882.

National Mind Mapping in Schools Week
The first full week in September promotes creativity and learning through mind-mapping in schools. *Sponsor:* The Innovative Thinking Network, Joyce Wycoff, 101 E. Victoria #33, Santa Barbara, CA 93101; 805-963-9151; Fax: 805-963-8220.

Saint Agricola of Avignon Feast Day
Patron saint of misfortune. He is also patron saint of Avignon, France.

U.S. Treasury Department established (1789)
Contact: Department of the Treasury, 1500 Pennsylvania Avenue NW, Washington, DC 20220; 202-622-2960; Fax: 202-622-0073.

V-J Day (official surrender of Japan in 1945)
Also known as Victory over Japan Day or simply Victory Day. Japan signed the peace treaty officially ending World War II.

Yesterday Today
In 1965, the Beatles released their hit single "Yesterday."

September 3

First bowling league in the U.S. (1921)
For a free booklet on Tips for Young Bowlers, send a business-size SASE to American Bowling Congress, 5301 South 76th Street, Greendale, WI 53129; 414-421-6400; Fax: 414-421-1194.

First lawyer to be disbarred in U.S. (1639)
Massachusetts attorney Thomas Lechford was the first lawyer to be disbarred in America.

First penny newspaper success (1833)
Benjamin Day began publishing the *New York Sun.*

First professional football game (1895)
The first professional football game was played in Latrobe, Pennsylvania, with quarterback John Broiler.

Saint Gregory the Great Feast Day

Saint Gregory is patron saint of musicians and teachers. The Gregorian chants are named after this pope.

Treaty of Paris ended the Revolutionary War (1783)

Signed by Americans John Adams, Benjamin Franklin, and John Jay.

World War II declared by England and France (1939)

Prime Minister Neville Chamberlain announced a declaration of war against Germany after Germany had invaded Poland the day before.

September 4

Beatles record their first single (1962)

They recorded "Love Me Do" and "P.S. I Love You" in London. The songs were re-recorded on September 11th.

Cook a Great Meal Day

On the birthday of Craig Claiborne, cookbook author and TV chef, prepare a great meal. Claiborne was born in 1920 in Sunflower, Mississippi. *Sponsor:* The Life of the Party. ✉

Day of the Edsel

The famous automobile failure, the Edsel, was introduced in 1957. *Contact:* Ford Motor Company, American Road, Dearborn, MI 48121-0000; 313-332-3000; Fax: 313-845-8981.

Do It! Day

Also known as Fight Procrastination Day, this is for those who need a little extra incentive to stop putting off doing what needs to be done. Always celebrated on the Wednesday after Labor Day. *Sponsor:* Corporate Improvement Group, Ethel M. Cook, 4 Hilda Road, Bedford, MA 01730; 617-275-2326; Fax: 617-275-7136.

First hotel with temperature controls in each room (1904)

First roll-film camera patented (1888)

George Eastman received a patent for his Kodak camera.

Hijacking airplanes was outlawed (1961)

Los Angeles' Birthday

In 1871, El Pueblo de Nuestra Senora La Reina de Los Angeles was founded. *Contact:* Los Angeles Visitors Bureau, 663 West Fifth Street #6000, Los ,CA 90071; 213-624-7300; Fax: 213-624-9746.

National Stearman Fly-In

Every September on the weekend after Labor Day, the world's largest gathering of Stearman airplanes takes place in Galesburg, Illinois. *Sponsor:* Galesburg Visitors Bureau, P.O. Box 631, Galesburg, IL 61402-0631; 309-343-1194; Fax: 309-343-1195.

Newspaper Carrier Day

In 1833, the *New York Sun* hired the first newsboy, Barney Flaherty.

Peter Rabbit's Birthday

Beatrix Potter first told the story of Peter Rabbit when she sent a get-well letter to 5-year-old Noel Moore in 1893.

September 5

Be Late for Something Day

Fight the compulsion to be on time. *Sponsor:* Procrastinators' Club of America, Les Waas, P.O. Box 712, Bryn Athyn, PA 19009; 215-947-0500.

First Continental Congress assembled (1774)

The forerunner to the U.S. Congress, the first Continental Congress first met.

Day Committee, Marian Mc-Quade, 140 Main Street, Oak Hill, WV 25901; 304-469-6884.

National Housekeepers Week
The second full week in September recognizes the contributions of house-keeping staff. *Sponsor:* NEHA, 1001 Eastwind Drive #301, Westerville, OH 43081-3361; 614-895-7166.

National Mind Mapping for Project Management Week
Brainstorm for success in handling projects during the second full week in September. *Sponsor:* Total Development Resources, Tim Richardson, 363-6 Atlantic Boulevard #201, Atlantic Beach, FL 32233-5251; 800-226-4473.

National Pet Memorial Day
Remember and appreciate your dead pets on the second Sunday in September. *Sponsor:* International Association of Pet Cemeteries, 5055 Route 11, Ellenburg Depot, NY 12935; 518-594-3000; 800-952-5541; Fax: 518-594-8801.

National Pledge of Allegiance Day
The first version of the Pledge of Allegiance appeared in *The Youth's Companion* in 1892. Francis Bellamy wrote the pledge in honor of the 400th anniversary of Columbus's arrival in America.

Nativity of the Blessed Virgin Mary
Celebrates the birthday of the Blessed Virgin Mary.

Pardon Day
In 1974, President Gerald Ford pardoned former president Richard Nixon.

Saint Adrian Feast Day
Saint Adrian was a Roman officer who was so impressed by the bravery of the Christians that he asked to be imprisoned with them. During his imprisonment, his legs were cut off. He is a patron saint of arms dealers, prison guards, and butchers.

Scotch tape developed (1930)
Richard Drew developed the first transparent tape. *Contact:* 3M Company, 3M Center, Maplewood, MN 55144; 612-733-1110; 800-362-3456; Fax: 612-736-3094.

Star Trek Birthday
The first *Star Trek* episode aired on NBC-TV in 1966. Paramount Communications produced the TV series, movies, and new TV series.

Contact: Paramount Communications, 15 Columbus Circle, New York, NY 10023; 212-373-8000; Fax: 212-373-8228.

September 9

California Admission Day
California became the 31st state of the U.S. in 1850. *Contact:* California Division of Tourism, P.O. Box 1499, Sacramento, CA 95812-1499; 916-322-3402; 800-462-2543.

Ellis Island Museum of Immigration opened (1990)
More than 12,000,000 people entered the U.S. through the immigration center at Ellis Island. *Contact:* Statue of Liberty–Ellis Island Foundation, 52 Vanderbilt Avenue, New York, NY 10017-3898; 212-883-1986; Fax: 212-883-1069. Ellis Island information: 212-363-3200.

Fearless Forecasts of TV's Fall Flops
Always made on the second Monday in September, the forecasts predict the new TV shows that will be cancelled before the year end. *Sponsor:* The Boring Institute, Alan Caruba, P.O. Box 40, Maplewood, NJ 07040; 201-763-6392; Fax: 201-763-4287.

First black to be U.S. men's single tennis champ
In 1968, Arthur Ashe was the first black U.S. men's singles champion.

First marathon (490 B.C.)

Phidippides, a Greek soldier, ran 26 miles to let the people of Athens know about the Greek victory against the Persians at Marathon. He died as he gasped, "Rejoice, we are victorious." The modern day marathon is based on this event.

First private rocket launched (1982)

Hot Dog Day

In 1884, Antoine Feuchtwanger invented the hot dog.

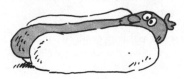

National Boss/Employee Exchange Day

The Monday after Labor Day, bosses switch jobs with employees so they can understand each other better. This means bosses must work today, and workers get the day off. Tell your boss I said that's the way it is today. *Sponsor:* Ann Chase Moeller, P.O. Box 71, Clio, MI 48420; 810-687-0423.

National Broadcasting Company Birthday

RCA created the National Broadcasting Company in 1926. For free tickets to NBC TV shows, write to NBC, Guest Relations Department, 30 Rockefeller Plaza, New York, NY 10020. On the West Coast, write to NBC, Guest Relations Department, 3000 W. Alameda Avenue, Burbank, CA 91523.

Party Party Day

An excuse to have a party once a month (when the day equals the month). *Sponsor:* Bonza Bottler Day. ✉

Saint Peter Claver Feast Day

Caretaker of over 300,000 black slaves in Cartegena, Columbia, he is patron saint of slaves.

U.S. Name Day

In 1776, the 2nd Continental Congress replaced United Colonies with the United States.

September 10

First coast-to-coast highway opened (1913)

The Lincoln Highway was the first coast-to-coast highway to open.

Gunsmoke premiered (1955)

Gunsmoke, the longest-lasting TV western, premiered in 1955 on CBS. *Contact:* CBS-TV. ✉

International Make-Up Day

Make up with someone who did you wrong or someone you treated badly. *Sponsor:* All My Events. ✉

Naval Sea Cadet Corps Birthday

The Corps was organized in 1962. *Contact:* Naval Sea Cadet Corps, 2300 Wilson Boulevard, Arlington, VA 22201; 703-243-6910; Fax: 703-243-3985.

Sewing machine patented (1846)

Elias Howe of Spencer, Massachusetts, was granted a patent for his sewing machine.

Swap Ideas Day

Exchange ideas for the betterment of humanity and to inspire creative imagination. *Sponsor:* Puns Corp. ✉

World's worst mid-air collision (1976)

A British Airways Trident collided with a Yugoslav charter DC-9 over Zagreb, Yugoslavia, killing 176 people aboard the two planes.

September 11

American Short Story Day

On the birthday of O. Henry (born in 1862), we honor all short story writers. His real name was William Sydney Porter. *Sponsor:* Book Marketing Update. ✉

Diocletian New Year

The Diocletian Era, an old way of measuring years, begins on September 12 (11th on leap years).

Under this system, 1996 is actually year 1713.

First Secretary of the Treasury (1789)

Alexander Hamilton was appointed the first treasury secretary. *Contact:* Department of the Treasury, 1500 Pennsylvania Avenue NW, Washington, DC 20220; 202-622-2960; Fax: 202-622-0073.

No News Is Good News Day

Don't read any news today. You'll feel much better that way. *Sponsor:* Wellness Permission League. ✉

September 12

Defenders Day (Maryland)

This public holiday commemorates the 1814 bombing of Fort McHenry in Baltimore, Maryland. *Contact:* Maryland Office of Tourism, 217 E. Redwood Street, 9th Floor, Baltimore, MD 21202; 410-333-6611; 800-543-1036; Fax: 410-333-6643.

Ethiopian New Years Day

A national holiday in Ethiopia. *Contact:* Ethiopian Embassy, 2134 Kalorama Road NW, Washington, DC 20008; 202-234-2281.

First spacecraft to land on the moon (1959)

The Soviet spacecraft *Luna 2*, was the first human spacecraft to land on the moon. *Contact:* NASA. ✉

Great Seal of the U.S. first used (1782)

National Day of the Working Parent

The second Thursday in September honors those who take care of children and elderly relatives. Formerly sponsored by the National Council of Jewish Women.

Taxi television show debuts (1978)

The comedy starred Judd Hirsch, Tony Danza, Andy Kaufman, and others. *Contact:* ABC-TV. ✉

World's first policewoman hired (1910)

The Los Angeles Police Department hired the first female officer. *Contact:* Los Angeles Police Department, 150 N. Los Angeles Street, Los Angeles, CA 90012; 213-485-3202.

September 13

Aloha Festivals

Celebrates the mixed cultural heritage of Hawaii with 300 events on 6 islands. This is the only statewide celebration in the U.S. It's held from September 13 to October 20, and 1996 marks the 50th anniversary of this event.

Blame Someone Else Day

The first Friday the 13th of each year is celebrated by passing the buck. *Sponsor:* A. C. Moeller, P.O. Box 71, Clio, MI 48420; 313-687-0423.

Commodore John Barry Day

Commemorates the death of Commodore John Barry (1803), the first American commodore to fight in the Revolutionary War. He is considered the father of the American Navy.

First automobile fatality (1899)

Henry Bliss was the first person to die as the result of an auto accident. He was run over as he stepped off a street car.

First helicopter flight (1939)

Igor Sikorsky invented the first practical helicopter. William Purvis and Charles Wilson of Goodland, Kansas, patented a helicopter in 1909.

Friday the 13th

Beware!

International Chocolate Day

Celebrate the birthday of Milton Hershey by eating a box or bar of chocolate. *Sponsor:* The Life of the Party. ✉

Ladies Professional Golf Association founded (1949)

Contact: Ladies Professional Golf Association, 2570 Volusia Avenue, Daytona Beach, FL 32114; 904-254-8800.

National P.O.W./M.I.A. Recognition Day

Recognizes prisoners of war and those missing in action in former wars. Celebrated on the second or third Friday in September.

Palestinian Self-Rule Anniversary

In 1993, Israel and the Palestinian Liberation Organization signed an agreement giving Palestinians limited self-rule in the Gaza strip and West Bank.

Saint John Chrysostom Feast Day

Patron saint of orators, speakers, and preachers.

World Championship Mud Bowl

Every year during the second weekend in September, a football game is played in the mud of Hog Colosium to raise money for charities. *Sponsor:* Mount Washington Valley Chamber of Commerce, P.O. Box 385, North Conway, NH 03860; 603-356-3171; 800-367-3364.

September 14

Byzantine New Year

The Byzantine Era year of 7505 begins on this day in 1996. The Grecian New Year (Selucidae) also begins (year 2308 in 1996).

Farmer-Consumer Awareness Day

The second Saturday in September is to educate consumers on the role farmers play in putting food on our tables. Tours of farms are part of this day's events. *Sponsor:* Quincy Valley Chamber of Commerce, P.O. Box 668, Quincy, WA 98848; 509-787-2140.

First American-born person to be canonized (1975)

Elizabeth Ann Seton was the first American-born Catholic to be declared a saint.

First human-made object to reach the moon (1959)

USSR *Luna 2* was launched on September 12th and reached the moon on September 14. *Contact:* NASA. ✉

First solo balloon crossing over the Atlantic

In 1984, Joe Kittinger left Caribou, Maine on the 14th and arrived over Capbreton, France, on the 17th.

International Cross-Culture Day

Celebrate the various cultures of the world. *Sponsor:* Window on the World, Robert Jackson, 322 First Avenue N #201, Minneapolis, MN 55401; 612-375-0141; Fax: 612-375-0143.

National Anthem Day

Celebrated in Maryland, commemorates the 1814 bombing of Fort Henry in Baltimore harbor that in-spired the writing of "The Star-Spangled Banner."

Rosh Hashanah (Jewish New Year)

Begins on the eve of the first day of the Jewish month of Tishri; also called the Day of Judgment and Remembrance. 1997: October --3, 1998: September 21–22.

Star Spangled Banner Day

In 1814, Fort McHenry was successfully defended against a bombing by English ships. This inspired Francis Scott Key to write the "Star Spangled Banner." For a History of the American Association, send 50¢ for postage and handling. *Contact:* Star Spangled Banner Flag Association, 844 E. Pratt Street, Baltimore, MD 21202.

Triumph of the Holy Cross

Also known as the Exaltation of the Holy Cross, this feast day celebrates the cross on which Christ died; celebrated on the day when the Basilica of the Holy Sepulcher was dedicated.

Typewriter ribbon patented (1886)

September 15

Agatha Christie's Birthday
This writer of mysteries was born in 1890 and died in 1976.

American Novel Day
This day honors the birthday of America's first major novelist, James Fenimore Cooper (born in 1789 in Burlington, New Jersey). *Sponsor:* Book Marketing Update. ✉

Battle of Britain Day
This English holiday celebrates the end of the largest aerial bombing raid of London by the German Luftwaffe in 1940. Surviving this raid was one of the turning points of the war for England.

Columbo's Birthday
One of the best detective series on TV, *Columbo*, premiered in 1971. *Contact:* NBC-TV. ✉

First national convention for blacks (1830)
Held at Bethel Church in Philadelphia, Pennsylvania. *Contact:* Philadelphia Visitors Bureau, 1515 Market Street, Philadelphia, PA 19102; 215-636-3300; 800-321-9563; Fax: 215-636-3327.

German-American Heritage Month
In 1683, 13 families from Krefeld, Germany founded Germantown, Pennsylvania. The month from September 15 to October 15 celebrates the history and culture of German-Americans. *Sponsor:* Society for German-American Studies, Don Heinrich Tolzmann, 3418 Boudinot Avenue, Cincinnati, OH 45211; 513-661-3310.

Greenpeace Birthday
The environmental activist group Greenpeace was founded in 1971 in Vancouver, British Columbia. *Contact:* Greenpeace, 1436 U Street NW, Washington, DC 20009; 202-462-1177; Fax: 206-462-4507.

International Priorities Week
Celebrated beginning two weeks after Labor Day. *Sponsor:* Priority Management Systems, Claire Dillon, 500 108th Avenue NE #1740, Bellevue, WA 98004; 206-454-7686; 800-221-9031; Fax: 206-454-5506.

Latin American Independence Day
In 1821, Costa Rica, El Salvador, Guatemala, Honduras, and Nicaragua gained their independence from Spain.

The Lone Ranger premiered (1949)
Clayton Moore and Jay Silverheels starred in *The Lone Ranger* TV show. *Contact:* ABC-TV. ✉

National Adult Day Care Center Week
During the third full week in September, celebrate those who help take care of the aged. *Sponsor:* National Institute on Adult Day Care, Betty Ransom, 409 Third Street SW, Washington, DC 20024; 202-479-1200; Fax: 202-479-6682.

National Chiropractic Day
Chiropractic was first discovered in 1895.

National Farm Animals Awareness Week
Appreciate the unique qualities of farm animals. Always celebrated the third full week in September. *Sponsor:* Humane Society of the U.S., 2100 L Street NW, Washington, DC 20037; 202-452-1100; Fax: 202-778-6132.

National Farm Safety Week
Always the third full week in September.

National Hispanic Heritage Month
September 15 to October 15. Began as a week to celebrate Mexican independence as recognized

by a 1968 proclamation by President Johnson. It later evolved into a month-long celebration of Hispanic heritage.

National Laundry Workers Week

During the third full week in September, say thank you to laundry workers. *Sponsor:* Nemaha Good Samaritan Center, Route 1, Box 4, Auburn, NE 68305; 402-274-4954; Fax: 402-274-4424.

National Mind Mapping and Brainstorming Week

The third full week in September promotes creativity and innovation in business and organizations through brainstorming and mind mapping. *Sponsor:* The Innovative Thinking Network, Joyce Wycoff, 101 E. Victoria #33, Santa Barbara, CA 93101; 805-963-9151; Fax: 805-963-8220.

National Rehabilitation Week

The third full week in September spotlights rehabilitation professionals and calls attention to the unmet needs of people with disabilities. *Sponsor:* Allied Services, P.O. Box 1103, Scranton, PA 18501; 717-348-1497; Fax: 717-348-1281.

National Singles Week

To make life more enjoyable and dignified for single people. Celebrated on the third full week in September. *Sponsor:* Singles Press Association, Janet Jacobsen, P.O. Box 6243, Scottsdale, AZ 85261-6243; 602-788-6001.

National Sports Junkie Week

We love our couch potatoes! Always celebrated during the week with the third Saturday in September.

National Tie Week

Celebrated the third full week in September.

Safety Awareness Week

Celebrated the third full week in September. *Sponsor:* The Weather Channel, 2600 Cumberland Parkway NW, Atlanta, GA 30339; 404-434-6800. *Co-Sponsor:* Johnson and Johnson.

Sock It To Me Day

In 1968, Republican presidential candidate Richard Nixon first appeared on *Rowan and Martin's Laugh-In* to utter those immortal words, "Sock it to me!"

USA Today first published (1982)

Contact: USA Today, 1000 Wilson Boulevard, Arlington, VA 22209; 703-276-3400; Fax: 703-558-3935.

William Howard Taft's Birthday

The 27th President of the U.S. was born in 1857 in Cincinnati, Ohio.

World's Largest Weather Vane Birthday

The World's Largest Weather Vane, at the edge of White Lake in Montague, Michigan, was dedicated in 1984. *Contact:* Muskegon County Visitors Bureau, P.O. Box 1087, Muskegon, MI 49443; 616-722-3751; 800-235-3866; Fax: 616-728-7251.

September 16

American Legion Day

The American Legion was incorporated by an act of Congress in 1919. *Sponsor:* American Legion, P.O. Box 1055, Indianapolis, IN 46206; 317-630-1200; Fax: 317-630-1368.

California Home-Based Business Week

First declared in 1994 by the California state legislature, this week is celebrated during the third work-week in September (Monday through Friday). *Sponsor:* Home Office and Business Opportunities

Association, 92 Corporate Park #C-250, Irvine, CA 92714.

Cherokee Strip Day

In 1893, the greatest land rush of all time was held on the Cherokee Strip in Oklahoma. A public holiday in Oklahoma. *Contact:* Oklahoma Tourism, P.O. Box 60789, Oklahoma City, OK 73146; 405-521-2409; 800-652-6552; Fax: 405-521-3089.

First animal heart transplant into a human (1984)

A baboon heart was transplanted into a human.

General Motors founded (1908)

William Durant founded General Motors in Flint, Michigan. *Contact:* General Motors, 3044 W. Grand Avenue, Detroit, MI 48202-0000; 313-556-5000; Fax: 313-556-5108.

Mayflower Day

The *Mayflower* brought the first English colonists to the New World. It sailed from Plymouth, England in 1620 carrying 102 passengers.

Mexican Independence Day

In 1810, Miguel Hidalgo Costilla, a Mexican priest from Dolores declared the independence of Mexico. Independence came in 1821. Celebrations begin just before midnight on the 15th and continue all day on the 16th. *Contact:* Mexican Embassy, 1911 Pennsylvania Av-

enue NW, Washington, DC 20006; 202-728-1600.

National Thank You Day

Oprah Winfrey established this day in 1994 to express thank yous to all those who have helped her out. She asked that everyone in the U.S. do the same by thanking those who helped them out. Celebrated on the third Monday in September. *Sponsor:* Oprah Winfrey Show, P.O. Box 909715, Chicago, IL 60690; 312-633-0808; Fax: 312-633-1515.

Stay Away From Seattle Day

People should not move to Seattle, America's Best Place to Live. *Sponsor:* Wellness Permission League. ✉

Typesetting machine patented (1857)

Wrinkled Raincoat Day

On the birthday of Peter Falk, who played the rumpled detective Columbo, wear a wrinkled raincoat

or do some investigating of your own. Falk was born in 1927 in New York City. *Sponsor:* The Life of the Party. ✉

September 17

Citizenship Day

In 1787, the U.S. Constitution was completed and signed.

Constitution Week

The U.S. Constitution was approved in 1787. The week of the 17th to the 23rd is, by presidential proclamation, known as Constitution Week.

First airplane fatality (1908)

Lieutenant Thomas Selfridge died after crashing in an airplane near Fort Myer, Virginia.

First black to be crowned Miss America (1983)

Vanessa Williams won the Miss America pageant. She was also the first Miss America to resign (as a result of nude photographs of her that appeared in *Penthouse* magazine).

First U.S. Secretary of Defense (1947)

James Forrestal was the first secretary of defense. *Contact:* U.S. Department of Defense, Public Affairs, Pentagon Room 2E-800, Washington, DC 20301; 703-697-9312; Fax: 703-697-1149.

International Day of Peace

The third Tuesday in September is dedicated to strengthening the idea of peace in the world. It is also the day that the United Nations General Assembly opens its annual session. *Sponsor:* United Nations. ✉

M*A*S*H premiered on CBS-TV (1972)

Contact: CBS-TV. ✉

National Constitution Day

In 1787, the U.S. Constitution was completed and signed. Today we recognize our civic rights and responsibilities and the freedoms we prize so much. *Sponsor:* National Constitution Center, 111 S. Independence Mall E #560, Philadelphia, PA 19106; 215-923-0004; Fax: 216-923-1749.

National Football League Birthday

In 1920, the American Professional Football Association, the precursor of the National Football League, was formed in Canton, Ohio. For a NFL Fan Package of goodies of your favorite team, send a business-size SASE to NFL Fan Mail, PO Box 25, Trenton, NJ 08650. *Contact:* National Football League. ✉

Saint Lambert of Maastricht Feast Day

Murdered when pierced by a javelin, Saint Lambert is patron saint of surgeons.

Whole Body Prayer Day

Commemorates the saintly Rabbi Mordecai of Lekhovitz who died in 1811. He taught that you should pray so deeply that each word arises from your heels upward. *Sponsor:* A Pilgrim's Almanac. ✉

September 18

CBS radio went on the air (1927)

For free tickets to CBS-TV shows, write to CBS-TV, Guest Relations Department, 524 West 57th Street, New York, NY 10019. Or, on the West Coast, CBS-TV, Guest Relations Department, 7800 Beverly Boulevard, Los Angeles, CA 90036.

Chiropractic Assistants Day

In 1895, Daniel Palmer of Davenport, Iowa, gave the first chiropractic treatment.

First black person in space (1980)

Cuban Arnoldo Tamayo was launched into space aboard Soviet spacecraft *Soyuz 38.* *Contact:* NASA. ✉

First spinet piano built in the U.S. (1769)

John Harris built the first spinet piano in the U.S.

Isolation Day

On the birthday of actress Greta Garbo (1905), famous for her isolation (I want to be alone!), throw a party. Invite over a lot of friends. *Sponsor:* The Life of the Party. ✉

Long playing record introduced (1931)

Introduced by RCA.

National Guitar Flatpickin' Championships

Founded in 1972, these championships are held on the Thursday through Sunday of the third weekend. *Sponsor:* Walnut Valley Festival, Winfield Fairgrounds, P.O. Box 245, Winfield, KS 67156; 316-221-3250.

New York Times began publishing (1851)

Contact: New York Times, 229 West 43rd Street, New York, NY 10036; 212-556-1234; Fax: 212-556-7389.

Saint Joseph of Copertino Feast Day

Because of his many experiences with levitation (more than 70 lift-offs were recorded during 17 years), he is considered patron saint of pilots and astronauts.

U.S. Air Force established (1947)

The Air Force was established as a separate service branch in 1947. *Contact:* Department of the Air Force, Pentagon, Room 4D-922, Washington, DC 20330; 703-697-4100; Fax: 703-697-1215.

U.S. Capitol cornerstone laid (1793)

George Washington laid the cornerstone for the U.S. Capitol.

U.S. government took out its first loan (1789)

The first loan was used to pay the salaries of the president and Congress. Alexander Hamilton, the first Secretary of the Treasury, negotiated this loan. *Contact:* Secretary of the Treasury, 1500 Pennsylvania Avenue NW, Washington, DC 20220; 202-622-2960; Fax: 202-622-0073.

September 19

First underground nuclear test (1957)

The U.S. conducted this test in Nevada.

Laundry Day

The first commercial laundry opened in Oakland, California in 1849.

Saint Nicholas of Tolentino Feast Day

Devoted to mothers and newborn babies, he is a patron saint of infants; also patron saint of the dying and of souls in purgatory.

Tuskegee Institute opened (1881)

Booker T. Washington founded the Tuskegee Institute in Tuskegee, Alabama. *Contact:* Tuskegee Institute National Historic Site, P.O. Box 10, Tuskegee, AL 36081; 205-727-3200.

World's first beauty contest (1888)

World's largest indoor display of grapes

Among other events, the Lodi Grape Festival features the world's largest indoor display of grapes, including many 8' × 12' murals made out of individual grapes. Always held the third week in September, from Thursday through Sunday. *Sponsor:* Lodi Grape Festival, 413 E. Lockeford Street, P.O. Box 848, Lodi, CA 95241; 209-369-2771; Fax: 209-369-9185.

September 20

Are You Somebody? Day

Celebrates all of us who are good but not yet "somebody." Celebrate you as you. Make a list of what you do, what you have done, and what you want to do. Build your self-esteem at the beginning of the school year. *Sponsor:* All My Events. ✉

Battle of the Sexes (1973)

Women's tennis player Billie Jean King defeated Bobby Riggs in 3 sets, winning the Battle of the Sexes.

The Cosby Show premiered (1984)

Contact: NBC-TV. ✉

Electric range patented (1859)

George Simpson of Washington, D.C., patented the first cooking range.

Equal Rights Party founded (1884)

Founded in San Francisco.

Everything I Have I Owe to Spaghetti Day

Celebrate the birthday of movie star Sophia Loren by eating a plate of spaghetti. Loren was born as Sofia Scicoloni in 1934 in Rome, Italy. *Sponsor:* The Life of the Party. ✉

Financial Panic of 1873 Anniversary

Due to a banking crisis, the New York Stock Exchange was forced to close for the first time in its history. *Contact:* New York Stock Exchange, 11 Wall Street, New York, NY

✉ Addresses for frequently cited organizations are gathered on pages vii–viii.

10005; 212-656-3000; Fax: 212-656-5725.

First meeting of the Association for the Advancement of Science

Held in Philadelphia, Pennsylvania in 1848. *Contact:* American Association for the Advancement of Science, 1333 H Street NW, Washington, DC 20005-4792; 202-326-6400; Fax: 202-682-0816.

Magellan began sailing around the world (1519)

Monterey Jazz Festival

Founded in 1958, this festival is the oldest continuously presented jazz festival in the world. Always held on the third weekend in September. *Sponsor:* Monterey Jazz Festival, P.O. Box Jazz, Monterey, CA 93942; 408-373-3366; Fax: 408-373-0244.

National Ballroom Dance Week

Celebrated from the third Friday in September to the fourth Thursday.

National Laundry Workers Day

On the Friday of the third full week of September, thank the people who wash our clothes and bedding. *Sponsor:* Nemaha Good Samaritan Center, Route 1, Box 4, Auburn, NE 68305; 402-274-4954; Fax: 402-274-4424.

World Grand Racking Horse Championship

The grand champion horse is crowned on the last night of this event, which is held on the last full week in September. A spring celebration is held on the last weekend in April. *Sponsor:* Racking Horse Breeders Association, P.O. Box 429, Somerville, AL 35670; 205-351-9242; Fax: 205-353-7266.

September 21

Biosphere Day

Recognizes the fragility of our biosphere (life on earth). List 5 things you can do to help our fragile biosphere, and do at least 1 today. *Sponsor:* Foundation for Environmental Conservation, 7 Chemin Taverney, 1218 Grand-Saconnex, Geneva, Switzerland.

Envelope seal patented (1897)

Black inventor F. W. Leslie patented the envelope seal.

First automobile manufacturer (1895)

Duryea Motor Wagon Company opened for business. The Duryea brothers built the first horseless carriage in 1893.

First daily newspaper in U.S. (1784)

The first successful daily newspaper in the U.S., the *Pennsylvania Packet and Daily Advertiser,* was published in Philadelphia, Pennsylvania.

First woman confirmed as Supreme Court justice

Sandra Day O'Connor was confirmed by the Senate in 1981. *Contact:* U.S. Supreme Court. ✉

Flashbulb patented (1930)

Johann Ostermeyer received a patent for the flashbulb.

Idaho Spud Day

Includes the World Spud Picking Championships, a tug-of-war in mashed potatoes, and plenty of potatoes. Celebrated since 1930. *Sponsor:* Idaho Spud Day Committee, P.O. Box P, Shelley, ID 83274; 208-357-7662.

International Flower Day

Bring bouquets of autumnal flowers into your home, business, school, or other places you frequent. *Sponsor:* All My Events. ✉

National Rich Villain Day

On the birthday of Larry Hageman, the actor who played the role of J. R. Ewing on *Dallas,* say something nice to a rich villain you know. Give them something to think about. Hageman was born in 1931 in Fort Worth, Texas. *Sponsor:* The Life of the Party. ✉

NFL Monday Night Football first broadcast (1970)

Contact: National Football League ✉ and ABC-TV. ✉

Perry Mason TV show premiered (1957)

This famous lawyer TV series premiered in 1957. *Contact:* CBS-TV. ✉

Saint Matthew Feast Day

A tax collector before he became a disciple of Jesus, Saint Matthew is patron saint of accountants, bankers, bookkeepers, tax collectors, custom officers, and security guards.

Tiffany's founded (1837)

Charles Tiffany established this retail store of jewelry, china, and other fine accessories. *Contact:* Tiffany and Company, 727 Fifth Avenue, New York, NY 10022-2503; 212-755-8000; Fax: 212-605-4465.

Watticism Day

In 1983, Secretary of the Interior James Watt slandered minorities in a speech before the U.S. Chamber of Commerce when he said that his committee had "a black, a woman, 2 Jews, and a cripple."

World Gratitude Day

Founded in 1965, this is a day to unite all people by simultaneously sharing a positive emotion, that of gratitude. *Sponsor:* Institute of Peace, Ann Heywood, 132 West 31st Street, Penthouse, New York, NY 10001; 212-629-4523; Fax: 212-594-9437.

September 22

American Business Women's Day

To celebrate the contributions of America's business women. Formerly sponsored by the American Business Women's Association.

Ancient Egyptian New Year

Some versions of the ancient Egyptian calendar celebrated the new year on the autumnal equinox.

Autumnal Equinox

Autumn begins at 3:04 p.m., Eastern Standard Time.

Dear Diary Day

Write in your diary today. *Sponsor:* Wellness Permission League. ✉

Fantasies Are Fabulous Day

The birthday of J. R. R. Tolkien is a day to create and celebrate fantasies. *Sponsor:* Book Marketing Update. ✉

Hobbit Day

Celebrates the birthday of Frodo and Bilbo Baggins. *The Hobbit* was published on this day in 1937. *Sponsor:* American Tolkien Society, Paul Ritz, P.O. Box 373, Highland, MI 48357; 813-585-0985; Fax: 813-585-0985.

Ice Cream Cone Birthday

Italo Marchiony filed a patent application for the ice cream cone in 1903.

Long Count Day

In a 1927 fight with a disputed long count, Gene Tunney won the world heavyweight championship from Jack Dempsey.

National Black Colleges Week

Howard University, the first all-black university, was created in 1867 by an act of Congress.

National Centenarians Day

Honor those you know who are now over 100 years of age. *Sponsor:* Williamsport Retirement Village, Meg Cliber, 154 N. Artizan Street, Williamsport, MD 21795; 301-223-7971; Fax: 301-223-6966.

National Dog Week

The Dogs on Stamps Study Unit promotes the relationship of dogs and people and the need for the proper care and treatment of dogs. DOSSU is a non-profit stamp club whose members collect dogs on stamps from around the world. Celebrated the last week in Sep-

tember. *Sponsor:* Dogs on Stamps Study Unit, Morris Raskin, 3208 Hana Road, Edison, NJ 08817; 908-248-1865.

National Good Neighbor Day
Do something good for your neighbor today. Celebrated the fourth Sunday in September. *Sponsor:* Good Neighbor Day Foundation, Richard and Rebecca Mattson, P.O. Box 379, Lakeside, MT 59922; 406-844-3000; Fax: 406-844-3000.

National Mind Mapping for Problem Solving Week
Brainstorm to solve problems during the last week in September. *Sponsor:* Total Development Resources, Tim Richardson, 363-6 Atlantic Boulevard #201, Atlantic Beach, FL 32233; 800-226-4473.

Proposal Day
This twice-yearly holiday encourages men and women to propose marriage to their true loves. Today day and night are of equal length—symbolizing that although men and women are as different as night and day, they are equal! *Sponsor:* Lady, Lad and Delia Company, John Michael O'Loughlin, 1333 W. Campbell #125, Richardson, TX 75080; 214-721-9975.

Religious Freedom Week
Celebrated the week that the Bill of Rights was submitted for consideration. Includes the 2 Sundays on either side of the 25th. If the 25th comes on a Sunday, then the week is celebrated the week before and up to the 25th. *Sponsor:* Religious Freedom Week Committee, Susan Taylor, 400 C Street NE, Washington, DC 20002; 202-543-6404.

Roller Skating Week
Celebrate roller skating during the last full week in September.

Tacy Richardson's Ride
In 1777, Tacy Richardson, a 23-year old woman, rode her horse several miles to warn General George Washington of the coming of British troops.

Tolkien Week
To promote appreciation of the writings of J. R. R. Tolkien. *Sponsor:* American Tolkien Society, Paul Ritz, P.O. Box 373, Highland, MI 48357-0373; 813-585-0985.

U.S. Postmaster General established (1789)
Congress established the fourth cabinet level department, the U.S. Postmaster General. *Contact:* U.S. Postal Service. ✉

World Maritime Day
Held during the last week in September. *Sponsor:* United Nations. ✉

You Light Up My Life Day
On the birthday of singer Debbie Boone, who sang the hit song "You Light Up My Life," light up someone's life. Do something special for them. Boone, the daughter of Pat Boone, was born in 1956 in Hackensack, New Jersey. *Sponsor:* The Life of the Party. ✉

September 23

Checkers Day
Recognizes dogs' contributions to presidential politics. In 1952, Richard Nixon saved his vice presidential nomination with his Checkers Speech (about his daughter's dog).

First air mail flight (1911)
Earle Ovington made the flight between Long Island and Mineola, New York. *Contact:* U.S. Postal Service. ✉

First woman to play a major pro team sport (1992)
Manor Rheaume played goaltender for the Tampa Bay hockey team.

Hearing aid patented (1879)
Richard Rhodes of River Park, Illinois, invented the first hearing aid.

National Multiple Wives Day
On the birthday of actor Mickey Rooney, famous for the number of wives he had, celebrate the beauty of women. Rooney was born as Joe Yule, Jr. in 1920 in Brooklyn, New York. *Sponsor:* The Life of the Party. ✉

Neptune discovered (1846)
Discovered by German astronomer Johann Galle.

Sign of Libra
The astrological sign of Libra, the balance (or scales of justice), runs from September 23rd to October 22nd. Librans are just, orderly, and persuasive.

The Jetsons' Birthday
In 1962, *The Jetsons* cartoon became the first program broadcast in color by ABC-TV. *Contact:* ABC-TV.

Victoria Woodhull's Birthday
The first female Presidential candidate was born in 1838.

Yom Kippur (Day of Atonement)
This Jewish holiday begins at sundown the day before. It is a day to ask forgiveness for any wrong you may have done during the past year. It is the 10th day of the Jewish High Holy Days, which begin with Rosh Hashana.

September 24

60 Minutes premiered (1968)
Contact: CBS-TV.

Bullwinkle's Birthday
The Bullwinkle and Rocky Show, starring Bullwinkle the Moose and Rocky the Flying Squirrel, premiered in 1961. Today is also Rocky's birthday.

Buy Nothing Day
This day provides a 24-hour moratorium on consumer spending and buyological urges.

Chapped Lips Day
The record for the world's longest kiss was set in 1984. How long was the kiss? 17 days, 10.5 hours. For a free sample packet of Blistex Lip Ointment, send a business-size SASE to Blistex Sample Offer, 1800 Swift Drive, Oak Brook, IL 60521. *Sponsor:* Open Horizons.

Discovery of tetracycline reported (1953)

First all-instrument airplane flight (1929)
Lt. James Doolittle flew a Consolidated NY2 Biplane.

First Judiciary Act (1789)
The Act provided for an attorney general and supreme court. *Contact:* Attorney General's Office, 10th Street and Constitution Avenue, Washington, DC 20530; 202-514-2001; Fax: 202-633-4371.

First nuclear-powered aircraft carrier launched
The *USS Enterprise* was launched in 1960 at Newport News, Virginia.

Miss Piggy Day
On the birthday of Jim Hensen, celebrate all of his creations—Miss Piggy, Kermit the Frog, Gonzo, Big Bird, Bert, and Ernie. Hensen was born in 1936 in Greensville, Mississippi. *Sponsor:* The Life of the Party.

National Bluebird of Happiness Day
Sing out about the joys of life. *Sponsor:* Tom Danaher, P.O. Box 1778, Las Vegas, NV 89125; 702-386-9115.

September 25

First American newspaper published (1690)
Benjamin Harris published *Publick Occurrences.* The first issue was the last issue of the newspaper. It was banned in Boston.

First black woman to be named a White House Fellow
In 1974, Barbara Hancock was named as a White House Fellow.

First major league baseball double-header (1882)

The first such double-header was played between the Providence, Rhode Island, and Worcester, Massachusetts teams. *Contact:* Major League Baseball. ✉

Food Service Employees Day

The fourth Wednesday in September recognizes the contributions of food service workers. *Sponsor:* Women and Infants Hospital of RI, Dietary Department, 101 Dudley Street, Providence, RI 02908-2499; 401-274-1100.

Howard University founded (1867)

The first all-black university was created by an act of Congress. *Contact:* Howard University, 2400 6th Street NW, Washington, DC 20059; 202-806-6100; Fax: 202-806-5961.

National Ask a Question Day

On the birthday of Barbara Walters, famous for her on-air interviews, ask any question you want. Walters was born in 1931 near Boston, Massachusetts. *Sponsor:* The Life of the Party. ✉

National One-Hit Wonder Day

Honors all recording artists who had a single hit. *Sponsor:* One Shot Magazine, Steven Rosen, 11667 Elkhead Range Road, Littleton, CO 80127; 303-979-2318; Fax: 303-820-1679.

New Horizons Day

In 1513, the Spanish explorer Balboa became the first European to look upon the Pacific Ocean.

September 26

Beverly Hillbillies TV show premiered (1962)
Contact: CBS-TV. ✉

First Attorney General and Chief Justice (1789)

Edmund Jennings Randolph was America's first Attorney General and John Jay was the first Supreme Court chief justice. *Contact:* U.S. Supreme Court. ✉

First Postmaster General (1789)

Samuel Osgood was appointed the first Postmaster General of the U.S. Previously, Benjamin Franklin had been Postmaster General for the colonies. *Contact:* U.S. Postal Service. ✉

First Secretary of State (1789)

Thomas Jefferson was appointed America's first Secretary of State. He took office on March 21, 1790. *Contact:* Department of State, 2201 C Street NW Room 6800, Washington, DC 20520; 202-647-6575; Fax: 202-647-5939.

Harvest Moon

The light of the full moon nearest the autumnal equinox extends the hours that farmers can use to harvest crops.

International Tool Time Day

Celebrate those who use tools and those who invented them. Take time today to buy new tools, refurbish your current tools, and use some tools. *Sponsor:* All My Events. ✉

Rocky Horror Picture Show premiered (1975)

This cult movie premiered in Westwood, California.

Saints Cosmas and Damian Feast Day

Patron saints of doctors, surgeons, and pharmacists.

Shamu's Birthday

Born at Sea World in 1985, Shamu was the first killer whale to survive after being born in captivity. *Sponsor:* Sea World, 7007 Sea World

Drive, Orlando, FL 32821; 407-351-3600.

Total eclipse of the Moon
One of 2 total eclipses of the moon in 1996, this will be visible in eastern and central North America. Watch for the total eclipse from 9:19 to 10:29 P.M. Eastern Standard Time.

Wine Moon
The full moon of September is the wine moon, symbolic of grape and fruit harvest, protection, confidence, strength, and life's blood.

September 27

Ancestor Appreciation Day
A day to learn about your family tree and all its branches. *Sponsor:* A.A.D. Association, P.O. Box 3, Montague, MI 49437.

Answering machine invented (1950)
Sorry, I'm not in right now, but if you leave a message, I'll get back to you real soon.

Contract with America Anniversary (1994)
Over 300 Republican congressional incumbents and challengers signed the Contract with America where they promised, if elected, to vote on 10 items within 100 days. On April 7, 1995, they fulfilled the contract. *Contact:* Republican National Committee, 310 First Street

SE, Washington, DC 20003; 202-863-8500; Fax: 202-863-8820.

First locomotive to haul a passenger train (1825)
George Stephenson's Stockton and Darlington railroad in England was the first to haul passengers.

Native American Day (American Indian Day)
First celebrated on May 13, 1916, and now celebrated on the fourth Friday in September, this day honors American Indians.

Saint Vincent de Paul Feast Day
Co-founder of the Sisters of Charity, the patron saint of charitable organizations and charitable giving.

The Tonight Show debuts (1954)
Steve Allen hosted the first version of the *The Tonight Show. Sponsor:* The Tonight Show, NBC-TV, 3000 W. Alameda Avenue, Burbank, CA 91523-0001; 818-840-4444.

U.S. Department of Education established (1979)
Contact: U.S. Department of Education, 400 Maryland Avenue SW #2089, Washington, DC 20202; 202-401-1576; Fax: 202-272-5447.

World's Largest Spinning Windsock
During the International Kite Festival held on the last full weekend of

September, the world's largest spinning windsock is launched. *Sponsor:* International Kite Festival, Lincoln City Chamber of Commerce, Lincoln City, OR; 800-452-2151.

September 28

Banned Books Week
Celebrating the freedom to read, held annually during the last partial week in September, from Saturday through Saturday. *Sponsor:* American Library Association. ✉

Cabrillo Day (California discovered, 1542)
Spanish explorer Juan Cabrillo entered San Diego Bay and discovered California. *Contact:* Cabrillo National Monument, 1800 Cabrillo Memorial Drive, San Diego, CA 92166; 619-557-5450; Fax: 619-557-5469.

First night football game (1892)
Took place in Mansfield, Pennsylvania. The game ended in a scoreless tie. *Contact:* Tioga Association for Tourism, P.O. Box 56, Mansfield, PA 16933-0056; 717-662-4466; 800-332-6718.

Indian Day (Oklahoma)
On the first Saturday after the full moon in September, this day recognizes the contribution of Native Americans to Oklahoma history and culture. *Contact:* Oklahoma

Tourism, P.O. Box 60789, Oklahoma City, OK 73146; 800-652-6552.

Kiwanis Kids' Day
On the fourth Saturday in September, make a fuss over kids, our greatest treasure. *Sponsor:* Kiwanis International. ✉

National Hunting and Fishing Day
Since 1979, celebrated by presidential proclamation on the fourth Saturday in September.

National Yo-Yo Championships
Always held the last Saturday in September. *Sponsor:* Bird in Hand, 320 Broadway, Chico, CA 95928; 916-893-0545.

Saint Wenceslas Feast Day
As the most notable saint of Bohemia (known for its beer), Saint Wenceslas is patron saint of brewers, beer, Bohemia, Moravia, and Czechoslovakia.

Sukkoth (Feast of Tabernacles)
This Jewish feast begins 5 days after Yom Kippur; celebrates the harvest and commemorates the journey of the Hebrew people through the wilderness. Also known as the Feast of Booths. 1997: October 16 to 22. 1998: October 5 to 11.

Teacher's Day (Confucius's Birthday)
On the birthday of Confucius, or Kung Futzu, China celebrates and honors all teachers. Confucius was born on the 27th day of the 8th lunar month in 551 B.C.

Walk for the Cure
September 28 to 29. This national event in over 80 cities raises funds for diabetes research and prevention. It is recommended the event be held on the fourth weekend in September, but some cities hold it on other weekends. *Sponsor:* Juvenile Diabetes Foundation, Walk Department, 120 Wall Street, New York, NY 10005; 212-785-9500.

September 29

First time Congress invoked the War Powers Act
In 1983, Congress gave permission to the President to extend the U.S. presence in Lebanon.

Gold Star Mother's Day
Since 1936, the last Sunday honors mothers of soldiers killed in wars.

Michaelmas (feast of St Michael the Archangel)
Saint Michael is patron saint of grocers, supermarket workers, paratroopers, security forces, battle, police officers, radiologists, and radiotherapists. If you eat goose on Michaelmas, you will never want for money during the entire next year.

National Chimney Sweep Week
During the week before Fire Prevention Week, we honor those who help prevent fires in chimneys.

Regular army established by U.S. War Department
The War Department established a regular army in 1789. *Contact:* Department of Defense, Public Affairs, Pentagon Room 2E-800,

Washington, DC 20301; 703-697-9312; Fax: 703-695-1149.

Scotland Yard established (1829)

London's police force was reorganized as Scotland Yard.

September 30

Ask a Stupid Question Day

There are no stupid questions. Ask your questions freely.

Black College Day

The last Monday in September celebrates the founding of Howard University on September 25, 1867. It spotlights America's traditionally black colleges and their role in helping African Americans advance in education. *Sponsor:* Howard University, 2400 Sixth Street NW, Washington, DC 20059; 202-806-6100; Fax: 202-806-5961.

Chewing Gum Day

Chew an entire pack of gum to celebrate the birthday of William Wrigley, Jr., the man who brought us "pure chewing satisfaction." *Sponsor:* The Life of the Party. ✉

First execution in U.S. (1630)

John Billington was hanged in Plymouth, Massachusetts after shooting a man.

First use of ether in a tooth extraction (1846)

William Morton was the first person to use ether to extract a tooth.

Happy Fiscal New Year Festival

Celebrates the beginning of a new fiscal year for the federal government. *Sponsor:* International Association of Professional Bureaucrats, James Boren, National Press Building, Washington, DC 20045; 202-347-2490; Fax: 202-456-6415.

Independent Publishers Day

Honors small independent book publishers. It is celebrated on the birthday of COSMEP (1963). *Sponsor:* COSMEP, P.O. Box 420703, San Francisco, CA 94142-0703; 415-922-9490; Fax: 415-922-5566.

Mozart's The Magic Flute premiered (1791)

Wolfgang Amadeus Mozart's musical play premiered in Vienna, Austria.

Saint Jerome Feast Day

Patron saint of scholars, students, and librarians because of his 22-year effort to write the Latin Vulgate version of the Bible.

The Flintstones' Birthday

The Flintstones, which premiered on ABC-TV in 1960, was the first TV cartoon show aimed at adults. *Contact:* ABC-TV. ✉

OCTOBER

American Magazine Month

Stop by the newsstand and pick up a periodical, or subscribe. *Contact:* Magazine Publishers of America, 919 Third Avenue, New York, NY 10022; 212-752-0055; Fax: 212-888-4217.

Arizona Book Month

Sponsor: Arizona Book Publishers Association, Gwen Henson, 4041 N. Central Avenue #750, Phoenix, AZ 85012; 602-274-6264.

Asthma Awareness Month

46% of asthma sufferers are allergic to cockroaches. Combat asthma by getting rid of cockroaches.

Auto Battery Safety Month

Learn how to safely jump-start your car battery so you don't injure yourself. *Sponsor:* Prevent Blindness America. ✉

Campaign for Healthier Babies Month

To focus on ways to prevent infant deaths. *Sponsor:* March of Dimes Foundation, 1275 Mamaroneck Avenue, White Plains, NY 10605; 914-428-7100; Fax: 914-997-7100.

Computer Learning Month

To focus on new ways to use computers in education. *Sponsor:* Com-

✉ Addresses for frequently cited organizations are gathered on pages vii–viii.

puter Learning Foundation, Sally Bowman, P.O. Box 60005, Palo Alto, CA 94306; 415-327-3347.

Consumer Information Month
To make people aware of resources that help consumers. *Sponsor:* Consumer Index to Product Evaluations, Pierian Press, P.O. Box 1808, Ann Arbor, MI 48106; 313-434-5530; Fax: 313-434-6409.

Cookbook Month
The Julia Child Cookbook Awards are given out in October. *Sponsor:* International Association of Culinary Professionals, 304 W. Liberty #201, Louisville, KY 40202; 502-581-9786; Fax: 502-589-3602.

Cooking, Crafts, and Home Books Month
Celebrates the authors and publishers of books on food, diet, crafts, hobbies, collectibles, antiques, home decorating, home re-

pair, beauty, and fashion. *Sponsor:* Book Marketing Update. ✉

Co-Op Awareness Month
Reminds retailers to use the co-op advertising money that is available. Each year more than $5 billion in co-op advertising money is left unspent by stores. *Sponsor:* Sales Development Services, 1335 Dublin Road #200A, Columbus, OH 43235; 614-481-3530; Fax: 614-548-0397.

Cooperative Month
Recognizes the contribution of electric cooperatives and other coops such as the Associated Press, Sunkist, and Florist Transworld Delivery.

Country Music Month
The Country Music Association Awards are given out this month. *Sponsor:* Country Music Association, 1 Music Circle South, Nashville, TN 37203-4312; 615-244-2840; Fax: 615-726-0314.

Crime Prevention Month
Challenges people to take individual and collective action to prevent crime and build communities that nurture and protect young people. *Sponsor:* National Crime Prevention Council, 1700 K Street NW, 2nd Floor, Washington, DC 20006-2817; 202-466-6272; Fax: 202-296-1356.

Cuts and Curls for Charity Month
Sponsor: TFA Communications, Kathleen Quinn, 9450 W. Bryn Mawr #300, Rosemont, IL 60018; 708-671-2900.

Domestic Violence Awareness Month
Send for their free domestic violence awareness pocket guide. *Sponsor:* National Coalition Against Domestic Violence, P.O. Box 18749, Denver, CO 80218-0749; 303-839-1852; Fax: 303-831-9251.

Ending Hunger Month
Presidential proclamation.

Energy Awareness Month
For a free teachers guide, Energy Education Resources, that lists more than 100 sources of free or low-cost materials on energy, write to the National Energy Information Administration, EI-231, Room 1F-048, 1000 Independence Avenue, Washington, DC 20585; 202-586-8800.

Energy Management Is a Family Affair Time
October 1st to March 31st of every year is a time to replace expensive energy-demanding appliances with energy-efficient ones. *Sponsor:* Home Improvement Time, J. A. Stewart Sr., 7425 Steubenville Pike,

Oakdale, PA 15071; 412-787-3233; Fax: 412-787-2881.

Family History Awareness Month

To spotlight the importance and fun of genealogy. *Sponsor:* Monmouth County Genealogy Club, 70 Court Street, Freehold, NJ 07728; 908-462-1466.

Fire Prevention Month

To teach people about fire safety. *Sponsor:* National Fire Protection Association, P.O. Box 9101, Quincy, MA 02269; 617-770-3000; Fax: 617-770-0700.

Gourmet Adventures Month

Try a new dish every day this month.

Healthy Lung Month

Focuses on the effects of childhood illnesses (asthma, flu, pneumonia) and indoor air pollution on the health of people's lungs. *Sponsor:* American Lung Association, 1740 Broadway, New York, NY 10019-4374; 212-315-6473; 800-LUNG-USA; Fax: 212-315-8872.

Hunger Awareness Month

Increases awareness of those who are hungry in the U.S. and the world. *Sponsor:* Food Industry Crusade Against Hunger, Fifth Floor, 800 Connecticut Avenue NW, Washington, DC 20006; 202-429-4555.

International Book Fair Month

Book fairs are great fund raising events for schools. *Sponsor:* School Book Fairs, Sharon Rice, 801 94th Avenue N, Saint Petersburg, FL 33702; 813-578-7600.

Italian-American Heritage and Culture Month

Presidential proclamation. During the month of the discovery of America by Christopher Columbus, an Italian, we celebrate all Italians.

Learning Disabilities Awareness Month

Lesbian and Gay History Month

Lock in Safety Month

Make sure your locks work. Check out security systems.

Lupus Awareness Month

Promotes awareness of Lupus disease and encourages its early detection. *Sponsor:* Lupus Foundation of America, 4 Research Place #180, Rockville, MD 20850-3226; 301-670-9292; Fax: 301-670-9486.

National Adopt A Dog Month

Encourages people to adopt pets, especially dogs, from animal shelters. Also known as Adopt a Shelter Dog Month. *Sponsor:* ASPCA, 424 East 92nd Street, New York, NY 10128; 212-876-7700.

National AIDS Awareness Month

Informs the public about AIDS and other sexually transmitted diseases. *Sponsor:* Pharmacists Planning Service. ✉

National Apple Jack Month

To honor America's oldest distilled beverage. *Sponsor:* Laird's Apple Jack, Ted Worner, 7064 Charleston Point Drive, Lake Worth, FL 33467; 407-439-4937; Fax: 407-439-4937.

National Arts and Humanities Month

Sponsor: National Cultural Alliance, Cynthia Lewis Schaal, 1225 Eye Street NW #200, Washington, DC 20005; 202-289-8286.

National Awareness Month for Children with Cancer

National Breast Cancer Awareness Month

National Car Care Month

A nationwide effort by businesses, civic groups, the government, and the media to focus motorists' attention on the need to maintain their cars for safer highways, improved air quality, fuel conservation, and investment protection. *Sponsor:* Car Care Council, Donna Wagner,

One Grande Lake Drive, Port Clinton, OH 43452; 419-734-5343; Fax: 419-732-3780.

National Clock Month
To celebrate the importance of clocks in America. *Sponsor:* Clock Manufacturers and Marketing Association, 710 E. Ogden Avenue #113, Naperville, IL 60563; 708-369-2406; Fax: 708-369-2488.

National Collector's Month
Promotes collecting collectibles as a family tradition. Sponsors include Enesco, Walt Disney Classics Collection, Silvestri, Kurt Adler, Bradford Exchange, and the major gift trade magazines. *Sponsor:* Disney Classic Collection, Retail Resource, 7502 Greenville Avenue #500, Dallas, TX 75231; 800-444-6474; Fax: 214-373-7110.

National Communicate with Your Kid Month
Tell your children you love them. Do this often. *Sponsor:* Parenting without Pressure. ✉

National Cosmetology Month
To encourage the use of cosmetics for increasing self-esteem. *Sponsor:* National Cosmetology Associa-

tion, 3510 Olive Street, Saint Louis, MO 63103-1015; 314-534-7980; Fax: 314-534-8618.

National Cut Out Dissection Month
To discourage dissections of animals for any reason. *Sponsor:* People for the Ethical Treatment of Animals, P.O. Box 42516, Washington, DC 20015; 301-770-7382.

National Dental Hygiene Month
Promotes the importance of oral health care. *Sponsor:* American Dental Hygienists Association, 444 N. Michigan Avenue #3400, Chicago, IL 60611; 312-440-8900; Fax: 312-440-8929.

National Depression Education and Awareness Month
To educate people about depression disorders. *Sponsor:* Pharmacists Planning Service. ✉

National Dessert Month
Desserts get rid of winter blahs. This is a time to celebrate with desserts. *Sponsor:* Martini and Rossi Asti Spumante, c/o Alden Advertising Agency, 52 Vanderbilt Avenue, New York, NY 10017; 212-867-6400; Fax: 212-986-5988.

National Disability Employment Awareness Month
People with disabilities can do a variety of jobs. *Sponsor:* President's

Committee on Employment of People with Disabilities, 1331 F Street NW, 3rd Floor, Washington, DC 20004-1107; 202-376-6200; Fax: 202-376-6859.

National Dollhouse and Miniatures Month
Sponsor: Miniatures Industry Association, P.O. Box 2188, Zanesville, OH 43702; 614-452-4541; Fax: 614-452-2552.

National Domestic Violence Awareness Month

National Down Syndrome Month

National Education Month

National Family Sexuality Education Month
Sponsor: Planned Parenthood Federation, Trish Torruella, 810 Seventh Avenue, New York, NY 10019-5882; 212-261-4627; Fax: 212-247-6269.

National Foster Grandparent Month

National High-Tech Month

National Kitchen and Bath Month
To spread info about kitchen and bath remodeling. Send for their free fact sheet, 31 Rules of Kitchen Planning. *Sponsor:* National Kitchen and Bath Association, 687 Willow

Grove Street, Hackettstown, NJ 07840; 908-852-0033; 800-367-6522; Fax: 908-852-1695.

National Liver Awareness Month

Our livers are important. Beware of liver disease. *Sponsor:* American Liver Foundation, 1425 Pompton Avenue, Cedar Grove, NJ 07009; 201-256-2550; 800-223-0179; Fax: 201-256-3214.

National Pasta Month

Celebrate pasta. Americans consume 3 billion pounds of pasta every year. For a free recipe booklet, *Endless Pastabilities,* send an SASE to Mueller's Endless Pastabilities, P.O. Box 307, Coventry, CT 06238. *Sponsor:* National Pasta Association, 2101 Wilson Boulevard #920, Arlington, VA 22201; 703-841-0818; Fax: 703-528-6507.

National Pizza Month

To promote the nutrition of America's Number One Fun Food. *Sponsor:* National Association of Pizza Operators, Gerry Durnell, P.O. Box 1347, New Albany, IN 47151; 812-949-0909; Fax: 812-941-9711.

National Popcorn Poppin' Month

Celebrates the economy, nutrition and fun of America's native snack. *Sponsor:* The Popcorn Institute, 401 N. Michigan Avenue, Chicago, IL 60611-4267; 312-664-6610; Fax: 312-321-6869.

National Pork Month

Sponsor: National Pork Producers Council, P.O. Box 10383, Des Moines, IA 50306; 515-223-2600; Fax: 515-223-2646.

National Quality Month

Devoted to improving the quality of America's products. *Sponsor:* American Society for Quality Control, 611 E. Wisconsin Avenue, Milwaukee, WI 53202; 414-272-8575; 800-248-1946; Fax: 414-272-1734.

National Roller Skating Month

National Sarcastics Awareness Month

(1) For those who realize they are sarcastic and want to get it under control; (2) for those who are sarcastic and want to get better at it; and (3) for those who are forced to live or work with people who are

WHAT A NICE SHIRT...

TOO BAD THEY DIDN'T HAVE IT IN YOUR SIZE....

sarcastic. *Sponsor:* Sarcastics Anonymous, Virginia Tooper, P.O. Box 10944, Pleasanton, CA 94566; 510-786-4567.

National Seafood Month

Enjoy the nutrition, variety, and taste of seafood. *Sponsor:* National Fisheries Institute, Emily Holt, 1525 Wilson Boulevard #500, Arlington, VA 22209; 202-296-5090.

National UNICEF Month

A month-long campaign to raise awareness in the U.S. of the needs of the world's children and to raise funds to help children in more than 135 developing countries. Call the toll-free number for a UNICEF fundraising kit. *Sponsor:* US Committee for UNICEF, 331 East 38th Street, New York, NY 10016; 212-686-5522; 800-252-KIDS; Fax: 212-779-1679; e-mail: mhirschhaut@unicefusa.org.

National Youth Against Tobacco Month

Sponsor: Tobacco Education and Prevention Coordinator, 1806 Cliff Drive #B, Santa Barbara, CA 93109; 805-899-3300; Fax: 805-899-3302.

Polish-American Heritage Month

No Polish jokes this month—or any month! *Sponsor:* Polish American Cultural Center, 308 Walnut Street, Philadelphia, PA 19106; 215-922-1700; Fax: 212-922-1518.

Spinal Health Month
To promote the importance of a healthy spine. *Sponsor:* American Chiropractic Association, 1701 Clarendon Boulevard, Arlington, VA 22209; 703-276-8800; Fax: 703-243-2593.

Sudden Infant Death Syndrome Awareness Month
Increase public awareness of SIDS, also known as crib death. *Sponsor:* SIDS Alliance, Phipps Cohe, 1314 Bedford Avenue #210, Baltimore, MD 21208; 410-653-8709; 800-221-7437; Fax: 410-653-8226.

Value of Play Month
Promotes safety and education in play. Co-sponsored by Educational Insights, Brio, and Small World Toys. *Sponsor:* Playthings Magazine, Frank Reysen Jr., 51 Madison Avenue, New York, NY 10010; 212-689-4411.

Vegetarian Awareness Month
A month to promote the many benefits of a meatless diet. *Sponsor:* Vegetarian Awareness Network, P.O. Box 321, Knoxville, TN 37901; 800-872-8343.

October 1

Federal fiscal year begins
The Federal Fiscal Year begins on October 1 and ends on September 30 each year.

Firepup's Birthday
To teach children fire safety in a way that does not scare them. *Sponsor:* National Fire Safety Council, P.O. Box 378, Michigan Center, MI 49254-0378; 517-764-2811.

First mass-produced tractors (1917)
The world's first mass-produced tractors were made in Dearborn, Michigan.

First postcards issued in Vienna (1869)
Contact: U.S. Postal Service. ✉

First rural free delivery of mail (1896)
Contact: U.S. Postal Service. ✉

First World Series baseball game played (1903)
Pittsburgh played Boston. *Contact:* Major League Baseball. ✉

Free Speech Movement launched (1964)
Students at the University of California at Berkeley launched the Free Speech Movement.

International Day for the Elderly
Focuses attention on the world's elderly. 1999 is the International Year of the Elderly. *Sponsor:* United Nations. ✉

Jimmy (James Earl) Carter's Birthday
The 39th President of the U.S. was born in Plains, Georgia in 1924.

Model T introduced by Ford (1908)
Henry Ford introduced the Model T automobile; it sold for $825.00. *Contact:* Ford Motor Company, American Road, Dearborn, MI 48121-0000; 313-332-3000; Fax: 313-845-8981.

National Book It! Day
Kicks off the largest reading incentive program in the U.S. Sponsored by Pizza Hut. For free materials for enrolling in Book It!, call 800-426-6548, or write to Book It!, P.O. Box 2999, Wichita, KS 67201.

The Night of the Living Dead premiered (1968)
The cult horror film *The Night of the Living Dead* premiered in Pittsburgh, Pennsylvania.

Saint Theresa of the Child Jesus Feast Day
Patron saint of missions and missionaries. Because she promised a shower of roses when she died, she is also considered a patron saint of

florists and flower growers; also a patron saint of France.

Special delivery mail service began in U.S. (1885)
Contact: U.S. Postal Service. ✉

U.S. Department of Energy established (1977)
The Department of Energy was created when President Carter signed the Energy Organization Act. The Department officially opened for business on October 1, 1977. *Contact:* Department of Energy, 1000 Independence Avenue SW, Washington, DC 20585; 202-586-5000; Fax: 202-586-4073.

Unicorn Questing Season
The first week of the unicorn questing season is for bow and arrow hunters.

Universal Children's Week
Inaugurated in 1985, the first 7 days in October promote the needs and rights of children. For a copy of the Declaration of the Rights of the Child, adopted by the UN General Assembly, send an SASE to the following address. *Sponsor:* International Society of Friendship and Good Will. ✉

Walt Disney World opened (1971)
Contact: Walt Disney World, P.O. Box 10000, Lake Buena Vista, FL 32830; 407-824-2222.

World Vegetarian Day
Take the day off from eating meat and see how it feels. *Sponsor:* North American Vegetarian Society, P.O. Box 72, Dolgeville, NY 13329; 518-568-7636.

October 2

Alfred Hitchcock Presents premiered (1955)
Contact: CBS-TV. ✉

Around the World in 80 Days
In Jules Verne's novel *Around the World in 80 Days*, Phileas Fogg made the trip around the world in 80 days, starting on the day of his wager, October 2, 1872, and ending a second less than 80 days on December 21, 1872.

Eyebrow Day
Celebrate Groucho Marx's birthday by trimming your eyebrows. *Sponsor:* The Life of the Party. ✉

Feast of the Guardian Angels
Guardian angels protect us from dangers. Their special duty is to watch over children.

First black Supreme Court justice sworn in (1967)
Thurgood Marshall was sworn in as a Supreme Court justice. He was

confirmed by the U.S. Senate on August 30, 1967. *Contact:* U.S. Supreme Court. ✉

First cartoon strip in a newspaper (1895)
Richard Felton Outcault created the first regular newspaper comic strip, *The Yellow Kid*.

Mahatma Gandhi's Birthday
This Indian national holiday celebrates the birthday of the man responsible for the liberation of India. Gandhi was born in 1869 in Porbandar, India. *Contact:* Government of India, Tourist Information Office, 30 Rockefeller Plaza #15, New York, NY 10112; 212-586-4901; Fax: 212-582-3274.

Name Your Car Day
Sponsor: KSDK-TV, John Pertzborn, Reporter, 1000 Market Street, Saint Louis, MO 63101-2060; 314-444-5119; Fax: 314-444-5119.

Snoopy's and Charlie Brown's Birthdays
The *Peanuts* comic strip by Charles Schulz first appeared in 1950. *Contact:* United Features Syndicate, 200 Park Avenue, 6th Floor, New York, NY 10166; 212-692-3700; Fax: 212-692-3758.

Twilight Zone premiered (1959)
You are now entering the Twilight Zone, the middle ground between

light and shadow, between science and superstition, between the pit of man's fears and the summit of his knowledge. *Contact:* CBS-TV. ✉

World Farm Animals Day
Fight against the ill treatment of animals grown for food. *Sponsor:* Farm Animal Reform Movement, P.O. Box 30654, Bethesda, MD 20824; 301-530-1737; Fax: 301-530-5747.

October 3

Adventures of Ozzie and Harriet, TV show premiered (1952)
The radio show had premiered on October 8, 1944. *Contact:* ABC-TV. ✉

Andy Griffith Show first broadcast (1960)
Contact: CBS-TV. ✉

Captain Kangaroo's Birthday
The kiddie TV show premiered on CBS-TV in 1955. *Contact:* CBS-TV. ✉

Cowboy Hall of Fame Day
The induction of new members into the Cowboy Hall of Fame always takes place the Thursday before Rex Allen Days (held the first weekend in October). Ride 'em, cowboy! *Contact:* Cowboy Hall of Fame, Museum of the Southwest, 1500 N Circle 1 Road, Willcox, AZ 85644; 602-384-2272.

Federal income tax signed into law (1913)
The first tax was only 1% of income. *Contact:* Internal Revenue Service. ✉

First black Major League baseball manager (1974)
Frank Robinson was named manager of the Cleveland Indians. *Contact:* Cleveland Indians, Cleveland Municipal Stadium, Cleveland, OH 44114; 216-861-1200; Fax: 216-566-1287.

First black radio station (1949)
WERD of Atlanta, Georgia, was the first black station in the country.

First woman U.S. Senator (1922)
Rebecca Felton of Georgia was appointed to serve out the term of Thomas Watson.

German Reunification Day (1990)
East and West Germany came together after 41 years apart. The first all-German elections were held on December 2, 1990. *Contact:* Federal Republic of Germany Embassy, 4645 Reservoir Road NW, Washington, DC 20007; 202-298-4000.

Mickey Mouse Club premiered (1955)
Contact: ABC-TV. ✉

October 4

Albuquerque International Balloon Fiesta
Founded in 1972, this festival is the largest in the world, with over 600 balloons and 800,000 spectators. It is also the most photographed public event in the world. Starts the first full weekend in October. *Sponsor:* Albuquerque Visitors Bureau, P.O. Box 26866, Albuquerque, NM 87125-6866; 505-842-9918; 800-733-9918; Fax: 505-247-9101.

Dick Tracy's Birthday
In 1931 Chester Gould's comic strip premiered.

First satellite to photograph moon's other side
Luna 3 of the USSR was launched on this date in 1959. It was the first to photograph the dark side of the moon. *Contact:* NASA. ✉

First successful human-made satellite launched
In 1957, the Soviet Union launched *Sputnik I.* *Contact:* NASA. ✉

First transatlantic passenger jet service (1958)
British Airways began the first transatlantic passenger jet service.

Guys and Dolls Day
On the birthday of Damon Runyon, celebrate the world of New York. Runyon, who chronicled the world of Manhattan Island in his short stories, was born in 1884 in

✉   Addresses for frequently cited organizations are gathered on pages vii–viii.

OCTOBER   **225**

Manhattan, Kansas. *Sponsor:* The Life of the Party. ✉

Leave It to Beaver premiered (1957)
Contact: CBS-TV. ✉

National Pickled Pepper Week
Celebrated the 10 days of the first two weekends (from Friday through Sunday), spotlights the extra zing of pickled peppers. *Sponsor:* Pickle Packers International, DHM Group, P.O. Box 767, Holmdel, NJ 07733; 908-975-9675; Fax: 908-946-3343.

National Storytelling Festival
Held on the first weekend in October, this festival is the premier storytelling event in the U.S. *Sponsor:* National Storytelling Association, P.O. Box 309, Jonesborough, TN 37659; 615-753-2171; 800-525-4514.

Piece of My Heart Day
On the anniversary of Janis Joplin's 1970 death (by heroin overdose), we honor all female blues singers. Janis Joplin was born in 1943 in Port Arthur, Texas.

Rutherford Birchard Hayes's Birthday
The 19th President of the U.S. was born in Delaware, Ohio in 1822.

Saint Francis of Assisi Feast Day
Patron saint of ecologists, animals, and animal welfare societies. He is

also patron saint of Assisi, Italy, and a patron saint of Italy.

Ten-Four Day
Recognizes radio operators who use "Ten-four" to mean "yes."

October 5

Alzheimer's Association Memory Walk
This annual fundraising and awareness-raising event is held in more than 200 communities around the country. Always held on the first weekend in October. *Sponsor:* Alzheimer's Association, 919 N. Michigan #1000, Chicago, IL 60611; 312-853-3060; 800-272-3900.

American Heart Walk
Held in more than 900 cities on the first weekend in October to promote physical activity and to educate about heart disease and strokes. Also raises funds for heart research. *Sponsor:* American Heart Association, 7320 Greenville Avenue, Dallas, TX 75231-4596; 214-373-6300; 800-242-8721; Fax: 214-706-1341.

Beatles' first hit released (1962)
The Beatles' first hit, "Love Me Do," was released in England.

Chester Alan Arthur's Birthday
The 21st President of the U.S. was born in Fairfield, Vermont in 1830.

First person to walk around the world (1974)

First radio broadcast of a World Series game (1921)
Contact: Major League Baseball. ✉

First televised presidential address (1947)
President Truman broadcast the first televised presidential address.

International Space Hall of Fame Day
New members of the International Space Hall of Fame are inducted on the first Saturday in October. *Sponsor:* International Space Hall of Fame, P.O. Box 533, Alamogordo, NM 88310-0533; 505-437-2840; 800-545-4021.

National Open House
All cultural organizations are invited to sponsor an open house for the public on the first Saturday in October. *Sponsor:* National Cultural Alliance, Cynthia Lewis Schaal, 1225 Eye Street NW #200, Washington, DC 20005; 202-289-8286.

National Rail Trail Day
The first Saturday in October celebrates the day 500 hiking and bicycling trails were created on former railroad rights of way.

PBS became a network (1970)
Contact: Public Broadcasting Service, 1320 Braddock Place, Alexan-

dria, VA 22314; 703-739-5000;
800-328-7271; Fax: 703-739-0775.

Unsolved Mysteries premiered (1988)

NBC's real-life mysteries program, hosted by Robert Stack, premiered on NBC-TV. *Contact:* NBC-TV. ✉

World Pumpkin Weigh-Off

On the first Saturday in October, weigh-ins are held around the world to find the world's largest pumpkin, squash, and watermelon as well as the tallest sunflower (and largest head), tallest corn stalk, largest cabbage, and longest gourd. *Sponsor:* World Pumpkin Confederation, Ray Waterman, 14050 Route 62, Collins, NY 14034; 716-532-5995; 800-449-5681; Fax: 716-532-5690.

World's Largest Guacamole Dip

During the first partial weekend in October, the California Avocado Festival always features the world's largest guacamole dip plus lots of other food, music, crafts, and arts.

Sponsor: California Avocado Festival, P.O. Box 146, Carpinteria, CA 93013; 805-684-0038.

October 6

American Indian Time of Thanksgiving

The second Sunday in October celebrates the heritage and way of life of the American Indian, especially the Lenni Lenape (Delaware Indians). *Sponsor:* Museum of Indian Culture, Route 2, Fish Hatchery Road, Allentown, PA 18103-9801; 610-797-2121.

American Library Association founded (1876)

Founded in Philadelphia, Pennsylvania. *Contact:* American Library Association. ✉

Birthday of the Soap Opera

The Faraway Hill soap opera premiered on the DuMont network in 1946.

Child Health Day

Since 1928 the first Monday in October has focused on children's health. For a free booklet of forms to track your child's medical history, write to Metropolitan Life Insurance, Attn: Your Child's Health Record, 1 Madison Avenue, New York, NY 10010.

Fire Prevention Week

The week of October 8th is dedicated to teaching people about fire safety. *Sponsor:* National Fire Protection Association, P.O. Box 9101, Quincy, MA 02269; 617-770-3000; Fax: 617-770-0700.

First talking picture (1927)

Al Jolson's *The Jazz Singer* was was the first successful talking picture.

First train robbery in the U.S. (1866)

The Reno Brothers carried out the first train robbery near Seymour, Indiana.

First Turkish bath in the U.S. (1863)

Get Organized Week

Always the first full week in October. *Sponsor:* National Association of Professional Organizers, 1033 La Posada Drive #220, Austin, TX 78752-3880; 512-206-0151.

Mental Illness Awareness Week

To raise the public's consciousness about mental illness. Always celebrated during the first full week of October. *Sponsor:* American Psychiatric Association, 1400 K Street NW, Washington, DC 20005; 202-682-6220. Also sponsored by the National Mental Health Association, 1021 Prince Street, Alexandria, VA 22314-2971; 703-684-7722; Fax: 703-684-5968.

National Coming Out Week

During the week of the 11th, celebrate those who come out as gay.

Sponsor: National Coming Out Project, 1101 14th Street NW #200 (20005), P.O. Box 34640, Washington, DC 20043-4640; 202-628-4160; 800-866-6263; Fax: 202-347-5323; e-mail: HRFC@aol.com.

National German-American Day

In 1683, 13 families from Krefeld, Germany founded Germantown, Pennsylvania. Sponsor: Society for German-American Studies, Don Heinrich Tolzmann, 3418 Boudinot Avenue, Cincinnati, OH 45211; 513-661-3310.

National Health Care Food Service Week

The first full week in October honors the people who provide food and nutrition for those in hospitals. Sponsor: American Society for Health Care, Food Service Administrators, 1 N. Franklin, Chicago, IL 60606; 312-422-3870; Fax: 312-422-4581.

National Metric Week

During the week of the 10th day of the 10th month, celebrate the metric system, which should be America's #1 method of measurement. Sponsor: National Council of Teachers of Mathematics, 1906 Association Drive, Reston, VA 22091-1502; 703-620-9840; Fax: 703-476-2970.

National Newspaper Week

The second week in October celebrates the role newspapers play in our everyday lives. Sponsor: Newspaper Association Managers, Mary Ann Gentile, P.O. Box 28875, Atlanta, GA 30358; 404-256-0444; Fax: 404-252-9135.

National Spinning and Weaving Week

Celebrated the first full week in October. Sponsor: Hand Weavers Guild of America, 2402 University Avenue #702, Saint Paul, MN 55114; 612-646-0802; Fax: 612-646-0806.

Naval War College established (1884)

The first such college in the world was established in Newport, Rhode Island. Contact: Naval War College Museum, Founders Hall, Naval Education and Training Center, Newport, RI 02840; 401-841-4052.

Ohio Art Company founded (1908)

Henry Simon Winzeler founded the Ohio Art Company, makers of the Etch-A-Sketch toy. Contact: Ohio Art Company, 1 Toy Street, Byran, OH 43506; 419-636-3141; Fax: 419-636-7614.

Physician Assistant Day

Celebrates the graduation of the first physician assistants from Duke University. Sponsor: American Academy of Physician Assistants, 950 N. Washington Street, Alexandria, VA 22314-1534; 703-836-2272.

Saint Faith Feast Day

Patron saint of pilgrims, prisoners, and soldiers.

World Prayer Meeting

Sponsored by the First Assembly of God churches, and held on the first Sunday in October.

World's Largest Enchilada

On the Sunday of the first full weekend in October, the world's largest enchiladas are served hot out of the oil. 50 lb. tortillas are just the beginning. Sponsor: Whole Enchilada Fiesta, P O Drawer 519, Las Cruces, NM 88004; 505-527-3939.

October 7

Birthday of the Bathtub

The bathtub was introduced in England in 1828. In 1945, it was banned in Boston.

Cats, the musical, opened on Broadway (1982)

Firefighters Week

The second working week (Monday to Friday) honors the brave firefighters who serve the public. Sponsor: Catherine Gallagher, 733 Avenue E, Bayonne, NJ 07002; 201-858-4889.

First black American Nobel Laureate in literature

In 1993, Toni Morrison received the Nobel Prize in literature.

First black singer hired by Metropolitan Opera

In 1954, Marian Anderson became the first black opera singer in the U.S. Her debut performance was on January 7, 1955. *Contact:* Metropolitan Opera Association, Lincoln Center, New York, NY 10023; 212-799-3100; Fax: 212-870-7416.

First made-for-TV movie shown on television (1964)

See How They Run, starred John Forsythe and Senta Berger.

First railroad in U.S. completed (1826)

Built in Massachusetts.

Home-Based Business Week

The week of the second Tuesday in October honors the home-based entrepreneur. *Sponsor:* American Association of Home-Based Businesses, Beverly Williams, 7601 Dew Wood Drive, Derwood, MD 20855; 301-963-9153.

Minority Enterprise Development Week

Encourages minority groups to improve their lives through education. Scheduled by presidential proclamation for the first full week in October.

National Customer Service Week

The first week in October (starting with Monday) helps companies celebrate the importance of customer service. The theme of this week is: Customers are really everything. *Sponsor:* International Customer Service Association, 401 N. Michigan Avenue, Chicago, IL 60611-4267; 312-321-6800; Fax: 312-321-6869.

National Flower Day

In 1986, President Ronald Reagan signed a bill making the rose the national flower of the U.S.

Supreme Court begins annual term

The U.S. Supreme Court begins its annual term on the first Monday in October. *Contact:* U.S. Supreme Court. ✉

World Habitat Day

The first Monday in October commemorates the 1976 conference on Human Settlements that was held in Vancouver, British Columbia. *Sponsor:* United Nations. ✉

October 8

Alvin C. York Day

In 1918, Sgt. Alvin York singlehandedly killed 25 German soldiers and captured another 132 during World War I. This is the greatest single military action by an individual.

Chicago Fire and Peshtigo Fire (1871)

Fires broke out in Chicago, Illinois, and Peshtigo, Wisconsin. The Chicago fire killed 200 people and burned 17,000 buildings. The Peshtigo fire killed 1,500 people and burned 1,280,000 acres of land and over 2 billion trees.

Dow Jones Industrial Average first reported (1896)

Contact: Dow Jones and Company, 200 Liberty Street, New York, NY 10281; 212-416-2000; 800-831-1234; Fax: 212-416-2658.

First movie shown on an airplane (1929)

Take a Fall Day

Celebrate the birthday of comedian Chevy Chase by taking a fall. Chase was born as Cornelius Crane in 1943 in New York City. *Sponsor:* The Life of the Party. ✉

Tube top designed (1975)

October 9

Calliope invented (1855)
Joshua Stoddard of Worcester, Massachusetts, patented the calliope.

First airplane flight (1890)
Clement Ader of France actually was the first person to fly an airplane. But his steam-powered plane only rose a few inches off the ground. It was not a sustained flight like the Wright Brothers later flight.

First woman to fly across the U.S. (1930)
Laura Ingalls completed the first cross-country airplane flight by a woman.

International Day for Natural Disaster Reduction
The second Wednesday in October is designed to foster international cooperation to reduce loss of life and property damage during natural disasters. The 1990s are the International Decade for Natural Disaster Reduction. *Sponsor:* United Nations. ✉

Leif Erikson Day
This Norse explorer discovered North America in the year 1000. This day is celebrated by presidential proclamation.

Mail-Order Business Day
Aaron Montgomery started the first mail order catalog business in 1872. *Contact:* Montgomery Ward, 619 W. Chicago Avenue, Chicago, IL 60671-0001; 312-467-2000; Fax: 312-467-7927.

World Post Day
Spotlights the work of the Universal Postal Union. *Sponsor:* United Nations. ✉

October 10

Bicycle frame patented (1899)
Black inventor I. R. Johnson recieved a patent for the bicycle frame.

Double Tenth Day
This Chinese holiday celebrates the anniversary of the revolution against the Manchu dynasty in 1911.

National Depression Screening Day
On the first Thursday of the first full week in October, check to see if anyone around you is depressed. If so, have them go in for a check up with a mental health professional. *Sponsor:* National Mental Health Association, 1021 Prince Street, Alexandria, VA 22314-2971; 703-684-7722; 800-969-6642; Fax: 703-684-5968.

National Dessert Day
Desserts get rid of winter blahs. Always celebrated on the second Thursday in October. *Sponsor:* Martini and Rossi Asti Spumante, c/o Alden Advertising Agency, 52 Vanderbilt Avenue, New York, NY 10017; 212-867-6400; Fax: 212-986-5988.

Party Party Day
An excuse to have a party once a month (when the day equals the month). *Sponsor:* Bonza Bottler Day. ✉

Porgy and Bess opened on Broadway (1935)
George Gershwin's musical premiered.

Tuxedo Birthday
In 1886, the tuxedo made its American debut at the autumn ball in Tuxedo Park, New York.

U.S. Naval Academy opened (1845)
Contact: U.S. Naval Academy, 121 Blake Road, Annapolis, MD 21402; 410-267-6100; Fax: 410-281-3734.

October 11

Adding machine patented (1887)
Dorr Eugene Felt's Comptmeter was the first accurate adding machine.

Casimir Pulaski Memorial Day
Celebrated by presidential proclamation, this day honors the Polish hero of the American Revolutionary War. Casimir Pulaski was killed on October 11, 1779, while fighting at Savannah, Georgia. Also known as General Pulaski Memorial Day.

Daughters of the American Revolution founded (1890)
The Daughters of the American Revolution was founded in Washington, DC.

Feast of the Motherhood of God
Because she was the mother of Jesus, Mary was given the title of the Mother of God by the Council of Ephesus in 431 A.D.

First American woman to walk in space (1984)
Kathy Sullivan was the first American woman to walk in space. *Contact:* NASA.

First political telecast in the U.S. (1932)

First roll film for cameras patented (1881)
David Houston of Cambria, Wisconsin, invented the roll film.

First steam-powered ferry (1811)
The *Juliana*, invented by John Stevens, was the first steam-powered ferry. It was put into service between New York City and Hoboken, New Jersey.

Kiss Your Car Day
On the birthday of Henry Ford, founder of Ford Motor Company, kiss your car (but only after you wash and wax it). *Sponsor:* The Life of the Party.

National Coming Out Day
This day commemorates the gay march on Washington in 1987 and is designed to increase the visibility of the lesbian, gay, and bisexual community and to help in dispelling negative stereotypes about gay people. *Sponsor:* National Coming Out Day, P.O. Box 34640, Washington, DC 20043-4640; 800-866-6263; e-mail: HRFC@aol.com.

National School Celebration
Unites and honors students as our future leaders. It also pays tribute to our American heritage and principles. The first National School Celebration took place on October 21, 1892. It is now celebrated on the second Friday in October. *Sponsor:* Celebration USA, 17853 Santiago Boulevard #107, Villa Park, CA 92667; 714-283-1892.

National Wild Turkey Calling Contest
During the second weekend in October, Yellville hosts its 51st annual wild turkey calling contest. *Sponsor:* Turkey Trot Festival, Chamber of Commerce, P.O. Box 369, Yellville, AR 72687-0369; 501-449-4676; 800-832-1414.

Saturday Night Live! premiered (1975)
NBC's weekend comedy program premiered on NBC-TV. George Carlin was the first guest host. *Contact:* NBC-TV.

World Championship Quartz Crystal Dig
Since 1987, the quartz crystal capital of the world, Mount Ida, has sponsored this event during the second weekend in October. *Sponsor:* Mount Ida Chamber of Commerce, P.O. Box 6, Mount Ida, AR 71957; 501-867-2723.

World's largest pizza baked (1987)
The pizza was cut into 94,248 slices. Yum, yum.

✉ Addresses for frequently cited organizations are gathered on pages vii–viii.

OCTOBER 231

October 12

America's Sexy Wives Contest

Held in Albuquerque, New Mexico, this contest judges wives on their commitment to marriage, their reason for feeling they represent sexiness, their charm and poise, and their creative expression. Always held on the second weekend in October. *Sponsor:* Married Mistress Association, Rose Smith, P.O. Box 81064, Albuquerque, NM 87198; 505-899-3121; Fax: 505-899-3120.

Columbus Day (original)

Celebrates the anniversary of the 1492 landing of Christopher Columbus in the New World. The legal holiday is now celebrated as Discovery Day on the second Monday of October.

Dia de la Raza (Day of the Race)

On the original Columbus Day, this Mexican holiday celebrates the shared heritage of the Spanish, Indian, and Hispanic people of Mexico. *Contact:* Mexican Embassy, 1911 Pennsylvania Avenue NW, Washington, DC 20006; 202-728-1600.

Indigenous Peoples Day

The city of Berkeley, California, celebrates the history and culture of the American Indian.

International Moment of Frustration Scream Day

Greenwich Time frustrated people should go outdoors to scream. *Sponsor:* Wellness Permission League. ✉

Interplanetary Confederation Days

The second Saturday and Sunday are designed to recognize the existence of other planets in the Milky Way Galaxy, to prepare people on Earth for the landing of spaceships in 2001, and to learn about the reality of interplanetary communications. *Sponsor:* Unarius Academy of Science, 145 S. Magnolia Avenue, El Cajon, CA 92020-4522; 619-444-7062; Fax: 619-444-9637.

National Gunfight Stunt Championships

On the second weekend in October, the Calico ghost town outside Barstow hosts a wild west parade, old prospectors burro run, and various 1880s games and stunts. *Sponsor:* Calico Days, Calico Ghost Town Regional Parks, P.O. Box 638, Yermo, CA 92398; 619-254-2122.

National Pasta Week

From angel hair to elbow macaroni, celebrate the versatile noodle during the second full week (Saturday to Friday). *Sponsor:* National Pasta Association, 2701 Wilson Boulevard #920, Arlington, VA 22201; 703-841-0818; Fax: 703-528-6507.

Nikita Khrushchev pounds UN desk with shoe (1960)

The Soviet premier gave new status to shoes when he used his to pound on a desk while giving a speech to the United Nations Assembly.

Pledge of Allegiance first recited in schools 1892

Recited to celebrate the 400th anniversary of Columbus' discovery. The first version of the Pledge was published in *The Youth's Companion* on September 8, 1892.

Taxpayer's Action Day

A day for taxpayers to be heard regarding waste in government. Local groups hold taxpayer rallys on the second or third Saturday in October. *Sponsor:* Citizen Against Government Waste, 1301 Connecticut Avenue NW #400, Washington, DC 20036; 202-467-5300; 800-BE-ANGRY.

Thanks, I'm Not Hungry Day

Commemorates the fasts that political activist Dick Gregory has undertaken to draw attention to important social issues. Gregory, also a comedian, was born on this day in 1932 in St. Louis, Missouri. *Sponsor:* The Life of the Party. ✉

Worker Empowerment Day

According to a Saturn television commercial, this was the day a line worker pulled the cord and stopped the entire production line to fix a small problem. Saturn gives it workers the power to make such decisions.

World Wristwrestling Championships

Begun in 1952 and held on the second Saturday in October, this event attracts over 500 contestants. *Sponsor:* World Wristwrestling Champions, Bill and Jane Soberanes, 423 E. Washington Street, Petaluma, CA 94952-3122; 707-778-1430.

October 13

B'nai B'rith founded (1843)

This Jewish organization was founded in New York. *Contact:* B'nai B'rith International, 1640 Rhode Island Avenue NW, Washington, DC 20036; 202-857-6600; Fax: 202-857-1099.

Credit Union Week

The week of the third Thursday in October spotlights the contributions of the world's credit unions. *Sponsor:* Credit Union National Association, P.O. Box 431, Madison, WI 53701; 608-231-4000; Fax: 602-232-8198.

Dictionary Week

During the week of Noah Webster's birthday (1843), we show our appreciation for all dictionaries and wordsmiths. Celebrated in Connecticut, New York, and Massachusetts.

First aerial photograph (1860)

The first aerial photograph was taken from a balloon above Boston, Massachusetts.

Getting the World to Beat a Path to Your Door Week

During the third week in October, improve your public relations. *Sponsor:* Barbara Gaughen PR, 226 E. Canon Perdido #B, Santa Barbara, CA 93101; 805-965-8482; Fax: 805-965-6522; e-mail: Barbara@bestsellers.com.

Modern Mythology Day

Explore modern myths in movies, television and paperback novels.

National Children's Day

By presidential proclamation, this day is held on the second Sunday in October.

National Pet Peeve Week

The second full week in October provides everyone a chance to air their minor grievances. *Sponsor:* Ad America Advertising, Kelly Fleming, 2215 29th Street SE #B7, Grand Rapids, MI 49508; 616-247-3797; Fax: 616-247-3798.

National School Lunch Week

The week starting with the second Sunday in October celebrates the nutritious, low-cost school lunch. *Sponsor:* American School Food Service Association, 1600 Duke Street, 7th Floor, Alexandria, VA 22314; 703-739-3900; 800-877-8822; Fax: 703-739-3915.

National YWCA Teen Week

The second full week in October promotes YMCA activities for teens nationwide. *Sponsor:* YWCA of the USA, 726 Broadway, 5th Floor, New York NY 10003; 212-614-2700; Fax: 212-677-9716.

Old Farmer's Almanac first published (1792)

Contact: Yankee Publishing, P.O. Box 520, Dublin, NJ 03444; 603-563-8111; Fax: 603-563-8252; e-mail: ofa1792@aol.com; World wide web: http://www.nj.com/weather.

U.S. Navy authorized (1775)

The Second Continental Congress authorized the acquisition of ships and the formation of a navy. *Contact:* Department of the Navy, Pentagon, Room 4E686, Washington, DC 20350; 703-695-0911.

White House Birthday

The cornerstone of the White House, the symbol of the American presidency, was laid in 1792.

World Wildlife Week

The week of the third Saturday is a time to appreciate the untamed creatures of the Earth. *Sponsor:* World Wildlife Fund, 1250 24th Street NW, Washington, DC 20037; 202-293-4800.

October 14

American Broadcasting Company formed (1943)
RCA sold the NBC Blue radio network to Edward Noble, who renamed it the American Broadcasting Company. For free tickets to ABC TV shows, write ABC, Guest Relations Department, 77 West 66th Street, New York, NY 10023, or ABC, Guest Relations Department, 4151 Prospect Avenue, Hollywood, CA 90027.

Be Bald and Be Free Day
The day for all bald people to go "shiny" and feel good about it. *Sponsor:* Wellness Permission League. ✉

Canadian Thanksgiving Day
Always celebrated on the second Monday. *Contact:* Canadian Embassy, 501 Pennsylvania Avenue NW, Washington, DC 20001; 202-682-1740.

Columbus Day (Discovery Day)
This legal holiday is held on the second Monday in October to celebrate Columbus's discovery of America. Also known as Discovery Day.

Discoverer's Day
This Hawaiian holiday, held on the second Monday in October, honors those who discovered Hawaii. *Contact:* Hawaii Visitors Bureau, 2270 Kalakaua Avenue #801, Honolulu, HI 96815; 808-923-1811; Fax: 808-922-8991.

Dwight David Eisenhower's Birthday
The 34th President of the U.S. was born in 1890 in Denison, Texas.

First live telecast from manned U.S. spacecraft
Apollo 7 transmitted the first live telecast in 1968. *Contact:* NASA. ✉

First person to fly faster than sound (1947)
Chuck Yeager flew an XS-1 rocket over the California desert.

Martin Luther King awarded Nobel Peace Prize
In 1964, Martin Luther King became the youngest person ever to receive the Nobel Peace Prize.

Monarch Day
On this day, millions of monarchs return to Natural Bridges State Beach near Santa Cruz, California. *Contact:* Santa Cruz Visitors Bureau, 701 Front Street, Santa Cruz, CA 95060; 408-425-1234; 800-833-3494; Fax: 408-425-1260.

national lower case day
celebrate the birthday of e.e. cummings by reading some great poetry. cummings was born in 1894. *sponsor:* the life of the party. ✉

National Occupational Therapy Day
Sponsor: American Occupational Therapy Association, Suzanne Carleton, 1383 Piccard Drive, Rockville, MD 20850; 301-948-9626.

Native Americans Day (South Dakota)
The second Monday in October is a legal holiday that honors Native Americans in South Dakota history. *Contact:* Indian Affairs Office, 500 E. Capitol Avenue #204, Pierre, SD 57501-5070; 605-773-3415; Fax: 605-773-4550.

Peace Corps Birthday
In a 1960 talk before college students, presidential candidate John F. Kennedy first spoke about his idea of a Peace Corps. *Contact:* Peace Corps, 1990 K Street, Washington, DC 20526; 202-606-6000.

October 15

First national lakeshore created (1966)
Pictured Rocks National Lakeshore was created in 1966. *Contact:* Pictured Rocks National Lakeshore, P.O. Box 40, Munising, MI 49862; 906-387-3700.

First weather report televised (1953)

Gourmet Coffee Week
Enjoy the companionship that only gourmet coffee can inspire. Always celebrated from the 15th to the

21st of October. Formerly sponsored by American Artists Studio.

I Love Lucy premiered (1951)

The first of many TV shows starring comedian Lucille Ball premiered on CBS. *Contact:* CBS-TV. ✉

Mata Hari executed (1917)

German spy Mata Hari was shot by a firing squad outside Paris, France.

Mushroom Day

National Grouch Day

Recognizes people who are chronically irritable. It doesn't necessarily accept these people or encourage them, and certainly doesn't honor them. It only recognizes that they exist. Bah, humbug! Held on the birthday of the founder, Alan Miller. *Sponsor:* Carter Middle School, Alan Miller, 300 Upland Drive, Clio, MI 48420; 313-686-0503.

U.S. Department of Transportation created (1966)

President Johnson signed the bill creating the department. *Contact:* Department of Transportation, 400 Seventh Street SW, Washington, DC 20590; 202-366-4000; Fax: 202-366-3937.

White Cane Safety Day

Celebrated since 1964 by presidential proclamation.

World Poetry Day

Formerly sponsored by Richard Falk, who died in 1994.

October 16

China became a nuclear power (1964)

China exploded its first atomic bomb, becoming the fifth nation to join the nuclear club. *Contact:* People's Republic of China Embassy, 2300 Connecticut Avenue NW, Washington, DC 20008; 202-328-2500.

Dictionary Day

On the birthday of Noah Webster, the creator of the first American dictionary, we show our appreciation for all dictionaries and wordsmiths. Webster was born in 1758 in West Hartford, Connecticut.

First birth control clinic (1916)

Margaret Sanger, Fania Mindell, and Ethel Burne opened the first birth control clinic in Brooklyn, New York.

First electric light bulb frosted on the inside (1928)

It's Safe to Breathe in the Sky Day

Commemorates the banning of smoking on domestic airlines in 1989. *Sponsor:* The Life of the Party. ✉

John Brown's Raid Anniversary

A militant abolitionist, John Brown seized the U.S. Arsenal at Harpers Ferry, West Virginia in 1859; 3 days later he and his cohorts were captured. Brown was hanged on December 2, 1859.

Learn a Word Day

On the birthday of Noah Webster (1758), take out your dictionary and learn a new word! *Sponsor:* All My Events. ✉

Let Them Eat Cake Day

In 1793, Queen Marie Antoinette of France was beheaded during the French Revolution. Earlier she had trivialized the hunger of the poor people of Paris who had no bread by saying, "Let them eat cake."

Maintenance Personnel Day

Honors those who maintain the nation's hospitals and other health care centers. *Sponsor:* Heartland Health Care Center, Dick Armstrong, Maintenance, 512 Draper Drive, Temple, TX 76501.

Missouri Day

The third Wednesday is a day for teachers and students to focus on the history, people, culture, and government of Missouri. *Contact:* Missouri Division of Tourism, P.O. Box 1055, Jefferson City, MO 65102; 314-751-4133.

National Boss Day

Give your boss a break—take the day off. Okay, plan a party too. You may celebrate on Friday if National Boss Day falls on a weekend. *Sponsor:* Patricia Haroski, 2871 F Walnut View Court, Winston-Salem, NC 27103; 910-765-2710.

National Train Your Brain Day

Exercise your brain, clean out the cobwebs, blast through the barriers, and click on the light bulbs! Give your brain a boost today. *Sponsor:* The Innovative Thinking Network, Joyce Wycoff, 101 E. Victoria #33, Santa Barbara, CA 93101; 805-963-9151; e-mail: staff@thinksmart.com.

Peace with Justice Week

Sponsored by 40 religious groups, promotes world peace. It is always held from the 16th (World Food Day) to the 24th (United Nations Day). *Sponsor:* National Council of Churches, 475 Riverside Drive #670, New York, NY 10115-0122; 212-870-2424; Fax: 212-870-2055.

World Food Day

The Food and Agricultural Organization was created on this date in 1945. This day focuses attention on world hunger and malnutrition. For free teaching materials, contact the National Committee for World Food Day, 1001 22nd Street NW, Washington, DC 20437.

October 17

Black Poetry Day

Celebrates the birthday of Jupiter Hammon (1711), the first American black to publish his poetry; also recognizes the contributions of black poets to American life and culture. *Sponsor:* Black Poetry Day Committee, Affirmative Action Office, State University College, Plattsburgh, NY 12901; 518-564-5250.

Cadillac's Birthday

The first Cadillac was completed in Detroit, Michigan in 1902. *Contact:* General Motors, 3044 W. Grand Avenue, Detroit, MI 48202-0000; 313-556-5000; Fax: 313-556-5108.

Credit Union Day

The third Thursday in October spotights the contributions of the world's credit unions. *Sponsor:* Credit Union National Association, P.O. Box 431, Madison, WI 53701; 608-231-4000; Fax: 608-232-8198.

International Day for the Eradication of Poverty

Devoted to eliminating poverty in all countries, especially developing nations. 1996 is the International Year for the Eradication of Poverty. *Sponsor:* United Nations. ✉

La Leche League International founded (1956)

Provides info to breastfeeding mothers worldwide. *Contact:* La Leche League International, 1400 N. Meacham, Schaumburg, IL 60173; 708-519-7730; 800-525-3243; Fax: 708-519-0035.

Mr. Smith Goes to Washington premiered (1939)

James Stewart starred in Frank Capra's film .

RCA created

The Radio Corporation of America was founded in 1919.

October 18

Alaska Day

Celebrates the anniversary of the transfer of Alaska from Russia to the U.S. in 1867. The purchase was made on March 30th. *Contact:* Alaska Division of Tourism, P.O. Box 110801, Juneau, AK 99811-0801; 907-465-2010; 800-200-1160; Fax: 907-465-2287.

Black Power Day

In the 1968 Mexico City Olympics, Tommie Smith and John Carlos were suspended for giving a black power salute during the victory ceremony.

First commercial long-distance phone line opened

Opened between New York City and Chicago in 1892.

First intercollegiate football rules (1873)

Persons Day

A Canadian celebration commemorating the 1929 ruling by the Judicial Council of England's Privy Council that declared women persons with rights.

Saint Luke Feast Day

Patron saint of artists, doctors, glassworkers, and painters.

Water Pollution Control Act passed (1972)

The act was passed over Nixon's veto.

World long jump record set (1968)

At the Olympics in Mexico City, Bob Beamon set the world long jump record of 29 feet, 2 1/2 inches.

Contact: U.S. Olympics Committee. ✉

October 19

Anniversary Day

In 1899, rocket pioneer Robert Goddard first envisioned a spaceship. *Contact:* NASA. ✉

Bridge Day

A day set aside for people to enjoy the world's longest steel arch bridge that spans 876 feet above the New River Gorge. Some enjoy the heights while others enjoy the food, crafts, and entertainment. *Sponsor:* New River Gorge Bridge, Fayetteville Chamber of Commerce, Fayetteville, WV 25840; 304-465-5617; 800-927-0263.

Concorde made its first landing in New York (1977)

The supersonic jet landed in New York City. It had previously landed in Washington, DC on May 24, 1976.

Evaluate Your Life Day

Check out your life—see where you're headed. *Sponsor:* Wellness Permission League. ✉

Lightening Is Electricity Day

In 1752, while flying a kite in stormy weather, Benjamin Franklin proved that lightning is electricity.

Mississinewa 1812

The largest War of 1812 living history event in the U.S. Includes a reenactment of the battle (December 17 and 18, 1812). Usually celebrated on the second weekend in October (due to cold weather later). *Sponsor:* Mississinewa Battlefield Society, 402 S. Washington #509, P.O. Box 1324, Marion, IN 46952; 317-662-0096.

National Mammography Day

National Off the Grid Day

To encourage self-sufficiency in home energy needs. Real Goods sponsors a National Tour of Independent Homes on this day. Always on the third Saturday in October. *Sponsor:* Real Goods Trading Corporation, Karen Hensley, 966 Mazzoni Street, Ukiah, CA 95482-3471; 707-468-9292; 800-762-7325; Fax: 707-468-0301; e-mail: realgood@well.sf.ca.us.

National Oyster Shucking Championships

During the third weekend in October, oyster shuckers from around the country compete for the national championship. Winners go to the world championships in Galway, Ireland. *Sponsor:* St. Mary's County Oyster Festival, P.O. Box 766, California, MD 20619; 301-863-5015; Fax: 301-863-7789.

Paint Pretty Day

On the birthday of pop artist Peter Max, paint a pretty picture. Max was born in 1937 in Berlin, Germany. *Sponsor:* All My Events. ✉

Sweetest Day

On the third Saturday in October, make someone happy. Remember that magic is hidden in the smallest act of unselfishness. *Sponsor:* Sanders Confectionery Products, John Sanders, 901 Wilshire Drive #360, Troy, MI 48084; 810-362-3223; Fax: 810-362-0878.

Worst 1-day stock market plunge (1987)

The Dow Jones Industrial Average dropped 508 points.

Yorktown Day

Celebrates the conclusive battle of the American Revolutionary War, where the Americans (led by George Washington) defeated the British (led by Lord Cornwallis) in Yorktown, Virginia in 1781.

October 20

America's Safe Schools Week

The third full week encourages programs for preventing campus crime and violence, increasing attendance, and suppressing drug abuse. *Sponsor:* National School Safety Center, 4165 Thousand Oaks Blvd #290, Westlake Village, CA 91362; 805-373-9977; Fax: 805-373-9277.

Birth of the Bab (1819)

Siyyid Ali Muhammad, the prophet/herald of the Baha'i faith, was born. *Sponsor:* Baha'i National Center. ✉

National Cleaner Air Week

The last full week in October promotes appreciation for clean air, a valuable resource. Formerly sponsored by the Air Pollution Control League.

National Collegiate Alcohol Awareness Week

Always celebrated the third week. Students on 3,000 campuses participate in educational activities that encourage respect for the law from those under age 21. Also promotes personal responsibility by adult students who choose to drink. Anheuser-Busch sponsors a poster competition. *Sponsor:* Anheuser-Busch, Inc., Department of Consumer Awareness, 1 Busch Place, St. Louis, MO 63118-1852; 314-577-9784; Fax: 314-577-9977.

National Consumers Week

The last full week is designed to alert consumers to potential fraud and misrepresentation. Also known as the National Consumer Protection Week. *Sponsor:* US Office of Consumer Affairs, 1620 L Street NW #700, Washington, DC 20236; 202-634-4329.

National Dental Hygiene Week

The third full week in October promotes the importance of oral health. *Sponsor:* American Dental Hygienists Association, 444 N. Michigan Avenue #3400, Chicago, IL 60611; 312-440-8900; Fax: 312-440-8929.

National Forest Products Week

By presidential proclamation, celebrated on the week beginning with the third Sunday in October.

National Pharmacy Week

The last full week in October honors pharmacists.

National Red Ribbon Week for a Drug-Free America

Wear a red ribbon during the last full week in October to create awareness and show support for alcohol and other drug prevention. For a free guide to more than 50 ideas for activities you can organize to celebrate this week, call the Bureau of At-Risk Youth at 800-99-YOUTH and ask for the Red Ribbon Week Idea Guide. *Sponsor:* National Family Partnership, 11159 B South Towne Square, St. Louis, MO 63123; 314-845-7955; Fax: 314-845-2117.

National Save Your Back Week

The last full week in October is designed to increase public awareness of proper back care. *Sponsor:* Daniel S. Romm, MD, Medical Arts Build-

---

✉   Addresses for frequently cited organizations are gathered on pages vii–viii.

ing, 890 Poplar Church Road #101, Camp Hill, PA 17011; 717-975-9994.

National School Bus Safety Week

Begins on the third Sunday.

National Shampoo Week

The third full week commemorates the history and evolution of shampoo. Formerly sponsored by Breck Shampoo.

National Shut-In Visitation Day

Take time to visit the sick and elderly on the third Sunday. *Sponsor:* National Society for Shut-Ins, Holy Rosary Church, 237 Franklin Street, Reading, PA 19602; 610-374-2930; Fax: 610-372-0130.

Saturday Night Massacre (1973)

Recognizes the anniversary of the major turning point in the Watergate fiasco, when President Nixon discharged Special Prosecutor Cox and Deputy Attorney General Ruckelhaus. As a result, Attorney General Mitchell resigned.

October 21

Battle of Trafalgar Anniversary

In 1805, the British Navy defeated the French and Spanish navies, preventing Napoleon from attacking Great Britain.

Camels' Birthday

In 1913, Camels became the first blended cigarette. *Contact:* R. J. Reynolds Company, 401 N. Main Street, Winston-Salem, NC 27101; 910-741-5000; Fax: 910-741-2214.

Can-Can Day

The dance was performed for the first time in Paris in 1858.

Electric Light Birthday

In 1879, Thomas Edison invented a successful light bulb in Menlo Park, New Jersey.

First commercial passenger airflight over the Pacific (1936)

Guggenheim Museum of Art opened (1959)

One of the greatest modern art museums opened in New York City. *Contact:* Solomon R. Guggenheim Museum, 1071 Fifth Avenue, New York, NY 10128; 212-423-3500; Fax: 212-423-3640.

National Biomedical Research Day

National Business Women's Week

The third full week honors professional and business women across the U.S. Inductions into the Business and Professional Women's Hall of Fame are also held this week. *Sponsor:* Business and Professional Women's Clubs, 2012 Massachusetts Avenue NW, Washington, DC 20036; 202-293-1100; Fax: 202-861-0298.

Saint Ursula and Her Companions Feast Day

Patron saint of teachers of girls.

October 22

Copycat Day

In 1938, Chester Carlson, inventor of xerography, made the first copy at his laboratory in Astoria, New York. *Contact:* Xerox Corporation, 800 Long Ridge Road, Stamford, CT 06902; 203-968-3000; Fax: 203-968-4525.

Cuban Missile Crisis Anniversary

In 1962, President Kennedy demanded that the Soviet Union remove missiles from Cuba. On October 28, after days of tension that had many people thinking World War III would result, the

You Bet Your Life premiered (1947)

The radio show starred Groucho Marx. *Contact:* NBC-TV. ✉

October 28

Cotton gin invented (1793)

Eli Whitney invented the cotton gin.

Fingerprints first used in crime investigations

In 1904, St. Louis police were the first to use fingerprints in a criminal investigation.

First baby born on an airplane (1929)

Mrs. T. W. Evans gave birth over Miami, Florida.

First ticker tape parade (1886)

Celebrated the dedication of the Statue of Liberty.

First woman U.S. ambassador appointed (1949)

Eugenie Anderson was appointed as ambassador to Denmark by President Truman.

International Space Rescue Agreement (1970)

The U.S. and the U.S.S.R. agreed to cooperate in any space rescues. *Contact:* NASA. ✉

Saint Jude Feast Day

Patron saint of lost causes and desperate situations. He is also the patron saint of police.

Statue of Liberty Day

In 1886 the Statue of Liberty was dedicated in New York harbor. Frederic Auguste Bartholdi designed the sculpture, which was paid for by the French and American people. The cornerstone of the statue was laid on August 5, 1884.

Turn Off the Violence Day

On the fourth Monday , turn off violent TV programs, don't listen to violent music, don't got to violent movies, and don't rent violent videos. Solve problems in a nonviolent way. *Sponsor:* Minnesota Citizens Council on Crime and Justice, P.O. Box 27558, Minneapolis, MN 55427.

October 29

Biographies Are Beautiful Day

On the birthday of James Boswell (1740), biographer of Samuel Johnson, we celebrate all biographies and biographers. *Sponsor:* Book Marketing Update. ✉

Black Tuesday (start of the Great Depression)

In 1929, the stock market suffered its most disastrous collapse.

First ballpoint pen sold in America (1945)

Gimbels Department Store sold the first ballpoint pens for $12.95 each.

First college fraternity founded (1833)

First peacetime military draft in U.S. (1940)

Held 2 years before the U.S. entered World War II. The Selective Service was organized on September 16, 1940.

National Organization for Women founded (1966)

Contact: National Organization for Women, 1000 16th Street NW #700, Washington, DC 20001; 202-331-0066; Fax: 202-785-8576.

Rock musical Hair opened off-Broadway (1967)

The musical was famous for celebrating long hair and other hippie cultural icons.

October 30

Bodybuilders Day

On the birthday of Charles Atlas, the original 97 lb. weakling, we celebrate all who strengthen their bodies. Atlas was born as Angelo Siciliano at Acri, Italy, on October 30, 1893.

Devil's Day or Mischief Night

The night before Halloween is a night for harmless pranks.

John Adams's Birthday

The 2nd President of the U.S. was born in 1735 in Braintree, Massachusetts.

War of the Worlds Day

In 1938, Orson Welles and the Mercury Players broadcast H. G. Wells' *War of the Worlds.* The broadcast caused panic among listeners who believed it was a real news report.

October 31

First person to land an airplane at the South Pole

In 1956, Admiral G. J. Dufek landed at the South Pole.

Halloween

Kids celebrate Beggar's Night by trick or treating door to door. Halloween celebrates an ancient Druid festival associated with ghosts, witches, and spirits. Also known as All Hallow's Eve and as Trick or Treat Night.

Mount Rushmore completed

Mount Rushmore was dedicated on March 3, 1933, and work stopped on the massive sculpture on October 31, 1941. *Contact:* Mount Rushmore National Monument, P.O.

Box 268, Keystone, SD 57751; 605-574-2523.

National Magic Day

The anniversary of the great magician Harry Houdini's death in 1926. *Sponsor:* Society of American Magicians, Anthony Murphy, 11 Angel Road, North Reading, MA 01864; 617-523-6434; Fax: 617-523-1814.

National UNICEF Day

A day for raising money for UNICEF to help the world's children. For free educational materials, write to the following address. *Sponsor:* U.S. Committee for UNICEF, 331 East 38th Street, New York, NY 10016; 212-686-5522; 800-252-KIDS; Fax: 212-779-1679; e-mail: mhirschhaut@unicefusa.org.

Nevada Admission Day

In 1864, Nevada became the 36th state of the U.S. *Contact:* Nevada Commission on Tourism, Capital Complex, Carson City, NV 89710; 702-687-3636; 800-638-2328.

Reformation Day

In 1517, Martin Luther nailed his 95 theses to the door of the church in Wittenberg, Germany, it denounced the selling of indulgences and sparked the Protestant Reformation.

Samhain (Druid New Year)

The ancient feast of Sacred Fire celebrates the reunion of Morrighan, a

Celtic goddess, with Dagda, the good god. It is also known as the Celtic Feast of the Dead, the Feast of Souls, or Calan Gaeaf.

Youth Honor Day

Celebrated in Iowa and Massachusetts.

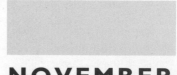

NOVEMBER

Aviation History Month

Commemorates the experiments of the Montgolfier brothers whose work led to the development of hot air balloons and aviation in general.

British Appreciation Month

Child Safety and Protection Month

Promotes the safety and protection of children. *Sponsor:* National PTA, 330 N. Wabash Avenue #2100, Chicago, IL 60611-3690; 312-670-6782; Fax: 312-670-6783.

Christmas Seal Campaign

The first Christmas Seals for researching tuberculosis were promoted in 1907. The Christmas Seal Campaign runs from November 1 to December 31. *Sponsor:* American Lung Association, 1740 Broadway,

✉ Addresses for frequently cited organizations are gathered on pages vii–viii.

New York, NY 10019-4374; 212-315-8836; 800-LUNG-USA; Fax: 212-315-8872.

Diabetic Eye Disease Month

Diabetes can lead to glaucoma and other forms of blindness. *Sponsor:* Prevent Blindness America. ✉

Good Nutrition Month

Refresh your memory on the 4 basic food groups.

International Creative Child and Adult Month

Designed to help people appreciate the importance of creativity in themselves and others. *Sponsor:* National Association for Creative Children and Adults, 8080 Spring-valley Drive, Cincinnati, OH 45236; 513-631-1777.

International Doll Collectors Month

Formerly sponsored by American Artists Studio.

International Drum Month

Encourages people to take up drumming. *Sponsor:* J and D Music Services, Jerome Hershman, 38 West 21st Street, 5th Floor, New York, NY 10010-6906; 212-924-9175; Fax: 212-675-3477.

Latin American Month

To bring closer ties between Latin America and the U.S. Formerly sponsored by Richard Falk, who died in 1994.

National Alzheimer's Disease Month

To help people learn about this disease and its care. *Sponsor:* Alzheimer's Association, 919 N. Michigan #1000, Chicago, IL 60611; 312-853-3060; 800-272-3900.

National Diabetes Month

Dedicated to reaching out to people with diabetes and their families with information about diabetes treatment. *Sponsor:* American Diabetes Association, 1660 Duke Street, Alexandria, VA 22314; 703-549-1500; Fax: 703-836-7439.

National Epilepsy Awareness Month

People with epilepsy can lead normal lives. Epilepsy occurs most often in young children and in adults over 65. There are 2,500,000 Americans with epilepsy. *Sponsor:* Epilepsy Foundation of America, 4351 Garden City Drive, Landover, MD 20785; 301-457-3700; 800-332-1000; Fax: 301-577-2684.

National Home Care Month

To show appreciation to home care providers. *Sponsor:* National Association for Home Care, Stanton Park, 519 C Street NE, Washington, DC 20002; 202-547-7424; Fax: 202-547-3540.

National Hospice Month

Honors those who provide care for those who are terminally ill. *Spon-*

sor: National Hospice Organization, 1901 N. Moore Street #901, Arlington, VA 22209; 703-243-5900.

National Neurofibromatosis Awareness Month

National Stamp Collecting Month

Cruise by the post office to see what's new in stamps. For a free Beginning Stamp Collector's Packet, send a business-size SASE to Junior Philatelists of America, P.O. Box 557, Boalsburg, PA 16827-0557. *Sponsor:* U.S. Postal Service. ✉

Native American Heritage Month

Celebrates the lives, history, and culture of the original Americans.

One Nation Under God Month

Reminds Americans of our rich religious heritage. *Sponsor:* The National Exchange Club, C. Neal Davis, 3050 Central Avenue, Toledo, OH 43606-1700; 419-535-3232; Fax: 419-535-1989.

Peanut Butter Lover's Month

Peanut butter was invented in November of 1895. *Sponsor:* Peanut Advisory Board, 1950 N. Park Place #525, Atlanta, GA 30309; 404-933-0357; Fax: 404-933-0796.

Project Red Ribbon

November 1 to January 1. Tie a red ribbon on your car to show concern for driving safely, especially during the holiday season. *Sponsor:* Mothers Against Drunk Driving, 511 E. John Carpenter Freeway #700, Irving, TX 75062-8187; 214-744-6233.

Real Jewelry Month
To encourage people to buy and use fine jewelry. *Sponsor:* Jewelers of America, 1185 Avenue of the Americas, 30th Floor, New York, NY 10036; 212-768-8777.

Religion and Philosophy Books Month
Promotes authors and publishers of religious, philosophical, and metaphysical books as well as Bibles. *Sponsor:* Book Marketing Update. ✉

Thanksgiving Canned Goods Drive
November 1 to 27. Many social organizations gather canned goods for needy people during the weeks before Thanksgiving Day.

November 1

All Saints Day
Honors all the saints who don't have a special feast day. First cele-

brated in 835. Also known as All Hallows Day.

Birthday of the Bra
New York debutante Mary Jacob invented the modern lightweight bra in 1914.

Ebony first published (1945)
John H. Johnson published the first issue of *Ebony*, the black general interest magazine. *Contact:* Ebony Magazine, 820 S. Michigan Avenue, Chicago, IL 60605; 312-322-9200.

First hydrogen bomb (1952)
The first hydrogen bomb was exploded at Eniwetok Atoll in 1952.

First medical school just for women (1848)
The Boston Female Medical School was founded by Samuel Gregory. It later merged with the Boston University School of Medicine. *Contact:* Boston University Medical Center, 88 E. Newton Street, Boston, MA 02118; 617-638-8000.

First weather reports from U.S. Weather Bureau (1870)
Contact: National Weather Service, 1325 East-West Highway, Silver Spring, MD 20910; 301-427-7689; Fax: 301-427-2610.

Forward Pass Day
Forward passes were first used when Notre Dame beat Army 35–13.

Money Order Day
In 1864, the post office introduced the first money orders. *Contact:* U.S. Postal Service. ✉

National Authors Day
Since 1928, celebrates American authors and also serves as an inspiration to new authors. Mrs. Cole is the granddaughter of the originator, Mrs. Nellie Verne Burt McPherson. *Sponsor:* Mrs. Sue Cole, 191 W. Cole Street, Macon, IL 62544; 217-764-3618.

National Fig Week
The week of the 1st to the 7th promotes eating figs for a nutritious, high-fiber taste treat. *Sponsor:* California Fig Advisory Board, P.O. Box 709, Fresno, CA 93712; 209-445-5626; 800-588-2344; Fax: 209-224-3449.

New Library of Congress opened (1897)
Contact: Library of Congress, 101 Independence Avenue SE, Washington, DC 20540; 202 707-5000; Fax: 202-287-5844.

Plan Your Epitaph Day
On the same day as the Day of the Dead, take time to think of the words you'd like to have on your tombstone. Write your own epitaph, and make it great! *Sponsor:* Dead or Alive, Lance Hardie, P.O. Box 4595, Arcata, CA 95521; 707-822-6924.

National Radiologic Technology Week

Celebrated the week of the 8th (the date on which Roentgen discovered X-rays), promotes public understanding of radiologic technology. *Sponsor:* American Society of Radiologic Technology, 15000 Central Avenue SE, Albuquerque, NM 87123-3917; 505-298-4500.

National Sandwich Day

The birthday of John Montague (1718), 4th Earl of Sandwich, who invented the sandwich in 1762 while playing a 24-hour game of cards. For recipe booklet of children's sandwiches, write Bread Winners, Ziploc Sandwich Bags, P.O. Box 78980, New Augusta, IN 46278. *Sponsor:* Ziploc Sandwich Bags, DowBrands, P.O. Box 68511, Indianapolis, IN 46268; 317-873-7000; Fax: 317-873-7319.

Saint Martin de Porres Feast Day

Patron saint of barbers and hairdressers. He is also patron saint of public health workers, people of mixed race, public education, social justice, and Peruvian television.

November 4

Black Solidarity Day

A national celebration held on the first Monday, encourages black students to share their common heritage. *Sponsor:* Afro-American Culture Center, Yale University, P.O. Box 3439, New Haven, CT 06520; 203-432-4131.

Cash register patented (1880)

James and John Ritty of Dayton, Ohio, patented the first cash register.

Celebrate Your Honeymoon Day

Go on a second honeymoon on the birthday of Art Carney, who won 6 Emmys for his work on *The Honeymooners* television show. Carney was born in 1918 in Mount Vernon, New York. *Sponsor:* The Life of the Party. ✉

First air-conditioned automobile (1939)

First migrant wagon train reached California from Missouri (1841)

First woman governor elected (1924)

Nellie Ross of Wyoming was elected governor after serving the last few months of her husband's term when he died.

Gatling gun patented (1862)

Richard J. Gatling patented a version the original version of the machine gun.

Hostages Day

In 1979 Iranian militants took 62 American hostages from the U.S. Embassy in Tehran, Iran.

King Tut's Tomb discovered (1922)

King Tutankhamen's tomb was discovered in Egypt. The tomb was filled with many treasures.

Peanut Butter Lover's Day

The first patent for the process of preparing nut meal from peanuts was applied for in 1895. *Sponsor:* Peanut Advisory Board, 1950 N. Park Place #525, Atlanta, GA 30339; 404-933-0357; Fax: 404-933-0796.

Saint Americus Feast Day

Son of King Stephen of Hungary, patron saint of America (because Amerigo Vespucci was named after him and America was named after Amerigo Vespucci).

UNESCO established (1946)

The United Nations Educational, Scientific, and Cultural Organization was established. *Contact:* UNESCO, 2 UN Plaza #900, New York, NY 10017; 212-963-5995; Fax: 212-355-5627.

Will Rogers Day (Oklahoma)

This public holiday celebrates the birthday of America's great humorist, Will Rogers. He was born in 1879 in Oologah, Oklahoma. *Contact:* Oklahoma Tourism, P.O. Box 60789, Oklahoma City, OK 73146; 800-652-6552.

November 5

Bridge Over Troubled Water Day

On the birthday of Art Garfunkel, singer of "Bridge Over Troubled Water," help someone through a tough time. Garfunkel was born in 1941 in Forest Hills, New York. *Sponsor:* The Life of the Party. ✉

Electric shaver patented (1923)

First automobile patent in the U.S. (1895)

George Selden was granted the first U.S. patent for a horseless carriage.

First FM-stereo broadcast (1935)

Edwin Howard Armstrong invented FM in 1933.

First mail carrier in the U.S. (1783)

Richard Fairfield delivered mail in Boston, Massachusetts. *Contact:* U.S. Postal Service. ✉

First U.S. transcontinental airplane flight (1911)

Calbraith Rodgers landed in Pasadena, California, after 49 days. He had taken off from Sheepshead Bay, New York.

November 6

First commercial TV station (1939)

WGY-TV of Schenectady, New York, was the first TV station licensed to broadcast commercially.

First intercollegiate football game (1869)

Rutgers beat Princeton, 6 to 4.

Jewish Book Month

During the month ending in Chanukah, read books by Jewish authors and books about Jewish interests. *Sponsor:* JWB Jewish Book Council, 15 East 26th Street, New York, NY 10010; 212-532-4949; Fax: 212-481-4174.

Meet the Press premiered (1947)

The longest-running show in TV history. *Contact:* NBC-TV. ✉

Saint Leonard of Noblac Feast Day

Because he helped a queen give birth while lost in a forest, Saint Leonard is patron saint of childbirth. For helping the queen, he was given land by the king, which he used to house escaped and freed prisoners; hence, he is also a patron saint of prisoners.

Saxophone Day

Celebrates the birthday of Adolphe Sax, inventor of the first brass woodwind, the saxophone. Sax was born in 1814 in Dinant, Belgium.

November 7

First black governor elected (1989)

L. Douglas Wilder of Virginia was the first black elected governor of a state since the Reconstruction. *Contact:* Office of the Governor, State Capital Building, 9th and Grace Streets, Richmond, VA 23219; 804-786-2211; Fax: 804-786-3985.

First black mayor of a major U.S. city (1967)

Carl Stokes was mayor of Cleveland. *Contact:* Office of the Mayor, 601 Lakeside Avenue, Cleveland, OH 44114; 216-664-2222.

First network to broadcast all programs in color

In 1966, NBC became the first TV network to broadcast exclusively in color. *Contact:* NBC-TV. ✉

First woman elected to Congress (1916)

Jeannette Rankin, a Montana Republican, was the first woman elected to Congress. She was formally seated in the U.S. House of Representatives on April 2, 1917.

National Notary Public Day

To recognize the contribution of America's notaries. *Sponsor:* American Society of Notaries, P.O. Box 5707, Tallahassee, FL 32314-5707; 800-522-3392.

PMS Stress Day

If you've got it, flaunt it. If not, get out of the way. This day was founded in 1995. *Sponsor:* KCAQ-FM, The Woody Show, Jewel Langway, Producer, 1701 Pacific Avenue #270, Oxnard, CA 93033; 805-483-1000; Fax: 805-483-6555.

Read Aloud Day

Held on the Thursday of the San Francisco Bay Area Book Festival. Read to your child on this day. *Contact:* San Francisco Bay Book Council, 555 DeHaro Street #220, San Francisco, CA 94107; 415-861-2665; Fax: 415-861-2670.

Republican Elephant Day

In 1874, illustrator Thomas Nast first used an elephant as a symbol of the Republican Party. *Contact:* Republican Party, 310 First Street SE, Washington, DC 20003; 202-863-8500; Fax: 202-863-8820.

November 8

Abet and Aid Punsters Day

Let the punsters have their day—for wordmeisters everywhere.

Originated by Earl Harris and William Rabe.

Days of Our Lives premiered (1965)

NBC's long-run soap opera premiered on NBC-TV. *Contact:* NBC-TV. ✉

First black popularly elected to the U.S. Senate

Edward Brooke of Massachusetts was elected in 1966.

First fatal train wreck in U.S. (1833)

Occurred near Heightstown, New Jersey in 1833. Two people were killed and many injured as a Camden and Amboy train derailed because of a broken axle.

First jet dogfight (1950)

Occurred during the Korean War.

First woman's college in the U.S. (1837)

Contact: Mount Holyoke College, College Street, South Hadley, MA 01075; 413-538-2000; Fax: 413-538-2391.

Home Box Office Birthday

In 1972, HBO premiered in 365 homes in Wilkes-Barre, Pennsylvania. *Contact:* Home Box Office, 1100 Avenue of the Americas, New York, NY 10036-6737; 212-512-1000; Fax: 212-512-5048.

Insect electrocutor patented (1910)

Louvre Museum opened (1793)

The famous art museum opened in Paris.

Merchant Sailing Ship Preservation Day

Commemorates the 1941 anniversary when whaler Charles W. Morgan began restoration in Mystic, Connecticut. *Sponsor:* National Maritime Museum, J. Porter Shaw Library, Fort Mason Building E, 3rd Floor, San Francisco, CA 94123; 415-556-9874; Fax: 415-556-3540.

Montana Admission Day

In 1889, Montana became the 41st state of the U.S. *Contact:* Travel Montana, 1424 Ninth Avenue, Helena, MT 59620; 406-444-2654; 800-548-3390; Fax: 406-444-1800.

Romances Are Rewarding Day

Celebrates the birthday of Margaret Mitchell, author of *Gone with the Wind.* Mitchell was born in 1900 in Atlanta, Georgia. *Sponsor:* Book Marketing Update. ✉

World Championship Goose Calling Contest

Among other events, the Waterfowl Festival features a contest for the world champion goose caller. Always held on the second full weekend in November. *Sponsor:* Waterfowl Festival, P.O. Box 929, Easton, MD 21601; 410-822-4567; Fax: 410-820-9286.

X-Ray Discovery Day

In 1895, Wilhelm Conrad Roentgen first verified the existence of X-rays.

November 9

Berlin Wall torn down (1989)

After 28 years the Berlin Wall was torn down.

Crystal Night (1938)

Nazis destroyed many Jewish homes and synagogues. It marked the beginning of the Holocaust. It is known as crystal night because of all the broken glass from the destroyed homes.

East Coast Blackout (1965)

An electric power failure caused a blackout over northeastern U.S. Nine months later, there was a large spurt of new births. Despite this curious side effect, the blackout brought out modern society's vulnerability to technology.

First neon sign (1911)

National Child Safety Council founded (1955)

Founded in Jackson, Michigan in 1955. *Contact:* National Child Safety Council, P.O. Box 1368, Jackson, MI 49204-1368; 517-764-6070.

Rolling Stone premiered (1967)

The first issue included a roach clip with every copy. *Contact: Rolling Stone Magazine,* 1290 Avenue of the Americas, New York, NY 10151-0002; 212-484-1616; Fax: 212-767-8203.

November 10

First long distance telephone call without an operator

Coast-to-coast direct dial telephone service began in 1951.

First motorcycle tested (1885)

Great American Warm-Up

Since the average American family of 4 has 10 wearable coats they are not using, clean out your closet today and take your extra warm coats to the nearest homeless shelter. Help them prepare for winter. *Sponsor:* All My Events. ✉

Hindu New Year (Deepavali)

Celebrated on the new moon near November 1st, this Festival of Lights celebrates the return of Lord Rama after a 14-year exile (symbolizing the triumph of light over darkness). Also known as Divali or Diwali, it honors Lakshmi, goddess of good fortune. *Contact:* Government of India Tourist Information Office, 30 Rockefeller Plaza #15, New York, NY 10112; 212-586-4901; Fax: 212-582-3274.

Hire a Veteran Week

Always celebrated the week of Veteran's Day.

International Week of Science and Peace

During the week of November 11th (Armistice Day), work to increase peace in the world through science. *Sponsor:* United Nations. ✉

Marine Corps Birthday

The forerunner of the Marine Corps was established on November 10, 1775. *Contact:* U.S. Marine Corps, Arlington Navy Annex #1134, Washington, DC 20380; 703-614-2958; Fax: 703-695-7460.

Martin Luther's Birthday

The leader of the Protestant Reformation was born in 1483 in Eisleben, Saxony (Germany).

Most expensive painting ever sold (1987)

Vincent van Gogh's *Irises* sold for $53.9 million.

National Split Pea Soup Week

During the week with the second Monday eat more split pea soup. *Sponsor:* USA Dry Pea and Lentil

Council, 5071 Highway 8 West, Moscow, ID 83843-4023; 208-882-3023; Fax: 208-882-6406.

National Women Veterans Recognition Week
Always the week of Veterans Day.

Operating Room Nurse Week
Celebrated the week of November 14th, anniversary of the first blood transfusion. *Sponsor:* Association of Operating Room Nurses, Janet Paulson, 2170 S. Parker Road #300, Denver, CO 80231-5711; 303-755-6300; Fax: 303-750-3212.

Saint Aedh Mac Breic Feast Day
Since Saint Aedh Mac Breic could take on the headaches of Saint Brigid as his own, he is considered a patron saint of headache sufferers.

Sesame Street Birthday
The long-lasting children's TV show began on PBS. This day also marks the birthday of Children's Television Workshop, the producers of Sesame Street. *Contact:* Children's Television Workshop, 1 Lincoln Square Plaza, 3rd Floor, New York, NY 10023-7170; 212-595-3456; Fax: 212-875-6106.

November 11

Civil Rights Memorial dedicated (1989)
Dedicated in Montgomery, Alabama. *Contact:* Montgomery Chamber of Commerce, 401 Madison Avenue, Montgomery, AL 36104; 205-240-9455; Fax: 205-240-9290.

First compulsory school law in the U.S. (1647)

God Bless America Day
Kate Smith first sang Irving Berlin's "God Bless America" on network radio in 1939.

Party Party Day
An excuse to have a party once a month (when the day equals the month). *Sponsor:* Bonza Bottler Day. ✉

Saint Martin of Tours Feast Day (Martinmas)
Patron saint of France, soldiers, horses, riders, geese, wine-growers, beggars, the homeless, and impoverishment (because he gave half his cloak to a beggar).

Veteran's Day
Also known as Armistice Day, Victory Day, Remembrance Day (in Canada and Great Britain), or World War I Memorial Day. Honors soldiers of all wars. It commemorates the day the Armistice was signed ending World War I in 1918.

Washington Admission Day
The Evergreen State became the 42nd state of the U.S. in 1889. *Contact:* Washington State Tourism, 101 General Administration Bldg, Olympia, WA 98504-0613; 206-586-2088; 800-544-1800.

November 12

Baha'u'llah Birthday
The founder of the Baha'i Faith was born in 1817 as Mirza Husayn Ali. *Sponsor:* Baha'i National Center. ✉

Exotic Dancers League of America formed (1963)
The League operates the Burlesque Hall of Fame (open daily, free admission) as well as the Miss Exotic World Pageant (in early May). *Sponsor:* Exotic Dancers League of America, Dixie Evans, 29053 Wild Road, Helendale, CA 92342; 619-243-5261.

First autobank (1946)
The first autobank opened in Chicago, Illinois, in 1946.

First happy hour held (1745)
Held in a pub in Ireland.

First professional football player (1892)
Pudge Heffelfinger was paid to play for the Allegheny Athletic Association.

First space salvage (1984)
Astronauts Dale Gardner and Joe Allen salvaged a satellite. *Contact:* NASA. ✉

First spacecraft launched for Second mission in orbit
Space shuttle *Columbia* was launched for a second orbital mission. *Contact:* NASA. ✉

✉ Addresses for frequently cited organizations are gathered on pages vii–viii.

254 NOVEMBER

November 13

Artificial snow invented (1946)
Vincent Schaeffer spread the first artificial snow on Mount Greylock, Massachusetts.

First radio symphony orchestra (1937)
NBC formed the first full-sized symphony orchestra to be broadcast over radio. *Contact:* NBC. ✉

First sit-down strike (1933)
Workers struck the Hormel Packing Company plant in Austin, Minnesota. *Contact:* Hormel Foods, P.O. Box 800, Austin, MN 55912; 507-437-5611; Fax: 507-437-5489.

First spacecraft to orbit another planet (1971)
Mariner 9, was the first human-made object to orbit Mars. *Contact:* NASA. ✉

Holland Tunnel Anniversary
Opened in 1927, it connected New York City and Jersey City. It was the first U.S. tunnel to be built under water.

Press-on fingernails first marketed (1952)

Saint Frances Xavier Cabrini Feast Day
Mother Cabrini, the first American saint, is patron saint of emigrants.

Saint Homobonus Feast Day
A merchant who gave away large portions of his profits, he is a patron saint of business people, tailors, and clothesworkers.

Vietnam Veterans Memorial dedicated (1982)
Dedicated in Washington, DC. A later statue, Three Servicemen, was dedicated on November 9, 1984. *Contact:* Vietnam Veterans Memorial, 23rd and Constitution Avenues, Washington, DC 20020; 202-634-1568.

Walt Disney's Fantasia premiered (1940)
Contact: Walt Disney Company. ✉

Winter Weather Awareness Day
Get your home ready for winter on the second Wednesday.

November 14

Dow Jones average first hit 1000 (1972)
Contact: Dow Jones and Company, 200 Liberty Street, New York, NY 10281; 212-416-2000; 800-831-1234; Fax: 212-416-2658.

First airplane flight from deck of a ship (1910)

First blood transfusion (1666)
The first transfusion was performed on a dog.

First streetcar goes into operation (1832)
The first streetcar was a horse-drawn vehicle and operated in New York City.

Great White Whale Day
In 1851, one of the world's greatest novels, *Moby Dick,* was published. Moby Dick was a great white whale.

Operating Room Nurse Day
Sponsor: Association of Operating Room Nurses, Janet Paulson, 2170 S. Parker Road #300, Denver, CO 80231-5711; 303-755-6300; Fax: 303-750-3212.

November 15

American Enterprise Day
Celebrates the benefits of the free market system in America. *Sponsor:* Future Business Leaders of America, Edward D. Miller, P.O. Box 79063, Baltimore, MD 21279-0063; 703-860-3334.

American Federation of Labor founded (1881)
First founded as the Federation of Organized Trades and Labor Unions in Pittsburgh, Pennsylvania. It was later reorganized in 1886. *Contact:* AFL-CIO, 815 16th Street, Washington, DC 20006; 202-637-5000.

Doublespeak Day

The Doublespeak Award is given to American public figures who have used language that is grossly deceptive, evasive, euphemistic, confusing, or self-contradictory. Awarded at the National Council of Teachers of English convention on the third Friday in November. *Sponsor:* Committee on Public Doublespeak, Keith Gilyard, 241 Lafayette Road #109, Syracuse, NY 13205; 315-443-9314.

First black professional hockey player (1950)

Arthur Dorrington played hockey for the Atlantic City Seagulls.

First unemployment check approved by SSA (1939)

Free postal delivery was inaugurated (1869)

Contact: U.S. Postal Service. ✉

George Spelvin's Birthday

Born in 1886 in the Broadway production of *Karl the Peddlar*, George Spelvin is a fictitious character who is listed in play programs to conceal the fact that an actor or actress (as Georgina) is playing more than one role.

Holidays Are Pickle Days

From November 15 to December 31, keep pickles on your holiday tables. *Sponsor:* Pickle Packers International, DHM Group, P.O. Box 767, Holmdel, NJ 07733; 908-975-9675; Fax: 908-946-3343.

National Broadcasting Company debuts (1926)

NBC made its radio debut. For free tickets to NBC-TV shows, write to NBC-TV, Guest Relations Department, 30 Rockefeller Plaza, New York, NY 10020. Or, on the West Coast, write to NBC-TV, Guest Relations Department, 3000 W. Alameda Avenue, Burbank, CA 91523.

National Philanthropy Day

By presidential proclamation, the third Friday in November is set aside to encourage giving to others.

Pikes Peak sighted (1806)

American explorer and soldier Zebulon Pike first sighted Pikes Peak in Colorado in 1806.

Saint Albert the Great Feast Day

Patron saint of scientists, science students, medical technologists, and philosophers.

November 16

Birth of the Blues

W. C. Handy, father of the blues, was born in 1873 in Florence, Alabama.

First salute to the American flag by a foreign country

In 1776, the government of St. Eustatius in the West Indies, saluted the American flag at Fort Orange.

First satellite on the planet Venus

The Soviet spacecraft *Venera 3*, which crashlanded on the planet Venus, was launched on this day in 1965; it landed on Venus on March 1, 1966. *Contact:* NASA. ✉

National Federation of the Blind Day

Contact: National Center for the Blind, 1800 Johnson Street, Baltimore, MD 21230; 410-659-9314; 800-638-7518; Fax: 410-685-5653.

Oklahoma Admission Day

In 1907, Oklahoma became the 46th state of the U.S. *Contact:* Oklahoma Tourism, P.O. Box 60789, Oklahoma City, OK 73146; 405-521-2409; Fax: 405-521-3089; 800-652-6552.

Sound of Music opened (1959)

This Rogers and Hammerstein musical opened on Broadway.

Touch-tone telephone introduced (1963)

November 17

Alascattalo Day

Named for a mythical beast (a genetic cross between a moose and a walrus), the third Sunday celebrates Alaskan humor. Steven Levi is author of *Alascattalo Tales: A Treasury of Alaskan Humor*. *Sponsor:* Parsnackle Press, Steve Levi, Editor, P.O. Box 241467, Anchorage, AK 99524; 907-337-2021.

American Education Week
Since 1955, honors America's education system. Always celebrated during the week before Thanksgiving week. *Sponsor:* National Education Association, 1201 Sixteenth Street NW, Washington, DC 20036; 202-822-7200.

Clock patented (1794)
Ely Terry patented the first clock.

First postage stamps depicting the American eagle (1851)
Contact: U.S. Postal Service. ✉

Homemade Bread Day
To promote the pleasure of homemade bread. *Sponsor:* Homemade Bread Day Committee, P.O. Box 3, Montague, MI 49437.

National Culinary Week
The full week before Thanksgiving celebrates culinary excellence. *Sponsor:* American Culinary Federation, Brent Frei, 10 San Bartola Drive, Saint Augustine, FL 32085; 904-824-4468; Fax: 904-825-4758.

National Geography Awareness Week
The week before Thanksgiving promotes geography lessons in schools. The National Geographic Society publishes a packet for K-12 teachers that includes posters, maps, lesson plans, and other resources to use during this week.

Cost: $3.50 each. *Sponsor:* National Geographic Society, Geography Education Program, P.O. Box 1640, Washington, DC 20013-1640; 202-775-6577.

National Stamp Collecting Week
Celebrated the third week in November. *Sponsor:* U.S. Postal Service. ✉

Saint Elizabeth of Hungary Feast Day
Patron saint of bakers.

Suez Canal opened (1869)

November 18

American Woman Suffrage Association founded (1869)
Worked exclusively for the right of women to vote, it was superceded by the League of Women Voters. *Contact:* League of Women Voters, 1730 M Street NW, Washington, DC 20036; 202-429-1965; Fax: 202-429-0854.

Antarctica discovered (1820)
Discovered by Captain Nathaniel Palmer of the U.S. Navy.

Ben Hur premiered (1959)
The biblical movie starring Charlton Heston premiered in New York.

Mickey Mouse's Birthday
In 1928, Mickey first appeared in the first sound-synchronized animated cartoon, *Steamboat Willie.* Today is also the birthday of Minnie Mouse. *Contact:* Walt Disney Company. ✉

National Children's Book Week
Promotes reading books with your children. It starts on Monday the full week before Thanksgiving week. *Sponsor:* Children's Book Council, 568 Broadway #404, New York, NY 10012; 212-966-1990; Fax: 212-966-2073.

National Hunger and Homeless Awareness Week
The week before Thanksgiving Day (Monday through Friday) promotes awareness of hunger and homelessness and also promotes active solutions to both problems. *Sponsor:* National Student Campaign Against Hunger and Homelessness, 29 Temple Place, Boston, MA 02111.

Superman died (1992)
In *Superman* comic #75, Superman died in a battle with Doomsday. He

later was resurrected. *Contact:* DC Comics, 1325 Sixth Avenue, 27th Floor, New York, NY 10019; 212-636-5400; Fax: 212-636-5430.

Teddy Bear Birthday
In 1902, Brooklyn toymaker Morris Michton named the teddy bear after Teddy Roosevelt.

November 19

First insurance policy on a woman's life issued (1850)

First Presidential Library (1939)

Gettysburg Address Anniversary
In 1863, Lincoln delivered one of the most famous and shortest political speeches of all time.

James Abram Garfield's Birthday
The 20th President of the U.S. was born in 1831 in Orange, Ohio.

Modern pencil invented (1895)

National Community Education Day
Promotes strong bonds between communities and schools; always held on the Tuesday of American Education Week. *Sponsor:* Community Education Association, 3929 Old Lee Highway #91-A, Fairfax, VA 22030-2401; 703-359-8973; Fax: 703-359-0972.

Pop Tarts Birthday
Pop Tarts, a great breakfast junk food, was created in 1965. *Contact:* Kellogg Company, 235 Porter Street, Battle Creek, MI 49016; 616-961-2000; Fax: 616-961-2683.

Puerto Rico Discovery Day
Christopher Columbus landed in Puerto Rico in 1493. *Contact:* Puerto Rico Tourism, 575 Fifth Avenue, 23rd Floor, New York, NY 10017; 212-599-6262; 800-223-6530; Fax: 212-818-1866.

Women's Christian Temperance Union formed (1874)
The WCTU was organized in Cleveland, Ohio. *Contact:* Women Christian Temperance Union, 1730 Chicago Avenue, Evanston, IL 60201.

November 20

200 Million People in the U.S. (1967)
The Census Clock at the Commerce Department hit 200 million people.

Africa Industrialization Day
Intended to mobilize the commitment of the international community to the industrialization of the continent of Africa. *Sponsor:* United Nations. ✉

DDT use outlawed in residential areas (1969)

Declaration of the Rights of the Child adopted
Unanimously adopted by the UN General Assembly in 1959. *Contact:* United Nations. ✉

First state to ratify Bill of Rights (1789)
New Jersey was the first to ratify the Bill of Rights.

Mexico Revolution Day
Celebrates the anniversary of the social revolution begun by Francisco Madero (1910). *Contact:* Mexican Embassy, 1911 Pennsylvania Avenue NW, Washington, DC 20006; 202-728-1600.

National Clean Out Your Refrigerator Day
On the Wednesday of the week before Thanksgiving Day, take time to clean and organize your refrigerator before the holiday season. Make room! *Sponsor:* Whirlpool Corporation, Dana Donley, 2000 N. State Route 63, Benton Harbor, MI 49022; 616-923-5298; Fax: 616-923-5486.

National Commission on Product Safety founded
Contact: Consumer Product Safety Commission, 4330 East-West Highway, Bethesda, MD 20814; 301-504-0500; Fax: 301-504-0124.

National Educational Support Personnel Day
The Wednesday of American Education Week salutes all school em-

ployees, especially secretaries, bus drivers, cafeteria workers, maintenance personnel, and other support people. *Sponsor:* National Education Association, 1201 Sixteenth Street NW, Washington, DC 20036; 202-833-4000.

National Young Reader's Day

The Wednesday of Education Week is a day to encourage young readers. It is sponsored by the Center for the Book in the Library of Congress and Pizza Hut. *Sponsor:* Pizza Hut, Book It! Program, Eunice Ellis, P.O. Box, Wichita, KS; 316-681-9000; 800-426-6548; Fax: 316-687-8937.

Timecard clock invented (1888)

William Bundy invented the timecard clock.

Traffic light patented (1923)

Garrett Morgan, a black inventor, patented the automatic traffic light.

Twiglet Bank opened (1987)

The first bank founded, operated, and used only by children.

November 21

Alcan Highway to Alaska opened (1942)

First Flight Day

In 1783, Frenchmen Jean Francois Pilatre de Rozier and the Marquis Francois Laurent d'Arlandes, went aloft for a 25-minute flight. They were the first humans to fly.

First human cannonball (1871)

The first performer to be shot out of a cannon was Emilio Onra.

First solo rowboat crossing of the Pacific Ocean

In 1991, French rower Gerard D'Aboville rowed across the Pacific Ocean from Choshi, Japan, to Ilwaco, Washington. He began his trip on July 11, and completed it on November 21.

First woman to serve in the U.S. Senate (1922)

Rebecca Felton of Georgia was sworn in as the first female U.S. Senator.

Great American Smokeout

On the third Thursday, encourage smokers to quit for at least 1 day. *Sponsor:* American Cancer Society, 1180 Avenue of the Americas, New York, NY 10036; 212-382-2169.

North Carolina Ratification Day

In 1789, North Carolina became the 12th state to ratify the U.S. Constitution. *Contact:* North Carolina Tourism Division, 430 N. Salisbury Street, Raleigh, NC 27611; 919-733-4171; 800-847-4862; Fax: 919-733-8582.

Phonograph invented (1877)

Thomas Edison announced the invention of the talking machine or phonograph.

Verrazano Bridge opened (1964)

Who Shot J. R. Day

In 1980, 83 million viewers tuned into CBS's *Dallas* to find out who shot J. R. Ewing. His sister-in-law Kristin did it. *Contact:* CBS-TV. ✉

Wild Bikini Day

On the birthday of Goldie Hawn, the bikini news lady from *Laugh-In*, wear a wild bikini or, since it might be cold where you live, shop for one. Hawn was born in 1945 in Washington, DC. *Sponsor:* The Life of the Party. ✉

World Hello Day

Make the world a friendlier place by greeting 10 people today. *Sponsor:* McCormack Brothers, P.O. Box 993, Omaha, NE 68101.

November 22

First trans-Pacific airmail flight (1935)

Carrying 100,000 letters, the *China Clipper* flew the first trans-Pacific airmail flight from San Francisco, California, to Manila, Philippines. *Contact:* U.S. Postal Service. ✉

Nation of Islam founded (1930)

Elijah Muhammad founded the Nation of Islam in Detroit, Michigan.

National Farm-City Week

Since 1959, the week ending with Thanksgiving Day commemorates the reliance that farms and cities have upon each other.

National Hockey League established (1917)

The League started with 4 Canadian teams. *Contact:* National Hockey League, 75 International Boulevard #300, Rexdale, Ontario M9W 6L9 Canada; 416-798-0809; Fax: 416-798-0852.

National Stop the Violence Day

On the anniversary of President Kennedy's assassination in 1963, radio and TV stations across the country promote a 1-day cease-fire on gang violence. *Sponsor:* Promotional Rescue, Cliff Berkowitz, Paradigm Radio, 309 O Street, Eureka, CA 95501; 707-443-9842.

Saint Cecilia Feast Day

A Roman virgin and early Christian martyr, she is patron saint of music and musicians.

Snowmobile Birthday

The snowmobile was patented in 1927.

SOS adopted (1906)

The universal distress signal, SOS, was adopted by the International Radio Telegraph Convention in Berlin.

Start Your Own Country Day

World's largest solar-powered power plant started

The plant opened at Carrizo Plain, California, in 1983.

November 23

Billy the Kid's Birthday

Billy the Kid was born as Henry McCarty in 1859. Use this day to relive the days of the old West.

Color photographs patented (1863)

Dr. Who's Birthday

The science-fiction TV show premiered in Great Britain in 1963.

First play-by-play football broadcast (1919)

Franklin Pierce's Birthday

The 14th President of the U.S. was born in 1804 in Hillsboro, New Hampshire.

Jukebox Birthday

Invented by Louis Glass, the jukebox made its debut in San Francisco, California, in 1899.

Life magazine first published (1936)

Contact: Life Magazine, Time-Life Building, Rockefeller Center, New York, NY 10020; 212-522-1212; Fax: 212-522-0907.

National Black Independent Party founded (1980)

The National Black Independent Party was founded in Philadelphia, Pennsylvania.

National Moms and Dads Day

On the Saturday before Thanksgiving Day, working spouses take time off from their children, jobs, and other duties. Formerly sponsored by Sunny 105.

Pencil sharpener patented (1897)

J. L. Love patented the first pencil sharpener.

Read Across America Day

On the Saturday before Thanksgiving Day, encourage everyone to read. Take some time today to read something yourself. *Sponsor:* Children's Book Council, 568 Broadway #404, New York, NY 10012; 212-966-1990; Fax: 212-966-2073.

Saint Clement Feast Day

Patron saint of blacksmiths, farriers, shoe tanners, and stonecutters.

Saint Felicity Feast Day

A rich Roman woman who had given birth to seven sons, she is solicited by women who want to bear sons, she is their patron saint.

Sign of Sagittarius

The astrological sign of Sagittarius, the archer, runs from November 23rd to December 21st. Sagittarians are practical, imaginative, and mature.

November 24

Barbed Wire Day

Joseph Glidden received a patent for barbed wire in 1874.

Brady Bill passed by Congress (1993)

Established a 5-day federal waiting period for handgun sales.

Comedy Hall of Fame first members inducted (1993)

Darwin's Origin of Species published (1859)

Darwin's thesis described his theory of evolution.

John F. Kennedy Day (Massachusetts)

The last Sunday honors the U.S. president from Massachusetts (1960–1963). *Contact:* Massachusetts Tourism Office, 100 Cambridge Street, 13th Floor, Boston, MA 02202; 617-727-3201; 800-447-6277; Fax: 617-727-6525.

National Adoption Week

Celebrate adoption successes during the week of Thanksgiving. *Sponsor:* National Committee for Adoption, Mary Beth Seader, MSW, 1930 17th Street NW, Washington, DC 20009-6207; 202-328-1200; Fax: 202-332-0935.

National Bible Sunday

On the Sunday before Thanksgiving day, encourage Bible study. *Sponsor:* American Bible Society, Rev. Fred Allen, 1865 Broadway, New York, NY 10023; 212-408-1200; Fax: 212-408-1512.

National Bible Week

To encourage Bible study and to increase awareness of the Bible's place in our country's history. Celebrated from Sunday to Sunday of the week of Thanksgiving Day. *Sponsor:* Laymen's National Bible Association, Thomas R. May, 1865 Broadway, 12th Floor, New York, NY 10023-7503; 212-408-1390; Fax: 212-408-1448.

National Eating Disorders Week

The week of Thanksgiving Day promotes the treatment of bulimia and anorexia.

National Family Caregivers Week

Always celebrated the week of Thanksgiving.

National Family Week

During the week of Thanksgiving, we honor all families.

National Game and Puzzle Week

During the last full week, enjoy your family and friends while playing games or doing a puzzle. *Sponsor:* Patch Products, Tim Walsh, P.O. Box 268, Beloit, WI 53512-0268; 608-362-6896; Fax: 608-362-8178.

National Rifle Association founded (1871)

Contact: National Rifle Association, 11250 Waples Mill Road, Fairfax, VA 22030; 703-267-1000; Fax: 703-352-6408.

Snow Moon

The full moon of November is the snow moon, symbolic of frost faeries, protection, hope, warmth, and healing. It is also known as the fog moon (in England) and beaver moon (in American backwoods tradition).

Universal Children's Day

First celebrated in 1953, this day makes children's needs known to governments around the world. The date may vary in different countries, but in the U.S. it is celebrated on the Sunday before Thanksgiving Day. *Contact:* United Nations. ✉

Win Friends and Influence People Day

Dale Carnegie, author of *How to Win Friends and Influence People,* was born in Maryville, Missouri, in 1888. His book was published in 1936 and has sold over 5 million copies. Also known as Stand Up and Give a Speech Day.

Zachary Taylor's Birthday

The 12th President of the U.S. was born in 1784 in Orange County, Virginia.

November 25

Automobile Speed Reduction Day

In 1973, to cut back America's reliance on Mideast oil, President Nixon issued a presidential order mandating a national maximum speed limit of 55 miles per hour.

Christian Science Monitor first published (1908)

Contact: Christian Science Monitor, One Norway Street, Boston, MA 02115; 617-450-2652; Fax: 617-450-2317.

National Military Families Recognition Day

Celebrated on the Monday of National Family Week (the week of Thanksgiving Day).

Saint Catherine of Alexandria Feast Day

Patron saint of maidens, students, philosophers, mechanics; also patron saint of those who work with wheels.

November 26

Casablanca premiered (1942)

One of the best movies of all time starred Humphrey Bogart and Ingrid Bergman. It premiered in New York City just weeks after the Allies landed in Casablanca.

First college social fraternity (1825)

Kappa Alpha was formed at Union College in Schenectady, New York.

Shopping Reminder Day

24 shopping days until Christmas (not counting Sundays and Christmas eve).

Sojourner Truth Day

Commemorates the death of Sojourner Truth in 1883. A former slave, she was an advocate of abolition and women's rights. Sojourner was born in 1790.

November 27

Army War College established (1901)

Established in Washington, DC.

Black Wednesday

The day before Thanksgiving Day is the busiest airline travel day of the year.

Save the Record Player Day

Celebrates the 1992 publication of *Turntable Illusions,* the book designed to save the record player. You can use your record player to spin discs of optical illusions! *Sponsor:* Open Horizons. ✉

November 28

English Poetry Day

Celebrates the birthdays of English poets William Blake (1757) and John Bunyan (1628). *Sponsor:* Book Marketing Update. ✉

First automobile race in the U.S. (1895)

Took place between Chicago and Waukegan, Illinois.

First public skywriting exhibition (1922)

RAF Captain Cyril Turner wrote "Hello USA. Call Vanderbilt 7200," over the skies of New York City.

Grand Ole Opry made its radio debut (1925)

Nashville station WSM broadcast the Opry. It was originally called the WSM Barn Dance. *Contact:* Grand Ole Opry, 2808 Opryland Drive, Nashville, TN 37214; 615-889-3060.

Thanksgiving Day

Give thanks for the harvest and your many blessings. Thanksgiving is always held on the fourth Thursday in November.

November 29

Black Friday
The opening of the Christmas shopping season, the day after Thanksgiving is the busiest retail day of the year. Christmas Eve is next busiest.

Computer Security Day
Celebrated on the last working day in November. Protect your computer and your data. For a free computer security poster, write to CSD Committee at the following address. *Sponsor:* Association for Computing Machinery, P.O. Box 39110, Washington, DC 20016; 202-874-2426; e-mail: computer-security-day@acm.org.

First airplane flight over the South Pole (1929)
Richard Byrd made the first airplane flight over the South Pole in 1929.

Frozen Americans Day
Thirteen Americans are currently frozen in hope of being brought back to life when a cure can be found for their diseases. *Sponsor:* A Pilgrim's Almanac. ✉

International Day of Solidarity with the Palestinian People
Sponsor: United Nations. ✉

Invisible ink used for the first time (1775)
Sir James Jay invented invisible ink; Silas Deane was the first to use it.

King Tut Day
In 1922, Lord Carnarvon and Howard Carter discovered the tomb of King Tutankhamen, one of the richest archeological finds ever recorded.

National Council of Churches founded (1950)
Contact: National Council of Churches, 475 Riverside Drive, New York, NY 10115; 212-870-2511; Fax: 212-870-3112.

National Red Kettle Kick-Off
Thousands of volunteers begin to ring the bells to encourage people to donate money for the holiday relief efforts of the Salvation Army. *Sponsor:* The Salvation Army, 615 Slaters Lane, Alexandria, VA 22313; 703-684-5500.

Sinkies Day
On the day after Thanksgiving, enjoy the leftovers while eating over the sink. Sinkies are people who eat over the kitchen sink because they are in a hurry to eat.

Enjoy a quick meal of leftovers before going out to shop. *Sponsor:* International Association of Sinkies, Norm Hankoff, Founder, 1579 Farmers Lane #252, Santa Rosa, CA 95405.

Ski Patrol Day
Celebrated on the Friday after Thanksgiving Day, traditionally the beginning of the winter skiing season. *Contact:* National Ski Patrol, Ski Patrol Building #100, 133 S. Van Gordon Street, Lakewood, CO 80228; 303-988-1111; Fax: 303-988-3005.

World Championship Duck Calling Contest
On the Friday and Saturday after Thanksgiving Day, Stuttgart sponsors the world championship duck calling contest as part of its Wings Over the Prairie Festival (held from Wednesday through Saturday). *Sponsor:* Stuttgart Chamber of Commerce, 507 S. Main Street, Stuttgart, AR 72160; 501-673-1602; Fax: 501-673-1604.

Worst traffic accident in U.S. history (1991)
A severe dust storm caused a massive traffic pileup on Interstate 5 near Coalinga, California; 17 people were killed and 104 vehicles were damaged.

You're Welcomegiving Day
This holiday on the day after Thanksgiving, when added to

Thanksgiving, creates a 4-day weekend. *Sponsor:* The Fifth Wheel Tavern, Richard Ankli, 639 Fifth Street, Ann Arbor, MI 48103; e-mail: rankli@umich.edu.

November 30

Exaggerated Death Day
Samuel Clemens, whose pen name was Mark Twain, was born on this date in 1835 in Florida, Missouri. In response to news that he had died, he sent the following note to the Associated Press: "The report of my death was an exaggeration."

Michael Jackson's Thriller released (1982)
The best-selling album of all time.

Perpetual Youth Day
On the birthday of Dick Clark, we celebrate all the people who never seem to age. Clark, host of *American Bandstand,* was born in 1929 in Mount Vernon, New York. Also known as Dorian Gray's Day.

Saint Andrew Feast Day
Patron saint of fishermen, sailors, and spinsters; also patron saint of Scotland, Greece, and Russia.

Stay Home Because You're Well Day
A day for calling in well and celebrating health. *Sponsor:* Wellness Permission League. ✉

DECEMBER

Art and Architecture Books Month
Promotes books about art, architecture, photography, buildings, and other fine arts. *Sponsor:* Book Marketing Update. ✉

Colorectal Cancer Education and Awareness Month
To spread info about the early detection of colorectal cancer. *Sponsor:* Pharmacists Planning Service. ✉

International Calendar Awareness Month
Most calendars are purchased in the month of December. January and November are also big selling months. *Sponsor:* Calendar Marketing Association, 621 E. Park Avenue, Libertyville, IL 60048; 708-816-8660; 800-828-8225; Fax: 708-816-8662; e-mail: calendars@aol.com.

Made in America Month

National Drunk and Drugged Driving Awareness Month
Contact: Mothers Against Drunk Driving, 511 E. John Carpenter Frwy #700, Irving, TX 75062-8187; 214-744-6233.

National Stress-Free Family Holidays Month
Take time out with your family to do some things that don't involve the hectic frazzle of holiday plans. *Sponsor:* Parenting without Pressure. ✉

Read a New Book Month

Safe Toys and Gifts Month
Choose your gifts carefully so they are safe for children. During this month, Prevent Blindness America issues a list of toys that are hazardous to eyesight. They also distribute tips on how to choose age-appropriate toys. *Sponsor:* Prevent Blindness America. ✉

Universal Human Rights Month
Since 1985, this month promotes the Universal Declaration of Human Rights. *Sponsor:* International Society of Friendship and Good Will. ✉

December 1

Becky Thatcher Day
Honors girls and women who have written or inspired great fiction; held on the birthday of Laura

Hawkins (1836), who was Samuel Clemen's first serious girlfriend and the model for Becky Thatcher in Clemen's books.

Bingo's Birthday
Bingo, the fund-raising game, was invented by Edwin Lowe in 1929. *Sponsor:* Bingo Bugle, Roger Snowden, P.O. Box 527, Vashon, WA 98070; 509-463-5656; 800-327-6437.

Christmas Lights Day
Also known as My Husband's Strung the Christmas Lights and Now I Can't Open the Garage Door Day, which commemorates an actual event experienced by Mary Jo, a listener of *The Good Neighbor Show. Contact:* WHBY-AM, The Good Neighbor Show, Kathy Keene, Producer, 2727 E. Radio Road, Appleton, WI 54915; 414-733-6639.

Day without Art
Focuses on the needs of people with AIDS, revealing the devastation of the disease.

First black woman to edit a major newspaper (1992)
Pearl Stewart edited the *Oakland Tribune.* She was appointed on November 3rd. *Contact: Oakland Tribune,* 409 13th Street, Oakland, CA 94612; 510-645-2000; Fax: 510-645-2285.

First chartered mutual life insurance company (1843)

First drive-in automobile service station (1913)
Opened in Pittsburgh, Pennsylvania.

First Sunday of Advent (Liturgical New Year)
The season of Advent begins with the fourth Sunday before Christmas and ends with Christmas Day. It is a preparation time before the celebration of the birth of Christ. It is also the beginning of the new liturgical year for Christians of the western world.

First voyage via hydrogen balloon (1783)

National Autism Week
Celebrated the first full week in December.

National Home Care Week
During the week after Thanksgiving, show appreciation to home care providers. *Sponsor:* National Association for Home Care, Stanton Park, 519 C Street NE, Washington, DC 20002; 202-547-7424; Fax: 202-547-3540.

Nebbish Pride Day
On the birthday of Woody Allen, celebrate all the wonderful crazy people in your life. Allen was born Allen Stewart Königsburg on December 1 in 1935 in Brooklyn, New York. *Sponsor:* The Life of the Party.
✉

Rosa Parks Day
In 1955, Rosa Parks of Montgomery, Alabama, was arrested for refusing to give up her seat on a bus to a white man. Her act sparked a bus boycott and began the modern-day American Civil Rights Movement.

Travelers with Disabilities Awareness Week
On the week after Thanksgiving, become aware of the accessibility problems faced by handicapped travelers. Call to confirm dates. *Sponsor:* Society for the Advancement of Travel for the Handicapped, 347 Fifth Avenue #610, New York, NY 10016; 212-447-7284; Fax: 212-725-8253.

U.S. Civil Air Patrol established (1941)

World AIDS Day
In 1988 the World Health Organization dedicated this day to increasing awareness of the HIV/AIDS virus. *Sponsor:* American Association for World Health, 112 20th Street NW #400, Washington, DC 20036; 202-466-5883; Fax: 202-466-5896.

December 2

First controlled self-sustaining nuclear reaction
The reaction was obtained in 1942 on the campus of the University of Chicago. *Contact:* University of

Chicago; 5801 S. Ellis Avenue, Chicago, IL 60637; 312-702-1234; Fax: 312-702-5846.

First permanent artificial heart transplant (1982)

Dr. Barney Clark received the artificial heart at the University of Utah Medical Center in Salt Lake City, Utah. He died on March 23, 1983, having survived 112 days.

First transatlantic telephone wedding (1933)

Bertil Clason of Detroit, Michigan, married Sigrid Carlson of Stockholm, Sweden, in a telephone ceremony.

Mars Landing Day

In 1971, the Soviet Union's *Mars 3* sent down a capsule equipped with a TV camera that landed on Mars and sent back pictures for 20 seconds. *Mars 3* was launched on May 28, 1971. *Contact:* NASA. ✉

Monroe Doctrine declared (1823)

President James Monroe's Doctrine stated that the U.S. would not approve Europe extending quarrels to the Western Hemisphere.

Pan American Health Day

Celebrated by presidential proclamation since 1940.

December 3

Bake a Biscuit Day

On the birthday of Charles Pillsbury, bake a biscuit, a cake, some cookies, or other goodies. Then send the author of this book some of those goodies: John Kremer, P.O. Box 205, Fairfield, IA 52556. Thanks. *Sponsor:* The Life of the Party. ✉

Day Without Crime

Today, give up your crimes of impulse. No white lies, petty stealing, or yelling at family or friends. No drug use. To stop major crime, start at home by stopping the little crimes so many of us do every day. *Sponsor:* All My Events. ✉

First co-educational college (1833)

Oberlin opened and admitted its first women on September 6, 1837. *Contact:* Oberlin College, 173 W. Lorain Street, Oberlin, OH 44074-1023; 216-775-8121; Fax: 216-775-8886.

First successful heart transplant (1967)

Dr. Christian Barnard of Cape Town, South Africa, performed the first successful heart transplant (though the patient died 18 days afterwards). A second heart transplant operation performed on another person on January 2, 1968, was more successful.

Illinois Admission Day

Admitted as the 21st state of the U.S. in 1818. *Contact:* Illinois Bureau of Tourism, 100 W Randolph Street #3/400, Chicago IL 60601; 312-814-4732; Fax: 312-814-6581; 800-223-0121.

International Day of Disabled Persons

Encourages integrating the disabled into society. *Sponsor:* United Nations. ✉

Saint Francis Xavier Feast Day

Perhaps the greatest Christian missionary is patron saint of foreign missions and tourism. He is also patron saint of India, Japan, Goa, and Outer Mongolia.

Telescope Day

Galileo invented the telescope in 1621.

World's largest bar opened (1829)

World's worst industrial accident (1984)

A gas leak in a Union Carbide plant in Bhopal, India, killed over 2,000 people. *Contact:* Union Carbide Corporation, 39 Old Ridgebury Road, Danbury, CT 06817; 203-794-2000; Fax: 203-794-6269.

December 4

Day of the Artisans

Honoring all workers.

First black naval officer to die in combat (1950)

Jesse Leroy Brown, the first black American naval aviator, was also the first black naval officer to die in combat. He was shot down over Korea. *Contact:* Department of the Navy, Pentagon Room #4E686, Washington, DC 20350; 703-695-0911.

First human-made satellite to orbit Venus (1978)

The *Pioneer Venus I*, was launched on May 20, 1978, and began to orbit Venus on December 4, 1978. *Contact:* NASA. ✉

Freedom for Hostages Day

In 1991, the final American hostage held in Lebanon was released. Terry Anderson, an Associated Press reporter, was taken hostage on March 16, 1985.

Manila paper patented (1845)

National Grange founded (1867)

This agricultural movement began in 1867. *Contact:* National Grange Headquarters, 1616 H Street NW, Washington, DC 20006; 202-628-3507.

Saint Barbara Feast Day

Patron saint of mariners and architects. According to tradition, if a young girl places a cherry twig in water on this day and it blooms by Christmas eve, she shall marry during the coming year.

December 5

AFL-CIO founded (1955)

The American Federation of Labor and the Congress for Industrial Or-

ganizations merged in 1955 to form the AFL-CIO. A merger agreement had been previously announced on February 9th. *Contact:* AFL-CIO, 815 16th Street NW, Washington, DC 20000; 202-637-5010.

Blue Jeans Thursday

Blue jeans were designed by Levi Strauss on this date in 1880. *Contact:* Levi Strauss and Company, 1155 Battery Street, San Francisco, CA 94111-1264; 415-544-6000; 800-USA-LEVI; Fax: 415-544-3939.

First nudist group in the U.S. (1929)

The first nudist group in the U.S. was the American League for Physical Culture, founded in New York City in 1929.

First scholastic fraternity in U.S. (1776)

Phi Beta Kappa was organized at William and Mary College. *Contact:* Phi Beta Kappa, 1811 Q Street NW, Washington, DC 20009; 202-265-3808.

International Volunteer Day for Economic and Social Development

This day commemorates the 1970 establishment of the UN Volun-

teers program. *Sponsor:* United Nations. ✉

Martin Van Buren's Birthday

The 8th President of the U.S. was born in 1782 in Kinderhook, New York.

Montgomery Bus Boycott began (1955)

Four days after Rosa Parks was arrested for not giving up her seat on a bus, the black community of Montgomery, Alabama, began a boycott of bus service in the city. The boycott lasted over a year.

Pipe wrench patented (1876)

Prohibition repealed (1933)

The 21st Amendment to the U.S. Constitution was ratified. It repealed prohibition, thus allowing Americans once more to drink alcoholic beverages to their heart's content.

December 6

13th Amendment to the Constitution ratified (1865)

This amendment abolished slavery. Congress passed it on January 24, 1865. Ratification of this amendment by the states was proclaimed on December 18, 1865.

Altamont Concert Tragedy (1969)

At a free concert held at the Altamont Speedway in Livermore, California, a spectator was stabbed to death by a Hell's Angel who was guarding the stage. Performers included the Rolling Stones; Crosby, Stills, Nash, and Young; Jefferson Airplane; and Santana.

Chanukah (Festival of Lights)
December 6 to 13. Also known as Hanukkah, this freedom festival celebrates the Jewish victory over the Syrians in 165 B.C. As the temple of Jerusalem was rededicated, a small amount of olive oil miraculously continued to burn; hence, the festival of lights. 1997: December 24 to 31; 1998: December 14 to 21.

Microwave oven patented (1945)

Saint Nicholas Feast Day
Patron saint of children, unmarried women, brides, bakers, merchants, apothecaries, pawnbrokers, brewers, Greece, and Russia. In the Netherlands, gifts are exchanged on this day. Saint Nicholas is the basis of Saint Nick or Santa Claus.

U.S. Border Patrol founded (1924)
Contact: U.S. Border Patrol, 425 Eye Street NW #6023, Washington, DC 20536-0001; 202-515-1689; Fax: 202-633-3296.

December 7

Celebration of an X-Rated Holiday
As late as 1856, Christmas celebrations were banned in Boston. Indeed, as late as 1870 Boston children had to attend school on Christmas. *Sponsor:* A Pilgrim's Almanac. ✉

Delaware Ratification Day
Delaware was the first state to ratify the U.S. Constitution on December 7, 1787. This day is a public holiday, Delaware Day, in Delaware. *Contact:* Delaware Tourism Office, P.O. Box 1401, Dover, DE 19903; 302-739-4271; Fax: 302-739-5749; 800-441-8846.

First instant reply during televised sports event (1963)

Gas refrigerator patented (1926)

National Candlelight Vigil of Remembrance and Hope
This event gives people who have lost a family member or friend to a drunk driver a chance to mourn them and, at the same time, work for ways to prevent more killings by drunk drivers. Held on the first Saturday in December. *Sponsor:* Mothers Against Drunk Driving, 511 E. John Carpenter Frwy #700, Irving, TX 75062-8187; 214-744-6233.

National Fire Safety Council founded (1979)
The council was formed to encourage fire prevention. *Contact:* National Fire Safety Council, P.O. Box 378, Michigan Center, MI 49254-0378; 517-764-2811.

New York Philharmonic first performed (1842)
Contact: New York Philharmonic, Avery Fisher Hall, 10 Lincoln Center Plaza, New York, NY 10023; 212-875-5000; Fax: 212-875-5717.

Night of the Ascent (Lailatul Mi'Raj)
On the 27th day of the 7th month of the Islamic Lunar Year, the Prophet Muhammad ascended into Heaven aboard a winged horse named Buraq.

Pearl Harbor Day
In 1941, the U.S. Naval Base at Pearl Harbor was attacked by the Japanese. This attack drew America wholeheartedly into World War II.

Saint Ambrose Feast Day
Patron saint of learning; also patron saint of beekeepers, geese, and orators.

December 8

American Bird Banding Association founded (1909)

American Federation of Labor founded (1886)
Samuel Gompers reorganized several trade unions to form the Amer-

ican Federation of Labor in Columbus, Ohio. *Contact:* AFL-CIO, 815 16th Street NW, Washington, DC 20000; 202-637-5010.

Beach Boys released their first single (1961)
Their first single was "Surfin'."

Bodhi Day (Enlightenment of Buddha)
This Mahayana Buddhist feast celebrates the day when Gautama Buddha found enlightenment while sitting under the bo tree. Buddhists of some other sects celebrate Buddha's enlightenment in May on the feast of Vesak. *Contact:* Buddhist Churches of America, 1710 Octavia Street, San Francisco, CA 94109-4341; 415-776-5600.

Civil Rights Week
Celebrated the week of the 10th and is observed in Massachusetts.

Coaxial cable patented (1931)

Commonwealth of Independent States organized (1991)
The Soviet Union dissolved as the Commonwealth of Independent States was established.

Feast of the Immaculate Conception
Acknowledges that Mary was a virgin when she became pregnant with baby Jesus.

First person to die of AIDS from a health care professional
In 1991, Kimberly Bergalis died from the AIDS virus after having contracted it from her dentist.

First treaty doing away with nuclear missiles
In 1987, the U.S. and Soviet Union took the first step towards a nuclear-free world by banning 2 classes of nuclear missiles.

Human Rights Week
The Universal Declaration of Human Rights was adopted by the United Nations on December 10, 1948. Celebrated the week of December 10th. *Sponsor:* United Nations. ✉

John Lennon Remembrance Day
In 1980, John Lennon was shot outside the Dakota apartment building in New York City.

National Drunk and Drugged Driving Awareness Week
Always the second full week in December.

December 9

America's first formal cremation (1792)
Henry Laurens, a colonial statesman, was cremated near Charleston, South Carolina.

Ball-bearing roller skate patented (1884)
Levant Richardson of Chicago, Illinois, patented ball-bearing roller skates in 1884. In-line roller skates had been previously designed and used in Holland since the early 18th century.

Christmas Card Day
Henry Cole created the first Christmas cards in 1843. Send your Christmas cards out today (or sooner, if you are a friend of the U.S. Post Office).

Christmas Seals' Birthday
The first Christmas seals were sold in Wilmington, Delaware in 1907. *Contact:* American Lung Association, 1740 Broadway, New York, NY 10019-4374; 800-LUNG-USA.

Genocide Convention approved (1948)
The UN General Assembly unanimously approved the Genocide Convention, designed to prevent and punish the crime of genocide. On February 19, 1986, the U.S. Senate finally approved the Convention. *Contact:* United Nations. ✉

Most Boring Celebrities of the Year
These awards are announced on the second Monday in December. Past winners of this award have included Madonna and Roseanne. *Sponsor:* The Boring Institute, Alan Caruba, Founder, P.O. Box 40,

Maplewood, NJ 07040; 201-763-6392; Fax: 201-763-4287.

December 10

Dewey Decimal Day
On the birthday of Melvil Dewey, we honor all librarians. Dewey invented the Dewey Decimal System for classifying books, he was born in Adams Center, New York in 1851.

First black awarded the Nobel Peace Prize (1950)
Dr. Ralph Bunche was the first black to receive the Nobel Prize for peace.

First domestic passenger jet flight (1958)
A Boeing 707 made the first domestic jet flight from New York to Miami.

First U.S. postal service announced (1672)
Contact: U.S. Postal Service. ✉

Gift of the Magi published (1905)
O. Henry's great short story was published.

Great Native Americans Week
December 10 to 15. During the week that Red Cloud (December 10, 1909) and Sitting Bull (December 15, 1890) died, we honor all great native Americans.

Human Rights Day
The Universal Declaration of Human Rights was adopted on this date by the United Nations in 1948. *Sponsor*: United Nations. ✉

Mississippi Admission Day
In 1817 Mississippi became the 20th state of the U.S. *Contact*: Mississippi Division of Tourism, P.O. Box 849, Jackson, MS 39205; 601-359-3297; 800-927-6378; Fax: 601-359-5757.

National Sarong Day
On the birthday of Dorothy Lamour, featured actress in the Road pictures of Bob Hope and Bing Crosby, wear a sarong. Lamour was born in 1914 in New Orleans, Louisiana. *Sponsor*: The Life of the Party. ✉

Nobel Prize Ceremonies
Held on the anniversary of Alfred Nobel's death. Nobel, a Swedish chemist who invented dynamite, endowed these awards for physics, chemistry, medicine, economics, literature, and peace. The first ceremonies were held in 1901.

Playboy's Birthday
Playboy magazine was first published in 1953. *Contact*: *Playboy* magazine, 680 N. Lake Shore Drive, Chicago, IL 60611-3088; 312-751-8000; Fax: 312-751-2818.

December 11

Aurora Borealis first described (1719)

First radio message sent (1901)
Guglielmo Marconi, the inventor of the radio, sent a wireless message from England to Canada (the Morse code for the letter S).

Indiana Admission Day
Indiana became the 19th state of the U.S. on December 11, 1816. *Contact*: Indiana Tourism Development, One N Capital #700, Indianapolis, IN 46204-2288; 317-232-8859; 800-469-4612.

Magnum P. I. premiered (1980)
The detective series, set in Hawaii, starred Tom Selleck. *Contact*: CBS-TV. ✉

UNICEF founded
The United Nations International Children's Emergency Fund was founded in 1946. It is now known simply as the United Nations Children's Fund. *Contact*: United Nations Children's Fund, 3 UN Plaza, New York, NY 10017; 212-326-7000; Fax: 212-888-7465; 800-553-1200 (ordering number).

December 12

Blue Eyes Day
Frank Sinatra, old blue eyes, was born in 1915 in Hoboken, New Jersey. *Sponsor*: The Life of the Party. ✉

Boys Town founded (1917)
Father Edward Flanagan founded Boys Town in 1917 near Omaha,

Nebraska. *Contact:* Boys Town, 14100 Crawford Road, Boys Town, NE 68010; 402-498-1300; Fax: 402-498-1348.

Feast of Our Lady of Guadalupe

Mary, mother of Jesus, is the patron saint of Latin America. In 1533, Mary appeared in a vision to a peasant outside the Mexican town of Guadalupe.

First black U.S. Representative (1870)

Joseph H. Rainey of South Carolina became the first black to serve in the U.S. House of Representatives.

First motel opened (1925)

Golf tee invented (1899)

George Bryant of Boston, Massachusetts, patented the wooden golf tee.

Party Party Day

An excuse to have a party once a month (when the day equals the month). *Sponsor:* Bonza Bottler Day. ✉

Pennsylvania Ratification Day

Pennsylvania became the second state to ratify the U.S. Constitution in 1787. *Contact:* Pennsylvania Bureau of Travel, 453 Forum Building, Harrisburg, PA 17120; 717-787-5453; 800-847-4872; Fax: 717-234-4560.

Poinsettia Day

Celebrates the anniversary of the death of Joel Roberts Poinsett, the man who introduced this Christmas plant to the U.S. He died in 1851.

December 13

Ban a Silly Superstition Day

Always celebrated on Friday the 13th. *Sponsor:* All My Events. ✉

Clip-on Tie's Birthday

The clip-on tie was designed on this date in 1928.

First savings bank opened (1816)

Friday the 13th

The second of two Friday the 13ths in 1996. Beware. Beware!

Lights On for Life Day

On the Friday of National Drunk and Drugged Driving Awareness Week, put your automobile lights on for safety.

Susan B. Anthony dollar coined (1978)

This was the first U.S. coin to honor a woman.

December 14

Alabama Admission Day

Alabama was admitted as the 22nd state of the U.S. in 1819. *Contact:* Alabama Bureau of Tourism, P.O. Box 4309, Montgomery, AL 36103-

4309; 334-242-4169; 800-252-2262; Fax: 334-242-4554.

Day of Prophecy

On the birthday of Nostradamus, celebrate all who foretell the future. Michel de Notredame was born in 1503 in St. Remy, France.

DNA created in a test tube (1967)

First black world heavyweight boxing champion

In 1915, Jack Johnson became the world heavyweight boxing champion.

Halcyon Days

The 7 days before and 7 days after winter solstice are calm and tranquil. They are named Halcyon Days because the mythical halcyon bird was thought to calm the wind and the waves during these days.

Saturday Night Fever movie premiered (1977)

Screw patented (1798)

South Pole discovered (1911)

Raold Amundsen and 4 companions reached the South Pole in 1911.

Women Politicians Day

On the birthday of Margaret Chase Smith, the first woman elected to both houses of Congress, we honor all women politicians. Smith was born in 1897 in Skowhegan, Maine.

December 15

Bill of Rights Day (1791)
Celebrates the anniversary of the ratification of the Bill of Rights in 1791.

First law school in the U.S. (1791)

First rendezvous in space (1965)
Spaceships *Gemini 6* and *Gemini 7* moved within 10 feet of each other. *Contact:* NASA. ✉

First sex-change operation (1952)
Christine Jorgenson became the first person to undergo a sex-change operation.

Gone with the Wind premiered (1939)
The movie premiered at Lowe's Grand Theater in Atlanta, Georgia.

International Language Week
Designed to educate people about the international language of Esperanto. It is always celebrated from December 15 (the birthday of Dr. Ludwig Zamenhof, developer of Esperanto) to December 21. *Sponsor:* International Society of Friendship and Good Will. ✉

International Shareware Day
Take time on the third Sunday in December to send checks to any shareware authors whose software you are using. *Sponsor:* Online Today, David Lawrence, 2816 Saddlebred Court #200, Glenwood, MD 21738-9740; 301-854-5006; Fax: 301-854-5085; e-mail: OLT-David@aol.com.

National Firefighters Day
By presidential proclamation, this day is always celebrated on the 15th.

Sitting Bull died (1890)
The great Sioux leader, died in a skirmish at Grand River, South Dakota.

Tell Someone They're Doing a Good Job Week
During the week before Christmas, give positive feedback on job performance every day of the week. *Sponsor:* WCMS Radio, Joe Hoppel, 900 Commonwealth Place, Virginia Beach, VA 23464; 804-424-1050; Fax: 804-424-3479.

December 16

Beethoven's Birthday
In 1770, Ludwig von Beethoven, the first star of the musical world, was born in Bonn, Germany.

Boston Tea Party (1773)
As a protest over a tea tax and monopoly granted by the British Parliament, American patriots boarded a British vessel and dumped 350 chests of tea. *Contact:* Boston Visitors Bureau, P.O. Box 490, Boston. MA 02199; 617-536-4100; Fax: 617-424-7664.

Coin-operated liquid vending machine patented
In 1884, William Fruen of Minneapolis, Minnesota, patented the vending machine.

Eat What You Want Day
Eat whatever you want. Splurge today, diet tomorrow. *Sponsor:* Wellness Permission League. ✉

Humans Will Never Fly Society Meeting
Since 1959, this meeting is held every year in Kitty Hawk, North Carolina, the evening before the anniversary of the Wright Brothers flight. *Sponsor:* Man Will Never Fly Society, Al Jones, P.O. Box 1903, Kill Devil Hills, NC 27948; 919-441-2424; Fax: 919-441-2424.

Las Posadas (Mexico)
December 16 to 24. This is a nine-day Mexican Christmas celebration that commemorates Mary and Joseph's search for lodging (posada) right before the birth of Christ. *Contact:* Mexican Embassy, 1911 Pennsylvania Avenue NW, Washington, DC 20006; 202-728-1600.

New Madrid Earthquake Anniversary

In 1811, the largest earthquake in American history took place near New Madrid, Missouri. *Contact:* City of New Madrid, P.O. Box 96, 560 Mott Street, New Madrid, MO 63869; 314-748-2866.

New World Symphony premiered (1893)

The New World Symphony by Anton Dvořák was one of the first classical pieces to draw upon the folk music and black spirituals of the U.S. It premiered at Carnegie Hall in New York City.

Take a Tribe to Lunch Day

On the birthday of anthropologist Margaret Mead, who lived for many years among primitive people, take a tribe out to lunch. Mead was born in 1901 in Philadelphia, Pennsylvania. *Sponsor:* The Life of the Party, K Callan. ✉

Variety's Birthday

Variety, an entertainment trade journal, published its first issue in 1905. *Contact: Variety* Magazine, 5700 Wilshire Boulevard #120, Los Angeles, CA 90036; 213-857-6600; Fax: 213-857-0494.

World's Largest Office Party

Office parties are held in every major city (with a Hyatt Hotel) on the third Monday or Tuesday of December. The parties benefit children's charities. *Sponsor:* Hyatt Regency Chicago, 151 E. Wacker Drive, Chicago, IL 60601-3709; 312-565-1234; Fax: 312-565-2966.

December 17

First one-way street (1791)

Created in New York City.

First world championship football game (1933)

The Chicago Bears beat the New York Giants 23 to 21. *Contact:* National Football League. ✉

Pan American Aviation Day

Since 1940, this day celebrates the first flight made by the Wright Brothers in 1903.

Saturnalia

December 17 to 23. This ancient Roman festival honored Saturn, the god of planting, harvesting, and the unknown. It was a time to give gifts (a forerunner of our current Christmas custom of giving gifts).

Wright Brothers Day

In 1903 the Wright Brothers were the first to achieve controlled, machine-powered flight. For a free pamphlet, *The Story of the Wright Brothers,* send a postcard to Wright Brothers National Memorial, P.O. Box 457, Manteo, NC 27954; 919-473-2111.

December 18

Feast of Our Lady of Solitude

Mary, Our Lady of Solitude, is also patron saint of the lonely.

First nuclear facility to generate electricity

The first such facility opened in 1957.

First radio broadcast of a livestock auction (1924)

First Sunday newspaper in the U.S. (1796)

Phillip Edwards of Baltimore, Maryland, published *The Monitor.*

Mother Goose Day

In 1719, Thomas Fleet of Boston, Massachusetts, published his mother-in-law's tales, *Mother Goose.*

New Jersey Ratification Day

New Jersey became the third state to ratify the U.S. Constitution on December 18, 1787. *Contact:* New Jersey Division of Tourism, 20 W. State Street CN 826, Trenton, NJ 08625; 609-292-2470; 800-537-7397; Fax: 609-633-7418.

Pantomime Day

On the birthday of Joseph Grimaldi, the greatest clown in history as well as a king of pantomime, celebrate all pantomime artists. Grimaldi was born in 1778 in London, England.

✉   Addresses for frequently cited organizations are gathered on pages vii–viii.

Steven Spielberg's Birthday

Creator of the *Star Wars* trilogy, *Jurassic Park, The Color Purple,* and *Schindler's List* was born in Cincinnati, Ohio, in 1947. Also known as Close Encounters Day.

December 19

A Christmas Carol first published

Charles Dickens's yuletide tale was published in 1843. Bah, humbug!

Almanac Day

In 1732, Benjamin Franklin began publishing his *Poor Richard's Almanac.*

Can't Get Up Day

1985 marked the first broadcast of the famous "I've fallen, and I can't get up" commercial.

Corrugated paper patented (1871)

First radio voice broadcast from space (1958)

President Eisenhower recorded the message, wishing everyone peace on earth and goodwill to all. *Contact*: NASA. ✉

U.S. invasion of Panama (1989)

The U.S. invaded Panama to capture Manuel Noriega, who surrendered on January 4th.

Women awarded Rhodes Scholarships for first time (1976)

December 20

American Poet Laureate established (1985)

Robert Penn Warren was the first Poet Laureate.

Christmas Bird Count

December 20 to January 5. 40,000 people go out during the holiday season to count bird species. 1997: December 19th to January 4th. *Sponsor:* National Audubon Society, 700 Broadway, New York, NY 10003; 212-979-3000; Fax: 212-353-0508.

Electric light first demonstrated (1879)

Thomas Edison demonstrated his new incandescent light.

First successful cotton mill in the U.S. (1790)

The first cotton mill was in Pawtucket, Rhodes Island.

First U.S. scientist to receive Nobel Prize (1907)

The first U.S. scientist to receive the Nobel Prize was physicist Albert Michelson, known for the Michelson Effect.

I've Got My Big Fat Guy Pants on Day

Wear anything you want on this day, as long as it's comfortable and roomy. *Sponsor:* WIMS-AM, Chris Carey, 685 East 1675 North, Michigan City, IN 46360; 219-874-9467.

Louisiana Purchase Day

In 1803, the U.S. bought the Louisiana Territory from France. At a cost of less than $20.00 per square mile, it was one of history's greatest real estate deals.

Mudd Day

Recognizes the birthday of Dr. Samuel Mudd (1833), who gave medical attention to John Wilkes Booth after the assassination of President Lincoln. Mudd was imprisoned for almost 4 years. "Your name is Mudd," came from this event.

National Flashlight Day

Because the day before the winter solstice has the year's longest night, flashlights are necessary. *Sponsor:* James Morgan, 589 Elma Street, Akron, OH 44310.

Underdog Day

To salute the second bananas of history and literature, from Sherlock Holmes's Dr. Watson to Robinson Crusoe's Friday. *Sponsor:* Peter Moeller, Chief Underdog, P.O. Box 71, Clio, MI 48420; 810-687-0423.

December 21

California Kiwifruit Day

On the first day of winter, enjoy the flavor and nutritional benefits of kiwifruit. *Sponsor:* California Kiwifruit Commission, 1540 River Park Drive #110, Sacramento, CA 95815.

Crossword Puzzle's Birthday

The first crossword puzzle (with 32 clues) was created by Arthur Wynne and published in the *New York World* on this date in 1913.

Exercise Day

Get ready for holiday meals by taking off some weight now, especially by doing some exercise on Jane Fonda's birthday. Fonda, an actress now better known for her best-selling exercise videos, was born in 1937 in New York City. *Sponsor:* The Life of the Party. ✉

First basketball game played (1891)

Played at Springfield College (then the YMCA Training School) in Springfield, Massachusetts. James Naismith, an instructor at the school, wrote down the rules of the game that morning. *Contact:* Basketball Hall of Fame, 1150 W. Columbus Avenue, P.O. Box 179, Springfield, MA 01101; 413-781-6500.

First feature-length silent film comedy (1914)

Tillie's Punctured Romance was the first such comedy film.

First junior high school established (1909)

It opened in Berkeley, California.

First moon voyage (1968)

Apollo 8 orbited the moon on December 24th and returned to Earth on December 27th. *Contact:* NASA. ✉

Forefathers' Day

Observed primarily in New England, commemorates the Pilgrims' arrival at Plymouth Rock in 1620.

Homeless Memorial Day

On the shortest day of the year, we memorialize the homeless.

Humbug Day

Yell 12 "humbugs" to vent Christmas-preparation frustrations. *Sponsor:* Wellness Permission League. ✉

International Flower Day

Bring bouquets of winter flowers (such as poinsettas) into your home, business, school, or other places you frequent. *Sponsor:* All My Events. ✉

Look on the Bright Side Day

On the first day of Winter, we can take comfort in knowing each day will get a little longer.

Om Celebration: A Global Peace Meditation

Meditate on world peace for an hour at noon your time. You can do it on any equinox or solstice. *Sponsor:* The Global Peace Foundation, Beverly Baby Shivia; 415-924-7281.

Pilgrims landed at Plymouth Rock (1620)

Also celebrated as Forefather's Day.

Radium discovered (1898)

French scientists Marie and Pierre Curie discovered radium.

Shortest Day of the Year

Also the first day of winter in the Northern Hemisphere.

Snow White and the Seven Dwarfs premiered (1937)

It was the first full-length animated cartoon. *Contact:* Walt Disney Studios. ✉

Winter Solstice

The winter solstice is also the shortest day of the year in the Northern Hemisphere. Winter begins at 9:07 A.M., Eastern Time.

December 22

First Christmas tree lights (1882)

Thomas Edison created the first Christmas tree lights.

First gorilla born in captivity (1956)

Colo was born at the Columbus, Ohio zoo. *Contact:* Columbus Zoo, 9990 Riverside Drive, Powell, OH 43065; 614-645-3550.

Sign of Capricorn

The astrological sign of Capricorn the Goat runs from December 22nd to January 19th. Capricorns are ambitious, blunt, and loyal.

U.S. Golf Association founded (1894)

Contact: U.S. Golf Association, Liberty Corner Road, Far Hills, NJ 07931; 908-234-2300; 800-336-4446; Fax: 908-234-9687.

December 23

A Visit from St. Nicholas first published (1823)

Clement Moore's *The Night Before Christmas* was first published as *A Visit from St. Nicholas* by the *Troy Sentinel.*

Federal Reserve System created (1913)

For a free booklet, *Fundamental Facts about U.S. Money,* write to the Federal Reserve Bank of Atlanta, Publications Department, 104 Marietta Street NW, Atlanta, GA 30303-2713. *Contact:* Federal Reserve System, 20th and C Streets NW, Washington, DC 20551-0000; 202-452-3000; Fax: 202-452-3819.

First non-stop world flight without refueling

Dick Rutan and Jeana Yeager completed the trip in 1986 when they landed at Edwards Air Force Base.

First serialized novel on the Internet (1994)

Time/Warner became the first electronic publisher to serialize a novel on the Internet. At 5:00 P.M. EST on December 23, 1994, Douglas Cooper's *Delirium* began to appear in weekly installments as Cooper wrote them. *Contact:* Time/Warner Electronic Publishing, 75 Rockefeller Plaza, New York, NY 10019; 212-484-8000; Fax: 212-489-3347; World Wide Web: http://www.pathfinder.com.

Metric Conversion Act adopted (1975)

This act made the metric system America's basic system of measurement.

Transistor invented (1947)

Invented by Bell Lab scientists Bardeen, Brattain, and Shockley.

December 24

Christmas Eve

The night before Christmas and all through the house, not a creature was stirring, not even a mouse.

First music program broadcast via radio (1906)

Reginald Fessenden of Brant Rock, Massachusetts, was the first to broadcast a music program via radio.

First surface-to-surface guided missile (1942)

German rocket engineer Werhner von Braun launched the first such rocket.

Ku Klux Klan founded (1865)

The KKK was founded in Pulaski, Tennessee, by Confederate Army veterans.

Matzo Ball Day

Provides a holiday celebration for single men and women of the Jewish faith.

National Cozy Night

On the night before Christmas, take some time to cuddle with someone special next to a fire. *Sponsor:* The Life of the Party. ✉

National Roof Over Your Head Day

Organize efforts for the homeless on the local level.

Oak Moon

The full moon of December is the oak moon, symbolic of protection, love, good will, and peace. Also, sometimes known as the cold moon or long nights moon.

Saint Adam Feast Day

Adam, the first man, is considered a patron of gardeners. Other saints named Adam also celebrate their feast day on this date.

✉ Addresses for frequently cited organizations are gathered on pages vii–viii.

Silent Night Anniversary

In 1818, Franz Gruber of Oberndorf, Germany, composed the music for the Christmas carol "Silent Night." Joseph Mohr wrote the words. The song was first sung the next day.

Treaty of Ghent

Signed in 1814 in Ghent, Belgium, the treaty ended the War of 1812.

December 25

Christmas

The first recorded celebration of this biggest Christian holiday took place in Rome, Italy, in 336 A.D.

First successful ovarian tumor operation (1809)

Dr. Ephraim McDowell of Danville, Kentucky, performed the removal of an ovarian tumor.

Gravity Day

Celebrates the birthday of Isaac Newton (1642), the first to describe gravity.

Papal States New Year

Before 1582, the Papal States and other Italian city states celebrated New Year's Day on Christmas Day.

Play It Again, Sam Day

On the birthday of Humphrey Bogart, who uttered these immortal words in the movie *Casablanca*, do something again that you've done before and enjoyed. Bogart was born in 1899 in New York City. *Sponsor:* The Life of the Party. ✉

December 26

Boxing Day

On the first working day after Christmas, give gifts to servants, mailpeople, paper delivery people, and others who render public services. This day is a national holiday in Great Britain, Canada, and some other countries.

Coffee percolator invented (1865)

James Nason of Franklin, Massachusetts, invented the percolator.

God-Awful Tie Day

A day to wear the ties we get for Christmas. Formerly sponsored by the National FRUMPS of America.

Kwanzaa

December 26 to January 1. This 7-day cultural festival, founded by Dr. Maulana Karenga (now a professor at California State University at Long Beach), celebrates African and African-American heritage.

Largest execution in the U.S. (1862)

38 Dakota Indians were executed in Mankato, Minnesota, for murdering unarmed citizens.

National Whiner's Day

For people who whine, especially while returning Christmas gifts. The most Famous Whiners of the Year are announced on this day. In Canada, this day is held on December 27th. *Sponsor:* National Whiner's Day, Kevin Zaborney, 1418 22nd Street, Port Huron, MI 48060; 810-982-8436.

Return All of Your Ugly Christmas Gifts Day

Saint Stephen Feast Day

Patron saint of bricklayers, horses, and care for the poor.

Soviet Union broke up (1991)

The Soviet Union broke up one day after Mikhail Gorbachev

resigned. *Contact:* Russian Federation Embassy, 1125 16th Street NW, Washington, DC 20036; 202-628-7551.

Umoja—Unity Day
The first day of Kwanzaa.

December 27

Carry Nation smashed a saloon for the first time (1900)
Carry Nation, a militant prohibitionist, smashed her first saloon in the Hotel Carey in Wichita, Kansas.

Father of Aerodynamics Day
Sir George Cayley, English scientist and inventor, was born on this day in 1773. As a designer of airplanes, helicopters, and gliders, he is considered the father of aerodynamics. He was also the pilot for the first manned glider flight.

Howdy Doody's Birthday
The children's TV program *The Howdy Doody Show* premiered on NBC-TV in 1947. *Contact:* NBC-TV. ✉

Kujichagulia—Self-Determination Day
The second day of Kwanzaa. This is the day to take control of your own life.

Modern Astronomy Day
In 1571, German mathematician and astronomer Johannes Kepler was born in Wurttemberg, Germany. Kepler is often called the father of modern astronomy.

Modern Medicine Day
Louis Pasteur, the founder of modern innoculation methods and pasteurization, is often known as the father of modern medicine. He was born in 1822 in Dole, Jura, France.

National Pageant of Bands
On the Friday before the Fiesta Bowl, the top 10 high school bands in the nation compete for the Grand Master Trophy. *Sponsor:* Fiesta Bowl, Tempe Visitors Bureau, 51 West 3rd Street #105, Tempe, AZ 85281; 602-350-0900; 800-283-6734.

Radio City Music Hall opened (1932)
Contact: Radio City Music Hall, 1260 Avenue of the Americas, New York, NY 10020; 212-247-4777.

World Bank created (1945)
On this day in 1945, 28 nations signed an agreement creating the World Bank. *Contact:* World Bank, 809 UN Plaza #900, New York, NY 10017; 212-963-6008; Fax: 212-697-7020.

December 28

Bairn's Day (unluckiest day of the year)
Folk tradition considers this the unluckiest day of the year. It is not a day to start a new job or any sort of new work.

Chewing gum patented (1869)
William Semple of Mount Vernon, Ohio, patented chewing gum.

Feast of the Holy Innocents
The Holy Innocents are the patron saints of foundlings. They were the male children under the age of 2 who were killed in Bethlehem in an attempt by King Herod to try to kill the baby Jesus.

First test-tube baby in U.S. born (1981)
Elizabeth Carr of Norfolk, Virginia, was the first U.S. test tube baby.

Iowa Admission Day
In 1846, Iowa became the 29th state of the U.S. *Contact:* Iowa Tourism Bureau, 200 E Grand Avenue, Des Moines, IA 50309; 515-242-4705; 800-345-4692; Fax: 515-242-4749.

National Quilter's Day

Poor Richard's Almanack first advertised (1732)
Benjamin Franklin, using the pen name Richard Saunders, first advertised his *Poor Richard's Almanack* in the *Pennsylvania Gazette* in 1732. He continued to produce the almanac for another 26 years.

Ujima—Collective Work and Responsibility Day
The third day of Kwanzaa. Work together with others on this day. Take responsibility for your actions.

Woodrow Wilson's Birthday

The 28th President of the U.S. was born in 1856 in Staunton, Virginia.

December 29

Andrew Johnson's Birthday

The 17th President of the U.S. was born at Raleigh, North Carolina, in 1808.

Bowling Ball's Birthday

The bowling ball was invented in 1862.

First movie serial premiered (1913)

The Adventures of Kathlyn was first shown in Chicago, Illinois.

First YMCA in America formed (1851)

Formed in Boston, Massachusetts, in 1851. *Contact:* Young Men's Christian Association, 101 N. Wacker Drive, Chicago, IL 60606; 312-977-0031; 800-872-9622; Fax: 312-977-9063.

Saint Thomas Becket Feast Day

In 1170, the Bishop of Canterbury was murdered in his cathedral.

Texas Admission Day

Texas became the 28th state of the U.S. in 1845. *Contact:* Texas Tourism Division, P.O. Box 12728, Austin TX 78711; 512-462-9191; 800-888-8839; Fax: 512-320-9456.

Ujamaa—Cooperative Economics Day

The fourth day of Kwanzaa. Share something with someone today.

Wounded Knee Massacre (1890)

The U.S. 7th Calvary killed more than 200 Indians, including women and children, at Wounded Knee, South Dakota. The massacre followed the death of Sitting Bull on December 15th.

December 30

First freeway in California (1940)

The Arroyo Seco Parkway opened between Los Angeles and Pasadena, California.

First oil company incorporated (1854)

Nia—Purpose Day

The fifth day of Kwanzaa. Set a purpose for yourself on this day.

December 31

Annual World Peace Meditation

Think about world peace for an hour at noon Greenwich mean time. *Sponsor:* Rhea Giffin, Coordinator, P.O. Box 1151, Coeur d'Alene, ID 83816-1151; 208-664-1691.

Check the Smoke Alarms Day

Make fire safety one of your New Year's resolutions. Check your smoke alarms today! *Sponsor:* Judith Bates-Gorman, 1731 Morton Street, Lafayette IN 47904; 317-742-4480.

Kuumba—Creativity Day

The sixth day of Kwanzaa.

Leap Second Day

Seconds are added or subtracted to adjust atomic time to astronomical time. *Contact:* Bureau International de l'Heure, Paris, France.

Make Up Your Mind Day

When procrastinators have to make a decision (before New Year's). *Sponsor:* Ann Chase Moeller, 12079 Belann Court, P.O. Box 71, Clio, MI 48420; 810-687-0423.

New Year's Eve

No Resolution Day

Be creative. Don't make a New Year's resolution today—or tomorrow! *Sponsor:* Creative Ways, Marcia Yudkin, P.O. Box 1310, Boston, MA 02117; 617-266-1613.

You're All Done Day

Pat yourself on the back and savor your year's accomplishments.